Riddles of Belonging

Riddles of Belonging

INDIA IN TRANSLATION AND
OTHER TALES OF POSSESSION

Christi A. Merrill

FORDHAM UNIVERSITY PRESS

NEW YORK 2009

Library of Congress Cataloging-in-Publication Data

Merrill, Christi A.
   Riddles of belonging : India in translation and other tales of possession / Christi A. Merrill. — 1st ed.
     p. cm.
   Includes bibliographical references and index.
   ISBN 978-0-8232-2955-0 (cloth : alk. paper)
  1. Indic literature—Translations—History and criticism.
2. Folk literature, Indic—Translations—History and criticism.
3. Dctha, Vijayadanna—Translations—History and criticism.
I. Title.
   PK5409.M47 2008
   891.409—dc22   2008037466

Printed in the United States of America
10 09 08   5 4 3 2 1
First edition

For Dorothy Freeman, whose keen habits of reading and of living have inspired me at every turn, and for her twin sister and my mother, Dolores Miller, who passed away while this book was being completed and whose memory has left its mark on every page.

CONTENTS

Riddles of Belonging started with translation riddles posed by the stories of Vijay Dan Detha; I am grateful to him for the rare aesthetic and political sensibility he brings to his work, which has so inspired me over the years, and for his unfailing enthusiasm in encouraging my attempts to do the stories justice in English. Likewise, I thank his Hindi translator and my collaborator, Kailash Kabir, for sharing so many incisive perspectives on Detha's stories, translation more generally, and the global circuits of exchange in our practices as writers. I thank as well Detha's best friend and lifelong collaborator, Komal Kothari, whose easy graciousness and keenness of intellectual and moral vision brought together a vibrant international community of scholars, artists, and activists poised to carry on his work after his passing in 2004. I am also grateful for the generosity and verve with which so many of the extended families and close friends of Detha, Kabir, and Kothari have welcomed me into their homes in Borunda and Jodhpur, especially Chandrakala, Mahendra, Nirmala, Prakash, Suman, and Swathi Detha. I also wish to thank the storytellers in Rajasthan who continue to keep these oral traditions alive and who have been so generous in sharing their work with me, particularly Bhola Ram and Shankar Singh.

I would not have found myself translating at all if my first Hindi teacher, Virendra Singh, had not made learning the language such an exciting adventure. More than that, over the years he and his family have made me feel I had a home in Banaras and Jaipur when I most needed it. A special thanks to his wife, Sushila, for her reliably commonsensical counsel; to Kashika, Anu, Sujata, and Sandesh for reviving my faith in the beauty of pancakes and wishing on stars; and to Rajendra and Surendra Singh and their families in Jaipur who helped me find a sure footing in a new city. Likewise, I wish to express my gratitude to John and Faith Singh for their ongoing work in making the world a lovelier place for all and for making me part of the charmed life in the garden at Anokhi. It was through them that I was able to work at Digantar School with Reena Das and Rohit Dhankar, who introduced me not only to Detha's stories but to a revolutionary approach to teaching that I continue to draw on today. And it was through them that I met Dharmendar Kanwar, who has taught me so much about bringing together the best of local and global culture and whose friendship has been a ballast to me over the years. My life has been much enriched by sharing food and laughter with her and her family, including Abhijit Jhala, Mukul Shekavat, and N. P. Singh, as this book was being researched and written.

I am especially indebted to my mentors at the University of Iowa, Stavros Deligiorgis, Maureen Robertson, and Daniel Weissbort, who were so adept at bringing together translation theory and practice with sophistication and good humor. Likewise, Philip Lutgendorf has been integral in helping me find my place in South Asian Studies, as was Steve Ungar in encouraging me to argue for the importance of translation to Comparative Literature. All my writing teachers helped me establish a daily practice that made the creative and the critical inseparable, especially Carol de Saint Victor, Paul Diehl, Patricia Foster, Carl Klaus, Sara Levine, and James McPherson. I also wish to thank Janet Altman and Jon Wilcox, who first encouraged me to articulate the connection between humor and translation; Latika Bhatnagar and Sawai Singh Dhamora for teaching me Rajasthani; Anne Donaday and Geeta Patel, who made the impossible issues of postcolonialism endlessly compelling; fellow translators Prasenjit Gupta, Chris Mattison, and Elena Reeves, whose wild ambitions give us all a good name; fellow writers Marilyn Abildskov, Faith Adiele, Mary Allen, Eileen Bartos, Sam Chang, Ellen Fagg, Sue Futrell, Kate Gleeson, Susan Gray, Will Jennings, Maria Nilsson, and Steve Willard, whose dedication and artistry have renewed my faith in the literary enterprise countless times; Jenny Anger, Amy Petersen, and Lara Trubowitz, whose rich, thoughtful lives in and through the academy have provided worthy models; and Asmita, Radhika Desai, and Facundo Montenegro for their deep and joyous commitment to issues of social justice and for proving to me that our idealistic work in Iowa City was only the start. Facundo's untimely death in 2005 has only strengthened my conviction that meaningful change is possible.

Robert Hueckstedt's spirited, exciting work as a translator and scholar of South Asian literature has made him an invaluable mentor and colleague.

First in Winnipeg and then in Charlottesville, the daily example he and Nazen Merijian set made me believe in the importance of maintaining one's principles through generosity and humor. I also wish to express my gratitude for the dedication and good work of the other colleagues I overlapped with at the University of Virginia, especially Griff Chausee, Dan Ehnbom, Jeffrey Grossman, Djelah Hajibashi, Walter Hauser, Mushirul and Zoya Hasan, Anne Kinney, Priya Kumar, Farzaneh Milani, Anne Monius, Mohammed Sawaie, and Michiko Wilson; for the serendipitous, bicontinental overlaps with Syed Faiz Ali; and for the ebullient, dancing ways of Adrian Gaskins, and Sarah and Deborah Lawrence that made Charlottesville such a wonderful place to be.

At Michigan I have been fortunate to work in the Department of Asian Languages and Cultures and the Department of Comparative Literature with colleagues whose active commitments to rethinking the legacies and possibilities of our fields have been a tremendous source of inspiration. I am grateful for the generous mentoring I have received over the years from Madhav Deshpande, Nancy Florida, Ken Ito, Vassilios Lambropoulous, Lydia Liu, Don Lopez, Markus Nornes, Yopie Prins, Anton Shammas, Bob Sharf, Tahsin Siddiqi, and Tobin Siebers; for the regular insights provided in conversation with Bill Baxter, Catherine Brown, Deirdre de la Cruz, Henry Em, Maki Fukuoka, James Robson, Youngju Ryu, Ruth Tsoffar, and Jonathan Zwicker; and for the input of those who took part in the workshop of this manuscript in November 2005—especially Ken Ito for organizing that event and panelists Alina Clej, Markus Nornes, and R. Radhakrishnan for the extraordinarily helpful feedback that emboldened me to make these creative experiments central to my theorizing.

The subsequent manuscript workshop organized by Liansu Meng and Nicholas Theisen on behalf of the graduate students of Comparative Literature generated an especially lively discussion of disciplinary issues that has helped me as I revise. I am grateful to all who attended that session, especially Neil Doshi and Corine Tachtiris for their leading comments. The Center for South Asian Studies and Kitab Mandal at Michigan have provided numerous circles for thinking through the ideas in several of these chapters; I would like to acknowledge especially the help of Sharad Chari, Don Davis, Will Glover, Jayati Lal, Barbara Metcalf, Farina Mir, Mary Rader, Sumathi Ramaswamy, Lee Schlesinger, Carla Sinopoli, and Rachel Sturman. The staff at the Hatcher Library, particularly Richard Saran, have been extremely efficient at tracking down the obscure titles I needed and generous with their time and expertise in helping me decipher them. I have also been helped by the discussions with undergraduate students in "Writing World Literatures," "South Asian Literary Humor," and "Translating Asia to the American Academy"; the graduate students in "Decolonizing the Tongue," "Translating in an Uneven World," "Writing on the Edge," and "Translating Theory into Style"; and also those I have had the opportunity to work with as this manuscript took shape, especially Vandana Baweja, Tamara Bhalla, Sayan Bhattacharyya, Efrat Bloom, Neil Doshi, Alexandra Hoffman, Clara Seunghei Hong, Belinda Kong, Christopher Love, Janam Mukherjee, Sheshalatha Reddy, Pavitra Sundar, Corine Tachtiris, and Taymiya Zaman. A special note of thanks for all the help I have gotten from Gerrie Brewer, Vicki Davinich, Jen Eshelman, Carla Mickler-Konz, Karen Munson, and Sonia Schmerl in seeing that grant money and manuscripts went to the proper places, as well as to my collaborators Lynne Crandall, Molly des Jardins, and Neil Doshi for helping me to think in broader ways about the implications of Web 2.0 technologies for the work we do in Asian Studies.

A National Endowment for the Arts literature fellowship combined with the support of my departments at the University of Michigan made it possible for me to spend a much-needed year in 2002 and 2003 in Rajasthan selecting and translating many of the stories I write about in these chapters; in addition, a Rackham Summer grant and fellowship allowed me to interview storytellers and record oral versions of the written stories I discuss. I am grateful as well to all those who so generously hosted me; in addition to those mentioned above, I would like to acknowledge Brajesh Samarth for his help in understanding the history of the Rajasthani language; Aruna Roy, Shankar Singh, and all those involved in the MKSS, who prove daily that working for meaningful social change can be both revelatory and fun; as well as Bijju Matthews, who made their translations to America even more salient.

A year-long fellowship at Cornell University's Society for the Humanities during a theme year on translation in 2004 and 2005 provided an extremely convivial and provocative environment in which to rethink the shape of this project. A special thanks to the director Brett de Bary and to all those who became reliably insightful interlocutors during that year in Ithaca, including Anne Blackburn, Martin Bernal, Saurabh Dube,

Ann and Dan Gold, Karuna Mantena, Natalie Melas, Catherine Porter, Naoki Sakai, Keith Taylor, Jon Solomon, and John Whitman; to Mary Ahl, Linda Allen, and Lisa Patti for their extra care; and to those who helped me improve not only my writing but my bowling and hiking skills: David Agruss; Jody, Marivi, and Sofia Blanco; Kim Kono; Sherry Martin; Anna Parkinson; Helen Petrovsky; and Tim Webster.

I am grateful, too, for invitations from colleagues at other institutions than those mentioned above who have given me the opportunity to get feedback on earlier versions of these and related chapters: Kirin Narayan at the Center for South Asia at the University of Wisconsin in Madison; Peter Bush of the British Centre for Literary Translation at the University of East Anglia; G. J. V. Prasad at the School of Language, Literature and Cultural Studies at Jawaharlal Nehru University in Delhi; Theo Hermans on behalf of the Arts and Humanities Research Board at the School of Oriental and African Studies and University College London; Sherry Simon in the Translation Program at Concordia University in Montreal; Ann Gold of the South Asia Center at Syracuse University in New York; Aditya Behl and Walter Hakala at the Department of South Asian Studies at the University of Pennsylvania; and Louis-George Schwartz at the Department of Cinema and Comparative Literature at the University of Iowa. An earlier version of the closing chapter appeared as an article in *The Translator*, and I am grateful for the helpful suggestions of the editors and anonymous readers in revising the essay, and for Mona Baker's kind permission to republish it here. In addition to those already mentioned, I wish to acknowledge the crucial support of colleagues working in Translation Studies such as Rita Kothari, Carol Maier, V. Narayana Rao, Harish Trivedi, and Lawrence Venuti. I am also grateful to those who have made working in Hindi-Urdu literature so relevant and exciting and who have collaborated in rethinking the bases of our field: Laura Brueck, Allison Busch, Carlo Coppola, Iftikhar Dadi, Vasudha Dalmia, Neil Doshi, Mehr Farooqi, Syed Akbar Hyder, Kathryn Hansen, Pamela Lothspeich, Sheetal Majithia, Ali and Raza Mir, Fran Pritchett, Sean Pue, Daisy Rockwell, Bali Sahota, Simona Sawhney, and Milind Wakankar.

I would not have been able to able to generate the necessary first, second, and third drafts of these chapters if it were not for my writing buddies Heidi Kumao, Nadine Naber, Julia Paley, and Sarita See, as well as those readers who waved me away from unfortunate formulations and cheered me on toward better articulations of my better ideas: Carol Bardenstein, Kirsten Barndt, Ross Chambers, Joshua Miller, Rachel Sturman, Jennifer Wenzel, Patsy Yaeger, and Andrea Zemgulys. I also wish to thank Emily Apter, Rebecca Tolen, and two anonymous reviewers for their enthusiastic and edifying comments on earlier drafts of this manuscript; Kathe Johnson for her wizardry with indexing; Gill Kent, Eric Newman, Kate O'Brien, and Katie Sweeney of Fordham University Press for proving in practical ways that a published work is indeed a collaborative enterprise; and especially Helen Tartar, who has understood better than I what this project was meant to be.

And finally a heartfelt note of gratitude to my circle in Ann Arbor, who made sure I continued to eat well and generally live well even during the most stressful times: the Aikens boys, Vandana Baweja, Laurie Blakeney, Catherine Brown, Valerie and David Canter, Matt Degenero, Deirdre de la Cruz, all my neighbors and especially Karen, Terry, Logan, and Mara Farmer, Linda Diane Feldt, Nancy Florida, Michael Flynne, Holly Hughes, Amy Kehoe, Amanda Krugliak, Heidi Kumao, Alexa Lee, Nadine Naber, Julia Paley, Loren Ryter, Sarita See, Cam Vozar, Jennifer Wenzel, Patsy Yaeger, and Andrea Zemgulys; to my fellow traveler from the Gamma Quadrant, Venky Nagar, who kept my sights trained on finishing, as well as to his family, whose *ashirwad* via cell phone seem to have been heard; to Dan Cutler, Matt Degenero, and Heidi Kumao, who have contributed their skills to the book jacket; and to those family members and old friends whom I have always been able to count on to support me: Dorothy and Bill Freeman; Danna Liebert; Andrea Merrill; John, Claire, Abigail, Lilly, and Ella Merrill; Philip and Gay Merrill; Melinda Papowitz; Karen Schiff; Jeff, David, and Lee Weiss; and Jessica, Pat, and Francis Wickham.

And to Pause and Minsky, who made it a more appealing option to stay in my seat and keep working until it was done.

Riddles of Belonging

Can the Subaltern Joke? (to open)

People say that on one of his later visits to England leading up to Independence, M. K. Gandhi was asked by a reporter, "Mr. Gandhi, what do you think of British civilization?" In past speeches and interviews, Gandhi had been quite critical of Western modernity as a capitalist, industrialist system, especially as exported to the Indian colony. This time, however, he is said to have replied to the question of British civilization cheerfully, as if in all earnestness, "I think it would be a very good idea."[1]

It is perhaps easy to imagine why this exchange has been repeated so often in the intervening years, and with such glee: here, contained in a clever, sassy quip, is a most damning critique of the uneven political and economic relationship between colonizer and colonized. Rather than assuming "civilization" to be a static, fixed entity that the British have possessed as a matter of course since time immemorial (or at least since the waning of the Roman empire) and rather than assuming that the British are necessarily in the superior position to help people in India (re)acquaint

themselves—somewhat derivatively—with their own version of "civilization," Gandhi's response points playfully to an imaginary future—mischievously conditional—with no such fixed logic of relation. This little bit
of dialogue between the upstart Indian nationalist and the straight-man
British journalist draws attention to the precarious positionality of each
speaker in relation to one another. We understand at the outset that they
both cannot but represent the larger historical forces at work at the time;
the wordplay reveals that the engagement between them (the civilizations,
the men), while pretending to be fixed and static, is actually quite dynamic
and has been all along. It is in this moment that we can sense most vividly
that "civilize" is a transitive verb and that Indian speakers need not necessarily always be the object of British imperial grammar but might instead
repeat such a sentence with themselves in the nominative and the British,
the accusative.

Not just the mirthful subversion of the expected grammatical relation
but the fact that this bit of dialogue has been recounted so often through
the decades should make us see that its power then and now derives from
our conventions of ongoing repetition and can be understood only as part of
its larger discourse network. Quick as a breath, Gandhi's playful response
invites us to think through a more basic and thus provocative set of riddles
raised by the unexamined grammar of colonialism: What is it to be civilized? Does a people that has enslaved another have a right to call itself
civilized? What might a just response be to the wholesale takeover of one's
country when done in the very name of justice and civility? That is, how
should one respond civilly to incivility? How should one respond ethically
to injustice?

Of course, Gandhi asked a more particular version of this riddle openly
and directly in his role as nationalist leader: How can one respond nonviolently to colonial violence? The very act of calling the British system
unjust, uncivil, and violent introduced a new vocabulary for addressing the
situation—justly, civilly, nonviolently. One might argue that the humor
in evidence above is but one such tactic of nonviolent resistance and thus
shares with it both the successes and limitations of that strategy. Indeed, at
the time and in the years since, a range of politicians, scholars, and activists
have asked whether Gandhi's movement was as inclusive and empowering
for all Indian citizens as has been claimed.[2] More recently, postcolonial
theorists have looked once more to Gandhi's work to provide alternative

understandings of indigenous resistance to colonial authority.[3] My interest in the topic is more particular: I begin with this playful repartee not in
an attempt to analyze the historical details of Gandhi's leadership, nor to
debate the legacy of nonviolent resistance, but instead to analyze it as an
example of the useful deployment of playfulness as a political tool. How do
we explain the procedures by which Gandhi's rhetoric has empowered not
only the isolated speaker but generations of speakers in turn?

To start, we might notice that this playful parley, like so many exchanges—
verbal, cultural, or economic—is most handily described as taking place
between two parties, even though we know instinctively that more must be
involved. The insight is not mine alone: Sigmund Freud famously described
the joking process not in terms of a two-way exchange but as a triangle.[4]
In Freud's scenario of a rejected sexual advance, the desirous male joker
and the complicit male listener use laughter to make an alliance against the
desirable, rejecting female, objectifying her and silencing her by rendering
her the butt of a joke they share. Significantly, Freud notes that "it is not
the person who makes the joke who laughs at it and who therefore enjoys its
pleasurable effect, but the inactive listener."[5]

I introduce Freud's simple geometry because it allows us to see quite
starkly that in the example of the exchange between Gandhi and the
straight man, at any given point in time that inactive listener would be us.
It follows then that it is as useless to try to ascertain once and for all who
that "us" might be, since that variable is as variable (as in: constantly changing) as the other terms of the exchange when seen in the larger context of
this evolving network of meaning. Instead of trying to fix these terms, I ask
how we might discuss the ethics and operations of our own complicity in
an exchange such as this, which, like every exchange, constantly finds itself
in the process of being displaced—displaced, that is, because when we try
to track the practical aspects of such a parley, we find ourselves drawing an
increasingly complex network of listeners and speakers extending across
time and space, zigzagging back and forth between an undefinable present
and a collectively, dynamically imagined past that itself points to a future
mischievously conditional. How do we map such an energetic, constantly
transforming system?

The interactive, collectively created sites of the Web 2.0 are only the
latest in successive waves of technological innovation that encourage us to
treat these discourse networks we participate in as fluid, flexible, fun. We

might understand intuitively that the technological innovations of the years from 1800 to 1900 challenge our Babel-anxious distinctions between language orderly and disorderly, unified and not; nevertheless, I would venture that Friedrich Kittler's observation that "Tradition produces copies of copies of copies and so on endlessly, until even the concept of the original is lost," might elicit not so much melancholy over the loss as a sense of adventure and delightful possibility in this age of Creative Commons licenses and collectively authored Wikipedia posts.[6]

In *E-Crit: Digital Media, Critical Theory, and the Humanities*, Marcel O'Gorman argues enthusiastically that Kittler's approach "draws on a single scene as an inlet into a network of discourses that circulate through the text" and thus offers "a generative, multi-directional passageway onto a research project" critical to reconfiguring our relationships to texts in this digital age.[7] O'Gorman invites us to focus our scholarly energies on "re-imagining the academic apparatus in the context of a techno-scientific culture where the humanities have lost their market value," by tapping the revolutionary potential of the repressed forces he calls "the monstrous 'other' of the conventional academic discourse" and thus by allowing ourselves to "join in the games that they play."[8] As I show in the pages that follow, these spirited "others" have been playing games with us for centuries, even if we have only recently rediscovered an academic idiom for pointing to the nonlinear, multidirectional paths of these ludic discourse networks.

Centuries before the advent of the maya that is the Web, storytellers in India were offering mischievous insight into the ways we might "surf" these tossing, overlapping, and certainly nonlinear reservoirs of knowledge they called—in the eleventh-century Sanskrit version—*Katha Sarit Sagara* ("the ocean of the streams of stories").[9] More recently, the postcolonial British writer Salman Rushdie appropriated this phrase into his own tale, *Haroun and the Sea of Stories*, to counter the logic of absolute silence in the Ayatollah's fatwa threatening his life. In turn, Edward R. Tufte appropriated the English-language version of the title for a chapter in *Visual Explanations* that challenges the implicit linearity characteristic of our thinking today.[10] Such a genealogy—and the fact that Tufte cites Rushdie and not *Katha Sarit Sagara* author Somadeva or nineteenth-century translator C. H. Tawney, who was responsible for coining the phrase in English—only serves to make an even more interesting point about how very erratic and multidirectional the movement of these reservoirs of knowledge is. The genealogy of this well-circulated phrase demonstrates that "the ocean of the streams of story" is apt both literally as well as metaphorically. In the process, such a figure makes the demand that we rework the conventions of our academic discourse to allow us to see that the scene in which the origin of such a phrase is imagined is not an origin at all but performs in multiple media, in multiple times and places (such as the "creative commons"), and is therefore intrinsically plural, empirical, other.[11]

When we consider the various translations of this oral-based storytelling cycle, we might notice—as I argue in more detail in the following chapters—that we are forced to conceptualize these plural texts not as material property to be exchanged but as a series of "tellings" being passed along from one person to the next. Such a distinction conforms to the Sanskrit etymology of the Hindi word for translation, *anuvad*, as a "telling in turn," as opposed to the Latin-based English understanding of translating as "a carrying across." Regarding a text as a "telling in turn" and thus as a verbal performance assumes that we, too, are part of this ocean of the streams of story, contributing to it and redirecting its flow. In these pages, I focus on texts—like the phrase "the ocean of the stream of story" or Gandhi's civilization quip—that have invited us to play along; I focus on these texts in a way that aims to draw on a single scene as an inlet into a network of discourses that circulate through the text and thus might offer a generative, multidirectional passageway onto any given inquiry.

Even if we try to isolate the text in a single site of exchange at a particular moment, we see that it is paradoxically there and yet here at the same time, then and now, us and them. Whether we imagine the complicity of a given exchange as occurring in a vaguely ahistorical past or in a constantly deferred present, we must acknowledge that for a quip like Gandhi's, for example, to be passed along requires that each listener become a raconteur in turn, just as a game can be meaningful only if it is played by multiple generations in turn.

Rather than tracing such genealogies, here I will focus on the procedures by which such humor performs by performing my own version of the humor, acting the part of a raconteur myself. I do this on the assumption that a joking communication always works on a number of different levels at once and that participants cannot by definition be conscious of the more compelling depths at which the exchange occurs. Unlike my predecessors who work to strip away layers of silence burying a secret, I maintain that attempts at direct and serious-minded revelation will not be as successful as those that play with—and play along with—such displacements. That is, if we agree with Freud that playful communication must necessarily be premised on displacement—one that is relational, dynamic, and therefore collectively negotiated—then in the case of exchanges that work across languages, cultures, continents, and media, I argue that we must analyze carefully the terms by which such a "place" is established rhetorically: How are the divisions of here and there, now and then, us and them, announced in such a performance? While displacement, by definition, cannot be understood directly, I contend that the very figures used to frame this imaginary space reveal much about the fraught historical contexts and ideological motivations of the individual tellings.

We might notice, for instance, that in our narratives of Gandhi, for this colonized subject to participate in this verbal exchange on English soil required him to translate his own person as much materially as culturally, if not linguistically. We know that the symbolism—and implicit contradictions—of such translations were carefully managed at the time. It is not beside the point that the visual vocabulary we have learned to rely on through the years draws scenes of his arrival by boat, a frail man, wrapped loosely (even scantily) in summer-weight cottons, waving to the assembled crowds from the deck. It is not the friendly shine of his eyes through the round spectacles or his tight, mischievous smile but often the skin he chooses to reveal that is most talked about and thus becomes the focus of public attention. We can see that his insistence on wearing nothing more than a *dhoti* and shawl with sandals on his feet has been read as a display of one of the more obvious irreconcilable differences between East and West. Rather than feeling ashamed, Gandhi is said to have joked about the political import of such questions of habitus: to another straight-man reporter's query about going to Buckingham Palace so "underdressed," he is said to have replied, "Her Majesty had on enough clothes for both of us."

In this repartee as well, as in the scene of Freud's joking triangle, humor is used to make alliance across a range of differences and in the process to renegotiate the implicit balance of power between the players. While in Freud's example, the effect of the humor might be understood to conserve the status quo of patriarchy, Gandhi was able—in part through such playful challenges—successfully (and repeatedly) to galvanize public opinion against the colonial regime. He did so by exposing the implicit double standard that since the late eighteenth century had posited the Indian colonial subject as both British citizen and not, one with inalienable natural rights and not.[12] He responded to what Homi Bhabha has since called the "sly civility" of the British by speaking their own language back to them, repeating it in such a way that common sense was revealed to be nonsense, and thus called into question the divisions between one and the other.[13] It is only when we recognize the play on words that we become conscious of the ways a word such as "underdressed" can have multiple senses. Even then, we might not be aware that we sense such multiple senses in sensual detail.[14] Overtly Gandhi's exposed ("underdressed") body is compared to the queen's lavishly cloaked person, and we are seemingly unaware of the journalist who is fabled to have made such a comparison. However, if the journalist appeals to a British idea of propriety in condemning Gandhi's choice of outfit, Gandhi in turn offers a different way of counting two against one by drawing attention to the travesty that serves to set the queen in a class by herself. The sense the two share is indeed revealed to be common when the underdressed body of a figure like Gandhi is distinguished from the overdressed queen, in comparison to the unmarked figure of the journalist.

It is only when we recount this triangular exchange in turn that we assume identifying attributes for the three speakers in such a way that the bodily sense of each speaking voice becomes posited as a source of historical legitimation and thus part of the story of its meaning that we might share. Gandhi is depicted as repeating the rhetoric of colonial discourse—a discourse in which, as Homi Bhabha points out, "that space of the other is always occupied by an idée fixe: despot, heathen, barbarian, chaos, violence"—and plays with the very fixed categories available through that language so it becomes clear that the common ground they thought they shared was not solid, as they assumed, but shifty, not static and fixed but dynamic and flexible.[15] Such an example shows that we need to engage with a more complex version of the standard postcolonial riddle—Can the subaltern speak?—and examine more carefully examples of playful exchange that unsettle and even displace the fixed categories by which we often frame such issues.

We might start by acknowledging that each instance of exchange can never function in isolation but is linked in an ongoing chain of collective meaning-making. In the example of Gandhi's quip about British civilization, we could look today to interviews with Amartya Sen or stray references on the Web by other public intellectuals such as Ramachandra Guha to see evidence of the ways this playful exchange has been repeated since then in forms both spoken and written, moving flexibly between various media.[16] When we consider a text such as this, which is reported to have circulated from spoken word captured on film to printed book, to spoken word, to Web page, we see that the distinction over technologies—between "spoken" and "written," for example—is not as salient as that between text which is fixed and that which is flexible. This project examines the networks that give such a text meaning over the years across a range of differences (language, nation, race, class, gender, ethnicity, faith).

Trying to trace the genealogy of Gandhi's retort allows us to inquire into the fuller range of meanings associated with a word such as "exchange." The Oxford English Dictionary definition—"the action or act of reciprocal giving and receiving"—reminds us that while such an idealized condition of commensurability is assumed at the outset, it can be achieved only in ongoing, dynamic relation. My suggestion in this book is that analyzing the temporal and spatial narrative structures of playful exchange as they repeat across a range of differences allows us to look more closely at the idioms available to us for participating in these performances in dialogic engagement with a range of interlocutors. Common rhetorical ground should be understood not as a fixed space given to us but as one we continually recreate. I advance such a notion in conversation with colleagues in postcolonial studies who see a link between issues of entrenched incommensurability and our own practices of comparison.[17] I purposely focus on playful narratives that challenge the status quo because they force us to account for our own complicity and resistances to such displacements. I take seriously Lydia Liu's warning that:

> a cross-cultural study must examine its own conditions of possibility. Constituted as a translingual act itself, it enters, rather than sits above, the dynamic history of the relationship between words, concepts, categories and discourse. One way of unraveling that relationship is to engage rigorously with those words, concepts, categories, and discourses beyond the realm of the common sense, dictionary definition, and even historical linguistics.[18]

To examine its own conditions of possibility, this particular study must dispense with categorizations that see "theory" as separate from other modes of writing and "oral" as distinct from "written." My contention—as performed here in my own writing as well—is that each of our delivery styles offers its own theoretical positioning which we must learn to read more attentively. How, then, may we engage critically with such displacements when our very interpretive act is itself multiply displaced?

Even if we try to isolate Gandhi's exchange with the British reporter in a single imaginary and generalized moment in time, we soon discover that the triangle has a fourth (that is, temporal) dimension: for the joke to be funny, we must locate its relevance both here and there, now and then, with regards both to us and to them. To wit: a speaker such as Gandhi can twist the meaning of "British civilization" only if there is a current understanding of the phrase already in place to work against, and a public ready to do that work. It thus should seem obvious that a joke, like language more generally, finds meaning in relation to prior usage and subsequent repetition. Meaning is thus made in the plural, on common ground necessarily temporary and provisional, even if it pretends that the understanding they currently share is singular, stable, timeless. Freud, for example, might very well present his joking scenario as if it could occur in a historical vacuum where differences of language, faith, race, nationality, and ethnicity seem not to exist, but, as I discuss in the following chapter, such an approach ignores the fact of, for example, the colonizer-colonized relationship on which his own disciplinary practice is premised.[19] I say this not to claim that we could ever meet up in some neutral zone outside history, lambasting this or that influential critic who has preceded us—as has been the unhappy convention in too much postcolonial criticism—but instead to suggest that our most fraught scholarly exchanges might be compared productively to such playful encounters.

In the humorous scene of colonial wrangling I open with, for instance, we might see that we have two men—ostensibly representing civilizations Eastern and Western—in conversation over not a sexually desirable woman but an equally desirable and even fetishized Mother India: Who has a right to call her his own? In whose hands will she fare better?[20] Such questions have no doubt been addressed in important ways over the decades by a phalanx of serious-minded experts. My project is slightly different: Gandhi's playful retort interests me for the ways it has been passed along through the generations, repeated in such a way that it has given us a dynamic and mutable language for posing afresh some of the larger—and largely unanswerable—riddles of colonial and postcolonial exchange.

The power of such repetitions can be understood only by combining the tools of analysis available to us from a number of disciplines—literature, anthropology, history, rhetoric, cultural studies, translation, folklore—to analyze in detail the complex comparison of one version to the next, especially those that are connected multiply, dynamically, and certainly nonlinearly across time and space. Velcheru Narayana Rao, for instance, acknowledges that riddling exchange "needs a community . . . a shared acceptance of a world," but that it "brings a community into existence, while allowing the members of this community to believe that it existed prior to their creating it."[21] What shared acceptance of a world is forged in individual relationships that cross accepted borders of language and culture?

We might notice that Gandhi does not seem to present to the British public an absolute nativist position in matters of language as he does in clothing and therefore does not force speakers of English to confront our own provinciality as it manifests in the discourse we share. He may have railed in print against the "evil wrought by the English medium" in India, but in newsreels and in lore Gandhi is seen conversing easily and directly with the British public in his well-trained English.[22] Javed Majeed makes clear that at home Gandhi made an effort to be conversant in his native tongue, Gujarati, as well as in the nonsectarian version of the north Indian idiom, Hindustani, which he wanted recognized as India's national language.[23] In the versions of the exchanges with the British reporters that have come down to us, however, neither English-speaking interlocutor is shown to be conscious of Gandhi's multilinguality; after all, Gandhi did not declare absolutely—as Ngũgĩ wa Thiong'o would decades later—that he was renouncing the colonizer's language entirely in order to begin "decolonising the mind."[24] Gandhi did not insist on conversing with the reporter exclusively in Gujarati or Hindustani.

The ideological link between such language issues and the effects of colonialism cannot be overemphasized. Indeed, it has received insufficient attention in much postcolonial theory—especially as it has been formulated in monolingual contexts. We might notice, for example, how easy it is for those of us analyzing this encounter in English to forget that we are reading a multilingual speaker monologically and therefore are limiting our discussion to terms available in the standard language we share.

Analogously, it would help us little to confine the site of meaning-making to a singular prior event—the "original"—forever lost to us, for such a melancholic approach not only fails to take account of our own part in the ongoing exchange but silences the speaker in the process. (Can the subaltern joke?) As I argue in the following chapter, the pervasive institutional fixation on what is "lost in translation" has implications for a wide range of intercultural encounters—whether understood as the bodily displacements of migrancy or as the textual recreations of interlingual transfer. My interest in this example, as in this book more generally, is to investigate our own responses as the silent public to such translational performances in an effort to rethink the very terms we use to delineate this space. I suggest that our English-language theories of postcoloniality need more sophisticated critical tools for mapping these complex networks of meaning-making and the common ground on which they are provisionally sited rather than ones that dismiss multilinguality as so much babble.

I am inspired in large part by the work currently going on today in India that understands issues of translation as a reading and writing practice in the context of postcoloniality: these scholars, publishers, creative writers, translators, teachers, and activists create communities that rethink and rework the conventions we rely on as we circulate texts.[25] In a direct challenge to pervasive monologically minded theorizations, for instance, Ganesh Devy describes the (post)colonized subject moving fluidly between a number of languages at once, traversing a complex linguistic terrain she rarely maps in fixed, discrete units. Such a formulation challenges the very way we figure the speaking subject spatially and temporally. While in America most particularly we might be familiar with the neatly demarcated and certainly binaristic DuBoisian model of "double consciousness" that in early twentieth-century America powerfully articulated the interior experience of a man of African descent at odds with the European-American society surrounding him, in late twentieth-century India Devy takes careful note of the confusing multilinguality that a (post)colonized subject experiences in conforming to Eurocentric hierarchies in both international and national arenas; Devy sees such interior experiences instead as an example of an alienated "translating consciousness."[26] Devy's project has been to rethink the very ways we frame in our own (decolonizing) minds the relationships of our various languaged selves to those of others, as a way of contesting not only English's supremacy in India but the more fundamental, pervasive assumption that monolingualism is of a higher, neater order, multilingualism of a lesser.

Given such an insight, let us return to my suggestion that a speaker such as Gandhi can twist the meaning of "British civilization" only if there is a current understanding of the phrase already in place to work against and a public ready to do that work. If you agree that a joke such as this, like language more generally, finds meaning in relation to prior usage and in subsequent repetition, then how do we frame the resulting colonial and postcolonial narrative relationships premised on such a current understanding, especially those that are read as monological when they are clearly multilingual? I argue here and in the following pages that in order to understand the spatial and temporal dimensions of the figurative common ground that is posited in such an exchange, we must take into account their fleeting, fluid nature and their dynamic relationality across time and space. It is for this reason that I will read "current" ("premised on a current understanding") in the more literal sense of being fleeting and fluid, a slender stream in the greater roil of ongoing circulations we take part in. The play in the metaphor helps us to recognize that the common ground we imagine we share at any point in time is constantly and necessarily moving. Attention to this dynamic engagement helps us to understand how the translated texts we read might be riddled ("with gaps") but are also riddling us, as Yopie Prins points out in the case of *Victorian Sappho*.[27]

As we see in Chapter 3 ("Framed"), the troping of displaced narrative exchange as riddling not only is relevant now but has been part of a self-reflexive, transgressive, and certainly mirthful literary vocabulary in South Asia for well over a millennium—at least since the days of the *Katha Sarit Sagara*. Both in written versions and oral, the framed narratives discussed in the second and third chapters imagine the dimensions of this exchange in terms of an ongoing and exceedingly contentious storytelling relationship—one that trades in riddles. Like Freud's joking triangle, the surface play allows the shared limits of difficult social quandaries to be explored—such as spouse abuse, caste-based discrimination—without naming the issues as such. Part of what gets negotiated in these playful exchanges is the boundaries of the precarious triangular alliance established through the exchange, and it is this fluid commitment to finding provisional common ground that allows difficult issues to be negotiated without fixing—or fixating on—them. Displacement, then, is the shifting ground on which all productive exchange must take place, especially in an uneven world.[28] In the following chapters I show that our interpretive methods need to be as quick and clever, as dynamic and responsive, as the performances that inspire them and should thus look to the methods and methodologies of these playful narrative texts themselves to narrate their procedures.

In Chapter 1 ("Humoring the Melancholic Reader of World Literature"), I show that even our own as-if-outside-the-bounds discussions of these issues necessarily assume a common understanding and therefore locate themselves on a precarious common ground whose fixed bases I interrogate through play. I frame the discussion for this opening chapter in a query of the displaced anxiety over originality that pervades much of our literary discussions today, focusing on texts that, like Gandhi's quip, defy easy division into categories of oral and written, translated and original, literary and nonliterary, even academic and nonacademic. Thus suitably framed, Chapters 2 and 3 ("A Telling Example" and "Framed") analyze framed narratives from contemporary and classical India that also defy easy division into available categories but feature contentious, riddling, storytelling relationships that comment metatextually on the frame story's own narrative devices. The embedded, riddling narratives I discuss negotiate delicate ethical questions—What rights does a woman have when being abused by her husband? How far does a husband's dominion over his wife extend?—and thus give us as readers an opportunity to investigate our own responses to such dialogic engagement and in the process to pose a set of analogous riddles: How do we identify a person's rights when reading a story that traverses the bounds of language and nation? How far does a narrative community's dominion extend?

My argument is that we need a more complex and responsive set of analytic tools in order to delineate this constantly shifting common ground that is our interpretive community today. Throughout these chapters I ask how we might reconcile the recent calls for the salve of translation with the lessons of colonialism when trying to formulate a critical vocabulary for justice that we might participate in as academics today. I look carefully at examples like Gandhi's clever retort and Vijay Dan Detha's politically engaged and certainly mirthful stories because their playfulness encourages us to move away from the fixed conceptual frames that threaten to render static an otherwise dynamic conversation and offers instead an approach that might be as attentive to past injustices as to present possibilities for temporarily correcting those imbalances.

I test this suggestion in Chapter 4 ("A Divided Sense") by comparing twelve translations of a story that itself plays with divisions between common ground and alien ground, common sense and nonsense, and I go on to demonstrate how we might best read a story of displacement when the story itself is translated and therefore displaced. The chapter not only shows how a work in translation might be read in the plural but argues that the literary frames we adopt must themselves be dynamic and responsive in that pluralism to allow us to think more critically and ethically about the shifting relationships we establish in narrative exchange.

To follow from that lesson, Chapter 5 ("Passing On") argues that even stories that are not readily identified as translated are themselves the product of such complex and paradoxically overlapping networks of interpretation that to understand the common ground established through these constantly evolving literary communities, we must take into account their temporal dimension. In this and Chapter 6 ("Narration in Ghost Time"), I pursue the suggestion offered in Chapter 4 that we must examine more carefully the technologies of literary analysis we adopt when reading translated texts. I look at the grammatical relations established in fanciful, oral-based ghost stories that are narrated in *bhoot kaal* (literally "ghost time" and so "past tense") to show how a Hindi story and a Rajasthani tale offer sophisticated tools for understanding nonlinear narrative relations. I then close my own frame (in "A Double Hearing") by concluding that these spirited literary encounters have much to teach us about the limits and possibilities of our own rights and responsibilities as literary citizens of this translated, globalized world.

Here and throughout I understand "spirited" in the sense of fun and exuberant but also in the sense of haunted, a play on words that applies similarly to the multiple meanings in English of "possession." In short, I argue that understanding how a translated text is possessed (as haunted, or as temporarily owned) requires us to examine more closely our own spirited engagements with the texts—in dynamic displacement.

While each chapter does indeed draw on oral performances (including a written translation of one of my own oral performances, once upon a time), the book takes advantage of its own medium of production and invites readers to skip through the text in any order, picking at fragments that seem interesting and relevant to them.[29] Each chapter is organized to read as a discrete piece in its own right and is further broken down into discrete sections to allow for the kind of agential movement I celebrate otherwise in the chapters that follow. My sincere hope is that you, my dear reader, will find your own way of putting together these fragments so that you can tell your own version in turn.

Humoring the Melancholic Reader of World Literature

"All Is . . . Lost!"

If in the previous chapter I argue that we must join in the games others play, in this chapter I do one better—by beginning with a riddling tale of translation. The story I have in mind is of origins so obscure that I am sure few know it; I turn to it here merely because the provocative questions it raises address almost too perfectly my own theoretical interests (an overlap that will, no doubt, provoke some well-warranted skepticism in the cautious reader). One can assume the reason for the story's obscurity is that it is not readily available in English and is written by a name few would know. I'd like to think of the author as a latter-day Borges, this one writing in a language (and in a country) that has inspired some of the world's most popular fictions.

The story tells of an earnest translator named Mr. Worth who, not unlike Borges's character Pierre Menard, sets out to complete a collection of stories that contain perfect translations.[1] Before Mr. Worth can even embark on such an undertaking, however, he must ascertain how one might judge perfection in translation. Answering such a question soon becomes a project in its own right, one that propels the narrative. The story details Mr. Worth's struggles against those subtle cultural forces that assert translational standards more and more persuasively in terms set out by critics in the home country than in the source: some less than encouraging words from an editor here, a few well-reasoned but still passionate scholarly appraisals there, not to mention the kind but certainly not neutral advice from a group of fellow writers in the source culture that perhaps those readers over there don't really understand us. "Us"? Indeed. This, in a word, is precisely the question the story raises.

As a character he's made to be likable enough, and so you hardly notice the gradual shift of alliance, hardly notice the shift in pronouns, in point of view. If you had heard me tell it (as I did in my own academic version of an oral performance, one early spring afternoon in Ithaca, New York), you might have assumed this to be yet another of those inevitable tales of a translator's divided loyalty. *Traduttore, traditore*, as they say (not just any "they"—Freud, too, repeats this little adage across languages).[2] In the story the translator begins making modifications to the stories he writes, thinking his interventions will render them more readily understood in their own terms, a course of action our increasingly unreliable narrator seems reluctant to protest. The very narrative style no doubt makes us uneasy— playing, as it does, along the edge separating fiction and nonfiction, teasing our sense of right and wrong. Are we meant to be responding with outrage? With mirth? The story seems to be setting up some kind of trap, but it is not clear who or what is being trapped, for what ends. What is the point of a telling such as this?

Within the story it soon becomes clear that in the name of being faithful to the original, Mr. Worth commits perhaps the most egregious act of infidelity. Not all at once but gradually. At first the modifications seem slight, a mere act of interpretive decisiveness where there had been ambiguity; a rhetorical flourish that allowed the translation language to stretch its limits in a way it could be imagined the original had stretched its own language; some background provided where it was presumed there might be confusion. Soon enough, however, Mr. Worth finds he is writing not the stories the authors had so dutifully written and published for distribution to the original readership but the ones they told by way of example—over dinner, in heated discussion, in informal, intimate settings.

Before too long he has begun recreating stories he heard from the authors' families, their neighbors, and finally his neighbors. It seems he would take up any story that conveyed a particularly rare or insightful point of view. The final capitulation comes when he begins writing not stories he'd actually heard told but ones he imagines would have been, had the authors met the kinds of critics the translator knew needed to be addressed to have these stories circulating more widely in global markets abroad. These were the stories, the narrator rationalized, that could serve to introduce the writers' creative worlds to readers unfamiliar with these foreign contexts, making way for more complex, more culturally specific stories in due time. We're told that the translator felt he had been infused with the spirits of the authors he was translating and thus had an obligation to cultivate an ongoing relationship with his readers directly. He was working toward a larger goal, toward a time in the future when those faraway readers would be more receptive to the kinds of challenges this body of stories posed. At least, this was the way our protagonist rationalized his creative and therefore ideological choices, conveyed to us via the narrator in third-person close.

We find out that the translator's instinct turned out to be at least partially right. Mr. Worth prepares an anthology of new writing from the country where he resides, in which he combines stories that were translations in the strictest sense of the word with those that were recreations of work we might say—to be delicate—had no *tangible* originals. Some he attributes to the authors from whom he had heard the stories in some form, and for those two or three stories where such a connection was really not possible, he invents an author named "Pata Nahin." The anthology, we learn, becomes a runaway success. What makes these newly discovered authors especially compelling, the narrator tells us, is the trenchant manner in which they offer critiques of the oppressive state in which they dwell, critiques that conform uncannily to sentiments those faraway readers most readily endorse.

In the final scene we watch the translator reading a letter from the publisher quoting lines from enthusiastic reviewers and literary scholars who speak authoritatively of the "startling truths" contained in this collection of short stories. The publisher goes on to suggest that it might be good for sales and perhaps lead to future contracts for collections by the individual authors if they could organize a book tour around the target country with a few of these "new voices" she is sure readers would want to hear more from—to let the readers know exactly "who is speaking," as she phrases it, and in what context. She does not stop to think that in any case, the "new voices" she heard as she read the words on the page were all written by Mr. Worth in various degrees of creative inventiveness.

And, as you're no doubt anticipating, when the letter goes on to specify the stories the publisher deems most worthy of further attention, she names those works that we would in all truthfulness identify as the translator's owns fictions: she wishes to send the author Pata Nahin on a book tour. The tale ends with Mr. Worth writing back to the publisher a version of that famous 1968 pronouncement in words published originally by Richard Howard after a subsequently published French version by Roland Barthes: "With a full heart I must inform you of the death of the author." The translator stops, realizing he must say something more about what this news might signify, and so elaborates in a tone he means perhaps to be consoling but which I must say struck me as musing, even amusing:

> We can never know, for the good reason that writing is the destruction of every voice, every origin. Writing is that neuter, that composite, that obliquity into which our subject flees, the black-and-white where all identity is lost, beginning with the very identity of the body that writes.[3]

He then murmurs to himself a quotation attributed to Voltaire that he remembers having read in Bouvard and Pécuchet's *Dictionary of Received Ideas* and particularly liked: "Even if he did not exist, it would be necessary to invent him."[4] The story ends with the translator leaning over his desk, laughing uncontrollably.

Why is the translator laughing?

The Scandalized Subject

To begin trying to solve such an endlessly teasing riddle, we might notice that the story of Mr. Worth touches on two anxieties still very much alive in our institutions of literary interpretation today: one Lawrence Venuti has aptly dubbed "the scandals of translation," the other Shoshona Felman (in the most recent English version by Catherine Porter) calls "the scandal of the speaking body."[5] The scandal, for an outraged Venuti, has been in treating the work of translation as marginal, derivative, false. Felman, for her part, delights in the scandal she subtitles a "seduction in two languages," comparing the work of speech-act theorist J. L. Austin to Don Juan to insist that for these two upstarts "Language . . . is performative and not informative; it is a field of enjoyment, not of knowledge. As such, it cannot be qualified as true or false, but rather quite specifically as *felicitous* or *infelicitous*, successful or unsuccessful."[6]

I would venture that Venuti and Felman each identify scandal because the performance in question—whether translation or speech act—plays with the line separating the false from the real and in the process forces us to question the very validity and even solidity of that demarcation. We might then understand how very unnerved a reader might be by Mr. Worth's successful—even felicitous—attempts to translate the speech acts of his dinner companions if that reader previously had full and complete faith in the authority of our literary institutions to detect the difference between a true translation and a fake. Considered this way, the translator's laughter leads us to a riddle that more closely considers these questions of scandal (and which propelled Mr. Worth's quest in the first place): What exactly constitutes a true translation?

As a published translator I find myself considering versions of this same riddle nearly every day, pursuing not just the pragmatic, if-I-were-to-stray-who-is-there-to-stop-me, safety-net set of questions but a more subtle inquiry that asks how and where we agree to draw the line separating the faithful act from the transgressive. As many practicing translators will no doubt agree, in matters of literary recreation the distinction between the two is never so very stark and clear. Few besides practicing translators, however, seem to see the task of the translator as anything but straightforward and mechanical and so have trouble apprehending the most urgent implications of these complex creative decisions we make.

In these many pages, I not only ask how and where we might draw that neat line but also explore what is at stake in the (contentious, collective, constantly shifting) mapping of these imaginary conceptual borders. To do so, I must begin by interrogating the very division between true and false, original and derivative, that such a judgment assumes. I will do so by bringing together Felman's concern for reading texts as dynamically performative rather than statically informative and Venuti's suggestion that a close reading of translation allows us to articulate what he calls in his title "an ethics of difference." If we agree that Mr. Worth's performance was scandalous, then what does such a judgment tell us about the boundaries of the rhetorical and therefore ethical ground we hold in common? Such a question works the same conceptual territory discussed in regard to Gandhi's playful parley in the opening. Here, however, I ask a more particular and provocative version: How do we proceed when we realize we mark our lines at slightly or even radically different points? That is, I would like to spend the remaining chapters asking what metacritical language we might rely on to negotiate our divergent readings of such performances, especially in instances where humor is used to address thorny ethical questions.

Venuti has commonsensically argued that we cannot begin to engage critically with translated literary texts when the work of the translator producing those texts has been rendered invisible. I further his argument by playing with the broader scandals he identifies, framing them in such a way that allows them to riddle us productively. We might, for instance, regard the fictional Mr. Worth as a most worthy literary upstart, in that he has successfully (albeit wickedly) played with the literary establishment's infuriating habit of treating a text as belonging exclusively to a single author. I suggest this because I myself have been caught by the same paradox he has: even though I wrote the English-language version of "Chouboli" or "*Dovari Joon*," our discursive conventions—not to mention our publishing protocols—would have us refer to the work as being authored singly by the famous, award-winning Indian writer Vijay Dan Detha.

I'm not complaining about my invisibility as translator for the reasons you might think, however. In some ways, I have found this temporary erasure to be a useful fiction for me to maintain, especially when representing controversial scenes of domestic violence and cross-dressing duplicity to an American audience. With me rendered silent and invisible, readers seem more convinced that the perspective they are being offered through the story is exclusively Indian or even Rajasthani. The problem is this: however irreverent and mischievously playful this translated work might be, with Detha's authorial imprimatur it ends up being treated as authentic commentary on South Asian culture—flat, humorless, static. Invisible is the wry, goading relationship Detha establishes with the traditional Rajasthani storytelling cultures he writes from and for. Invisible, too, is the admiring, amused, and slightly scandalized relationship I establish with the Hindi and Rajasthani stories I write from as reader. What is literary about the resulting performance? Instead you, the reader, might as well be greeted on the page with a two-in-one version of Mr. Worth, Detha and I silently submitting to this jargon of authenticity we are both doomed to repeat as if in a single voice.

Such laughing dialogism masquerading as somber monologism suggests a version of the riddle posed by Mr. Worth toward the end of the story; if we agree with him that "all identity is lost, beginning with the very identity of the body that writes," then we need to ask: Which writing body is referred to as lost?[7] We might follow the old conventions of literary criticism vis-à-vis translation and pursue one of those endlessly fascinating and maddening projects, intent on recovering something we never really had in the first place. (This is more or less the aporia Judith Butler plays with in her work on gender and melancholy.) But here, in the realm where fictional worlds overlap with the nonfictional, I want to suggest that if we stop looking for elusive origins, we might notice we already have quite a lively exchange going on—across time, place, languages, genre, even media. For instance, when I refer to "the body that writes," I could be asking about the identity of the author within the fiction framed by the story (Pata Nahin), which itself is a ready allusion to Barthes's riddling, translated essayistic voice asking about Balzac's lost identity, a reference we could imagine was made by the author of this story in the "real" world (whom some suppose to be Lillian Virginia Mountweazel),[8] or we could be referring to me, the person framing this story for you here, who not only repeats it now in this ambiguous and constantly shifting space of a written present tense, but claims to have told the story originally in March of 2005—as a living, breathing, speaking, tangible body in my avatar as translation scholar at a conference at Cornell University called "Tasking the Translator." Shouldn't such lively circulations be worth something?

Let's pretend for a moment that I'm an old party faithful, happy to practice criticism the usual way. And let's say we know the original author of the story of Mr. Worth to be a translator herself caught in a similar predicament. Does it help us solve any of the most interesting riddles raised by the story? Does it help us explain why, for instance, the translator in the fiction is laughing? Does it convince us to laugh along with him? If so, at what? At his own fallibility in committing such an unforgivable transgression? At the transnational institutions of literature that are not able to draw a clear line distinguishing the real from the fake? At this circuit of production called "world literature" that does not seem to know how to read fiction as fiction? Or perhaps at the community of readers who would recoil in horror at the thought of such travesty? How can we know? (Here, the translated voice of Barthes is speaking to us again: "We can never know, for the good reason that writing is the destruction of every voice, every origin.") I am sure there are many good reasons to insist on the authority of the original: at least with the verifiable evidence of a writing body—even if as dead as Balzac—we imagine we can somehow *place* the story's creation—culturally, politically, aesthetically, even ethically. We have already considered such a question in regard to the Gandhi repartee. And I know from my own experiences that smart, playful, spirited critiques of domestic violence like the one we find in "Chouboli" or *"Dovari Joon"* can't float outside time and space. They live in a particular Rajasthani context. How are we to understand the continued life of that critique when translated into Hindi or English, if not in strict comparison to its original?[9]

We find ourselves in a similar bind when we consider a writer of oral-based tales such as Vijay Dan Detha. Here in his work we have the same anxieties over originality: the stories he writes are perhaps too derivative to be considered true literature by some detractors and too embellished to be considered authentic folklore by others. The result is that he sits uneasily in designated categories such as "author" or "folklorist." He told me that when he started writing in the 1960s he thought of himself as a folklorist in the tradition of the Brothers Grimm. In the heady Nehruvian days following Independence in 1947, he returned to his village with college friend and musicologist Komal Kothari to found an organization called Rupayan Samsthan that would work with the community to document and preserve the folk traditions of their native Rajasthan. Then, as now, he held an abiding belief in the power of local cultural forms to express the most democratic (and some say communist) will of the people. Unlike the Grimm Brothers, however, and like Ngũgĩ wa Thiong'o's commitment to "decolonising the mind," Detha began writing not in the language of the former colonizer (English), nor in the national language (Hindi) which citizens of Rajasthan were officially declared to speak, but in the spoken idiom he had grown up with, which at the time had no name or official status but which his publications helped define: Rajasthani.[10] He combined elements from different versions he heard, elaborated on others, and reworked the versions to be as powerful as he was able. The stories, like the language, belonged to Detha as much as to his neighbors. The irony is that so many of us have had trouble finding a ready critical idiom for describing such a straightforward relationship between a vernacular, postcolonial writer and the culture he writes from and to.

One could accuse Detha of translating local forms in a neocolonial version of the British-Orientalist appropriations that have received so much criticism.[11] To be sure, throughout his career, Detha has written down stories he heard from thieves in his village, stories he heard from politicians, prostitutes, farmers, potters, housewives, and wandering mendicants and claimed them, in part, as his own. He has framed the stories with invocations and singsong rhyming verses called *chouga* that are signatures of Rajasthani oral convention. To make these simulated storytelling performances come alive from the page, he has taken care that the characters speak in the local idioms of their castes; has inserted proverbs and expressions he found particularly colorful; has combined fragments of various versions of stories he heard; he'd take the seed of a story like "Duvidha," which in the telling was only a few lines, and draw it out to more than thirty pages. And his versions were so effective that they garnered audiences in both oral and written contexts: people began reading them out loud in storytelling sessions or retelling stories they had read in *Baatan ri Phulwari* (his fourteen-volume collection of stories) at political rallies, putting these stories back into circulation in the oral tradition, even adapting them to film. I heard a hilarious version of a story Detha had written down told in Hindi at a political gathering in Ann Arbor, Michigan—the English-language translator then attributed the story to Detha.[12]

If Detha's main objective was to ensure that the idioms and the stories of Rajasthani would live on, then his writings by most accounts have been felicitous. Or are we looking for something else when we insist upon such standards? Would we rather be given a name, any name, that allows us to fix the text once and for all than be told that these stories belong as much to Detha as to the people who have told them in the past and might in the future?[13] To mark this line separating his from theirs, the real from the fake, requires that we move beyond vague assertions of scandal (whether of translation or of the speaking body). Instead we need to address a more complex riddle: How do we read texts authored in the plural?

We might imagine this to be an entirely postmodern, even postcolonial, riddle until we consider that James Macpherson's *Poems of Ossian* caused a similar quandary in its day: a few decades before Goethe began making enthusiastic claims for the establishment of a "world literature," Macpherson collected fragments of what he considered an ancient epic circulating in the oral traditions of the Scottish Highlands, which he then translated into English and published in various versions from 1760 to 1765. Nowadays scholars on nationalism such as Eric Hobsbawm refer glancingly to the *Ossian* when offering illustrative (even originary) examples of "invented tradition," slotting it not under the more ambiguous category of "semifiction" but of outright "forgery."[14] Folklorist Alan Dundes likewise uses the example of Macpherson to worry at the distinction between the false and the real—as "fakelore" versus folklore—proposed by Richard Dorson in 1950 and bids us see such inventions as an understandable reaction to feelings of "national inferiority" as common in twentieth-century America (Paul Bunyan) as in eighteenth-century Scotland (the Ossian), nineteenth-century Germany (the Grimm fairy tales) or nineteenth-century Finland (the Kalevala).

It is no coincidence that all the works mentioned here—like the tales of Detha or even the story of Mr. Worth—are based on oral narratives. These examples signal an interpretive process Katie Trumpener has quite insightfully labeled "bardic nationalism," whereby a figure such as Macpherson becomes a "mouthpiece for a whole society" and the oral-based literature he has written, "a vehicle of collective expression and historical justice."[15] Literary writing becomes an answer to power in the name of justice and equality, a reaction to imperial conquest. In Trumpener's Romantic examples, the bard becomes "a figure who represents the resistance of vernacular oral traditions to the historical pressures of English imperialism and whose performance brings the voices of the past into the sites of the present."[16] Significantly, she argues that such reactions are related to the new terms of ownership the English instituted in their bid for political and economic control in the eighteenth and nineteenth centuries; she sees the Scottish and Irish expressions of nationalist consciousness—documenting masters of the oral traditions, mapping sites of historical significance—as attempts to speak back to this new ownership order. As intangible objects such as oral stories and sayings began to be considered cultural inheritance, they became increasingly figured as valuable property whose veracity was vouchsafed by linking them to specific owners—variously as authors or as folklorists. I would suggest, then, that the very attempt to insist upon the existence of a more authentic, more innate (real rather than fake) version of these oral traditions lost to us plays into the very rhetoric of colonial possession that I suggest we need to call into question.

The equation Trumpener makes of "vernacular oral traditions" with "voices of the past" helps make clear how identitarian concerns with linguistic mapping might look sideways to fellow contemporaries in the very gesture of looking back at one's own heritage—in the process of defining and delineating the culture as one and as one's own. Naoki Sakai describes this obliquely comparative gesture as an example of what he calls (using Japanese examples) the "schema of cofiguration" whereby linguistic communities as self-contained unities (read: nations) "can only be figured in translational exchange."[17] According to Sakai, the operation of translation becomes a primary tool for mapping national boundaries that mark off "us" from "them" and in the process fix expressions of indigenous culture as real and enduring (as opposed to fake and temporary) in relation to other cultures deemed comparable and therefore worthy of emulation. It is not only the implicit hierarchy of such a comparison but the pressure to fix a culture as timeless, homogeneous, and authentic that makes these figurations so objectionable. The result, as Lydia Liu and Timothy Brennan have both shown, is that writers of folklore in imperial regimes have felt pressured to represent their vernacular oral cultures as real, indigenous, timeless, and worthy of nationalizing and thus fix these texts in a manner that loses the dynamism and responsiveness innate to the form.[18]

Trumpener contends that the nationalist antiquaries (later called folklorists) would look to bardic work "to express its very different yearnings for independence and a lost feudal unity," and in the process would adopt a universalizing rhetoric not so much of "imagined community" (in Benedict Anderson's much-repeated formulation) as of "lost community."[19] If we keep in mind the Freudian insight that the melancholic responds to loss by identifying with fixed aspects of that lost object in a manner that can never be resolved, then we might see what an impossible bind it is to base an entire nationalist project on those intangible aspects of a past culture—oral epics, daily mundane rituals, folk sayings—that are as fleeting as they are essential.

For Ranjana Khanna, such melancholic attachment to the past—as loss—becomes a type of haunting whereby the postcolonial intellectual, like

Hamlet, is compelled by specters of (colonial) violence to heroic gestures of justice-seeking that can never be fully realized.[20] Khanna understands melancholia to be "an affective state caused by the inability to assimilate a loss, and the consequent nagging return of the thing into psychic life."[21] She argues that because the development models of psychoanalysis both inform and are informed by the colonial relationship, instead of a common sense of reality that continually and dynamically integrates a flexible and variously constituted notion of the past, the postcolonial nationalist can only incorporate a version of the past that has been fixed through the colonial encounter by possessing ("swallowing") it whole and unassimilated.[22] I would make a distinction here, however, that this postcolonial gesture be read not as ownership but as temporary possession of someone else's property. Such an insight allows us to take advantage of the double meaning of "possession" in English to understand these postcolonial hauntings in both senses of the term: the postcolonial subject is trying to assimilate a version of the past that belongs and yet does not belong to him and thus appears stricken because he has been taken over by spirits of another time and place.

How do these terms of possession work? Khanna explains that the epistemic violence of colonialism—which includes, as Dipesh Chakrabarty, among others, points out, narratives of development that render the colonized subject childlike and chronically lagging behind[23]—results in the colonized subject being powerless, split between a past and a present not of his creation, thus leading to an acute moral dissatisfaction that Khanna associates not only with melancholia but with double consciousness.[24] In a deft move, she turns this analysis of splitting back on the analyst himself and shows the ways Freud's *Civilization and Its Discontents*, for example, claims to speak generally for humankind while positing an irreconcilable difference between the West (as strong, modern, individuated) and the non-West (as weak, backward, as dependent as a child). Her reading thus shows that a melancholic relationship between the powerful and the powerless is neither based on essential criteria nor fixed in its positionality. Instead, she shows it to be a peculiar dynamic, one that needs to conceal its underlying arbitrariness to its participants in order to make the system appear all the more static and natural; the result is that it increases the feeling of loss for all.

We might, then, understand Mr. Worth's laughter to be a helpless response to just this feeling of loss. Not just in this fictionalized case, but in the case of Macpherson as well, these regimes of lost unity primarily serve to put impossible pressure on the writer to conform to expectations of a fictional authenticity.[25] "Apparently," Dundes writes, "the feelings of inferiority are so strong as to compel some of the pioneering figures in folklore to drastically alter the folklore they collected so as to 'improve' it, thereby making it the intellectual equal of the classic literary heritages of what are deemed more advanced cultures."[26] The express concern of being thought of as an "advanced" culture reveals that these artifacts are being used to plot oneself along a scale in a globalwide model of development (also known as a narrative of "progress" or "transition"): postcolonial critics have shown how impossibly such narratives fix cultures in static relation to one another, with the colonized culture positioned implicitly as the inferior "other," always a step or more behind. Looking to Sakai's "schema of cofiguration," however, we see how arbitrary and vulnerable even the seemingly superior position is and therefore why the operations of folklore and translation are mobilized to assert a fixity and inevitability that is so anxiously guarded.

In the example of *Ossian*, for instance, Scottish ethnologist James Porter points to the vulnerability of the British, suggesting that Macpherson was writing at a time when Gaelic "began to be considered inferior to English" and so "the poems of Ossian, written by a Gaelic-speaking Highlander who had been educated in English . . . communicate[d] to a now 'British' audience the harmless, politically defanged, but still 'wild' and 'sublime' quality of Gaelic culture with its apparently Homeric qualities."[27] Here, once again, Venuti's scandal of translation meets Felman's scandal of the speaking body. Certainly, Macpherson's performance should be considered felicitous, even if not entirely faithful. Porter claims that Macpherson's success in English influenced generations of luminaries, including not just Goethe (whose best-selling *Die Leiden des jungen Werthers* was, Porter claims, modeled on the "elegiac mood" created by Macpherson's poems) but figures as diverse as Napoleon, Diderot, Jefferson, and the Brothers Grimm.[28] "Indeed," Porter claims:

> it is no exaggeration to say that the poems of Ossian are not just the key to European Romanticism—with its emphasis on individual sensibility and the sense of loss associated with a glorious past—but the key also to the beginnings of interest in a collective cultural history and oral tradition.[29]

It is the "sense of loss" Porter mentions that has particular relevance for this study, for I would argue that in this day and age it has become a central—and committedly melancholic—mode of reading any text of world literature as "national allegory."

Unwittingly, we have been taught to participate in our own version of a developmental narrative, whereby oral forms composed in ongoing plurality are depicted as being premodern and crude, while authored forms are considered modern, inimitable, and thus valuable. Timothy Brennan argues that such narratives underwrite the story of the relationship between the nations of world literature. He points out that literary historians (Mikhail Bakhtin and Georg Lukács, for example) regard oral forms such as the epic as necessary precursors to the modern novel. Rousseau's idea of the "collective personality" of the people united in common destiny was transformed into the German idea of the *"Volksgeist,"* so that by the end of the nineteenth century "the 'folk,' the 'plebeians,' the 'people,' the 'working class' were now important components for any inclusive treatment of the nation in fiction."[30]

Yet these nationalist readings of literary histories depend on the written texts being representative of a collective vision of the world, a plurality in the singular. The result in the twentieth century, Susan Bassnett notes wryly in *A Critical Introduction to Comparative Literature,* is that as "emergent nations had to establish a tradition and a canon," they began to turn to folklore as an "idea of a cultural heritage that sprang from the people, from the 'genuine,' 'authentic' voices of the collective upon which the nation was based."[31] The paradox she outlines is important: oral cultures were denigrated as being of lower status, and yet, "because of the importance of the written epic in the European tradition, those cultures which had no epic . . . were also downgraded."[32] Which is to point out that if there is a national longing for form today, it is for the imagined storytelling communities of the past, which a death-drive discipline such as Comparative Literature deems lost to modern society.[33]

Voices in the Republic of Scholars

We might speak as if such communities of the past have nothing in common with us as literary scholars and postcolonial theorists, but the very tropes of our own disciplinary discourses repeat such themes, linking death with loss of speech in ways that serve only to fix and fetishize individual performance.[34] The most frequently repeated riddle of postcolonial theory, for instance—written in three successive versions by Gayatri Spivak—revolves around the figure of a dead subject who can no longer tell her own story: "Can the subaltern speak?"[35] Judith Butler, too, tells the story of a death (Walter Benjamin's, in fact) to ask how we frame life-and-death questions in our literary debates today: "Who was speaking there?"[36] Like Spivak, Butler is relying on the trope of translation from the oral to point to the ethical dimensions of our own values of performativity. Roland Barthes, for his part, both in his essay "The Death of the Author" and in *S/Z*, frames the storytelling relationship in the Balzac story *Sarrasine* by discussing the relationship of the narrative text to the performing (narrating) body: "Who is speaking?" Barthes uses this riddle to formulate an opposition between the modern, writing-based societies of the author-god and the premodern, oral-based societies of the shaman-storyteller:

> once a fact is *recounted* . . . this gap appears, the voice loses its origin, the author enters into his own death, writing begins. However, the affect of this phenom-enon has been variable; in ethnographic societies, narrative is never assumed by a person but by a mediator, shaman, or reciter, whose "performance" (i.e., mastery of the narrative code) can be admired, but never his "genius." The *author* is a modern character, no doubt produced by our society as it emerged from the Middle Ages.[37]

If so many otherwise insightful and engaging narrative theorists turn to the image of the speaking subject to voice disciplinary concerns of justice, then I would like to read these interventions as if beyond a melancholic attachment to a lost speaking subject. Instead, I would have us rely on the concept of the performative to invert the hierarchy Barthes presents (and maybe parodies) so that in Comparative Literature we might learn to read an author's writing as shamanistic performance, recitation. Theo-retically, such a move would call attention to the way literary frames bring into relief the utterly constructed status of the so-called spoken original. Thus, speaking would be to writing *not* as original is to copy but, rather, as copy is to copy. The parodic repetition of "the original" would then reveal the original to be nothing other than a parody of the *idea* of the lost original.[38]

After all, we can never be sure that the translated text we read isn't the creation of a different writer from the one named, someone who perhaps shares our tongue with us but is laughing at us for believing so earnestly in the stability of the ground of commensurability we think we stand on. Instead of trying to police the categories of authored or unauthored, oral or written, real or fake, we might learn to play along according to the rules of texts whose primary interest in being read as authored, real literature is to make fun of (and sometimes take advantage of) such expectations.[39] If we accept that stories by a writer like Detha are, like nationalist discourse, necessarily derivative, then I am interested in formulating how we might begin to read each version—be it translated from oral or written, from Rajasthani to Hindi or English—as a performance in its own right. Examples like Macpherson's *Ossian* and Detha's tales that do not sit tidily in the available well-disciplined literary categories should force us to wonder at our own evaluative practices: Do we have a clear sense of what it would mean to be faithful to such a source? Anyone who has read recent reviews of contemporary literature knows that the same vague criteria of fidelity are still used to judge translated work as to judge folklore. In the nineteenth century Nietzsche may have written of the death of God, in the twentieth century Barthes of the death of the author, and recently in this new century Spivak of the death of a discipline (i.e., Comparative Literature), but readers of world literature today are still applying the same limited but seemingly critical term used in the days of James Macpherson: fidelity. In what are we expressing faith?[40]

The story of Mr. Worth is charged with scandal because it reveals in part the unfortunate pressures on writers to offer literary works for global consumption that might serve as representative. Historically, we are taught to understand literary crossings in oversimplified geographical terms. The titles on publishers' lists, for example, like the literature courses offered in colleges, are often organized in neatly bounded, colorful groupings that together look suspiciously like the political maps of the world. The assumption is that a good literary work can speak reliably on behalf of the nation from which it hails, in a latter-day version of the *translatio studii et imperii* ideology of the Roman empire that made translating and imperial conquest synonymous.[41] Aijaz Ahmad has articulated this problem similarly as a riddle of translation. He asks (facing off with Fredric Jameson): Must all Third World writers be read only in terms of "national allegory"—that is, the same narrative, "rewritten, over and over again, until the end of time" in "the poststructuralist world of Repetition with Difference"?[42]

Ahmad, like Partha Chatterjee (in his own face-off with Benedict Anderson), rails against a system that maps originals in the European metropole, derivatives in the Third World.[43] What outrages is the implicit hierarchy operating: origins are assumed to be superior, and derivatives inferior. Since the days when the interested first began discussing in English the relationship of the derivative to its original, translators have been told to follow faithfully, even slavishly, in their masters' footsteps.[44] We should note that it is precisely the epistemological constructions of such hierarchical relation that Ahmad and Chatterjee are critiquing most strenuously: while there is no doubt a long list of entrenched inequalities and injustices resulting from this arrangement that motivate their scholarship on this topic, what they focus on in each of their critiques are our own scholarly habits of reiterating such simpleminded hierarchies. I point out that reading the trope of repetition as a performance of hierarchical relation makes sense only if we maintain the belief that such repetitions are mindless, slavish mimicry, dime-a-dozen examples of lifeless, mechanical reproduction.[45] Such an assumption, I should add, is not only ethically but logically suspect. My purpose here is to propose methods for reworking our thinking on such translational relationships.

Homi Bhabha, for one, has argued vociferously against the fixed hierarchies underwriting these projects of what he calls—drawing on Salman Rushdie's example—"cultural translation."[46] He has helped articulate a more complex and potentially practical, even agential, notion of universality under the name of cultural translation, one that Judith Butler has quite prominently and successfully taken up in the struggle for human rights. And indeed, these two are certainly not the first to wax utopic when discussing the possibilities of translation for enhancing human life on the planet. Goethe's much-cited formulation of a *Weltliteratur* in early nineteenth-century Europe emphasized, as Antoine Berman suggests, the "contemporaneity, or simultaneity" of what Goethe calls the "living . . . community" of "men of letters," whereby—as Goethe explains—"these connections between original and translation . . . express most clearly the relationship of nation to nation."[47]

At its most ideal, then, an egalitarian community of "world literature" has promised to eschew the asymmetry inherent in these uneven relationships formed across the divides of space and time. Literary theorists writing on the phenomenon of "world literature" in the globalized literary market of today, however, remain skeptical of the global phenomenon Berman calls *Weltliteratur* functioning as *Weltmarkt*.[48] In such a schema, Pascale Casanova notes, the translator becomes "not only an intermediary but also a creator of literary value" in the effort to promote what Goethe calls "this universal spiritual commerce."[49] Writers are thus under pressure to offer literary works for global consumption that might serve this unquenchable and unself-conscious need for universal spiritual commerce that replicates familiarity but is sold under the name of difference. Surely this is not the grand, transcendent project to which we would want translators and readers of translation to be faithful.

Faithful, then, to what instead? The image of universal humanity as a *spiritual* project reveals contradictions not only in Judeo-Christian theological arguments over formulations of harmonious and unified community post-Babel (as we might expect) but also at the heart of the most secular, Marxist visions of a more equal world. As David Damrosch makes clear in his riddling monograph, *What Is World Literature?*, Marx and Engels issued a call in the name of "world literature" that believers today are endeavoring to answer afresh in this new millennium: that "national one-sidedness and narrow-mindedness [should] become more and more impossible."[50] They never stopped to consider, however, the preferred economy of such translations and have left believers arguing over the details of nationalism versus (or even as) internationalism in much the same way literary theorists argue over the details of linguistic mapping.

Damrosch successfully demonstrates that we have already begun creating community through our circuits of world literature and so are not "fated to disintegrate into the conflicting multiplicity of separate national traditions" nor to "be swallowed up in the white noise . . . [of] 'global babble.'"[51] To engage seriously with such a pronouncement, we first need to attend to the tropes Damrosch relies on to describe such an opposition: these interrelated fall-of-the-Tower-of-Babel fears are written into much of our current discourse on translation and link to the melancholic yearning for lost unity discussed in the previous section. In this project I thus rely on Indian examples in the belief that the diverse literary traditions of multilingual, partitioned South Asia in particular have useful strategies to teach us for reading such "babble" metacritically. I, too, work from the fundamental premise of Bhabha, Butler, Damrosch, and other theorists that to articulate a theory of translation is to articulate a theory of ethical citizenship in our globalized world. The riddle from the beginning of this chapter is relevant here once more: What do we want the rules of our exchanges to be?

Bhabha's work on cultural translation goes far in offering a corrective to traditional literary scholarship that seals itself off completely from real-world concerns of justice and equal rights; nevertheless, I am concerned that this version of "afterlife" he advances does not rethink the terms of translation sufficiently to respect and even protect those very lives it is committed to helping. In his landmark essay on cultural translation, for instance, Bhabha conflates the plight of fictional characters (*The Satanic Verses*'s Saladin Chamcha) with stories of real-life threat (the fatwa against Salman Rushdie, for one) to delineate what he calls "the performativity of translation as the staging of cultural difference."[52] In this case, "performativity" means that Rushdie's very body (as well as the bodies of other, nameless migrants) serves as the original to which all criticism must then refer. As the infamous "Rushdie affair" demonstrates most powerfully, we need instead a space where the crucial issues of our day might be negotiated—fiercely, honestly, playfully—without life-and-death consequences to its living members. Here I do not mean to insist on empty and perhaps self-serving notions of "free speech"; instead I would have us use our critical tools to analyze not the translated (speaking) bodies but the translated (speech) acts themselves. That is, to make the study of such performances more equitably relational, dynamic, and dialogic, we need to theorize the terms of these one-to-one exchanges between speakers and listeners in the plural as an ongoing, interactive process that necessarily takes place on uneven, shifting ground.

To do so requires rethinking the definitional bounds of the "continued life" of translation to which so many—including Bhabha—refer when attempting this crucial task. Bhabha is not the only one; the list is long of noteworthy critics who work from Walter Benjamin's "Task of the Translator" essay to meditate on the contradictory promises of literary community across borders of language and culture, particularly the impossible demand that we transcend difference in the very gesture of reinscribing it.[53] Among these intelligent and engaged readings, I find Andrew Benjamin's work particularly insightful and relevant to this project, for he is able to show how inextricably Walter Benjamin's ideas of translation are bound up with his ideas of storytelling—or, in the phrasing introduced earlier, the connection between the task of the translator and that of the storyteller shows that the scandal of translation cannot be addressed without engaging with the scandal of the speaking body.[54]

Andrew Benjamin argues that the "continued life" of such performances—whether understood as translated literary texts or as orally performed speech acts—depends on the work being translated generation after generation. The work, then, is both singular and plural at the same time and maps a complex temporality that evades the linear. Such an approach helps us address afresh the concern, outlined in the previous section, that oral performances be fixed, authentic, eternal. For Andrew Benjamin, there need not be a binaristic choice between authored and unauthored, eternal and temporary. He argues that the task of the storyteller, like the task of the translator, is to work toward a unity that "does not involve the retrieval of the past, but a futural projection," one that is "always—always already—displaced."[55] Such a reading rejects the Babel myth of an innocent, prelinguistic unity and instead accepts that "difference may be original and in the end can never be synthesized."[56]

Community, then, is not something lost to us in a linear progression of time, not something somewhere there, but what we are performing right here, right now. Community is always—always already—in translation. Such an approach helps us to move away from a melancholic attachment to an original text—including a speaking body—and instead to suggest strategies of treating texts as temporally possessed. Regarded this way, the not-quite-utopic no-place of translation might be analyzed using literary tools that help us understand its complicated temporality as if a distinct and perhaps even translated narrative mode (as I show in my discussions in Chapters 5 and 6 of the past tense—*bhoot kaal* as "ghost time"—of Hindi and Rajasthani translation). A playful, performance-based theory of translation would have us think more carefully about the critical language we use to describe the terms of this displaced temporality as an endless series of present tenses. Such a strategy should allow us to ask what kind of community we create for ourselves metatextually in our very exchanges over translation. How do we ourselves frame these ongoing discussions of uneven exchange?

Tales of Possession

Until now, much of our scholarly discourse on translation concerned with issues of equality and justice tends to polarize along two stark camps: some—such as Talal Asad, Eric Cheyfitz, Rita Kothari, Lydia Liu, Tejaswini

Niranjana, Vicente Rafael—see such exchanges as premised on inherent incommensurabilities that can never be overcome; others—such as Homi Bhabha, Judith Butler, James Clifford, Robert Young—acknowledge these historical, systematic inequalities but insist in the face of them on a future-oriented praxis that sees in translation possibilities for a utopic space that Butler calls "proleptic and performative, conjuring a reality that does not yet exist, and holding out the possibility for a convergence of cultural horizons that have not yet met."[57]

That this utopia exists in no place is exactly the point that interests me, for it draws attention to the trope's potential as a heuristic device in and of itself: the figurative language of translation performs a network of relation that we take part in through each and every exchange and as such orders these networks as much spatially as temporally without our being aware of the terms of the agreement. That is, the grounds of such exchanges are negotiated in the very act of such translations and must be understood to be always—always already—displaced. Butler, for example, takes care to cite a real-life example of back-and-forth, face-to-face translational exchange—that of a group of English-speaking AIDS activists in America who learn that Spanish-speaking migrants identify more readily with terms other than "homosexual."[58] These complicated riddles of belonging ask us to map our ethical investments and moral values across exceedingly ambiguous terrain; in this example, as in so many, it is not clear that the exchange offers possibilities for the dynamic, nonlinear, and nonhierarchical shifts I would like to think possible through translation (in the best sense of the word).

More than anything, the example recalls the warnings of a number of respected scholars—Eric Cheyfitz, Rita Kothari, Tejaswini Niranjana, Lydia Liu, and Vicente Rafael among them—who have traced the ways translation historically has been part of the larger epistemological project of imperialism that has relied on similar universals to deny colonized subjects their rights.[59] Just because we might agree with a group of activists' contemporary efforts to secure human rights, it does not mean their interventions are very different from English colonial officials railing against the Indian practice of "suttee" or *sati*, which Gayatri Spivak, for one, reduces to the self-consciously simplistic narrative of "white men saving brown women from brown men" (which we consider in the next chapter),[60] or from the work of the Spanish missionaries in the Philippines, which Vicente Rafael describes as "setting and sustaining the conditions for a history of conquest and salvation."[61]

It is precisely the colonial history of conquest announcing itself as salvation that has made so many rightfully wary of translation and the universalizing projects it represents. Lydia Liu has pointed out that the rhetoric of human rights has historically proven to be a series of translated negotiations cloaking more nefarious (and, of course, unspeakable) designs on power that colonial historiography (and later Marxist criticism) has colluded with.[62] These exchanges pose an unsolvable riddle that we do our best to ignore: How do we reconcile the recent calls for the salve of translation with the lessons of colonialism when trying to formulate a critical vocabulary for justice we might participate in as academics today? I propose we start by interrogating the uneven grounds on which such exchanges are imagined to take place; we need to join in the conversations already taking place that use humor to remap the set boundaries in this virtual no-place of translation.

I am not the only one to suggest looking toward the playful edginess of the present moment as a healthy antidote to a gloomy, fixed attachment to the past. In an early monograph not on translation but on the revolutionary potential in the work of Walter Benjamin, Terry Eagleton suggests that we must all in our historical moment choose between a melancholic fixation on the revolution (never) to come and a humorous understanding of the stakes here and now. Eagleton puts Benjamin's blasted-out-of-the-continuum-of-history idea of a "time filled by the presence of the now" in conversation with Bakhtin's carnivalesque celebration of Marx's "let the dead bury their dead," thus rescuing the comical dimension of historical materialism which—ironically here—Eagleton charges "Western Marxism has damagingly lost."[63]

I point to Eagleton's work here and now because his formulation helps us understand the esprit (understood as spirit and as humor) with which we might place the bodies that write on the common ground ("no place") of translational unity, one that we now know, paraphrasing Andrew Benjamin paraphrasing Walter Benjamin, to be always—always already—possessed. Eagleton tells us that in socialist collectivism, the "the simple ironic structure that we are both individuals and interrelated" has the potential for a comic rather than tragic reading if we learn to approach it with the appropriate sense of humor.[64] He singles out one of what I am calling the riddles of belonging, one that, he says wryly, Bakhtin built a whole theory of language around, that "in social dialogue what I say to you already includes what you say to me, which in turn includes what I have said and may say to you."[65] If we were to try mapping the agents and locations described in this riddle, we would see that, as in the paradoxical temporality of the riddle discussed by Narayana Rao in the opening chapter, not just the dream of revolution but the very means of expressing it belong as much to the individual as to the collective, as much to the past as to the present and future.

Such paradoxes are amplified exponentially when we consider this ironic theory of language in the multilingual context of our globalized world today or even in multilingual postcolonial India. Such a move would necessarily—as Eagleton goes on to suggest—"explode the authoritarian solemnities of the monolingual and hegemonic."[66] Such a riddle helps us understand intuitively that language (of storytelling, of translation, of revolution) cannot be mastered individually, cannot be owned, but only temporarily possessed. The playfulness I am advocating would allow us, then, to locate these performances in time and space without fixing them or fixating on them. How might such an insight apply to our current institutions of reading practice, which themselves are premised on unity as much past as potentially present and future? That is, how do we understand the "continued life" of such a performance?

I suggest we begin by interrogating our understanding of the conceptual limits of that life we express interest in protecting. Recent academic discussions strain to find a way of understanding the global community we are now part of beyond notions of authenticity and originality, but these debates invariably assume a dualistic, Christian attitude toward the nature of being under discussion, employing what Pheng Cheah calls (after Derrida's "hauntology") a "vitalist ontology" whereby "the nation is not only conceived in analogy with a living organic being but is also regarded as the enduring medium or substrate through which individuals are guaranteed a certain life beyond finite or merely biological life, and hence, beyond mortality and death."[67] Emily Apter, too, notices how much the rhetoric of Comparative Literature is indebted to an early twentieth-century "bio-organicist vision of linguistic life."[68] We can see the pressure on a minority writer such as Detha to reproduce faithfully the most vital aspects of Rajasthani language and culture in order to keep it alive and to put it on the world map.[69] In a particularly postcolonial narrative twist, the success of Detha's own writing career has become virtually synonymous with the success of the Rajasthani language as a political entity. If, as Cheah claims, "all forms of political community . . . rely on ontological metaphors that subordinate the dead to the living," then here I wonder if the most effective strategy for a living writer interested in being translated abroad has been to play dead.[70]

Our fictional Mr. Worth is not the only one to have tried some version of this strategy; George Chapman, who rendered both of Homer's epics into the English language at the turn of the seventeenth century, contends quite fantastically that the spirit of Homer possessed him as he wrote.[71] Literary historians writing on the Homeric spirit haunting Chapman often describe the process as one of "metempsychosis"; the word refers to a spirit or life force changing bodies and thus is understood to refer to a singular being embodied in plural forms. The contradiction suggested here is telling, for it indicates that theorizing translation leads us to the discrepancies between our very understandings of "life."[72] After all, metempsychosis also happens to be the technical term used for the migration of a soul from one body to the next, as in the Hindu concept often called "rebirth."

The two meanings differ in an important respect: one refers to the spirit taking possession for the duration of that particular body's lifetime, while in the other the residence is of an additional spirit that itself is only temporary—for the duration of that particular creative act (as in the case of Homer's ghost writing through Chapman). What they have in common, however, is a philosophy reminding us how arbitrary and fleeting this identification is between spirit and body, an insight we must keep in mind when metaphorizing the act of translation in terms of "continued life." Like translation, our very discussions of "life" are predicated on the unspoken answers we provide to important but unanswerable questions of faith: What spirits do we imagine animating these material forms we inhabit? How do they move from one realm to the next? Where do we mark the line between the two? Our very exchanges over such questions reveal disparate, even contradictory understandings of the boundaries of said "life."

For the period in which Chapman's hand penned the *Odyssey* in English, for instance, we are asked to picture two spirits inhabiting a single writing body: the spirit of Homer temporarily possessing a body that belonged otherwise to George Chapman. Similarly, we might notice that the spiritual/material split in the very metaphors we use—for example, my own phrase, "belonged otherwise to George Chapman"—refers to an identity we ordinarily assume to be stable. I use the example to point out that even Chapman, one of the most foundational—and, not incidentally, Christian—figures in the canon of literature in English translation, subscribed to a notion of plural authorship that I hold to be in conflict with the neat, linear, postlapsarian narrative positing a single (transcendent) original followed by a (lowly, necessarily flawed) derivative. Not just the story of Chapman or of Mr. Worth but every tale of translation relies on a similarly complex narrative of possession.

How then to explain more precisely the process by which these spirits animate various authorial corpi? Which spirits shall we designate as belonging to which bodies of texts? I contend that a translator like George Chapman had to invoke this particular tale of possession because he worked in a time (like today) when textual authority was believed to reside in the original (dead) author who lived once upon a time. I, too, find myself trapped by this critical language: our literary institutions teach us to think of the English version of the epic as belonging to Homer even though we know it to have been written by Chapman.[73] For centuries we have been participating in conventions of reading that treat texts as singularly authored even though on some level we know them to be multiply possessed. My proposition here is that the ghosts haunting these translation projects will be revealed only if we play with them—riddle them.

Riddle them how?

By way of an answer, I would have us look briefly at another irreverent, riddling story written in Rajasthani by Vijay Dan Detha, one that interests me in part because it appears only in the form of afterlives. "*Duvidha*" is based on a tale told commonly in Rajasthan as a way to exorcize fevers: a ghost falls in love with a beautiful woman and takes on her husband's form so that he might be with her; the husband and the ghost look identical, so it is impossible to know which is the real and which one the fake; the riddle is finally solved when a clever shepherd (a common motif in Rajasthani folktales) tricks the ghost into performing impossible feats and thus exposes the act of possession.

In Detha's longer, literary treatment, the terms of good and bad reverse: the wife is portrayed sympathetically as neglected by her money-obsessed husband, who leaves without her soon after their wedding to pursue business abroad. Under social pressure to remain loyal to a man in name only, she submits readily to the ghost's tender seductions and becomes complicit in this uncanny act of duplicity. I am told—by Detha and others in his family—that in the folk version, it is seen as a good thing when the ghost's identity is discovered and he is driven off. (This is the moment when the fever is supposed to break.) In Detha's version, the ending of their unlikely affair is seen as nothing short of tragic, since duty triumphs over love. What critical vocabulary is required for us to explain the compelling circumstances of such transgressive acts of possession—that it might be equated with true love?[74] With whom do we side when accusations fly that one of these two is a fake?

I use the example to point out that the lesson of this story comments on itself metatextually: it makes a clever and certainly spirited argument that it is unhelpful and perhaps even detrimental to insist on the authority of a single, prior original. After all, in the real circulations of this story, it is Detha's literary adaptation that has inspired a host of other similarly spirited afterlives: in 1973, the celebrated independent filmmaker Mani Kaul adapted the story to the screen to create in black-and-white film a spare but moving account of patriarchal oppression in rural Rajasthan; in 1979, Kailash Kabir published an elegantly Rajasthani-inflected Hindi translation as the title story of a volume from the prominent publisher Rajkamal Prakashan that alerted the Delhi literary establishment to the powers of Detha's prose and Rajasthani literature more generally; in 1991, Ruth Vanita worked from Kabir's Hindi version to create an English translation called "The Dilemma" that was published in the prominent feminist magazine *Manushi* to testify to the experiences of rural women; in 2005, the Bollywood actor and director Amol Palekar worked from a new Hindi version by Kabir to create a glitzy, fantastical version of the story called *Paheli* ("The Riddle"), which was so popular that it was chosen as India's sole nomination in 2006 for an Academy Award.

While the simple chronology outlined might suggest a linear, unidirectional narrative of influence between versions, I would like to suggest that in practice the uneven realities of cultural exchange make them relate to each other in unexpected, atemporal ways. It shouldn't surprise us to learn that a generation of new readers has gone to libraries and bookstores in search of Detha's tale in Hindi and English translation so that they might read the version on which Palekar's film was based,[75] nor that in 2003 Detha and Kabir encouraged me to incorporate elements of Kabir's proposed

Hindi screenplay of "Duvidha" into the English translation I was doing.[76] Detha and Kabir seemed to recognize in advance that more people would be introduced to the tale through Palekar's movie than had ever heard of it through the printed media (especially the Rajasthani volume published in a hand-cranked press in Detha's hometown).[77] They were eager to have me complete a collection of the stories in English for similar reasons. Their attitude forced me to theorize in new ways the relationship of original to derivative; rather than regarding Palekar's movie adaptation or my English translation as a threat to the authority of Detha's Rajasthani version or a desecration of its loftier artistic purposes, they envisioned the various versions working in complementary force to revitalize one another. In part, Detha might have been responding to the realities of writing in a minority language (Rajasthani) without state recognition or support. In part, too, I imagine Detha's anticapitalist idealism made him bridle at the thought of conforming to bourgeois notions of literature which treated a story—in the singular—as property.

Such an anecdote should have us consider afresh the tendency to consider translation synonymous with the act of possession in the sense of hierarchical appropriation. In the case of colonial examples most particularly, the act of possession should be understood in the legal sense of laying claim to property, seizing land, exchanging goods. After all, the English rules of copyright—that is, owning the rights to the original literary text to be copied—were established by analogy with the laws for translating tangible property.[78] I find it significant that the Latin root of the most common term for translation, *trans-latus* ("carrying across") suggests a transaction in the most material sense, as goods being transported across distances through networks that exist by and for such exchanges. While scholars in the field of economic history have traced in some detail the systems by which people involved in those trade networks have negotiated the (constantly shifting) value of these translated objects, literary scholars have seemed reluctant to see the translated text in terms of both tangible and intangible currency, reluctant to see the ways the political and the aesthetic come together in the rendering of value, and therefore have not been able to acknowledge the ways our evaluative tools, too, have to be negotiated in constantly shifting networks of the trade. In order to articulate a (meta)critical idiom more dynamic, incisive, and relational, I would not have us conceptualize translation in terms of material property to be exchanged but would have us focus instead on the relationship that is formed as the text is passed along from one language speaker to the next. Translation should be understood, then, as a performance in the sense of a "telling," as the act of passing along a text from one to the next, as we do when we repeat a joke or a riddle.

Understood as a telling, a translation can be decentered, dialogic, even while being paradoxically agential. I am reminded of this dynamic, interactive possibility most acutely when I am asked to describe my own work in Hindi, one of the languages I translate Detha's work from: the word for translation, *anuvad*, emphasizes my role as translator actively recounting a story. Hindi speakers might very well dismiss such etymology as being overly creative, but I cannot but find it significant that the Sanskrit roots *anu* (after, in turn, alongside) and *vad* (to tell or say) figure translation as an oral performance. If *trans-latus* can be read as a "carrying across," then I would gloss *anuvad* as a "telling in turn."[79] For this puts emphasis on the task of the translator in a slightly different way from what is often understood in property-based readings of translation: I must first take in a story and then pass it along, so act the part of both reader and writer in turn. Likewise, we might understand Benjamin to be suggesting that a text's afterlife depends on it being translated generation after generation. A playful, performance-based theory of translation would have us think more carefully about the critical language we use to describe the terms of this displaced temporality as an endless series of uncanny present tenses whose temporary rhetorical ground must be negotiated afresh in each round.

In the next two chapters I will look more closely at the ways we frame that storytelling space by focusing on the narrative relationships formed between performer and audience. This in finer pursuit of the riddle posed earlier: If we rely on the trope of translation to question the ways we form community via the literary text across a range of differences, then how might we imagine community through performances that cross languages, cultures, media? I rely primarily on examples of Indian literary texts in the assumption that the contentious language politics of multilingual India has much to teach the world community about negotiating difference in translation.

A Telling Example

The Value of Speech

Few stories in contemporary cultural criticism have been more compelling, it would seem, than those that assert a people has been silenced. Often these narratives are delivered in such stark, life-and-death terms that the audience is left with little room to engage dispassionately with the details of the situation and therefore to make a reliable moral assessment of its complexities. The political battles being waged over recognition of the Rajasthani language, for example, rely on the same polarizing rhetoric perhaps familiar from other places and times.

That citizens' nationalist loyalties would be expressed as reverence for their language as "mother tongue" is not perhaps so surprising, given the Romantic idea of the vitality of the nation figured so prevalently in biological metaphors (as Pheng Cheah points out).[1] India's multilingual situation presents an unusual version of such life-and-death, nationalist-minded devotion, since the limits of any single language's territory cover only a small portion of the map of the nation; the bid to recognize every language group divides fellow citizen against fellow citizen and in the process threatens to dismember the very India such nationalists are asked to pledge their loyalty to. Moreover, the pulls of regional identification become further intensified by other identitarian allegiances. Language nationalists seem to gain power by identifying the language's limits and concerns in terms synonymous with a caste group's, to the exclusion of the others, often claiming shrilly that the silence of the group is equivalent to the extinction of the language, and vice-versa.

Lisa Mitchell has shown that during the struggles for recognition of the southern Indian language of Telugu as distinct from Tamil, for example, low-caste speakers were urged to die for a language whose claims and attitudes eventually and overwhelmingly represented Brahmin interests.[2] In such a climate, academic distinctions between a language and a dialect do indeed have life-and-death consequences for their speakers as they fight to defend the honor of their language in terms that might be politically successful.

Often, then, the revered figure of the mother tongue vies with religion— as Paul Brass notes—to produce a particularly potent symbol of national unity.[3] To take one strident but typical example, the Rajputana Liberation Front (RLF) in its recent introductory Web site material pits its own high-caste group—the ruling, landowning Rajputs—over another—the priestly Brahmins—to make a claim of persecution:

> Ever since the establishment of the neo-Brahminist state in 1947 under Pandit Nehru, the Rajasthani language has been targetted for complete destruction. The alien Sanskritic Devanagari was enforced upon the helpless Rajputs, whilst the ancient indigenous Rajput Marathi script was slowly choked to death. Now, our Mahajani only survives in remote regions. A large number of Sanskritic words were enforced upon the Rajputs, leading to a suffocation of the Rajasthani language. Finally, Rajasthani was declared a dialect of Hindi, meaning that the very language of the Rajputs had been taken away from them. Indeed, the Brahmin-Occupied-Government still refuses to accpet [*sic*] that Rajasthani is or even ever was an independant [*sic*] language.[4]

Part of the logic of the nation-state seized on (quite shrewdly) by the RLF is that power legitimizes certain sectarian interests at the expense of others;

the decision to make Rajasthani secondary to Hindi is figured here in terms of caste. This same logic might break down infinitely into any number of categories: Rajasthani nationalism, for instance, can be thought of as consonant or competing with Hindi nationalism or with Indian nationalism; likewise, within the contentious category of Rajasthani, groups identified along geographical region, class, and caste vie for hegemonic control of this particular brand of unity. It is in this regard that the RLF publicly applauds the efforts of seemingly like-minded organizations to establish secessionist movements on behalf of the Gujarat cause and the Maratha Hindutva cause, as well as for a free Dalitstan and Mughalstan for the downtrodden (formerly "untouchables") and Muslims respectively.[5] As we investigate in more detail in Chapter 4, the very gesture of mapping these linguistic (as cultural, ethnic) territories separately—as "not us"—creates problems in the name of solving them.

While it is worthwhile understanding in more detail how these divisions of belonging and exclusion become written into the critical idiom we use today to negotiate these issues, one of the paradoxes of modern political rhetoric we should note first is that one achieves power for those linguistic identities by claiming a gendered powerlessness. We see that the RLF passage above figures the language—and therefore culture—as "helpless" and female ("Mahajani" is a title of affectionate respect for the language in the feminine). This trope has been particularly effective in the Indian context, as Sumathi Ramaswamy has argued in the case of Tamil: she shows that speakers came to identify so strongly with the cause of Tamil as revered mother tongue that it became a source of "devotion" (in her words) that they would die for.[6]

We might look once more to Pheng Cheah's observation that such "vitalist imagery" of nationalism promises to outlive and outlast the individual members and see that nationalists repeating the stories of such sacrifices only serves to render a figure such as Tamiḷttāy in Ramaswamy's example or the Mahajani mentioned here that much more worthy of dying for. Such an insight makes the postcolonial riddle, "Can the subaltern speak?" more meaningful, for it forces us to ask: Speak in whose tongue? As I investigate below, the very grammar of biologically fragmented possession used to frame such riddles—"whose tongue?"—plays into the anxieties of belonging that such nationalist movements draw on. In this chapter I look more closely at the sacrifice being demanded in the name of such a cause and how that rhetoric is then shaped when discussing the elusive, transitory, and multiform texts of oral-based fictions.

In this regard we might read Vijay Dan Detha's decision to translate the local *boli*, or spoken idiom, of his native Rajasthan into written, literary form most fundamentally as an effort to give voice to a subaltern version of Rajasthani. (She shall not be silenced! She shall not die!) After all, as Bassnett, Brennan, and Trumpener argue, the translation of the oral into the literary realm is a necessary part of any nationalist power play. Certainly, Detha's recognition by the Sahitya Akademi reinforces such a perception and could even make the cynical conclude that his work has achieved national recognition precisely because it so well represents the heterogeneous and yet fixed, ideologically vibrant image of Rajasthani familiar to English and Hindi speakers in Delhi. We thus find ourselves presented with a version of the impossible contradiction Mr. Worth encountered on the stage of world literature, but here working regionally (and might we say dialectically?) within India.

In the following pages I work to show that Detha's writing plays *into* such nationalizing discourse while at the same time playing *with* these categories, making fun of the very idea of such sacrifice for the mother tongue. In his version of the traditional Rajasthani storytelling cycle "Chouboli," for instance, Detha adopts a frame narrative centered on the same riddle seen in countless other versions of "Chouboli" and now quite familiar to us: How can we make the unspeaking subaltern subject speak?[7]

Not just in his but in most versions the frame story features a beautiful Rajput princess (therefore ruling-class, but because female—by Spivak's logic—subaltern) who has taken a vow of silence: she will not marry until she finds a suitor who can make her speak four times. (*Chou* means four, and *boli* can be understood as speech, dialect, talk. Thus Chouboli's name could be translated as "four-speak.") The protagonist then tells entertaining, riddling tales to the princess designed to make her (and metonymically the audience) interested enough to speak out and thus participate in the ongoing dialogue established by the storytelling tradition. Another riddle is being asked: How do we ensure the language will not be silent? The answer to the riddle asked by the frame story becomes the answer to larger, metatextual riddles of community: Who are we, and what matters to us? In the process, the storytelling community also looks for an answer to the question: What do we matter?

Detha answers such riddles in a most curious way, for he weaves into the standard frame narrative a complex plot in which a young, rebellious, female protagonist dresses in drag to seduce the princess with her-as-his stories and through the telling convinces her to marry her-as-him. The stories this spirited cross-dressing storyteller recounts within the frame narrative revolve around spouse abuse and caste-based discrimination and so interrogate entrenched forms of injustice in a playful, captivating, storytellerish way. The stories are so entertaining and vexing that they provoke the silent subaltern subject to speak out against these forms of silencing and in the process to fall in love with the gifted, irreverent storyteller who has successfully induced her to take part in these regular forms of human intercourse.

Such a narrative strategy inherently challenges the pat, nationalist-minded formulas through which we often read traditional oral-based texts of world literature. As we see in more detail below, Detha recuperates traditional oral conventions in such a way that teases the common nationalist narratives: he begins the storytelling cycle with a playful, rhyming *chougou*, a conventional bit of nonsense that ordinarily marks the beginning of storytelling performance in Rajasthani oral tradition;[8] he ends with the same-sex couple posing a final question that riddles the very grammar of possession we so often rely on—whether applied more literally to the grammar of heterosexual union or metatextually to our grammar of text as property: "*Chouboli kin ri?*" ("Chouboli is whose?" or "To whom does Chouboli belong?") That "Chouboli" is one of the most traditional and beloved oral storytelling cycles of Rajasthan only makes such paradoxically antitraditional political questions posed by the narrative that much more potent. This final riddle of belonging not only challenges traditionalists within the Rajasthani movement but also forces those of us who wish to reflect on the lessons of literary and cultural studies to rethink those institutional conventions that rely similarly on traditionally defined, nationalistic constructions.[9] Each of these translated conventions jar because they reveal just how provincial our discussions of rights often are.

With every word, Detha's version questions the sense (and therefore senselessness) of these boundaries of belonging that mark out the traditional storytelling performance. By adapting the conventional *chougou* to written form, for example, he establishes a sense of common ground as provisional as it is dynamic: the rhyming *chougou*'s familiar nonsensicalness marks the boundary between common sense and nonsense and therefore between those in this narrative community that he establishes through the telling and those who are not, but in such a way that invites his audience in and teaches them the rules of interpretation they need to know in order to be included. His work demonstrates that the elusive sense of unity discussed in the previous chapter does depend on recovering something lost and in the past, but in such a way that we might participate in the performance here and now.

We see a similar strategy employed shortly after the recitation of the *chougou*, when the narrator moves quickly into the prose portion of the performance by repeating the popular invocation:

> *tou rama bhale din de ke chouboli ri aa baat tou khasi jooni hai, pana inanai sunun wala ara banchana wala jugjugantar tai nava ra nava raivaila.*

> [May Lord Ram bless us that, however old, this tale of Chouboli might become fresh and new to listeners and readers age after age.]

In a delightful moment of cheeky self-referentiality, the invocation announces the importance of the story being renewed and by that very act of repetition is participating in such a renewal in the translation from oral medium to written. I would claim that such a line offers to teach its audience how to engage with the text interactively across time, a lesson as reassuring in its repetitions to those familiar with the oral traditions as instructive to those who are not. Such a lesson applies equally to those translations from oral to written as to those from written Rajasthani to written English, for example. After all, in Detha's written Rajasthani version he mischievously includes *"banchana wala"* ("readers") in his audience of imaginary listeners and thus adapts the storytelling formula for the era and medium in which he works.

Such an inclusion should be seen as not just an adaptation of the oral tradition but an innovative adaptation of the strategy of cultural revitalization that German nationalists like Herder and the Brothers Grimm espoused (and that Cheah so roundly critiques): rather than fixing the oral tradition in a beautifully crafted but static literary form, Detha's written versions sound as though they are designed to be repeated and thus to be reborn again—in either written or oral form—age after age.[10] There is a crucial difference here: the dialogically charged vitality he writes into his versions depends not on a linear dialectic between a romanticized individual agent ("the author") and an undifferentiated, anonymous plurality ("the folk") but on an ongoing lineage of performers agential age after age.

In Detha's work the category of timeless becomes a collective enterprise that requires ongoing individual contributions, whether oral or written. Such an approach is consonant with Andrew Benjamin's reading of Walter Benjamin's fragmented storytelling culture as translation community, one that accepts that "difference may be original and in the end can never be synthesized."[11] The very form the story takes in Detha's version challenges the hierarchical relationship of the folk to the literary, just as it challenges the hierarchical relationship of a nonstandardized language like Rajasthani to a national language like Hindi or an international language like English.[12]

Such an innovative, complex approach to the folk traditions of Rajasthan, I have come to understand, has been carefully thought through as part of Detha's ongoing collaboration with others in Rajasthan through the folklore institute Rupayan Samsthan. He told me more than once of his decision in 1958 to move back to his village: he joined forces with a college friend named Komal Kothari, who was equally eager to document the folk culture of Rajasthan—to showcase the art and therefore the thinking of "the people."[13] This was a little over a decade after Independence, when the idealism of the nationalist movement was still strong and hopeful. Together they convinced Detha's neighbors to donate land, applied for grants and permits, and cofounded a thriving folklore institute that would come to serve as a central node for musicians, puppeteers, storytellers, hut-makers, dancers, writers, and scholars from around the world to meet together.

Eventually they would receive funding for their work from national and international organizations such as the Indira Gandhi National Centre for the Arts and the Ford Foundation. Detha was a writer and so would collect folktales; Kothari was an ethnomusicologist and so would work with the folk musicians. The institute bought a clunky hand-cranked press and hired someone to run it. Detha decided it would be better to write the stories he was collecting not in Hindi, the newly minted national language that the people of Rajasthan were officially purported to speak, but in the rich local idiom people actually told the stories in. At first, Detha wrote down the stories just as he heard them.

During our first set of interviews in 1989, he told me the stories were everywhere, vibrating in the air; his pen couldn't move fast enough to record them all. He grew animated as he described carrying page after page of prose, carefully—the ink still wet—holding up the sheet of paper between thumb and forefinger as he trotted down the hall of the Samsthan to the waiting printer. He tried writing out the stories exactly as he heard them; he was so excited to discover such a vibrant but sadly overlooked tradition in Rajasthan that he could hardly sleep at night, could hardly stop writing. Rupayan Samsthan distributed the books to local schools and bookstores at a price that scarcely covered their costs, interested only in realizing the progressive ideals of a writer like Premchand—their greatest hero—who used art to voice the dreams and realities of the people of India.[14]

It did not take long, however, before their engagements with "the people" as an abstraction (an anonymous collective that they, following convention, called "*lok*," "the folk") became personalized, specific, complex. Both Kothari and Detha were worried about how these folk arts would fare in the breakdown of the traditional feudal system of patronage (*jajman*) and felt that organizations like Rupayan Samsthan could be critical in establishing a newly democratic version of support for the artists. Eventually Kothari would organize trips to Japan, the United States, France, and the Soviet Union through the Festival of India and would produce a series of recordings of the musicians' best work, careful that these ventures not become facile lessons in self-exoticization. He took his role as critic seriously, pressing the musicians to teach him what the highest standards of their art might be, rigorously holding them to those ideals in practice. Vijay Dan Detha's efforts in collecting narrative folklore, of course, did not travel so easily. At least in musical performance you did not need to understand the words to appreciate its expressiveness.

One of the main differences between Kothari's work and Detha's was that Kothari nurtured an unmistakable and crucial feeling of play in the discerning way he encouraged others to perform, whereas Detha's very writing was a kind of performance itself: he translated the stories he heard into words on the page as if he were just another storyteller in a long line of storytellers. By the time he was working on the third volume, Detha told me, he realized that the quality of the stories was affected as much by the stories he chose to write as by the way he wrote them. He no longer thought of himself strictly as a "folklorist" but rather as an "author." Kothari cited Vladimir Propp and Carl Jung in his Hindi introductions to the various volumes of *Baatan ri Phulwari* ("A Garden of Tales"), Detha's collections of tales, to explain the meaning of the stories Detha wrote in universal, scholarly terms. But in conversation with me, Detha would compare his work to Anton Chekhov and Premchand more often than the Grimm Brothers.[15]

In the years since he began writing he has received many literary awards for his work—including a *purushkar* award in 1974 from the national Sahitya Akademi for Rajasthani prose, the first Rajasthani writer to be recognized by that body, as well as being named one of the twenty-four lifelong fellows of the Sahitya Akademi in 2004—and yet detractors have variously complained that he is not a real author or that he has not been *faithful* to his oral sources. Again I'll ask: Faithful to what? To the mother tongue?

A literary historian such as Ram Chandra Bora in his English-language *Contemporary Rajasthani Literature* is typical: he makes an effort to extol contemporary Rajasthani literature in strict comparison to earlier British writing, commending a writer like Narain Singh Bhati for "following the local tradition with a difference," the difference being Bhati's ability "to remain Victorian in approach and like poets of England of that period" who succeed in "maintaining the classical lead in their literary endeavor"; Bora then condemns Detha for writing work that he calls a "confused mixture of folk-literature and short story teller tradition."[16] The anxiety, I would surmise, is that such writing makes Rajasthani literature look backwards. Bora complains:

> His painstaking labour is admirable in gardening his volumes of *"Batoun ki Phulwari."* [*sic*] But one wonders why all this. These are but folk tales of Rajasthan, rather hazy and reflect a well known confounded confusion which Mr. Detha as a part of innovation has to introduce in the field of folk literature.[17]

Understandably, Detha bristles at such critiques. Partly, his work is victim of the inherent contradictions of the form called "folk literature" (*"lok sāhitya"* in Hindi): on the one hand, he has to defend his part in making the stories of the Rajasthani "folk" recognized in schools and other institutions of authority as a viable cultural inheritance rather than the disrespected, unlettered form folktales once were considered;[18] on the other, he has to defend his creative interventions to make these oral-based tales read as "literature." While such questions of aesthetic value have an unmistakably ideological component, these debates over reading practice are often expressed in terms not just of possession but of ownership: To whom do these stories belong? If they are considered literature, then the stories are thought to be authored by Detha and he is responsible for their content. If they are considered folklore, then they are of the people.

In his landmark essay, "What Is an Author?" Michel Foucault similarly questions these boundaries of belonging that we rely on to map our interpretations of texts. Like Benjamin, Foucault compares oral storytelling traditions to institutions of textual ownership that demand the ultimate sacrifice of their authors. He asks how we can possibly keep these narrative communities alive when we kill off the keepers of these traditions. Such a mortal demand, he suggests, is "What matter who's speaking?"[19] He looks to Shaharazad's imaginative storytelling strategies in the frame narrative of *The Thousand and One Nights* to show how storytelling performances might explicitly challenge these life-and-death logics threatening us all, and argues—in a move I'll admit is cloyingly nostalgic—that these healthy mechanisms of collective (cultural) survival in the storytelling communities of yesteryear have been corrupted in the move from oral to written narrative modes. The irony is that he relies on a written version of a multiply translated example—*The Thousand and One Nights*—that plays on the very boundary dividing the oral from the written, the fictional from the real, to champion the importance of the oral in the real world. By ignoring the conventional framing devices that distinguish these domains, he makes a much more complex argument about the fictional Shaharazad as storyteller than he announces on the surface:

> Storytellers continued their narratives late into the night to forestall death and to delay the inevitable moment when everyone must fall silent. Scheherazade's story is a desperate inversion of murder; it is the effort, throughout all those nights, to exclude death from the circle of existence. This conception of a spoken or written narrative as a protection against death has been transformed by our culture. Writing is now linked to sacrifice and to the sacrifice of life.[20]

The temporal structures of the prose itself make a different point, however: Foucault's narrative performance serves to exclude death from the circle of existence just as surely as he claims Shaharazad's did once upon a time, and so his writing is linked not so much to his life as an individual author as it is to his retelling of the tale of Shaharazad, a figure his version keeps alive and in the process is kept alive by. We might understand by this that Foucault, too, is part of a fragmented, ongoing storytelling community—might see that even these postmodern discussions are another version of a riddling exchange that (to quote Velcheru Narayana Rao once more) "brings a community into existence, while allowing the members of this community to believe that it existed prior to their creating it."[21] I focus on questions of authorship here and their relationship to nationalist-minded discourse to ask: How do we map the bounds of our storytelling communities? Where and when do we imagine these narrative exchanges to take place?

If we return to the question asked in the opening chapter with regard to Gandhi's quip—How are the divisions of here and there, now and then, us and them announced in a storytelling performance?—then we notice that Foucault's author, in analogy with Shaharazad, is figured as being both inside and outside the text because he claims that the proper name "moves from the interior of a discourse to the real person outside who produced it."[22] In a footnote the translators of the essay, Douglas Bouchard and Sherry Simon, suggest that not only does the single author himself become split across time through these institutional practices but—ironically here—the translators likewise become divided off and therefore excluded.[23]

In subsequent work countering Foucault's "What Is an Author?" riddle with her own version—"What is a translator?"—Simon writes that these modes of reading through implicit narratives of belonging (or what she calls a "modern conception of translation") are in practice "linked to the establishment of a series of boundaries" in terms of nationalist projects, ones that are mapped according to "boundaries defining national languages as complete and circumscribed units; boundaries surrounding the individual text and its meaning, and identifying the author as exclusive proprietor of the text."[24] The text pretends to belong exclusively to a single figure (in this case, "the author") even while being reworked and claimed collectively by various agents across time and place. Simon's discussion challenges us to ask how we might read these multiply possessed texts in a way that does not serve to consolidate boundaries of authorship, language, and text. How would we approach these texts without hinging the interpretation on the figure of a single originating subject like a Foucault or even a translator like Simon?

The "What Is an Author?" essay suggests that a reader relies on a complex interpretive operation to attribute discourse to an individual precisely so that she can imagine holding someone responsible for a text's ideas and propositions, as we do in a real-life situation where we hold an actual speaker to his word.[25] For Foucault, an authored text "always bears a number of signs that refer to the author," including personal pronouns, adverbs of time and place, and the conjugation of verbs, in contrast to an unauthored text, where "these 'shifters' refer to a real speaker and to an actual deictic situation."[26] This, then, is the matter who's speaking: these storytelling relationships within a text such as *The Thousand and One Nights* or "Chouboli" help us to understand the ways we map our own ethical projects onto our interpretations of these written literary texts.

Neither storytelling cycle—*The Thousand and One Nights* nor "Chouboli"—offers a simplistic moral of the story but instead asks riddles within the frame of the story (in a world not real) that provoke us to ask similar questions outside the frame of the story (in the real world). Such exercises in displacement are particularly fraught in contexts that confound or cross these nationalistically defined boundaries separating one language from another, since we must then translate, too, the conventions of ideological framing. How might we read these exchanges effectively without inadvertently participating in the simplistic sacrifices Foucault (in the name of the author), Cheah (in the name of the nation), and Ramaswamy (in the name of the mother tongue) warn us against? Detha's suggestion that every performer—whether a writer or an oral storyteller—must learn to make this story come alive age after age maps a complex narrative space of belonging, one whose ethical responsibilities demand attentive negotiation.

Narratives of Belonging

The invocation is but one example of the ways the storytelling cycle offers a playful, metacritical language for understanding how to read the ethics of agency involved in these performances as they extend across time and place. If we agree that a storytelling cycle such as "Chouboli" can be possessed only temporarily, then how do we expect ourselves to identify the agents of such crossings, especially when we veer into "the comic side of the truth," to quote Eagleton once more, "that in social dialogue what I say to you already includes what you say to me, which in turn includes what I have said and may say to you"?[27] How do we map such elusive networks of belonging?

Rather than securing the author's own eternality in the Romantic way we have seen Foucault, Simon, and others take issue with, Detha's version seems interested in exploring, even delighting in, the comic side of the truth of temporary possession as provisional, playful, and fragmented. Paradoxically, his is a version that is also not exclusively his. Balancing, as this version does, on the border between individual and collective possession, it asks us to imagine a different relationship with this figure who is neither entirely author nor folklorist.

Like so many of the versions of "Chouboli," the storytelling cycle invites us to consider complex questions of right and wrong, and in so doing, to question what matters most to us as a community. We grapple with these questions by asking ourselves: With whom do we imagine such a dialogue to be taking place? Like so many oral narratives, Detha's version is repeated by him in this storytelling space because it has been repeated in other storytelling spaces in the past, in ongoing cycles that extend into the future. Participating in this ongoing network of storytelling exchange asks us to subscribe to a notion of community with boundaries flexible, not fixed, inclusive rather than exclusive. The implicit answer to the metatextual riddle being asked through the telling—Who are we in this narrative community?—is necessarily in the process of ongoing redefinition age after age. Each version, then, performs a provisional answer to the riddles raised by the telling; Chouboli belongs to whoever is telling her tale at that moment. Which means that Chouboli speaks in whatever tongue the teller speaks at that moment—and that this subaltern therefore speaks in tongues.

After all, I learned from Detha that Chouboli spoke once upon a time through local Dalit storyteller Savalram's informal oral version recounted to Detha and his fellow villagers, which Detha translated into a written Rajasthani version, which I then translated into a written English version, which allows you, my reader, to know the story. She has spoken through another oral performance by a professional storyteller named Abdul Rahman that I recorded in 2003. She has spoken in a version written by the esteemed Rajasthani writer Lakshmi Kumari Chundavat in a collection of Rajasthani folk stories edited by the Rajasthani scholar Kanhaiyalal Sahal.[28] She has spoken in the version published in a collection of Rajasthani folk stories written and edited by Manohar Sharma and Shrilal Nathamalji Joshi,[29] and has spoken in Hindi in a version published in a collection of Rajasthani stories written and edited by Manohar Prabhakar.[30] She has even spoken in a version as part of an unpublished handwritten manuscript from the collection of Colonel James Tod collected in the early part of the nineteenth century. Even though Chouboli exists almost entirely in oral tradition, we have enough tangible evidence to know that she has spoken in countless settings and in countless ways through the centuries. What do each of these versions teach us about our relationship to the tradition from which they derive and of which they form a part?

With the exception of Detha's, most of these versions are primarily interested in documenting the existence of a story as it has persisted independently in oral tradition and not in taking advantage of the medium to see it carry on. Most of the stories seem interested only in whether the king (in some versions Raja Bhoj, in others Raja Vikramaditya) succeeds in getting Chouboli to speak. While Detha's version can be said to use the riddling conceit as an opportunity to riddle the very notion of uneven dialogue, the others invariably accept the hierarchical arrangement between man and woman, high-caste member and low-, without explicit commentary.

We notice this contrast in the embedded riddling stories the various performers tell as they recount the versions told to Chouboli. In one, a tale of switched heads, which Detha calls *"Malik kin ri?"* ("Who Is Her Lord?"), the riddle directly addresses questions of caste discrimination, as I discuss in detail in the last section of this chapter. The others, however, tell versions of this story that are equally provocative in asking whether the woman should be considered married to the man with her husband's head and someone else's torso or the man with her husband's torso and someone else's head. They do not, however, mention any caste differences between the characters. Likewise, they do not comment directly on and even tease the gender differences and certainly do not show how these gender differences speak through the grammar of possession, as Detha's version does. The other versions do not engage playfully and metacritically with the very medium in which they recount the story.

It is this playful aspect of the stories that makes them so crucial to include in nationalist narratives, in the best sense of the phrase. We see this more clearly when we consider the version of "Chouboli" transcribed by the controversial Scots-British adventurer and administrator, Colonel James Tod, at the start of the nineteenth century. In terms of plot, it differs little from the other versions, except that the storyteller frames the storytelling cycle by focusing on the adventures and dilemmas of a good-natured (and low-caste) shepherd named Phopsi, who eventually lands up in the kingdom of

Raja Bhoj and hears the story of Chouboli.[31] Less important is the fact that the story is found today in the Royal Asia Society in an unpublished manuscript handwritten in the dialect of Western Rajasthan and that it never found its way directly into Tod's foundational two-volume work *Annals and Antiquities of Rajasthan*; more important is that the story reads very much as a transcript of an oral performance and as such is but one of thousands of details Tod collected to form an impressionistic tableau of Rajasthan, one that succeeded in giving legitimacy to the idea of Rajasthan as an entity. Today, newly printed copies of *Annals and Antiquities of Rajasthan* are sold from the bookstalls of Jaipur.

In aggregate, Tod's work points to an interesting contradiction at the heart of such projects of cultural representation. Ronald Inden most notably has taken issue with Tod's efforts at purportedly objective research for being premised on a strictly hierarchical East-West division, one that glorifies the golden age of Hindu rule (whose "feudal states [were] comparable to those of the Holy Roman Empire") and castigates contemporary Muslim rulers (branded "Asiatic despots") with the aim of proving that even if restored to its former glory, the Hindu state would not be a "threat to British imperial aims."[32] In contrast, Norbert Peabody cautions us not to see Tod's work purely in terms of "oppositional essences" but to recognize that such Indological discourse was also "based on the idea that there was a fundamental unity, or single essence, underlying all humankind," which Peabody understands as being "expressed through the idiom of Romantic nationalism and the idea that the highest degree of human fulfillment is achieved through the complete manifestation of one's transcendent national identity."[33] Peabody argues that Tod's work was instrumental in defining a form of national identity that subsequent generations drew on to resist colonial rule.

Faced with the legacy of this monumental effort to catalogue the "antiquities" of Rajasthan, I would argue that we cannot dismiss Tod's success in advancing a narrative unifying the culture any more than we can ignore the self-serving and even damaging hierarchical divisions upon which such a narrative of Rajasthani unity was premised. That is, we cannot automatically assume that our own efforts at cultural representation are any different. In Chapter 1, I argue that these complicated riddles of translational exchange ask us to map our ethical investments and moral values across exceedingly ambiguous terrain; here I look to this example to interrogate once more how we draw the boundaries of the utopic space that is culture in translation.

We might notice, for instance, that Tod decided not to translate the storytelling cycle *"vat chouboli ri"* ("The Story of Chouboli") in his *Annals and Antiquities* and instead introduced his monumental study by celebrating the courtly writings of the Charan poet Chand as "the last of the great bards of India."[34] One can well imagine that if Tod had the literary ambitions of a James Macpherson combined with the democratic sensibilities of the Brothers Grimm, he might have turned that spirited, folksy version of the Chouboli tale into a verifiable "antiquity" celebrating the anonymous raconteur as bard. Instead, he chooses a celebrated, published writer and thus advances a different brand of bardic nationalism, commending writers like Chand for being "the primitive historians of mankind" who record "real events" but with such poetic license that their "peculiar tongue" must be "translated into the sober language of probability."[35] Tod uses the example to suggest that the courtly culture of the Hindu Rajputs is comparable to European elite cultures and that the fact that they already have a bard like Chand in their history proves they are closer to achieving a modern form of nationalism than perhaps other cultures, one that struggles with issues of "fidelity" (as he points out), just as European nations do.

It is for this reason, I suggest, that Tod thinks explicitly about the relationship of conventional institutions of literary exchange to statecraft. He argues, for instance, that the bards' "magniloquence" allows them an unequal freedom, for "there is a sort of compact or understanding between the bard and the prince" that allows the bard to be critical of the state in a manner both recognize to be healthy.[36] I would add that such an understanding is created not *ex nihilo* through individual authors' displays of genius but by those of us who participate in these literary institutions (as authors, readers, translators, publishers, scholars, even benefactors) and in the process make a choice whether and how to guard these inventive spaces where criticism of the state might be passed on. Moreover, such tools of criticism are not fixed objects to be found intact in the cultural landscape like a lost knife or compass. Our scholarly narratives call them into being— across languages, media, eras.

In her incisive study on the history of Hindi literature and its Hindu basis, *The Nationalization of Hindu Traditions*, Vasudha Dalmia suggests that "James Tod's glorification of Chand came to be of immense importance for the historiography not only of the Rajput royal houses but also of Hindi literature" because he recognized Chand's writing as the "poem with which Hindi literature could be said to commence."[37] Indeed, the Hindi literature historian Ramchandra Shukla, in his classic *Hindi Sahitya ke Itihas* ("The History of Hindi Literature") calls Chand "Hindi's first epic poet [mahākavi] and his *Prithvīrājarāsou* Hindi's first epic [*māhakāvya*]."[38] In a telling overlap, historians not only of Hindi but also of Rajasthani literature claim Chand as originary: Motilal Menaria assumes in *Rajasthani Bhasha aur Sahitya* ("Rajasthani Language and Literature") that Chand is a foundational figure in Rajasthani—not Hindi—literary history and argues more specifically that Chand writes in the Rajasthani bardic language, Pingal (a poetic idiom that relies on Marwari grammar) rather than Dingal (which has more Brajbhasha influence).[39]

Of these scholars, only Dalmia turns a critical eye to the work of Tod, whose "contribution to the construction of the early canon of Hindi literature," she asserts, "has not yet received sufficient scholarly attention."[40] She speculates little on the reasons Tod has received little attention post-Independence from literary historians but does offer the provocative suggestion that his narrative was successful because he framed the courtly idiom of Rajasthan as "a language of rank" that "was spoken by the cultivated," and thus worked to rescue it from "the usual assignment of the language to rustic environs."[41]

Such an observation does indeed offer insight into the complicated relationship of Rajasthani to Hindi and the many sectarian interests that come into play when overlapping nationalist narratives compete. In the process, it should help us see how often our own scholarship relies on a set vocabulary of assumed nationalist-minded equivalences—for example, the first epic poet, writing in a special courtly idiom, cultivated not rustic. How might we incorporate into our transnational, translingual, and even transtemporal discussions literary institutions such as the bard-prince compact that Tod describes when they have no easy equivalent in other nationalist narratives? Or more to the point, how do we discuss local literary institutions that challenge the very hegemony of these repeatable nationalist narratives?

The question is not only raised by the example of a twelfth-century poet like Chand but in reading the work of a contemporary writer like Detha, who also identifies as Charan even if he writes neither in Dingal nor Pingal and does not set out to uphold most of the courtly literary conventions of his caste. Detha's writing style and political sentiments bear little resemblance to the work of his predecessors, and yet in Detha's village I would hear members of his extended family speak of the need for poets to criticize the mistakes of the state. One even told stories about the legendary ability of the tongue of the Charan to utter curses more fearsome than the sword.[42] This recalled words I had read in the volumes of Tod though written almost two centuries earlier:

> these chroniclers dare utter truths, sometimes most unpalatable to their masters. When offended, or actuated by a virtuous indignation against morality, they are fearless of consequences; and woe to the individual who provokes them! Many a resolution has sunk under the lash of their satire, which has condemned to eternal ridicule names that might otherwise have escaped notoriety. The *vis*, or poison of the bard, is more dreaded by the Rajpoot than the steel of the foe.[43]

While the version of the legend I heard was recounted with a characteristically postcolonial mixture of pride and wry if not self-conscious amusement, I pondered how this story about the otherworldly might of the Charan's poisonous tongue has been repeated through the centuries, marking for the audience (be they readers or listeners) an imaginary protected space that guards the importance of satire. I suggest that such a framing device should be understood to follow the rules of play, as I discuss in some detail below, for it metatextually marks a border between that which is real (the effects of mismanaged statecraft) and that which is not real (satire), demanding that the "not real" be honored for the sake of the real.

Members of the community agree to such an outlandish scheme because stories of the poison of the bard reinforce the belief that these social mechanisms allow an arena for life-or-death political battles that have no actual consequences to living members of the community and so collectively protect them. The concerns Foucault and Walter Benjamin have both expressed ("what matter who's speaking?") about life-and-death issues in their own narrative communities share the same impulse as these bards and proponents of the bards such as Tod. How do we write these concerns into our histories of world literature? Rather than wring our hands as we fixate ineffectually on recovering a lost community, I would have us learn to laugh along at the comic side of the truth of these multiply mapped boundaries of belonging, as Detha does in his Rajasthani version of "Chouboli" and as

I do in my English version. Approaching these versions as an expression of unsynthesized difference suggests another reading of the riddle "*Chouboli kin ri?*" ("Chouboli is whose?" or "To whom does Chouboli belong?"): Who has a claim to the bard's poison? Who has the right to set the limits of the story's reach? The framing of the narrative thus calls into being the very storytelling community in question in a gesture of self-reflexivity, I argue, that the story itself plays with.

The story framing the storytelling cycle begins by introducing a husband who abuses his wife in a ritual made to seem as amusing as it is shocking:

> This story starts with a big *thakur* who ruled over a big *thikana*. Now, this *thakur*, each morning after doing his morning ablutions, washing his teeth and rinsing out his mouth, observed the most lamentable custom of shooting a hundred and eight arrows through his *thakurani*'s nose ring.

The narrator then asks a question of power in a confiding voice sympathetic to the wife: "*Thakurani kai jor karti?*" (Lit: What power could the *thakur*'s wife employ? That is: What could she say? How could she oppose him? What right did she have to object?) As readers, becoming involved in the story means becoming complicit in the solving of such a question: What power do we have over a situation where a fantastical Rajput wife of oral tradition is abused by her husband, enduring an arrow shot through her nose ring 108 times a day? The fiction allows us to inquire obliquely into other, related real-life questions: What power do we have over a situation where a Rajput wife dies on her husband's funeral pyre? *Thakurani kai jor karti?* What *jor* can we, as readers far away in place and time, have to object to such a ritual? To ask: Can the subaltern speak? is to ask a more specific version of the riddle: How might she express her *jor?*

Sakariya and Sakariya's Rajasthani-Hindi dictionary glosses "*jor*" as "1. *shakti* [which Stuart McGregor's Hindi-English dictionary glosses as 'power'], *bal* ['strength,' according to McGregor], 2. *kabu* ['control'], *vash* ['power' or 'state of subjection'], *adhikar* ['right' or 'authority']."[44] While the word has Persian roots and is used often in Hindi to mean power in the sense of persuasion, in this context I have rendered the Rajasthani word "*jor*" as "right" to emphasize the relational aspect of power, control, and subjection. This is not a story that assumes her "right" to object in the sense of moral correctness (human rights, right vs. wrong), nor does it assume her authority (as "*adhikar*" is often translated). Rather, this is a story that asks us to identify with a character in an inferior position and to ask how we participate in a system that renders her powerless: thinking through the terms of the storytelling relationship in a fictional world allows us to think through the relationships we form in the real world. Within the frame of the narrative, her *jor* becomes our responsibility in part, one we feel by being drawn into sympathy with her:

> What right could his wife have to object? Everyday she would take her place on the terrace under the awning exactly where her lord ordered her to stand—in the spot where he had had a pair of footprints painted in glowing *hingloo* red. He made her place her feet exactly on those prints and wait. Then he would go to his place one hundred and eight hands away, where he had had a pair of footprints painted for himself. He strode over to that spot, placed his feet exactly on those footprints, and stood there at the ready. Then he'd pull back the string of the bow to his ear and let the arrow go zinging through the air, whistling towards the *thakurani*, straight through her nose ring, to go whizzing out the other side. With each arrow the *thakurani* could feel her organs doing flips inside her. If he missed his mark by even a hair, there'd be nothing separating her from the beyond but the grace of Lord Ram.

It is important that the storytelling "we" constructed through this narrative be fantastical and provisional and thus allow us to approach the real-life question of *jor* in the most playful and yet confrontational of ways. This is the kind of power we need to understand when we speak about the subject position of the subaltern across ages, across languages and cultures. The question about our histories of world literature becomes more specific: How do we read Chouboli age after age?

We might begin answering that question by looking more closely at the convention of the *chougou* mentioned above, for it reveals how generic our discussions of rights often are. In Rajasthani storytelling traditions, the *chougou* marks the start of the oral performance, a transition from ordinary speech to stylized, in a parody of religious (devotional, even *bhakti*) recitation. Detha's published Rajasthani version presents the *chougou* as if he were transcribing word for word, even letter by letter or syllable by syllable, the same lines that are repeated at the start of countless oral storytelling performances.

Even after asking Detha and others fluent with the culture, I never understood how a *chougou* could combine a sense of the outlandish and the unremarkable, even perfunctory, until I heard one myself at an impromptu storytelling session one evening after dinner with friends. This was in 2003, when I was an assistant professor of South Asian literature at the University of Michigan and had the year off on fellowship to collect oral versions of the stories I was translating from Detha's written versions.

That particular evening I was in a town in Marwar district called Pipar, and was taking the evening to visit Yaseen Shahabuddin and his extended family, a community of hand-block printers I had become close to after interviewing them for a series of articles on vegetable-dye printing techniques more than a decade earlier. This was supposed to be my evening off from work, but they knew that I was interested in recording storytelling performances so, in a gesture both generous and larkish, sent for a popular storyteller in the neighborhood named Abdul Rahman to see if he might be free and willing to entertain us that evening. By the time Rahman arrived, we had already gathered in the front room of Yaseen-ji's house, all of us sitting cross-legged on the floor, curled up in woolen shawls, children in laps, well fed and settling in, slightly fidgety, waiting for the performance to start. After sitting down and composing himself, Abdul-ji looked over to Yaseen-ji, who, we had decided, would be the primary listener—that is, would give the *hunkarou*[45]—and asked his permission to start, then began to intone the same playfully nonsensical words of the chougou that I had read so many times but had never heard recited:

> *bhale din padhara, pendai paki bor*
> *ghar bhindak ghora jinera ladoo bhare chor*
> *bat ri bat khurapat ri khurapata*
> *khejari ro kantou sarhi solah hatha.*[46]

The chougou made more sense as musical convention than semantic communication. Suddenly everyone in the room focused; we seemed to cross an invisible line in our imaginations. Rahman's nasal voice filled the room. All our faces were turned toward him, but somehow we were not seeing him exactly; he was merely the medium for the sentences that would create the fantastic realms we all began to construct in the privacy of our minds. His manner was both self-effacing and dramatic. The everyday part of him seemed to step away from the performance, even as this performative side took over. When he started, it hardly mattered what words he was saying—this was just a preliminary shift toward the world of the story he was inviting us into. This was the narrative voice I always thought of as both repetitive and adaptive, formulaic and singular, when I read the Rajasthani words on the page Detha had written—oral storytelling conventions translated into written form.

I'd like to think that any person sitting in that room, even someone who didn't understand a word of Rajasthani, would probably feel something of the *chougou*'s spiritedness just hearing the music of the metrical, rhyming syllables.[47] Even if you couldn't recognize the meter (*doha*) or know its associations with the popular, populist, anti-Brahminical *bhakti* movement in early-modern South Asia, you might correctly guess from its singsong quality that the *chougou* offered a playful mockery of elite (literary) expectations. Did it matter what was being mocked or by whom? These were exactly the same lines I had read in the opening of the first volume of Detha's *Baatan ri Phulwari*, the same lines I would hear the storyteller Bhawani Bai repeat to start her much more informal and breathless story two weeks later, the same lines the professional genealogist and storyteller Omprakash would invoke to talk about the etiquette of the relationship formed through storytelling.[48]

When I had first asked Vijay Dan Detha and Kailash Kabir what the words meant, they told me it was playful nonsense. I asked the same question of the storytellers I interviewed; some offered contradictory explanations, others just shrugged. Those storytellers who did try to maintain that the lines referenced a complete narrative—as Durgaram Ratnam did—ended up telling stories so circuitous and laborious that the explanations only demonstrated how much of a jumble the narrative fragments were. This is how I decided to render the lines of the *chougou* that Detha began his collection with:

all is good, the days are fine, berries ripe on the way,
family cow birthed a jumpy colt, sweets killed thief that day.
some men sleeping, some are not,
they hold their turbans close to their cots,
lift sleepers' turbans and run off in the night,
skinny weak men don't have the fight.
it's all just talk, twisting in the sea,
streams dance wildly, spin excitedly.
worn-out little pony rider, oh so lean.
what is the sense? what does it mean?[49]

Like Lewis Carroll's famously nonsensical poem "Jabberwocky," the grammar follows just enough of the rules of meaning-making to make you conscious of the language's attempts to communicate. That is, the *chougou* makes us aware of our activity of finding meaning together. How do we understand the procedures of such playfulness?

Susan Stewart maintains that the function of such rhetoric is precisely its ability to reveal the metatextual and thus the ideological import of our unexamined conventions: "Nonsense," she writes in a book of that name, "is the realization of the possibility that the discourse of everyday life could become totally conscious of its own procedures."[50] Stewart maintains that nonsense does not function to provide a communication opposite of common sense but "always refers back to a sense that itself cannot be assumed."[51] Therefore, nonsense does not depend on common sense as much as make us aware of the ways we constantly and consciously depend on common sense and construct it even in our everyday language practices. Stewart writes: "because it gives us a place to store any mysterious gaps in our systems of order . . . nonsense can be seen to function as an aid to our sense making."[52] A convention such as beginning a storytelling performance with a *chougou* makes us aware of the line between order and disorder, sense and nonsense, and thus of the provisional ways we establish community by taking part in such a performance—whether as the teller or as the listener.

The way it helps us negotiate that line, Stewart suggests, is by signaling through metalanguage: "This is play." How? In his foundational work on the dynamics of play, Gregory Bateson asks how animals engaged in fighting behavior know to distinguish "fighting" from "not fighting" and concludes that it is not the content of the behavior itself that signifies playful "not fighting" but the way the content itself is framed.[53] Stewart applies this insight to intertextual moments of nonsense (which could be oral or written, categorized broadly as "folklore" or "literature"; the procedures are the same) and concludes that "play" is not "a shift within the domain of everyday lifeworld; rather, it is a shift to another domain of reality that refracts back on the everyday, suddenly revealing paradoxes of reflexivity and self-contradiction that are part of our communication acts."[54]

The salient difference Stewart identifies between the two domains is an important one to note: "play" is reversible and "not play" is not. That is, play allows us to find ways of adapting ourselves to difficult circumstances in a context with low stakes.[55] Theorists of humor such as Mikhail Bakhtin,

Henri Bergson, and Jo Anna Isaak assert that such acts are subversive in that they allow a time when those suppressed and repressed needs of the oppressed are allowed to be expressed in the public domain. One might worry that this safety-valve effect serves only to release built-up tensions without effecting any structural change and therefore ultimately serves the conservative needs of the ruling elite. Stewart refutes such charges, maintaining that "play and other types of reframing . . . prevent the organism from being trapped within one set of interpretive procedures."[56] We must understand by this that these storytelling conventions offer tools for the kind of awareness that might lead to social change, even if such a revolution never does take place in the end.

According to Stewart's thinking, playful, nonsensical texts like Carroll's "Jabberwocky" or the Rajasthani *chougou* allow language speakers to play at confronting everyday paradoxes and their possible resolutions in a version of reality that is reversible and therefore not "real" in the commonly understood sense of the term. A self-conscious awareness of this critical approach is signaled most explicitly by the lines "what is the sense? what does it mean?"—as if the *chougou* were making fun of itself or of our attempts to understand it. Of the many versions I heard recounted, only Detha's made explicit use of the formula's subversive potential. In his version, the cheeky question perfectly sets up the stories to come, which think through issues of caste discrimination and spouse abuse, all in a playful manner that pretends that such violence does not exist in the real world and that no one has ever had to face such situations. Detha is thus drawing on a storytelling tradition that uses these narrative conventions to play the line between the real and the not-real, even if others such as Abdul Rahman do not work its subversive potential so blatantly.

What Is the Sense? What Does It Mean?

When I heard Abdul Rahman open the storytelling session by reciting the nonsensical lines in a dutiful, breathless warm-up, it all went so fast that I scarcely had a chance to register the humor. I knew that the *chougou* was not meant to be read closely as if it were an intricately crafted poem but heard in a blur of fun to signal a transition to the imaginary realm of the storytelling performance—an atmosphere I clearly saw created in the hasty but spirited way Rahman called out the lines, in the way those gathered

seemed to register not so much the words as the convention he was uphold-
ing. The very point of the *chougou* was that it was exactly the same, line
for line, in every performance. But Detha's decision to translate this very
Rajasthani, very oral convention to a written, literary realm was an attempt
to adapt the convention to a new context in this new age. The worry was
that such rhyming banter would not be read as playful nonsense when you
did not have common sense in common—that the metatextual cues Stewart
describes would not be read as such, and so the implicit ideological critiques
would also not be expressed. How should one read this adapted storytelling
voice when its repetitions wouldn't necessarily be read as repetitions?

To start, Detha's version of the storytelling cycle borrowed as much
from the oral folk tradition as from the written literary tradition. While he
included an invocation and a *chougou* and adopted a narrative voice that was
more storytellerish than authorial, his descriptions and plots were much
more elaborate and involved. In contrast, Rahman, after telling a few other
stories, began narrating his version of Chouboli by announcing simply:

> *ek rājā rī larkī hī | unrou nīv hou chouboli*
>
> [Once there was a princess. Her name was Chouboli.]

Rahman then went on to explain in direct discourse that she would only
marry the suitor who could make her speak four times. Many men try, he
said, but none are successful. Not more than eight short lines into the story,
however, enters clever Raja Bhoj, come to win her hand. Rahman's version
was unusual in that he described Raja Bhoj creeping into the palace gar-
dens to win the princess's female attendants ("*saheliyoun*") over to his side.
Then he waits until night has fallen, enters the fort, and announces himself
to the princess's bed—on which she lies sleeping—with a friendly "Rama!
Rama!" and says that he can't sleep; would she mind if he tells a story?
Fantastically, the heretofore inanimate bed does her best to play the formal
part of listener in Rajasthani storytelling tradition, for she—not the silent
princess—assures him:

> *āp īj bāta kaivou mhai hunkārou deūn*
>
> [You tell the story and I'll give the *hunkarou*.]

I had learned by then that a "*hunkarou*" was the response an active listener was supposed to give at a storytelling performance. Nearly every

storyteller I spoke to told me that a performance would not start without someone designated to give the *hunkarou*. I soon learned the wisdom of such a tradition in humiliating detail when none of my friends versed in the rhythms of Rajasthani storytelling were able to go along with me to tape the stories and thus no one was there but me to give the *hunkarou*. The tradition involves not only urging the teller on with oh's and mm's but also repeating the last phrase spoken at a particularly dramatic moment or trying to answer a rhetorical question the teller asks the group. It also requires anticipating what the teller is going to say. For instance, at the point in Abdul Rahman's performance when he pretended to be the primary listener (that is, the bed) within the frame story, saying, "You tell the story and I'll give the *hunkarou*," Yaseen-ji, as primary listener in our actual storytelling session, gave an especially spirited *hunkarou*—an irony that made us all laugh, especially since I had asked him to give the *hunkarou* in my stead—as if I were playing the part of the silent Chouboli and he the part of the bed.

Here theory and practice were coming together in active, dialogic performance; both inside and outside the storytelling frame this narrative convention helped establish a dynamic relationship between teller and listener. Like the conventional singsong familiarity of the *chougou*, the back-and-forth dynamism of the storyteller-*hunkarou* call-and-response forms a playful repartee in the realm of the not-real that refracts back on the realm of the real.

To readers in the habit of being silent and isolated (as Lukács would argue), it might seem an odd premise to insist that a listener speak back. The storytellers I spoke to, however, agreed with the fictional premise within the frame story of the Chouboli narrative that a storytelling performance could not proceed without someone actively participating as a listener. Such an arrangement is even laid out explicitly in the version of the *chougou* that Detha begins his collection with (which I heard repeated by many tellers): after the line "What is the sense? What does it mean?" the couplets end on the triumphant, marching note that teaches interlocutors the importance of audible, active participation in a storytelling performance:

> *phouj main nagārou, bāta main hunkārou,*
> *hunkārai bāta pyārī lāgai,*
> *jīvai bāta rou kahanawāl,*
> *jīvai hunkārā rou denawāl*

[armies march to the beat of a drum,
stories flow to the rhythm of oh's and hm's.
hunkara make stories fun
long live the storyteller! long live the *hunkara*-giver!]

Rahman, however, did not include these lines in his opening *chougou*, perhaps under the assumption that it would not be necessary to explain such an obvious thing to a roomful of *hunkara*-giving listeners. Such a thing is anything but obvious, however, to a listener unfamiliar with Rajasthani traditions (to the point where I could find no English equivalent for the phrase "*hunkārā rou denawāl*"). Detha's written version is more specific about the terms of this relationship that pretends to be between both a reader-writer and a listener-teller at once. However displaced, then, the silent reader is still expected to be a *hunkarou*-giving participant in this dynamic exchange.

How might this work virtually? We might follow the logic of this bit of metatextual playfulness by considering that both Detha's written version of Chouboli and Rahman's oral version revolve around the issue of the *hunkarou*-giver. Once Raja Bhoj (in Rahman's version) has someone to give the *hunkarou*, he can then tell his riddling stories and trick the princess into entering the conversation. As in the other versions, she blurts out the answers to the riddles and happily loses the contest. In Abdul Rahman's version, Raja Bhoj gets to marry the princess and that is the end of the story.

Detha's more intricate plot introduces an implicit riddle in the frame story itself that diverges wildly from Rahman's oral version and all the others I read. Detha provides details about the daily abuses the *thakurani* must suffer as if to ask us, his *hunkara*-giving participants: What is to be done? As if in answer, we are introduced to a character who expresses outrage at this treatment. She is the niece of the *thakur*'s *seth*, or manager, who happens to be visiting from another town; she is the first character we see to speak out explicitly against the injustice—albeit in a fanciful (even ridiculous), storytellerish way:

If my rogue of a husband ever did that to me I'd feed him roasted chick pea fodder and serve him water I'd washed my feet in. Then I'd climb on his back and ride him around the bed seven times. If a husband shoots an arrow through his wife's nose ring a hundred times each day then he deserves to have a wife who would treat him this way.

She thus voices a protest that we as silent onlookers are as helpless to make as is the *thakurani*. Another riddle is implicitly posed by the story that has implications in the nonreversible world outside the storytelling frame: When we see injustice going on around us, is it more effective to stay silent or to register a protest? And if one decides to speak out, to whom and how? We watch and see that all the niece's fiery words do is remind the *thakurani* of her powerlessness:

> The niece's talk was like an arrow to the *thakurani*'s heart. But her strength had its limits. This was out of her hands. The wives of big men had to learn to walk through life head bowed down.

Again, the same word—*jor*—is used to talk about the limits of her power, strength, rights, and thus indicates that this state of subjection is relational. We understand that the narrator's voice—ostensibly of the *thakurani*—is not just repeating the *thakur*'s words heard previously but articulating a more pervasive common wisdom, one that we see here presented ironically. In this instance we can see that irony works not just to align three different individual subjectivities in relation to one another but to map the distance between these different versions of common sense—each a metonym for a plurality of people who might hold this moral view.

Linda Hutcheon describes such playful dynamism as the defining feature of irony: for her it is the ability of participants to imagine slightly or radically different points of view simultaneously and thus it creates the possibilities for negotiating difference in the worldwide community. She sees irony as a complex but potent political instrument, indispensable in the postcolonial world because it has a "cutting edge" (as with the edge in the title of her book), which might allow an English reader such as myself to imagine a range of ideological positions with a flexibility that allows temporary, humorous recognition of both the commonalities and divisions between each.[57]

Hutcheon critiques the work of such important thinkers on irony as Hayden White who see in it only a potential for challenging the hierarchy of the sites of discourse built upon the social relations of dominance.[58] Instead, she argues, irony might be used as a strategy as much for oppositionality as for complicity. She asks: How do we know what kind of effect irony might have in any given context? How would we know that this story, for instance, is meant to be read as oppositional, complicit, or something else? Hutcheon's suggestion—one that should be seen as an important contribution to the field—is that we figure these political dynamics by focusing less on the "intention" of the ironist than on the agential contributions of the interpreter;[59] that is, that we pay more attention to the multiple contexts of ironic interpretation that any work creates—that we see irony is not created by them, those authors there, but is made by us, here, in ongoing literary conversation. Such an approach starts by recognizing the vulnerability of those engaged in ironic exchange and thus fundamentally interrogates rather than guards the power of the ironist's position, as her predecessors do. Her work teaches us to see that all of us might participate in doing or undoing ironic readings and to decide to what ends such readings might be used.

Readers can see this kind of irony operating within Detha's version of "Chouboli" by attending to our own reactions. In addition to the status quo viewpoint we might expect, the storytelling performance also establishes the possibility of a viewpoint that might find fault with a marital arrangement that expects the wife to walk through life with head bowed down. While we cannot fix a singular narrative presence (whether distinguished as narrator or as implied author) with whom we might find common cause in this critique, it is clear that Detha's written version—here, too, in my English translation—relies on the same teller-listener camaraderie established in oral performance that Abdul Rahman's might. Thus we see how the dynamism and contingency that Hutcheon ascribes to literary irony might be read in the playful exchanges of the Rajasthani oral conventions that Detha adopts.

The phrase "head bowed down" seems all the more ironic when we imagine the *hunkarou*-giver repeating it in imaginary oral performance— and thus a sequence of three different pairs of interlocutors, real and imagined, repeating this phrase. The conceit of the storyteller–*hunkarou*-giver bond establishes even in the written text a playful mechanism for thinking through the importance and the means of establishing a community that is dynamic, contentious, various in its views. This story plays on such a contentious tradition, I would argue, in addition to playing it up. Looking closely at these playful storytelling strategies allows us to see that repetition in this tradition is anything but unthinking and mechanical. Each of these versions—Savalram's oral performance, Detha's written Rajasthani text, my translation into English—does not so much fix a singular viewpoint as bring together several in a single text and thus creates more possibilities for an ongoing, contentious plurality.

After all, we soon learn in the narrative that the *thakurani* does have her own brand of strength, one that—in a fun metatextual move—makes handy use of the ambivalent power of repetition:

> The *thakurani* could never have allowed words critical of her husband to come from her own mouth. Which is why she used the pretext of telling him what the *seth*'s niece had said about feeding such a rogue of a husband roasted chickpea fodder, serving him water used to clean her feet, sitting on his back and riding him around the bed seven times.

We consider in more detail the economics of the metaphor of borrowed speech in Chapter 5. For now it is enough to notice that the very figure encourages us to understand that the grammar of possession can be spoken in many tongues. Such a play on tropes allows us to see that the question of the value of the language discussed earlier in this chapter might serve an ideological purpose within the storytelling exchange. Here, then, we need to look closely at the rhetorical gesture of naming this critique as borrowed within the narrative frame in order to draw larger lessons about the story's narrative strategies outside the frame. After all, isn't a storyteller like Savalram or Detha simply repeating in turn someone else's critical words in order to play up a point of contention without taking direct and sole responsibility for such mischief? These acts of repetition necessarily establish a basis of provisional and yet ongoing relationality that requires a plurality of speakers to function. Their force is diminished if they are read in the singular. We thus need to develop a strategy for approaching a text as singular-plural—that is, a singular performance in complex, contentious dialogue with the ongoing plurality. In a recent meditation on the value of sense-making as collective enterprise, Jean-Luc Nancy insists that "There is no sense just for one. . . . What makes sense is what does not cease circulating and being exchanged, like coins in fact, but coins whose currency is incommensurable with any possible equivalent."[60] We find meaning in incommensurability, as we see likewise in Gandhi's ludic exchange.[61]

We can understand more clearly the value of reading for a dialogic plurality when we watch the *thakur*'s reaction to the words the *thakurani* has repeated. As any listener might have anticipated, the *thakur* is more than taken aback by this challenge to his power and thus to his entire way of thinking:

> The Graingiver never would have imagined in his wildest dreams that there would be anyone on this earth ready to criticize his daily practice. Hearing it made the blood start boiling in his veins. Now he'd be at peace only once he had married that insufferable girl. Instead of a hundred and eight arrows he was going to sling two hundred.

His character becomes increasingly, unbelievably ridiculous. The next scene shows him pounding on the *thikana* manager's door in the night, demanding that the manager allow his niece to be married to the *thakur* in punishment for her impertinence. (Marriage, in this narrative, is presented only mockingly in happily-ever-after terms.) Somewhat surprisingly, the niece who had earlier shown so much bravado quickly agrees to the arrangement. And so, by narrating the face-off that is their marital alliance, the storytelling cycle pursues the same question of a woman's *jor* that was introduced in a sympathetic, third-person, close observation of the first wife's baleful situation.

The injustice, the story suggests, is generalizable. Outside the frame of the narrative, readers must consider: How is power defined, who can access it, and how? The narrative sets up a spirited, outspoken, brave young woman paired with an impossibly intractable and egotistical man, with the storyteller and *hunkarou*-giver working together to understand and perhaps redefine the terms of their respective *jor* in relation to one another. How do we understand the moral framework established in a playful, plurally constructed narrative such as this, which is clearly one triangular relationship in an ongoing series?

We could ask this same question of any one of the versions available; of the six I have looked at closely, only Detha's version uses the storytelling conventions featured in the story to call into question the *thakur*'s masculine posturing. After the *thakur* takes the *thikana* manager's niece as his second wife in a hasty ceremony, impatient to start shooting arrows through her nose ring, he drags her up to the terrace to make her stand in the same marital red footprints as his first wife. He is quite proud of his prowess in being able to shoot arrows through a wife's nose ring, but the ingenious, spirited niece manages to flip the power balance by making fun of his manly pride over such an exploit:

His newest bride burst into gales of laughter and said, "Why is your chest all pumped up over such a small thing? You put on a nose ring and stand there so I can shoot a thousand arrows through your nose ring, easy as the flick of my left wrist. No, to do something truly extraordinary, you'd have to win the hand of the Chouboli Princess and bring her home to this fort. Seventeen times twenty rajas and lords have scrubbed their faces clean ready to make her speak four times so they could wed Chouboli and all but one of them are sitting in a dungeon right now grinding fodder for the horses. If you could pull off this feat that would be something truly wonderful—much more impressive than shooting an arrow through a nose ring."

Her announcement pretends to be naïve to this bit of intertextuality, but we can imagine that in performance, oral or written, anyone familiar with more conventional versions of the story of Chouboli would wonder if this hapless *thakur* were going to play the part of a hero on the level of Vikramaditya or Raja Bhoj. Even those unfamiliar with the Chouboli story become involved in the mounting narrative tension: Was this hapless lord going to be the one to win the beautiful princess's hand?

The narration soon goes in search of another love triangle: at the niece's urging, the *thakur* goes galloping off to win the hand of Chouboli. The narrative temporarily returns to the point of view of the first *thakurani*, who can only marvel at the feats of her new co-wife. ("After enduring life for twenty-five years, at last the *thakurani* felt she had started to live. The arrow of the manager's niece had hit its mark on the very first try!") We in the audience have established a relationship with the narrator about the scene of action within the story—that is, a narrative version of the joking triangle I discuss in the opening chapter (and which we will consider in more detail in the next chapter). The events within the narrative begin to comment on our own exchange. For we soon realize that the story of the eldest *thakurani* has been only a setup for the story of the struggle between the *thakur* and the niece, and this is the contentious relationship through which we are going to track our own ethical investments in the story.

It becomes increasingly difficult for readers to make alliance with the ridiculously heroic *thakur*: after arriving at the palace to win Princess Chouboli's hand, he puts on his best clothes and marches with much fanfare into the hall of the princess, where four drummers are stationed, ready to beat the drums in celebration each time the suitor succeeds in making her speak. But this particular suitor is so struck by her beauty, the narrator tells us, that "The *thakur* stayed in the doorway right frozen in his footsteps without saying a word, quiet as a stone statue. He came to get the princess to speak and here he himself forgot how to speak." (Can the subaltern's lord speak?) The *thakur* clearly is not up to playing the part of legendary leader in stories of days gone by. Instead he is thrown down into the dungeon to grind fodder for the horses along with the rest of the humiliated, unsuccessful suitors.

The narrative then begins to focus on the niece, who emerges to become the unlikely protagonist of the story:

> The junior *thakurani* knew very well that her lord didn't have the kind of character that would enable him to make Chouboli speak. So now it was up to her to come up with some clever stratagem to free him. She told everyone she was going on a pilgrimage and went straight to the town of the princess. She put on men's clothes and marched in banging every *nagaara* drum that came her way. When she banged on the drum closest to the Raj Mahal the attendant standing nearby taunted, "Looks like you've come straight from a spat with Mummy and Daddy. There are seventeen times twenty young men as vigorous as you whiling away their lives down in the dungeon grinding fodder. And you've still got the smell of mother's milk on your breath. Take my advice: turn around and leave."

In typical storytelling mode, the narrator plays along with this act and has us imagine the scene from the townspeople's point of view, describing the niece, even in close third-person, from the outside as a male suitor: "But he acted as if he hadn't heard a word they said." The scene might be read most productively as a travesty—understood simultaneously in all the interrelated meanings in English: as an outrage, a parody, an act of cross-dressing, and a translation.[62] After all, in Detha's Rajasthani version, the narrative participates in travestying itself, cross-dressing pronouns playfully so that sometimes we see the suitor as a male actor and sometimes we see her playing the part of a female agent. The niece thus plays at being the heroic male suitor of the legendary Chouboli, making fun of these traditional storytelling conventions by performing a new and fresh version of the story in this new and fresh age.

I would argue that the logic of such a travesty might best carry over as it crosses into English if we can allow the various kinds of travesty to play off against one another. Not just "Chouboli" but all of these cross-dressing, oral-based stories written by Detha and myself ("A True Calling," discussed later in the this chapter, and also, as we shall see in the closing chapter, "A Double Life") ask us to interrogate our own reading practices that try to secure meaning by comparing the "translation" to an "original" as if there were a single, stable original to be compared with. We can see in the example of this frame narrative that the story makes meaning in conversation with the others that both precede and will eventually follow—making a travesty of the idea of an original and also of a linear progression.

I would have us think, too, about the ways we read gender in this story in order to interrogate the ways we read stories in their various translations—showing how, as Judith Butler (once again) writes, "The parodic repetition of 'the original.' . . reveals the original to be nothing other than a parody of the *idea* of the natural and the original."[63] Just as simplistic Judeo-Christian narratives of man as original (with *jor*) and woman as derivative are being critiqued in recent gender theory, so should binaristic models of translation. It is not possible to read my English translation of Detha's version of this story by comparing it with a single, fixed original, for a story such as this has been circulating in various versions, oral and written, for centuries. The questions raised by this travesty (in all senses of the term) are analogous: What exactly is being travestied here, and by whom? I suggest it would be more productive to notice what differences it makes to your reading of the story if you imagine this playfulness being instigated for the first time by me, the English translator, or by Detha, the author of a written Rajasthani version, or by Savalram, the Dalit teller of an oral Rajasthani version, and then allow these various versions to play with each other across languages, media, space, and time.

Play them not just one against the other but against the more common versions of this story; as we know, these feature the prowess of a legendary prince like Raja Bhoj or Vikramaditya who succeeds in winning the hand of the beautiful princess Chouboli by his powerful rhetoric. These versions of the story are most interested in aggrandizing the wit of the male suitor. The English version produced collectively by Savalram, Detha, and me, however, flips the gender hierarchy so that we're on the side of a woman oppressed by hierarchy and rooting for a woman who pretends to be a man, thus implicitly posing another riddle (a variation of the seemingly real-life riddle posed of the *thakurani*): What right/power/*jor* do we—the members of the audience—have to object to the *thakur*'s treatment of his wife? What right/power/*jor* do we have to endorse such rhetorical travesties?

The frame story thus is interrogating the way we cross not only borders of male and female, the powerful and the less powerful, but those between the fictional and the real—not as a way of questioning the usefulness of playful fictions in sorting out real-life questions but rather to play at answering real-life questions in a context where the repercussions are—to borrow from Stewart—reversible. Such exchanges are far more effective when we read them in the plural, with every version crossing established boundaries of language and culture but also of belief systems.

We might notice, for example, our reaction to these various crossings when the narrator describes the niece-as-suitor entering the hall:

> When she first set her eyes on the princess the niece felt as if she had been blinded. Chouboli's beauty was truly such that men would risk spending all their days splitting fodder! Even questing after such beauty was a worthy end in and of itself. It would be as wonderful to have her come into your possession as not. It would be worth cracking chick peas for a thousand years just to behold her for an instant. Even this woman's heart became infatuated.

It might not seem extraordinary that the narrative describes the niece's interior reactions in close third-person, referring to her in the feminine. At first glance, rendering this beautiful princess a silent object to be possessed is not made to seem as remarkable as the niece's homosexual desire. Over the course of the narrative, however, it is the convention of treating a human being as a possession that is increasingly called into question, while the nature of their same-sex relations receives scant attention and to some extent is normalized. Such an observation should allow us to inquire more specifically into the ways the narrative creates this uncommon sense of common ground with its audience in a context that announces itself as traditional.

I would argue that it is the reliance on traditionally oral conventions such as embedded narratives and the giving of the *hunkarou* that invites the reader to accept an alliance with the niece, for in her role as male suitor she is playing along with familiar interpretive procedures. For example, Detha's version takes advantage of the same narrative trick we saw in Abdul Rahman's: when the protagonist sits down to begin telling stories, she-as-he is faced with a silent listener:

> The handsome young suitor sat down on the carpet before [the princess]. He looked up into Chouboli's face and started in, "Chouboli isn't going to urge me

on, isn't going to break her oath of silence, so who will give the *hunkarou* to my story? A story without *hunkarou* is like food without salt!"

While in oral performance this only serves to encourage the *hunkarou*-giver to respond that much more vociferously to make up for Chouboli's silence, in the written version the reader might remain just as silent outwardly. Happily, this story is more interested in narrating an inward experience where the fantastical elements of the story can come to imaginative rescue:

> Chouboli said neither yes nor no in response, so he repeated his question once more. Just then the colorful, pretty bed said he would be glad to give the *hunkarou*. Without proper *hunkarou*, a story had no flavor.

Admittedly, the image of a bed sitting down to a meal of bland food is as funny as that of it not being able to stay silent during a storytelling performance—or perhaps of a sentient human remaining as silent as an inanimate object. Such playfulness nicely echoes the *hunkarou* lines from the *chougou* and helps the audience of the written text feel carried along. For now the narrator must perform the role of niece-as-male-storyteller, superimposing one narrative frame over the other with the lines, "As soon as the bed agreed, the young man started the story." The metatextual doubling serves an important purpose: each of the four stories the cross-dressed protagonist delivers ends in a riddle that forces the silent listener (Chouboli, us as readers) to consider impossible questions about the logic of relation that then reflect on the relationship formed between teller and listener (as between writer and reader). We watch as common sense—and therefore community—is established between the two of them through storytelling performance, and thus we are given an opportunity to think through our own engagements with provisional community. Rather than functioning as provisional synthesis in an unsatisfactory dialectic, this kind of play emphasizes the necessity of a constant handing off and switching in ongoing performance.

The riddles, we soon see, are a gambit. The point is not the answer but to have the silent listener transformed into an active, speaking member of the community. Both within the frame of the narrative and outside it, a riddle gets worked out continuously in the various performances of the story itself. Various kinds of silence are being commented on at the same time: in actual oral storytelling performance (which is being commented on in an analogy with the beautiful Chouboli, whose silence must be broken); in the silence of the reader; and finally in a more dangerous kind of silence: when this story will not be "fresh and new," will not "find new readers and new listeners age after age." The *hunkarou* convention makes clear that this story doesn't just belong to a single teller but is a performance that is shared, transitory, continually regenerating (hence "be reborn . . . age after age"), and is thus asking larger questions about the ways such a story translates across media (oral to written, for example). So here the question about translation and community does not run along gendered, nationalist, or even nationalistically minded linguistic grounds but forces us to find a temporary, practical answer to the central question: To whom does this story belong?

The niece borrows these storytelling conventions in order to win the hand of the beautiful princess—in order, as she says, to possess her. Nevertheless, I would argue that the travesty of this frame story introduces a different grammar of possession—that an oral-based storytelling cycle like "Chouboli" is Detha's, say, or Savalram's, or mine only temporarily and relationally. "Chouboli" is translated not in the sense of *trans-latus* as a carrying across and thus tangible, something that can be owned only by a single person in a specific hierarchy, but in the sense of *anuvad* as a telling in turn. This is a temporary and temporarily constructed sense of belonging.

The frame story will eventually end by asking: "To whom does 'Chouboli' belong?" The implicit answer has been given at the start of the story: to new listeners and readers age after age—which asks another riddle: Who has the right/*jor* to tell this story? To give the *hunkarou*? To participate in solving the riddle—that is, to figure out the moral of the story? If we are looking for a solution, for a moral, we find that this is not a static, onetime, takeaway lesson but something that gets negotiated and renegotiated through the telling of the story as plurally owned. It is a process of creating community in translation. It implicitly asks a larger riddle about imagined community: What are the rules by which we negotiate such boundaries of ambiguous belonging?

The Irony of the Language

One couldn't own a story any more than one could own a language, as I discovered during the summer I spent learning Rajasthani. This was in 1992,

between my first and second years of graduate school. In my grant propos-
als I had written about my work translating Vijay Dan Detha's oral-based
tales and had explained that I wanted to read him directly in the language
he wrote in rather than in Hindi, the national language that his work was
translated into. I only briefly mentioned the complications: that Rajasthani
was not officially recognized as a state language by the constitution of India
and had been named as an official language by the governmental Sahitya
Akademi (Academy of Letters) only recently, and that this official recognition of Rajasthani as a literary language had actually been inaugurated with
an award to Detha in 1974. The very gesture to translate his work marked a
distinction between Hindi and Rajasthani that legally did not exist: the language Detha wrote in was officially considered substandard Hindi. I wasn't
sure the funding agencies I had applied to—the International Institute and
the Department of Asian Languages and Literatures—would agree to support me in learning a substandard dialect of Hindi.

I later discovered that Detha's refashioning of the folktales he had
heard told by family, friends, and neighbors in the local idiom had helped
define what has been come to be considered Rajasthani. Sitaram Lalas,
for example, selected entries for his five-volume dictionary by poring over
Detha's volumes.[64] I had been told that some people objected to this proposed version of the language; they thought that these efforts to standard-
ize Rajasthani were based primarily on grammatical and lexical models
provided by Marwari, the dialect of Rajasthani that Detha and Lalas spoke
and that some critics considered both provincial and hegemonic.[65] Others objected that the idiom Detha wrote in was too rustic and too local to
serve as a standardized language, a concern we have already seen Dalmia
address with the work of Chand. While they phrased their arguments in
geographical terms—advancing models they considered more versatile and
pan-Rajasthani—it was hard not to see in their suggestions an elitist vision
of what the language and therefore culture might be. This was the strain of
the Rajasthani movement that was uncomfortable with and even disdainful
of Detha's populist language formulations, no doubt because a democrati-
cally conceived language base would threaten the return of this former
feudal class to power.

Lisa Mitchell shows a similar mechanism at work in the example of
Telugu in the 1930s, when struggles over the definition of a language had
to negotiate political divisions based on class, caste, religion, and gender.[66]

In that case, Telugu speakers had managed to distinguish a Telugu identity separate from Tamil; here, Rajasthani speakers were less effective at unifying across class markers and therefore of classifying themselves as separate from the Hindi speakers. The result was that there was no established institutional space for its recognition and development. In the alternative school in which I taught in Jaipur in the late 1980s, for instance, we were told to scold the children speaking in Rajasthani for speaking incorrectly.

I discovered during that summer of 1992, after receiving grants from the university for intensive study, just how very difficult it was to learn a language that had none of the institutional apparatus I ordinarily took for granted: there were no textbooks to be had, few tutors trained to teach a beginner such as myself, and not even agreement on what might comprise standard Rajasthani.[67] The few courses in the Rajasthani language offered through universities (Jodhpur University, most particularly) assumed the student had knowledge as a native speaker that merely needed to be legitimized, codified, and historicized. Those courses recognized Rajasthani as a literary language extending back to the eleventh century, emphasizing the complex and certainly elegant literary contributions of the poets—primarily Charans, the bardic caste Detha was born into.[68] While I knew that I would eventually like to read these more literary works, I wanted to begin with the day-to-day language that might be spoken around me in Rajasthan; I wanted to be able to read Detha's stories but also to understand folktales written and told by others in Marwari and in the other contemporary dialects of Rajasthani.[69]

When I arrived back in Jaipur that summer, my friends introduced me to Sawai Singh Dhamora, an elderly man who worked full-time for the Rajasthan bureau of Akashvani, the state radio station. They told me he produced broadcasts of news items and dramas that would appeal to a range of Rajasthani speakers and so knew the dialects people actually spoke. They said he had been instrumental after Independence in fostering a sense of Rajasthani identity that transcended regional bounds. I soon learned that even the lines separating one dialect from another were somewhat ambiguous. There was a famous saying I heard repeated everywhere I traveled in Rajasthan: *har choubis kos pani aur boli badalta hai* (every twenty-four miles the water and the language change). *Boli* was an informal word for language, the everyday speech people actually spoke. It was a political act for Detha to write in *boli*, and that was the kind of Rajasthani I wanted to learn.

It was true that Sawai Singh Dhamora was extremely knowledgeable about spoken Rajasthani: I would read a line out loud from any of the Rajasthani stories I had managed to find in the market, and he could tell me right away that the story was written in a Mewari or Marwari, Shekhavati or Dhundari dialect. I would diligently write out the various versions of the simple sentences I had heard or read, trying to piece together the rules of grammar. Day after day I would coax him to teach me simple sentences, trying to build up a working vocabulary. But he was not a language teacher, and I was not a linguist. These simple exercises seemed pointless to him. As I would prompt and repeat and write, he would shake his head impatiently, the tail of his colorful, upper-caste turban tossing like a kite.[70] It didn't seem to either of us that these daily lessons were adding up to anything meaningful.

More disconcerting for both of us was that on the very first week of our meetings, when I tried to have him help me read through a story written by Detha, he told me flat out in Hindi that he had no respect for that communist poet and his upstart Charan ways. I knew that as bards, Charans were traditionally supposed to be subservient to Rajputs; Sawai Singh Dhamora was not the first Rajput I had met who seemed threatened by Detha's anti-feudal, democratic politics. What these erstwhile feudal lords seemed conveniently to forget was that Charans were traditionally also given the responsibility of using their fancy wordplay to offer eloquent and elegantly phrased critiques of the king's statecraft, as celebrated by Colonel Tod. It wasn't just the conventions of poetic exchange that protected the bard from reprisals: the lore I had heard claimed the curse of a Charan in particular was especially fearsome because it would follow you through several lifetimes; even powerful kings were wary of crossing a Charan.

I liked to think that Detha's decision to write for the people in the language of the people, offering humorous, political critiques of the people, was an adaptation of his traditional caste vocation: this was independent India, and now he was the bard of a democratic Rajasthan. It seemed that Dhamora's consternation with Detha was a reaction against Detha's ideological approach—Detha was adapting tradition to these new democratic realities in such a way that threatened the feudal yesteryear ways that Dhamora was hoping to revive through his own conservation of Rajasthani language and culture.

When I'd complain of Dhamora's politics to my roommate Dharmendar, she'd just shrug and tell me I wasn't trying to organize a political campaign with him but was just trying to learn a language. She was a Rajput, too, and, like many of my friends, worked for a nongovernmental organization whose means were very much keeping with the ends.[71] Years earlier she had also taught in the alternative school where I had worked, and that's where we had first met. That summer, two years into our friendship, we would laugh together as I learned basic Rajasthani, especially when I would purposely misuse the more ornate courtly formulations, narrating my simple actions—*mai padharou* (I have graced you with my presence), *mai jimarou* (I have feasted)—in the decorous language that was supposed to be used only in the third person to honor a guest of high standing.

Talking to Dharmendar helped me see that the differences in the language that I was learning to recognize weren't based only on geographical regions but on class and even gender. I trusted her evaluations of my attempts to make sense. When Dhamora corrected me, it wasn't always easy to know whether he was responding to incorrect grammatical usage or an ideological stance he disagreed with. With an unstandardized but highly hierarchical language like Rajasthani, the two seemed inseparable.

All along, my friend Dharmendar had teased me when I complained about Dhamora's conservative views, until the night he stopped by for tea, and we got into an argument about *sati*. The death of the teenage Roop Kanwar on her husband's funeral pyre was still much in the news, stirring controversy, and had served as a rallying cry for those on both sides of the battles lines: the traditionalists, who had begun worshipping her image in a gaudy display of national and caste pride, and the feminists, who mourned her as a tragic case of ritual murder. The event had taken place just a few years before in a Rajasthani village not far from the capital where we were, and people from all over India joined in this ideological battle.

I think the argument in Dharmendar's living room started when Dhamora muttered something that obliquely referenced Roop Kanwar, perhaps enlisting Dharmendar on his side as a fellow Rajput or perhaps testing her loyalties. Dharmendar's Hindi grew even more stately as her ire rose. She asked pointedly: "Do you really think that poor girl had any choice in the matter?" Dhamora's temper flared in turn: "This is a devi who has offered her life in the greatest sacrifice, and you dare question her honor? You are a disgrace to all Rajputs!" Previously I had only heard the various words for honor and disgrace in literary contexts, but here they were being used two or three to a sentence. Dharmendar retorted that he was a relic of history if he thought this is what being a Rajput was about. If you had to kill your women to feel secure, then there wasn't much to the tradition.

I was angry, too, but, more than that, awed by Dharmendar's rhetorical display. I opened my mouth to add tentative support to her argument, when Dhamora suddenly turned on me and shouted: "You be quiet! You are just like those English coming here and telling us what to do." The tactic worked better than he could have hoped. I shut my mouth quick and tight like a wooden puppet and didn't say another word.

He left minutes later in a huff, with Dharmendar shouting down the stairwell after him. She came back into the flat still raging, and was so energized that she ended up ranting and pacing for another few minutes until she finally sat down and dissolved in laughter. Then she looked up in surprise to see how deflated I was. I tried to explain: Not only was it upsetting to have this side of my teacher revealed so spectacularly, but his comment reinforced my worst concerns. I thought of Edward Said's damning critique of Orientalists like William Jones. I asked Dharmendar, "How am I any different from those English colonists coming in and telling people that their traditions are backward?" She tried to convince me that those colonists were completely different from me, but I didn't see how, exactly. "Did they help little children learn to read the tales they heard spoken around them?" she asked, trying to be helpful. She tried to explain that it came down to a subtle matter of the ways one conveyed respect. But Dhamora's outburst raised a question I had trouble answering: What right did I have to voice my opinion on the *sati* issue? What right did I have to give my opinion on any issue here in a place where I didn't grow up? I didn't necessarily believe nationalist definitions of belonging, but when faced with a believer like Dhamora, I had no argument in response.

Later I realized I could have asked: What right did a man like Sawai Singh Dhamora have to speak for a woman like Roop Kanwar after her death? It wasn't such a different question from the one asked by a scholar such as Gayatri Spivak two years before this actual post-Independence *sati*: Can the subaltern speak?[72] Lata Mani and Rajeshwari Sunder Rajan subsequently joined Spivak in writing on the *sati* issue to ask what our responsibilities are as scholars and as thoughtful citizens negotiating the rights and wrongs of what Lata Mani has famously called "contentious traditions."[73] We might ask: What right does a non-Rajasthani Indian woman have to speak for a Rajasthani woman like Roop Kanwar? What right does any of us have to speak for anyone else, living or dead? According to Dhamora's logic, a theorist such as Spivak or Mani could just as easily be accused of being English colonial patsies as could Dharmendar or myself. Sunder Rajan in particular admits to being caught in a quandary on the issue of Roop Kanwar, where she is pitted against fellow citizens of India and allied with the colonist of the nineteenth century.[74]

One of the reasons I was interested in translating Detha's prose was the way the stories he wrote establish a realm of playful fictionalizing that allows us to think through the contradictions and implications of these difficult and often divisive questions . . . together. And they make us all rethink what this project of creating community together might involve. Detha's stories question the various degrees of belonging we rely on in the very process of establishing that narrative relationship; his very choice to write in the *boli* spoken by people in his locale has forced his readers to rethink the categories of these different ways of identifying with one another and their attendant hierarchies. To me the operative question isn't *whether* a *sati* like Roop Kanwar could speak, but *how*.

After the argument with Dhamora, I thought again of Detha's Hindi version of a folktale I had translated called *"Rijak ka Maryada"* ("A True Calling"), which ended with an act of *sati*.[75] Now that I look back on it, I see that like "Chouboli," the story features a cross-dressing protagonist and quite playfully poses unanswerable questions of truth and our daily responsibility to uphold it. Detha had heard the tale from a barber and it showed a low-caste, uneducated barber outwitting the king's ministers and all his courtiers. In it a *bhand*, a traditional albeit clownish shape-shifter, takes on the guise of a bloodthirsty female demon and kills the queen's brother while in disguise. The queen demands revenge, but the courtiers are all helpless to do anything, because the *bhand* is protected by the rules of play (just as a Charan is protected by the rules regarding his profession). The barber then thinks up an ingenious solution: that the king ask the *bhand* to become a *sati*. The *bhand* is thus trapped by the rules of his own game and walks to his death.

Detha published a version of the story in 1972 as a strand of a Rajasthani storytelling cycle called *"Aath Rajkumar"* ("The Eight Princes") and then shortly after the Roop Kanwar incident—when I started working with him—took up that story again, writing in Hindi and focusing this time on the *sati* aspect. In this version, instead of extolling the smarts of the barber, he uses the tale to think about what he calls in the Hindi title *"rijak ka maryada"* (literally "the honor of one's profession," which I render "A True Calling"). The story implicitly asks: What is honor? What is respect? Rather than a simple reading of *sati* as being good or bad, legal or illegal, Detha's version of the story asks larger questions about our collective responsibilities when we are committed to a system that demands a mortal sacrifice of one of its members.

The story thus forces us to consider larger questions about this fictional sacrifice that we might apply to similar real-world sacrifices like Roop Kanwar's: Does the *bhand* really have a choice? What in the end does he die for? What do those around him believe he has died for? By translating the story from oral to written form, from Rajasthani into Hindi, Detha is asking us to think about the rhetorical conventions we rely on to think through such questions.

All of us—Dhamora, Dharmendar, Mani, Sunder Rajan, Spivak—were grappling with a similar basic but impossible riddle. How does a *sati* speak after her death? In this case I knew as a translator that such a fundamental question could only be answered by attending closely to a story's narrative technique—in written or oral form, in Rajasthani, Hindi, English: What kind of voice does the story's narrator assume? What was the quality of the relationship implied between the fictionalized storyteller and his imaginary audience? In the Hindi version of the story I translated, for instance, the narrator ends by describing the *sati* in a tone whose formal shifts convey a more complex ideology than could be summed up in newspaper banner headlines or even in shouted arguments over tea:

> Subsequently the incomparable *bhand* did just what he said he would. Thousands gathered to see a man assume the guise of a *sati*. Soon a cremation pyre was laid of sandalwood. She mounted the funeral pyre with the natural bearing of a true *sati*. Such was the power of her conviction that flames leapt up from the pyre of their own accord. The *sati* disguise turned out to be another great success.[76]

The narrator seems to believe the *bhand*'s shift from male to female guise so completely that he switches the gender of the pronoun from one sentence to the next without comment as if he has as much respect for this *bhand*'s art and sacrifice as he does for those who deem it a great success. It is this "as if" that is key to understanding the ethics of the story. I knew

Detha's work well enough to understand that the narrative voice is a bit of a playful setup, a guise he takes on in order to explore these issues, but how to explain such a rhetorical move?[77] This isn't so much ironic in the (mostly European) literary sense of the term as humorous in the (mostly Rajasthani) oral storytelling sense of the word. This narrator is putting on an act of being something other than what he claims. What then? He isn't exactly saying the opposite of what he means—as simplistic descriptions of irony in English would often phrase it (and which Hutcheon so elegantly critiques). Such a binaristic reading would make little sense in the case of a story such as "*Rijak ka Maryada*" or any of Detha's oral-based tales. What would be the opposite of a business-as-usual gender switch or a performance that is called successful precisely because it ends in the death of the performer? The style of the narrative plays with these switches in frame in such a way that it renders the very categories they establish unreliable. How can one explain a mode of playfulness whose critique depends on movement between more than one point of view?

If we look once more to Linda Hutcheon's work on irony, we see that while she is generally concerned with the inequality or unevenness of ironic encounters as figured culturally (whose boundaries she describes predominantly in ethnic if not geographical terms), she does not consider the specifics of cultural translation as it plays out in literary/linguistic terms. How might we discuss relationality and therefore community across such divides? This component is especially important to discuss when we, as interpreters, are called upon to consider the relative value of the languages in comparison to one another, as we do implicitly in any translated text. Consider for a moment the playful irony at work in the following example:

heer, ther solah aana, idhar-udhar baar,
ikde tikde aath aana, athe bathe chaar[78]

[Here, there sixteen annas, *idhar-udhar* twelve,
Ikde tikde eight annas, *athe bathe* four][79]

How we establish the "here" and "there" in a playful text is precisely what is being called into question "here" and "there" (and thus by "us" and "them"). Even in English translation, to understand the humor the interpreter must be able to evaluate the languages being compared: English's "here, there" is 16 annas and so worth full value, while Hindi's is 12 annas, 75 percent of the full value, Gujarati's is 8 annas or 50 percent, and Rajasthani's is a mere 4 annas, 25 percent of the value of English. A reading strategy that pretends all languages are commensurate and therefore does not attend to the operations of translation breaks down when faced with this example. Such playful accounting of these imaginary here-theres underscores the point Ganesh Devy has made most forcefully: that in multilingual India, all language speakers are translators, traversing categorical divisions between languages and cultures even when staying in one geographical place. Such interpretations are located in a critical landscape that brings together Hutcheon's insights into the "cutting edge" of irony with Devy's "translating consciousness."[80]

We should note that each of the performances of "here" in the above example overlaps with the other in this multilingual world, with the differences being counted primarily even while amorphously in terms of power (here figured economically). The humor of the rhyming couplet (a traditional *doha* meter, not coincidentally) depends on it being read as a plural voice—a group of people vital, anonymous, constantly in flux—by people who themselves are part of a plurality able to make these linguistic switches provisionally, *heer, idhar, itke, athe*. The English version challenges the pretense that English, Hindi, Gujarati, and Rajasthani could ever be considered commensurate by performing the instability of the very *bathe-ness* (not exactly *ther*-ness) that translation as an operation tries to pretend is stable. In this case, as Hutcheon notes, those who are excluded from the humor are the ones to who do not recognize *heer, idhar, itke, athe* as *here, idhar, itke, athe*.

To ask what right I have to try to understand how the subaltern speaks, I have to ask: How do we critically approach a playful rhyme that makes fun of the very project of translation in terms of marketplace value when we ourselves are engaged in that exchange? While Bakhtin describes Rabelais's folk borrowings as marketplace humor in the abstract sense of the term, here the imaginary performer of these *dohas* can be imagined as any number of a variety of people standing in front of a seller's cart somewhere, arguing about the prices of the languages for sale. How can we imagine that provisional somewhere "here" across languages in a manner that recognizes the implicit disparities being made fun of?

A more general question is being raised that applies not only to this couplet but to *"Rijak ka Maryada"* and any number of stories: How can we discuss the moral vision of translations whose values become negotiated through the very rhetoric of the exchange? We might begin answering this question by focusing more specifically on the relationality of the enterprise, following the example of Wayne Booth in *A Rhetoric of Irony*. Like Hutcheon, Booth does not extend his study to inquire into examples of translation (even while he does read texts in translation). He does show, however, that in the case of literary texts, finding a passage ironic means that a reader makes alliance with an implied author against the viewpoint of a narrator whom the reader finds morally untenable (and therefore unreliable).[81]

That we imagine the plurally constructed voice of Detha's story or this rhyming *doha* in terms of a singular figure becomes a strategically useful fiction (with its own dangers, as Foucault points out. What, after all, is an author?). This is a more specific inquiry into the rhetoric of irony—as Booth's title promises—than Hutcheon's insightful but ultimately abstracted discussions of the responsibility of the interpretive community. Booth's attentive reading of the reader–narrator–implied-author relation as triangular helps us see the ways such formulations negotiate the real and the imaginary concerns of all parties involved in the exchange and compare this three-way exchange to Freud's joking triangle, which I discuss in the opening section in terms of Gandhi's anticolonial humor.

Bringing discussions of irony together with questions of translation forces us to account for the relative value of the languages brought into such an exchange in our readings of the translated text—forces us to pay attention to the ways an implied author's viewpoint becomes more valuable than a narrator's, for instance, in our minds, or an English speaker's than a Rajasthani's, or an implied author's more than a translator's. These heated cultural negotiations that go on via a literary exchange are often silent and therefore not attended to. Can the translating consciousness speak?

In Detha's version of "*Rijak ka Maryada*," for instance, the narrative seems to take definite sides within a feudal context so local and outdated as to establish a fantastical "there" no matter who the reader is. In the quest to find an effective strategy for translating Detha's prose into English, I had to do more than learn basic Rajasthani; I had to find a way of explaining to myself the wisdom and complexity of the storytelling voice he had adapted to written form, and this involved recognizing the complex historical relationship of Rajasthani to Hindi, of Hindi to English, and of all its references to hierarchy. I knew of no narrative theory that accounted for such practical concerns of translation in the discussions of voice and the nation beyond simplistic constructions of here and there, us and them: On whose behalf was the story thought to be speaking? Such a question was answered differently whether you categorized it as a literature or as folklore, as part of the Hindi tradition or the Rajasthani.

To Whom Does Chouboli Belong?

Part of the trick of reading stories like the ones Detha wrote is in learning to read across categories usually kept distinct. Unlike the English word "literature," the Hindi word "*sāhitya*" suggests that literary exchange is premised not on the mechanical practice of writing but on the relationality of imaginative enterprise.[82] The Sanskrit of *sāhitya* is, according to Sir Monier Monier-Williams, related to *sahita*, which means "with, accompanied by," and so *sāhitya* is defined first as "association, connection, society, combination, union with," second as "agreement, harmony," and only third as the meaning commonly used in Hindi and other modern Indian languages: "literary or rhetorical composition, rhetoric, poetry."[83]

At its most ideal, then, the Hindi phrase "*lok sāhitya*" does not sound as contradictory to the ear as the English "folk literature," for it does not necessarily assume that the "*lok*" are rustic and unlettered, and that "*sāhitya*" is an elite enterprise requiring specialized training. Approaching a text as an "association, connection, society, combination, union with" a people does not ask us to think about how we might map that people regionally (as European Romantic ideas connecting literature and nationalism would teach us) but instead asks us to think about how we might map the relationship that is formed at that moment between storyteller and audience within that imaginary narrative space. Implicitly, this means comparing the conventions of narrative relation established in this particular performance with the other tellings said to exist across space and time, past, present and future.

Such a comparison is made explicit in a story such as "Chouboli," a metatextual cue that we see quite clearly when the cross-dressed niece begins her own performance within the frame narrative by asking someone to give the *hunkarou*. Such a move should make audience members wonder: How does their *hunkarou*-giver–storyteller relationship compare to ours?

Because Chouboli must remain silent, the niece finds volunteers among the hitherto inanimate objects around the room—the bed Chouboli is sitting on, the necklace around her neck, Chouboli's own veil, and finally the lamp lighting the room where they sit—and thus demonstrates that a storytelling exchange can never take place exclusively between two people. I have made this point already in the case of Gandhi's playful quip. Here the scene of *hunkarou*-giving demonstrates more particularly that a storytelling performance depends on being part of an ongoing cultural community and so is necessarily (in Andrew Benjamin's words) "always—always already—displaced."

We might understand the terms of displacement in a number of complementary ways; here we have what could be a real storytelling scenario but located in an imaginative realm, a realm in which the storyteller turns away from the nonspeaking subaltern subject and instead forms a narrative relation with a series of objects (therefore "displaced" in the classic psychoanalytic use of the term). This thus strengthens the impression that in any storytelling scenario certain protocol must be followed and that the resulting performance itself cannot but be translated from another time and place, which only serves to emphasize how very contingent this temporary experience of community truly is, how provisional the sense of common ground achieved through the narrative can ever be. Rather than react melancholically to such contingency, however, the narrative encourages us to play along with the displacements, to laugh at the comic truth that "what I say to you already includes what you say to me, which in turn includes what I have said and may say to you." These examples of *lok sāhitya* thus teach us a different grammar of possession from what we might otherwise learn in our literary exchanges and in the process teach us to map a different mode of belonging to one another through these very texts.

Not just the ritual negotiating the giving of the *hunkarou* but each of the four embedded tales poses a riddle that forces the displaced audience to reckon with the implications of such meaning-making in process. In Detha's version, each time the niece-as-suitor finishes telling one of the riddling stories, the *hunkarou*-giver hazards a guess at the solution. The storyteller wins the bet precisely because Chouboli cannot allow herself to remain excluded; she disagrees so passionately that she joins the conversation, turning the dialogue between *hunkarou*-giver and storyteller into a three-way argument.

Explicitly, each story relies on riddles to engage the listeners (both *hunkarou*-giving and silent) in thinking through impossible moral quandaries of trust and value in interpersonal relations: Which extraordinary talent of the four marvelous friends proves most valuable to the king? Which of the four involved in a ring of deceit—the neglectful husband, the conniving thief, the amorous merchant, or the wayward wife—can be blamed for a wife's near-infidelity? Whose magical powers are critical in bringing a lump of clay to life and thus who has the right to possess her as a wife? If a man's head is miraculously exchanged with another's, then to which—the head or the body—does the wife belong?

Each story effectively asks us to judge for our own time and place: Whose solution is most true? The solving of the riddles within the frame of the story thus teaches how to solve much more serious riddles outside the frame of the story, in our own lives, where friends really do compete for the favor of the king or the hand of a bride and where neglected or confused wives are blamed for their impossible choices. The frame story insists that these wives—the *thakurani* and the niece in the frame story as well as the female characters in the second and fourth embedded stories—do not have enough *jor* even to act on what they believe is right. Two of the four riddling stories ("*Sata Kin Mai?*" ["Who Is True?"] and "*Dhani Kun?*" ["Who Is Her Lord?"]) go so far as to make fun of those in power who assume there are easy distinctions between right and wrong and who try to insist on these facile schemas for their own limited ends. Instead, the stories teach us that truth is variable and context-dependent and thus that *jor* is contingent. The frame stories' riddles are made fresh and new age after age because of this contingency.

How does a story like "*Dhani Kun?*" ("Who Is Her Lord?") then work to locate such a contingency in the imaginative space they have in common? That is, how does the performance serve to map a different boundary of belonging from the one we might expect?

We might notice that the version of the story embedded in Detha's version of "Chouboli," like the storytelling cycle more generally, plays with the very grammar of textual possession that we rely on in English, for it can be said to belong to Detha and to the people of Rajasthan at the same time—including Savalram's oral performance which Detha based his written version on, as well as Abdul Rahman's oral performance which I recorded. Not only that, but this particular story has appeared as an embedded narrative in another storytelling cycle as well: in the riddling twelfth-century Sanskrit storytelling cycle, the *Vetalapanchavimshati* ("The Twenty-Five Tales of the Undead"), which we consider at length in the next chapter.

To understand the grammar of temporary possession, we must see how each version asserts its own ideological framework: the version told by Abdul Rahman, for instance, features two Rajput friends who are forced to protect the bonds of friendship in the face of marital responsibilities, while the version embedded in the *Vetalapanchavimshati* asks the wife to choose between a man who has the body of her husband and the head of her brother and vice versa, thus bringing issues of incestuous relation to the fore. Thomas Mann's novella *Die vetauschten Köpfe* ("The Transposed Heads")—purportedly inspired by a Heinrich Zimmer translation of the *Vetalapanchavimshati*—emphasizes the languorously romantic and thus tragically painful aspect of such a choice (in a writing style that seems influenced by nineteenth century Orientalism), whereas Girish Karnad's more recent Kannada play *Hayavadana* uses the story of two childhood friends— one a brawny laborer and the other a brainy teacher a woman falls in love with and marries—to tell a story of passion first of the mind and then of the body and the irresolvable conflict between them.

In each case, the story plays with a taboo issue that cannot be named directly, thus inviting the reader or listener to contemplate the competing implications of this situation through the storytelling exchange. In Detha's version of the Chouboli storytelling cycle, the riddle of the switched heads—"Who Is Her Lord?"—introduces not only the issue of friendship, as in Rahman's version, but the issue of the prohibition against the mixing of castes:

> Once there was a village where a Rajput and a Jat lived. They were the best of friends. They spent every moment of the day and every moment of the night as close to each other as shadows. They worked in the field together, grazed their cattle together, ate their *roti-bati* together. The two had their houses built next to each other on adjoining plots. The love they had for each other was deeper than brothers.[84]

Thus the concerns over belonging work on two levels simultaneously: on a metatextual level, we are asked to question the relationships we form as performers and audience through texts, and within the thematics of the narrative, we are asked to question the relationships we form as individuals through other cultural markers such as caste. In each case we are asked to wonder: What are the rules of such an alliance? How dependable should these limits be?

Not far into the narrative, first the Jat (someone who works the land and thus is often of lower status) and then the Rajput (a landowner or lord and thus of higher status) get married. The Jat ensures that his best friend is by his side for his *muklavau*, the ceremony when he goes to retrieve his bride from her parents' home. The narrator moves into the Rajput's point of view to confide that "his friend's in-laws treated him better than their own son-in-law" since "the in-laws knew what a deep bond there was between the two."[85] The narration thus opens up a space between the specific perspective of this character and the more general views offered by the narration. The paragraph concludes, "When the Rajput saw them paying more attention to him than their own son-in-law, he was infinitely pleased."[86] As it turns out, when the situation is reversed and the Rajput brings his Jat friend to his own *muklavau*, the higher-caste friend expects hospitality to trump caste hierarchy, going against tradition to demand social equality between the two friends:

> After a few days it came time to set out for the Rajput's *muklavau*. There was no question of the Jat not accompanying him. But if his in-laws didn't extend the same hospitality to his friend that his friend's in-laws did to him, then the Rajput would be sorely displeased. The Jat would hardly care about such things, but for the Rajput such a thing would be a disgrace worse than death. This is what he thought to himself.[87]

The narration thus turns the rhetoric of Rajput honor on its head through repetition, using it ("a disgrace worse than death") against the very traditions of caste hierarchy it was meant to uphold. To whom do these critiques belong?

We might claim simply that Detha is responsible for such anticaste discourse, or that the perspective belongs exclusively to Savalram, the Dalit on whose oral version Detha based his written text. As my discussion in the previous chapter of the story of Mr. Worth should make clear, I am calling for a more complex grammar of textual possession, one that can explain the ways such shifts in meaning can take place only within a collective enterprise of meaning-making. We need to find an alternative to the ideological stance adopted by the colonial officials described by Lata Mani in "Contentious Traditions: The Debate on *Sati* in Colonial India," who banned the practice of ritual widow immolation in 1829 as part of a "civilizing mission" they believed would allow India to participate more fully in the "modern" circulation of cultures and ideas. We need, too, to incorporate into our thinking Lata Mani's own complicated reactions to such a ban more than a century later, wanting to side with neither the traditionalist advocating the right of women to sacrifice themselves in the name of indigeneity nor with the presumptuousness of the colonial officials.

Mani admits, "even the most anti-imperialist amongst us has felt forced to acknowledge the 'positive' consequences of colonial rule for certain aspects of women's lives, if not in terms of actual practice, at least at the level of ideas about 'women's rights.'"[88] If we agree that Savalram and then Detha in turn have used a story outlining injustices against women to speak to broader issues of human rights and our responsibilities to work against discrimination, then how might we adapt our discussions of translation to approach these situations as impossible but worthwhile riddles and thus to use the fanciful fictions to recognize in play the competing interests and responsibilities at stake in our ongoing relationships? If these riddling storytelling cycles propose a way of thinking of community, then I would suggest we define community in translation in such a way that might challenge set boundaries of language, nation, caste, and gender. Part of the bind Mani describes is that the perceived consensus on human rights reveals a more entrenched and yet ambiguous pattern of discrimination inherited from colonial regimes, as we see in the previous chapter. The question this particular translation of *"Dhani Kun?"* forces us to ask is how we might form an interpretive community that uses translation to rethink the uneven terms of exchange inherent in such an act. What would it mean for the reception of translation to assert a different understanding of human rights proleptically and performatively, as Butler has suggested? What rights and responsibilities do we wish to negotiate in the space of community created through translation?

"Who Is Her Lord?" poses such questions in its own storytelling terms. It asks: Is the Rajput wrong to expect his in-laws to flout tradition? On the way to his in-laws' house with his Jat friend, he stops at the temple to Lord Shiva to pray for help in this matter:

> The Rajput stood before the image of Shankar Bhagwan with folded hands and prayed that his in-laws would attend to his friend with the same care and concern as they would to him. He pledged an eleven-rupee offering that everything might turn out as he hoped. But he vowed that if there were any discrimination, he would come back to take his life at that very spot.[89]

The irreverent narrator then adds: "Shankar Bhagwan would not be able to live down the disgrace of someone taking his own life before Him."[90] Yet, in typical storytelling mode, this is exactly what happens:

> The Rajput did everything he could to explain matters to his in-laws, but either the in-laws didn't understand what he was trying to tell them, or else they didn't care. They received the Jat as coolly as they would have a menial. They treated him just like a servant. They discriminated against him in the way they served the food, in the way they served the drinks, in the way they talked to him. The Rajput's heart went out like a snuffed candle. It was true, he was angry with his in-laws, but what good would it do to push? Instead he stored up his ire for his deity, Shankar Bhagwan.[91]

And so, as the Rajput is returning home with his wife and his best friend, he stops at the Shiva temple, pulls out his sword, and lops off his own head, just as he had vowed, exclaiming first to his intoxicated god: "If you didn't take the trouble to look after my honor, then why should I bother to look after yours?" Detha's version uses the oft-repeated Rajasthani word *lāj* (which I have translated as "honor") strategically: while Rajputs in ballads and epics are often extolled for making the ultimate sacrifice to defend the *lāj* of their clan, this intercaste definition of *lāj* is new, even somewhat scandalous. Traditionally it is said that a Rajput has a right to kill someone from another caste for daring to take water from his clan's well; here instead, this Rajput's *lāj* and therefore very life is staked on that taboo being overturned, on the two friends being treated equally, as brothers. This version of the story thus asserts a different version of alliance from traditional Rajasthani ballads, and so the story itself risks being outcast—that is, being considered inauthentic, un-Rajasthani nonsense. Who has a right to set these boundaries of belonging? How, then, are these set—especially in texts translated across languages and cultures?

As it happens, the image of intercaste mixing only gets more vivid as the narrative proceeds. We next see a scene narrated sympathetically through the Jat's point of view when he discovers his dear friend's corpse. It ends with a startling image of their merging, the narrator turning suddenly sentimental as he describes a scene of union more fundamental than sexual lovers:

> The Jat waited for a while and then went into the temple himself. And the sight he saw—no one should ever have to witness! When he saw the red blood

flowing from his friend's body, his face went white as a ghost. There was no need to think any further. He grabbed the same sword to slice his own neck and fell next to his friend. While alive, both friends' hearts beat as if one. Now even their blood had begun to mingle. They began to dissolve into one another.[92]

The riddle posed implicitly is a caste-tinged variation of one familiar to readers of the *Ramayana* and countless other tales: Is the bond between brothers more important than the bond between man and wife?[93] Who has a right to establish their relative values?

The story answers the question in its own way, for when the Rajput wife discovers the two corpses, rather than the plaintive prayers we see in the other versions of the story, she responds as bravely and resolutely as the legends of Rajput women promise, grabbing the sword by the hilt, as the narrator tells us, "ready to slice her own throat." At this point the goddess intervenes, first apologizing for her husband ("he was too high to know what was going on") and then directing the bride, "Just stick their heads back on their trunks, and they'll come back to life in the blink of an eye."[94]

The Rajput wife switches the heads as she puts them back on the bodies, and after they come back to life, the riddle the teller then asks touches not so much on an incest taboo or a prohibition against homosexuality, as in the other versions, but on a question of caste contamination. The cross-dressed storyteller asks: To whom does she belong? The one with the husband's head and the Jata friend's body, or one with the friend's head and the Rajput husband's body?

The riddle asks in binary terms: Is a person's caste identity located in the head or in the body? It prompts a whole series of questions that are not supposed to be spoken: What use is caste difference in our society? What is a woman's place? What is the meaning of friendship and of marriage-mediated sexual relation? It seems significant that the tragic and then miraculous scene takes place in a temple to one of the main gods in the Hindu pantheon at a moment when He has disappointed one of His worshippers. The story asks: What do we believe in? because if the riddle "Who is her lord?" becomes a question of faith, it applies as much to the lives of the fictional figures within the story as to those reading it. We might say in simple terms that we believe or do not believe in this or that god, but that helps us only partially understand our own rights and responsibilities as a provisional community of readers of world literature in answering this riddle. When we question the maintenance of caste and gendered hierarchies within this traditional society, do we try answering in terms of some imaginary community within Rajasthan, to an equally local imagined community of English speakers somewhere, as an even more nebulous universal? Who do we believe is posing these questions to whom and who has the right to answer in a story in so many ways displaced?

The question becomes even trickier when religious institutions are invoked in maintaining a hierarchical social order that benefits only a small minority. The story uses humor to critique such a tradition. The word "caste" or a perceived equivalent such as *jāti* is never mentioned in either the English or the Rajasthani version of the story, however. To frame the particular details of the story this way, as Nicholas Dirks points out in *Castes of Mind*, says as much about English speakers' preoccupations with hierarchy as it does about any empirically verifiable historical reality in India. And yet the fantastic context described in the embedded narrative, like the frame narrative, forces us to ask implicitly if such an institution is one we wish to maintain in the ideal world that we can imagine together through the narrative. If we take Judith Butler's point seriously, that "universality can be proleptic and performative, conjuring a reality that does not yet exist, and holding out the possibility for a convergence of cultural horizons that have not yet met," then, like her, we might arrive at "a second view of universality in which it is defined as a future-oriented labor of cultural translation."[95]

How might this definition of cultural translation apply to our reading of "Who Is Her Lord?"—especially if we take into account the contingent expectations and responsibilities of our own relation? Do we as readers in English have the *jor* to change the situation in the nonreversible world that we see described in this reversible world? How do we solve riddles about our own lives?

As it happens, the frame story of Detha's version of "Chouboli" ends with that very riddle. After all, with each story the cross-dressed niece tells, it becomes increasingly obvious that each of the answers is entirely arbitrary and subjective, that in the case of "Who Is Her Lord?" for example, a lamp would argue that caste identity resides in the trunk of the man because the lamp is mostly trunk, whereas a ruling-class human like Chouboli would insist that "Men recognize one another by their faces. Your face and your head are the most important parts of your person." As the audience, we come to learn that such disagreements become only a tool or even a tease the storyteller uses to engage the silent listener. Within the frame of the story, we understand that the goal is to make the silent Chouboli speak. Through the course of the narrative, we as readers realize we have fallen prey to a similar trick: telling riddling story after riddling story has been only a pretext to keep the narrative exchange alive—a notion I have adapted from Roland Barthes, and one that I will explore in more detail in the following chapter.

We might notice similarly that with each story, the no-longer-silent princess seems to become increasingly interested in this unnameable something else that the storyteller is leading her toward in the guise of a riddle. Given that "Who Is Her Lord?" is the fourth of the four embedded stories, like the audience outside the narrative frame, the silent listener, Chouboli, seems aware that this contest of wills has come to an end. The storyteller has tricked her into speaking a fourth time and thus has won the bet. Like Chouboli, then, we are not disappointed when the crossed-dressed storyteller-suitor, rather than arbitrating between the lamp and the princess to deem one answer right and the other wrong, proceeds to focus on his not-so-hidden agenda:

> The handsome young gentleman stood up with his hand on the hilt of his sword. He proclaimed loudly, "Beat the drums to a glorious beat! The unspeaking Chouboli has deigned a fourth time to speak!"
>
> The four drummers began pounding out a joyous beat: dham-dhamadham. The gentleman handed them each a necklace from his own neck in gratitude. The Raja-Rani went crazy with joy, jumping and dancing as they ran to the princess's *mahal*. The suitors grinding fodder got up from their grindstones and began raising a ruckus.
>
> The princess who had defeated thousands of nobles and made them her slaves had at last been defeated herself. But this defeat was also her victory. The drumbeats sounded pleasant even to Chouboli. Now her oath had been fulfilled.

Here, by suggesting that Chouboli's defeat might also be her victory, the narrative shows that the rules of this game of the oath she was engaged in were not so fixed that she was unable to step outside the fiction she was maintaining when the time came. Silence, it turns out, was merely a tool useful within a clearly delimited frame of play—a frame that was designed to turn inside out, not just commenting on the conventional expectations of alliance with a princess and expected heir but also agentially transforming them. Because she had changed the rules of the game within this delimited frame, she was able to change the rules of the game of her future welfare more generally.

Similarly, the narrative itself comments self-consciously on the relationship between the world within the riddling storytelling cycle and that without. Unlike all the other versions of "Chouboli," Detha's version of the frame story closes with an extra riddle once the winning suitor admits his secret to his trophy bride: that the suitor was only playing the part of the man to fulfill her own vow, that she is the new bride of a *thakur* who sits down in the dungeon with the other unsuccessful suitors grinding fodder. We might imagine a character from this mythical time in the soft-focus past to react to such a travesty with horror, but instead to Chouboli this is yet another riddle, one whose solution is only slightly more troublesome. She admits to being glad to discover that no man could defeat her in her oath, but then:

> Suddenly Chouboli felt confused. She threw her arms around her friend's neck and exclaimed, "Your four stories made me blurt out the right answers. But when it comes to the riddle of my own life, I'm all puzzled. Tell me, whom do I belong to? To you or to the *thakur*? You won my hand according to my oath. It was you I followed around the wedding fire."

The phrase she utters in Rajasthani, "*Chouboli kin ri*?" is the title of the last section of the story, and translates literally: "Chouboli whose?" The riddle can be read on a number of different levels at once.

The simplest, most obvious answer the successful suitor could make would be: "mine," since this is the standard grammatical way in Rajasthani of marking relation (unidirectionally) between a husband and his wife. So the riddle ends up asking: Who can speak this pronoun "*mari*" (as in "*Chouboli mari*")—that is, she is mine, belongs to me. The couple assume, somewhat playfully, that it would be impossible for a woman to repeat this phrase, even though the pronouns "whose" (*kin ri*) and "my" or "mine" (*mari*) are also nongendered on the part of the speaker, as in the English. Generally in Rajasthani, the word "husband" or "wife" is not used, just the possessive pronoun, so that it's clear that one person is supposed to be the possessor and one the possessed. Grammar is thus conspiring with convention to make possession automatically gendered in exactly the way the niece's parody submits to on the surface and therefore calls into question.

Likewise, we might wonder who is making this joke on the Rajasthani grammar of possession—especially in English translation. Rather than just ridiculing the *thakur*'s possessive nature, we are asked to turn the humor against ourselves and wonder more generally about these narratives of belonging that we subscribe to in our very approach to such texts: "Chouboli" belongs to whom? (*"Chouboli kin ri?"*) Whose story is this? A reader cannot be sure that this isn't a story I've made up myself and just created an imaginary genealogy for (like Mr. Worth in Chapter 1), nor that Vijay Dan Detha hasn't done the same thing, as the storyteller, Savalram, could have. Each genealogical narrative frames the story for us and thus gives it meaning. These metatextual framing devices that pretend to exist outside the frame establish an ethical relevance that we want to take seriously, even in the act of playing along with the fiction.

The storytelling conventions make us aware of this ongoing network of exchange we are participating in just by listening to the story: "May Lord Ram bless us that, however old, this tale of Chouboli might become fresh and new to listeners and readers age after age." The invocation thus teaches us a different grammar of possession, one that does not demand a fixed relationship between teller, listener, and story, located always and forever at the same point in time and space and relative positionality, but instead finds itself negotiating temporary alliances, temporary solutions, which must constantly adjust to new, ever-evolving contexts.

As it turns out, in the frame story of "Chouboli" the couple find themselves participating in a fiction partially of their own creation, one that they nonetheless have little control over:

> No one had any idea of what was taking place between these two friends. Princess Chouboli's farewell send-off went down with as much pomp and pageantry as her wedding had. The nobles who had been grinding fodder down in the dungeon were also sent off with farewell gifts. Chouboli asked the Rajaji to have the *thakur* who used to shoot arrows through his wife's nose rings accompany them. So he was seated in the carriage with her. But the *thakur* hadn't the faintest idea what was happening. He sat there staring at Chouboli's face, abject as a beggar, and didn't take his eyes off her even to blink.

We see the scene unfold in close third-person from the niece's point of view. ("Now there was no point in keeping the secret quiet, the *seth*'s niece thought to herself. She changed out of the men's clothes and got dressed up as a woman again.") Only when she is in her female guise does the *thakur* recognize her, with the result that "it was as if he had been struck by lightning." More than any of the characters of the story, we see, he is pathetic because he is unable to read these travesties on more than the literal level. The niece reads him expertly, and guessing the source of his anxiety, uses his myopia against him, reassuring him, "There's no reason to worry. You stop breathing and three women will have to suffer widowhood. Chouboli belongs all to you. She was wedded to your sword."

The *thakur*, of course, cannot believe his good luck. ("What did you say? . . . Chouboli is mine . . . Chouboli is really mine?") The niece lays out her condition—that he comply with her vow—and we are told:

> The *thakur* agreed right away. He happily gobbled down handfuls of roasted
> chick pea fodder and then slurped down water that had been used to wash
> her feet, as obediently as if this were a *charanamrat* ritual for the gods. He let
> himself be saddled up and ridden around the bed, and afterwards pleaded with
> hands clasped please to never let this secret spread anywhere in the *thikana*. If
> this matter were ever leaked to his subjects, what would it do to his standing?

At first, such a claim might have seemed silly and innocuous, but now when we see him comply with her whimsical threat, we understand that it displays her power over him. For we are told likewise that "The *seth*'s niece made him give up his daily practice of shooting arrows through his wives' nose rings." While he might continue to be the *thakur* in name, beneath the formalities, the niece—nominally his second wife—is clearly the person in charge. After all, she was the one who won Chouboli in marriage. The network of belonging laid out in this story is a complex one that connects realities and formalities in a manner whose irony it seems to delight in.

Indeed, the narrator pretends to be oblivious to such ironies when we're told:

> Rajaji had no other issue except Princess Chouboli. When he deemed it time
> to retire, he bequeathed the entire kingdom to his daughter and spent all his
> days saying his *mala* praying that Bhagwan would make him a *raja* again in his
> next birth. The guileless *thakur* had fumbled upon luck upon luck. He ruled
> over his kingdom for years upon years relying completely on the intelligence of
> the *seth*'s niece and Chouboli, and they lived like that playing the flute of bliss
> forever after.

The suggestion, of course, is that the *thakur* held this power in name only and that the two women had learned to play him like a flute, behind the scenes in the running of the kingdoms as well as in bed. In this way we see it is possible that the final riddle of the story—To whom does Chouboli belong?—might on the formal level of social presentation find a ready answer that corresponds with the common discourse (that is, they are co-wives subservient to their lord) while at the same time in practice find itself venturing into territory outside the bounds of acceptable language (the two are lovers, fronting with this hapless man). Our fictions allow us to negotiate the terms of just such complicated realities; to be faithful to a network of exchange that trades in such riddles of belonging requires we formulate a critical methodology as flexible and dynamic as the stories we tell in turn. And in turn to imagine a common narrative ground that is constantly shifting.

THREE

Framed

Out of Bounds

Detha's version of the story of the switched heads provokes a fundamental question: What ethical landscape does a community map for itself in its very framing devices? Common sense tells us that the exercise of translating a story as a telling requires in turn that members of a community use material inherited from the past to mark out a narrative space in the present that they envision future generations might happily and hopefully step into. The very bounds of the community are thereby established in such a gesture. I have already suggested that this space is neither the lost unity that Romantics pine for in nationalist movements, nor the utopia that revolutionaries dream of, but something more flexible, fluid, and as heterogeneous as its many speakers.

The riddle of belonging that we considered in Chapter 1—that what I say already includes what you say to me—reveals to speakers that they are necessarily, as Terry Eagleton puts it, "caught up in a pleasurable play of shifting solidarity with others" that assumes a form collectively imagined.[1] Thematically, the story of the switched heads teaches us to question the fixity of the line we draw distinguishing our bodily selves from those of others; Detha's version has us meditate on this riddle to question in turn the fixity of the line we draw distinguishing one value system from another. If the frame story of Detha's version of "Chouboli" were to be switched with four of the embedded narratives written eight centuries earlier by Somadeva in the *Katha Sarit Sagara* ("The Ocean of the Streams of Stories"), then what do we imagine the value system of the resulting narrative community to be? To ask about framing devices is to ask what kind of world is being created collectively in the ongoing storytelling process we are engaged in at that moment, in comparison to other possible performances located in various points in time and space. How do we map such fluid boundaries of belonging?

To begin addressing such a question, one might look at how these temporal relationships of past to present to future are posited in the narrative. Which past, present, and future do we wish to claim as our own? Here the paradoxical temporalities of Narayana Rao's riddling community referred to in the opening chapter assume a metaphorical locatedness in riddling framed narratives that Eagleton describes as a "semiotic puzzle": such repetitions create a space for themselves that seems both very much their own world, he observes, and yet intimately connected to the world outside.[2] To judge the effect of a story such as that of the switched heads requires we first set about solving this semiotic puzzle. When we look closely at the devices framing such insides and outsides, for example, we need to understand how these two distinctly demarcated worlds—imaginary and real, inside and outside—delineate themselves in the very telling. While in the previous chapter we were presented with a similar puzzle with regard to the narratives of belonging associated with language use and storytelling circulations, here I focus on Eagleton's concern with a different sort of revolutionary-minded appropriation—that of historical repetition.

I have already argued that the final riddling stories of the "Chouboli" cycle each in their own way have challenged and even subverted the inherited rules of possession by which we relate (in both cases: Which is her spouse? To whom does she belong?). In his book on Walter Benjamin and revolution, Eagleton is interested in the ways the subversive humor of such stories might tell a larger, metatextual story about our place in the world. He asks: How might we understand dialectical materialism as a big joke that history plays on us? Playfully transgressive stories such as "To Whom Does Chouboli Belong?" allow us to understand these rules of relation in a way that does not assume the tales can be categorized sui generis as strictly subversive nor ultimately conservative but that instead sees them as narrative rituals leading us to consider more carefully the function of playful transgression in the cultures in which they circulate (including our own).

Following Eagleton, Peter Stallybrass and Allon White have likewise dismissed the standard line of inquiry which asks whether the licensed release of carnival—especially as depicted in Mikhail Bakhtin's euphoric work on "marketplace humor" in Rabelais—foments ongoing and even institutionalized resistance to the dominant culture or whether it simply serves as a temporary release of built-up pressure that allows the hierarchical system to return to the status quo.[3] (That is, what is the "effect" of carnival, as we might ask what is the "effect" of the story?) Instead, they ask more generally how we participate in reversals that do not announce themselves as such, and thus how we are reinscribing the very divisions such dialectics depend on. They assert that a focus on what they call "the politics and poetics of transgression" (from the title of their book) "not only moves us beyond the rather unproductive debate over whether carnivals are politically progressive or conservative" but that attention to such binaristic discourses of the body "reveals that the underlying structural features of carnival operate far beyond the strict confines of popular festivity and are intrinsic to the dialectics of social classification as such."[4] The promise is that we might better understand the physical bounds of these dialectical, even hierarchical performances through attention to the laughing body. The story of the switched heads challenges us to consider afresh the question of the body of world literature, both figuratively and metatextually: Which laughing body? Starting and ending exactly where?

Bakhtin insists that festive laughter "is not an individual reaction to some isolated 'comic' event" but is instead "the laughter of all the people."[5] While such a vision of an unbridled and undifferentiated collectivity is beguiling, I am interested in the formulation for the way it depicts laughter as a bodily phenomenon in both the singular and the plural, as both individual and collective. In this quotation, as in his work more generally, Bakhtin constructs an individual (as an author, such as Rabelais) who can decide to take part in a mass movement or not, whose very material dimensions can become part of the greater "grotesque body" around him that is constantly in the process of becoming, is "continually built, created, and builds and creates another body."[6] In a move that resonates with the logic of the riddle of belonging, Bakhtin posits an individual *speaker* whose words are "actually a cry, that is, a loud interjection in the midst of a crowd, coming out of the crowd and addressed to it."[7]

This joyous expression of resistance requires us to think carefully about the ways we are defining a "you" in relation to a first-person subject position. How do we frame such a relationship? We might notice that the very posing of such a question establishes a division between the first and second persons that the riddle works both to defend and at the same time to abrogate. Here a Tantric understanding of the limits of subjectivity (that a practitioner's body both possesses and is possessed by tradition, as we consider below) finds itself in conversation with a reading of Freud's joking triangle that contends that the pleasure of laughter works only in relation with others: the use of the plural first-person pronoun is itself contentious, transgressive, unstable. Eagleton's semiotic puzzle mentioned above then leads to another, even more compelling puzzle: that the stories we tell change the world we live in, and the world we live in changes the stories we tell, in an ongoing loop with no distinct beginning or ending. I invoke Eagleton here in the interest of working from his suggestion that we can understand such revolutions only through humor.

Of course, some might be scandalized by the very idea that Marxist criticism is in want of guidance *spirituel* (here understood in the sense of both otherworldly and humorous). Eagleton is engagingly emphatic on this point: he begins his chapter on humor and revolution with Brecht's succinct observation: "I have never found anybody without a sense of humour who could understand dialectics."[8] He then goes on to show—even more provocatively—that Benjamin's attempts to seek "dialectical justice" were most successful when, like Bakhtin, he realized them through the image of the laughing communal body.[9] Lamentably, Eagleton does not question how this communal body might define its insides and outsides in terms established by the shifting language maps we investigate in the previous chapter—this project he allows scholars such as myself to elaborate on. He does, however, confine himself in that chapter entirely to thinkers who approach issues of dialectical justice through humor (hence the focus on Benjamin in comparison to Brecht and Bakhtin).

Eagleton assumes a fairly abstracted and yet individualized notion of language when he argues that for Benjamin language use is a sensuous, social practice; when the speaking subject inserts himself as signifying body "into the absent space between 'base' and 'superstructure,'" he provides "occasion for reconsideration of both terms."[10] Such an insight is not only helpful but crucial when one considers how the individual maps these translation acts through the very framing of such language performance (as we consider later in the chapter). The speaking body becomes, in Eagleton's words, "an ambivalent, 'undecidable' category," the site, I would add, where larger historical forces play out—playing in such a way that the individual speaking body and the collective, communal body are in uneasy but dynamic tension. It is this fluid, responsive force I use in this chapter to map in some detail, attentive in this case to the very ways such an undecidable category gets decided in the very act of narration.

In the "Storyteller" and "Task of the Translator" essays of Benjamin already mentioned, he might have fixated nostalgically on those storytelling communities now lost to us, but Eagleton points out that such melancholic meditations are blasted out of the continuum of history by Benjamin's attempts to "prise images loose from the authority of the past so that they might plurally interbreed," in a "raising of the dead" carnivalesque performance, as much travesty as parody, that Benjamin sees as "incipiently comic."[11] Playful versions of stories, that is, offer us a way of relinquishing a melancholic attachment to a vision of past unity. Like Bakhtin, Benjamin figures this laughing communal body as ongoing storytelling community (imagined, in his "Storyteller" essay, within the borders of a single, homogeneous language domain). Benjamin goes so far as to write in personal correspondence that "the critique of spiritual realities . . . isn't something that language can achieve other than by the detour of a deep disguise: humour."[12]

"'Humour,'" Eagleton admits playfully, "is hardly a familiar concept in Marxism, least of all in the work of the melancholic Benjamin."[13] And yet Eagleton is convincing in his argument that humor is a necessary element of social change and that such a strain is to be found in Benjamin's own work. After all, in the same letter Benjamin names Cervantes and Sterne as great writers who teach us to laugh at the "inauthentic," "counterfeit" aspects of a culture that, presumably, must be left behind in our search for dialectical justice.

It is in this regard Eagleton observes that "Bourgeois revolution are [*sic*] fictions that rewrite fictions; and it is difficult for us not to feel . . . that there is also something 'textual' in the model of socialist revolution that Marx counterposes to them."[14] We might notice that in Eagleton's retelling, Marx does sound less like a political historian and more than anything like a contemporary literary critic writing approvingly of our most engaged and self-reflexive storytellers:

> proletarian revolutions, like those of the nineteenth century, criticize them-
> selves constantly, interrupt themselves continually in their own course, come
> back to the apparently accomplished in order to begin it afresh, deride with
> unmerciful thoroughness the inadequacies, weaknesses and paltriness of their
> first attempts, seem to throw down their adversary only in order that he may
> draw new strength from the earth and rise again.[15]

How might we understand such political relationships in terms of storytell-ing exchange, especially ones written across time, place, language, genre, and even media? Here in Marx's writing, the collective body—"proletarian revolutions"—is acting as one to engage in ongoing acts of translation as agential, ethically attentive repetition, adapting material inherited from the past to mark out a space in the present that envisions a more equitable, just future. In Eagleton's thinking, such battles are waged most successfully in play, as the collective body engages in a catharsis through laughter that is "reconstructed by the very transgressive surge that deconstructs it," in the process giving birth to a new form of discourse.[16] Turning once more to our example, I wonder (as if) out loud how a retelling of a story like the switched heads succeeds in giving birth to a new form of discourse. Can such a retell-ing be considered revolutionary?

We might notice that the image of deconstruction and dismemberment that Eagleton refers to becomes quite vivid in a story such as this, where two bodies are literally beheaded before becoming whole once more, but with the crucial difference that the heads have been switched. Eagleton argues, that "it is only by dividing the body, grasping it as the decentred site of contradictions between this or that . . . , that some potentially redemp-tive meaning may be released from its delusive *Gestalt*."[17] If we pursue the implicit comparison with translation—Eagleton's body as "decentred site of contradictions between this or that" sounding very much like Homi Bhabha's liminal body "living on borderlines"—we might see that these acts of division not only force us to interrogate the borders we rely on to frame these entities as whole but also lead us to question the very integrity of either entity as fundamentally distinct.[18]

Such an insight applies both to the thematics of the story as well as to its methods: I could be the listener at one moment and the teller the next, just as could you, or anyone else. The awareness of the workings of this ongoing network of exchange influences the way a teller might tell the tale, just as much as readers might be influenced by the memory of previous versions. These links of influence are multiply sited, connecting not just listener to teller and teller to listener but past to present to future to past in a never-ending network that we imagine being located in the translated body (as a "decentred site of contradictions between this or that") so often described in linear, temporal terms. It is for this reason, I believe, that Eagleton calls for a "political somatics" that might offer "a study of the political-libidinal production of the historical body that attends not only, in negative fashion, to its past and present imprintings, but which may learn from such sources as Bakhtin something of its revolutionary potential."[19] While Bakhtin's image of the laughing communal body that Eagleton relies on needs to be complicated (as I argue later in this chapter), such an observation suggests that we must refine our most sophisticated tools of literary analysis in order to understand the ways the future is framed in the use of the narrative past and present and thus the ways our hopes and dreams are written through our translations in the present of stories from the past.

Through her own translation and discussion of the nineteenth-century Javanese text *Babad Jaka Tingkir*, for instance, Nancy Florida has shown convincingly that "the writing of history" (*mèngeti*) very actively "prophesies its own future in ways that work to bring that future about" and thus that the Javanese word *mèngeti* can be understood as "a prescient present's writing about a past which opens to a desired future."[20] How might we read the complex temporalities and ethical investments of an agential production of "historical consciousness" that contests present understandings of the past, present, and future by repeating versions of framed (fictional) narratives?[21]

We have already seen that the framed story of the switched heads appears in a number of versions, not just in the version of "Chouboli" that we considered in the previous chapter but most famously as an embedded story in the riddling eleventh-century Sanskrit storytelling cycle the *Vetalapanchavimshati* ("The Twenty-Five Tales of the Undead") as part of the sprawling *Katha Sarit Sagara*, which announced itself as a translation of the lost *Brhatkatha* ("Great Tale") and was translated into German by Heinrich Zimmer, in turn inspiring Thomas Mann's novella *Die vetauschten Köpfe* ("The Transposed Heads"), which in turn inspired Girish Karnad's more recent Kannada play *Hayavadana*. Each version in its own way has its readers consider the limits of the culturally coded idiom its audience relies on to determine a person's identity. We might agree that each version of the story invites readers to explore the import of confounding those neat boundaries separating one person from the next. The riddling nature of the story makes clear that such meaning is created not by individuals but interactively, collectively, in ongoing negotiation that not just the narrator but audience members past, present, and future actively take part in, in an ongoing dynamic relation that Bakhtin calls "dialogic." Thus the form itself helps work out the moral tension implicit in the act of repetition.

How might we find a critical idiom for discussing the dynamics of narrative exchange in a way that speaks to our conscience? Bakhtin maintains that a dialogic encounter between two entities (as individuals or as cultures) never allows either side to rest easy in its narrow views and assumptions nor advocates a complete merging with another viewpoint, but encourages a dynamic encounter where "each retains its own unity and open totality, but" in a way in which "they are mutually enriched."[22] For Bakhtin, the dialogic—as opposed to the dialectic—is lively, open-ended, full of rich, meaningful contradictions.[23] And while such a theory risks sounding as utopic as any other, it does encourage us to ask how we might participate in these exchanges in such a manner that we might learn from others involved and yet not forsake our own positions entirely.

Often critics describe such dangers in terms of unproductive narrowmindedness, on the one hand, and a disquieting cultural relativism, on the other.[24] Each in his own way, Eagleton and Bakhtin articulate these tensions more particularly in terms of textual issues, relying on close readings of the play of language. Eagleton's laughing dialectic and Bakhtin's dialogic laughter attempt to turn an exasperatingly infinite theoretical loop to productive use: we cannot articulate and thus challenge our own ideological positions except through a language that belongs to us as much as to others.

Here we find a related paradox that laughter reminds us of most vividly: a language can be said to belong to us only when it belongs to others, past, present, and future. The analogy with a story—especially a humorous one—would be equally obvious if our recent traditions of copyright did not teach us otherwise. Given the equalizing potential of laughter that we have seen Bakhtin in particular defend, I will have us assume for the space of this chapter that institutions of authorship have a purposeful intent complementary to more egalitarian and even collective concerns: that the metatextual narratives of single ownership of a text remind us to respect the ideological perspective and expressive intention behind a given performance of a text so that we might better be in dialogic relation with it.[25]

Ideally, the institutional framing of an individual author of great genius creates an authoritative "other" for the reader to identify with and against as she sets about creating meaning in conversation with the riddling story.[26] At its best, the figure of the author is a useful fiction for us to engage with, for the historical details of the actual life and writing process imply a limited temporal and spatial specificity that can never coincide completely with our own. That is, it creates the suggestion of a historical context, an actual event, that the reader is thus forced to engage with in playing the fictional world off against the nonfictional world—the author's against his own, the reader's against her own. Thus the author's collectively imagined corporeality situates him as the reader's other and in the process adds value to the story's implied lessons as they might pertain to the reader's present moment in analogy with the author's (in much the same way that Benjamin argues held true for storytellers in days of old and that we have already seen happen when we attribute the civilizing quip to Gandhi).

While I have already made clear how parochial and inaccurate I find the faithful-unfaithful binary, I do believe we must find a critical language for describing the degree to which a committed reader succeeds in allowing herself to be challenged by the ideological position she sees at work in any given text distinct from her own. Commensurability, I have already argued, is not a state we can assume at the outset but one we agree to work toward in these very narrative exchanges, engaging in these repetitions in such a way that we might criticize ourselves constantly, interrupt ourselves continually in our own course, coming back to the apparently accomplished in order to begin it afresh, deriding with unmerciful thoroughness the inadequacies, weaknesses, and paltriness of our first attempts, seeming to throw down our imaginary adversary only in order that we may draw new strength from the earth and rise again. Such collective work toward an ideal space of justice and equality must necessarily figure itself as already—always already—displaced. Attention to the rules of narrative framing teaches us, then, to understand the bounds of such continual and fluid displacement.

The tension Bakhtin describes as dialogic is quite useful here: How do we learn from this figure of the author as "other" in such a way that we do not merge overly with its ideological intentionality nor entirely reject the insights borne of difference? I repeat the insight in order to remind ourselves that such a tension is particularly complex to negotiate when investigating a text positing the figure of the author in the singular that in fact represents the collective efforts of several historical composers in the plural. (Ronald Inden in his introduction to *Querying the Medieval*[27] finds such a situation particularly crucial to address in South Asian texts, although his focus is entirely on the historical.) I contend that these plurally authored texts allow us to trace with more complexity some of the humorous workings of the phenomenon Bakhtin would call dialogic and Eagleton, dialectic. Moreover, I suggest that Eagleton's big joke (that is, historical dialectic) becomes most explicitly and thus potently expressed in a story that riddles us. In each case we might begin by asking: Who do we imagine asking these riddles, of whom, and to what ends? How might we map the complex relationship upon which such an exchange is based, especially as it adapts itself to new settings and new situations age after age?

I would have us start addressing such a question by considering the triangle of relations between three modern translations of the story of the switched heads: Girish Karnad, winner of the Jnanpith award, announces that his play written in Kannada, *Hayavadana*, was inspired by Nobel Prize laureate Thomas Mann's German novella, *Die vetauschten Köpfe* ("The Transposed Heads"), which itself offered a reading of the embedded story in the *Vetalapanchavimshati* ("The Twenty-Five Tales of the Undead") after Heinrich Zimmer's German version of the Sanskrit. As a set they nicely illustrate some of the contradictions implicit in trying to locate a literary work premised on displacement. In an insightful and richly argued essay analyzing all three versions in relationship to one another, Anand Mahadevan emphasizes Zimmer's flair in recreating this "Indian myth" as grand joke and thus—most unusually—analyzes the investments this particular translator had in presenting his version of the "retelling" (as Mahadevan calls it).[28] Mahadevan writes:

Like his predecessors, Zimmer recites the story within the context of Somade-va's *Kathāsaritasāgara*, but in his retelling the happy marriage of the other versions becomes sour. Zimmer pointedly asks whether the wife had a secret reason for changing the heads and speculates that an unhappy marriage may have led the husband to commit suicide.[29] In his version, the wife for the first time assumes a certain degree of culpability for the deed. In effect, Zimmer adds a touch of "Western realism" to the myth, and his alterations mark the beginning of the transposition of this ancient tale from parable to "meta-physical joke," [*metaphysicher Scherz*] the label Thomas Mann gave to his 1940 version of the story, *Die vertauschten Köpfe*, which was inspired in large part by Zimmer's research.[30]

It is no small matter that in his analysis Mahadevan makes clear that it is not the story as a fixed, unchanging essence but Zimmer's written per-formance that turns it into "metaphysical joke." Such a reading is particu-larly beguiling to me, for it suggests that the complex relationship among versions might be analyzed by adapting Freud's "joking triangle" to these network of repetitions extending across languages, times, places. Accord-ing to Mahadevan, Mann reads Zimmer's tale as "metaphysical joke" and reworks it to become a novella-long joke on Nazi society for venerating the Aryan race, which in turn inspires Karnad to combine elements of the high literary version with local folk-theater techniques to challenge play-fully traditional readings of the tale privileging the upper-caste mind over the lower-caste, working-class body.[31]

We might adapt Freud's atemporal geometry and imagine instead a series of interlinking triangles, whereby the attentive listener in one tri-angle becomes the engaged teller in the next; in each case, the object of the joke is the society in which they live. In each triangle of this ongoing joking chain, then, the imaginary listener becomes someone to whom the teller might offer this joking critique as appeal. Given that the ideal listener need not be of the society but simply participate in this alliance, how do we mark the geographical and temporal bounds of each historical location as it translates across these set boundaries? Such a riddle introduces another semiotic puzzle, this one concerned particularly with our disciplinary hab-its of reading literary texts across borders of language and nation: How can this cultural territory be considered both ours and yet theirs at the same time, as the universalizing and yet nationalizing mandates of world litera-ture often dictate? Upon what grounds, for example, does a story advance commonly shared notions of justice and equality? How is such a common ground framed in the story's very narrative?

Mahadevan's methodological strategy similarly asks us to consider upon what basis we might judge (non-Indian author) Mann's appropriation of this "Indian myth" in comparison with (Indian author) Girish Karnad's, especially when these writers are working "to subvert [the very] traditional ideas" that constitute such categories.[32] Given that Somadeva's eleventh-century storytelling cycle was written in a language now considered nonaggressively cosmopolitan, while Mann's twentieth-century novella was written in the national language of Germany during a time when it was most aggressively hegemonic and Karnad's play was written post-Independence in a regional language called Kannada (one of the seventeen languages of India officially recognized by the India constitution at the time) whose linguistic borders had established the right for the state of Karnataka to be recognized, we might wonder how these literary crossings should be mapped in relation to one another.[33]

When we look closely, we see that Mahadevan's literary analysis of the Karnad text against the Mann assumes that in Mann's work, the interesting dialectic involves crossing a line separating German literary traditions from Indian myth (he is careful not to describe the play in terms of a more general, Orientalist, East-West divide), and in Karnad's, the line is between elite and folk traditions. Mahadevan points to Karnad's own essay, "Theatre in India" to argue that Karnad's play incorporates the traditional *yakshagana* (a Karnataka folk theater) technique of putting all the characters in a single plane, thereby ending the formal class segregation conventionally performed in elite Indian theater. Karnad claims that the appropriation of folk forms allows for more divergent views to be presented in an egalitarian manner in what he calls "a genuine dialectic."[34]

Such a pronouncement serves only to raise questions rather than answer them, however. When we look to the example of Bakhtin's Rabelais translating "folk" culture into a high literary form, it becomes clear that to the person working in the culture, there is not necessarily a clear line separating folk culture from high literary or the individual from the collective he draws from and speaks to—even when, as Stallybrass and White argue, a strict hierarchical system undergirds much Western literary criticism.[35] We cannot assume these hierarchical positions are essential and fixed but are defined (and redefined) relationally through performances that posit an "other" (as lower-class, as foreign) that we distinguish ourselves against.[36] Instead, we must work with examples that might teach us—in the words of Stallybrass and White—to "move beyond Bakhtin's troublesome *folkloric* approach to a political anthropology of *binary extremism* in class society."[37] My argument is that attention to these details of narrative framing also helps us see play with the classificatory systems we rely on in our approach to these literary texts. Karnad himself argues that "Every theatre is rooted in the culture of its own language, so there are as many theatre situations as there are languages."[38]

Karnad's essay makes clear that language is only one such marker of the diversity of Indian theater. Indeed, this actor, playwright, and director, who also happened to be chairman of India's Sangeet Nathak Akademi (Academy of Music and Drama) at the time of the essay's publication, may have organized his engaging and seemingly disparate musings under the title "Theatre in India," but more than anything he makes a case that the category of "*a* traditional Indian theatre" is a bit of a puzzle in and of itself: puzzling not only for the ways "modern" Western conventions such as realism collide with indigenous theater traditions but because the very category of indigeneity needs to be contested and complicated as a homogeneous space.[39] Karnad complains:

> Standard, official art history is based on the assumption that there is such a
> thing as a homogeneous "Indian culture," within which Indian theatre, Indian
> dance, Indian music, and so on find their own homogeneous identities without
> conflict. According to this theory, when applied to the field of performing
> arts, all traditional forms are merely expressions of a basic philosophy, an
> attitude toward life and the arts, which is common to all Indians and which
> has remained unchanged through the centuries, so that no history needs to be
> taken into account.[40]

He goes on to explain that often this vaguely articulated notion of Indian philosophy makes inchoate references to the classical treatise on dramaturgy, the *Nāṭyaśāstra*, to fold all traditions into a single Brahminical order so that "even folk and tribal material—if studied at all—is studied in the light of Sanskrit texts."[41] For Karnad, such an attitude diminishes the possibilities offered by engagement with these traditions, for what is most important about such non-Brahminical forms is that "The energy of folk theatre comes from the fact that while it seems to support traditional values, it is also capable of subverting them, looking at them from various points of view."[42] His question of the scope of "a traditional Indian theatre" raises an important methodological consideration similar to the one I began the chapter with: How do we ascertain for what ends any particular folk culture is being appropriated? How are such ideological positions framed? How might we as engaged, critical readers frame these various cultures to understand their dialogic relationship to one another?

Karnad is not the only one to address these riddles of translation. Recently, for example, the leftist writer, actor, and street-theater director Sudhanva Deshpande not only has pointed to the variety of languages to speak to the rich diversity of India's prolific, lively, and engaged theater traditions but has singled out the work of Karnad to ask provocatively, "How do we understand the so-called 'folk' theatre done almost exclusively by urban directors and actors, for urban (and often foreign) audiences, in proscenium spaces?"[43] The implicit riddle that Deshpande joins others in post-Independence India in asking goes beyond tidy distinctions of subversive or conservative: Whose story is this? Who has a right to tell it this way?

Writing for a Comparative Literature journal published in America, Mahadevan does not question Karnad's authority to appropriate folk elements and reads the dialectic he identifies in unabashedly idealistic terms: "The folk theater–based play thus becomes an ideal way to return the story of the transposed heads to India by exposing modern Indian audiences to an alternative explanation of the traditional tale."[44] Unlike Karnad in his own writing (which also happens to be published in an American journal), Mahadevan does not question the equation between folk theater and Indian tradition nor defend Karnad's authority in framing the story with a tale he claims to base loosely on *yakshagana*. It is only his analysis of the novella written by Thomas Mann that invites such scrutiny. The example illustrates the disciplinary dilemmas we face when understanding such exchanges: it is necessary to acknowledge the inherent unevenness in a comparison between the work of Karnad and Mann but also to understand that the very acknowledgment of such differences threatens to fix them. How, then, in our own practice might we frame the multilingual, multicultural workings of the dialogic in such a way that allows it to flow over the bounds of the very categories we rely on to analyze its moves?

A Playful Particle of Comparison

A professedly fluid text such as the eleventh-century *Katha Sarit Sagara* offers some insight into the importance of approaching transgressive framing devices through strategies dynamic and flexible. Somadeva begins his text by acknowledging his debt to a previous version, announcing—in the words of the 1880 English translation by C. H. Tawney—that his collection "contains the pith of the Brihat-Katha" and "is precisely on the model of that from which it is taken . . . [without] even the slightest deviation."[45] We are soon alerted to accept such claims of fidelity with some mirth.

Within the frame story of Somadeva's *Katha Sarit Sagara*, the narrating "I" ("I compose this collection")[46] tells us he has written this version from one told by a *paishach* ("goblin") that was then written in blood in the Paishachi ("goblin") dialect by Gunadhya, a fallen immortal and former attendant to the gods ("*gana*") who in his previous birth had been cursed by Lord Shiva's wife Parvati to become a mortal in punishment for overhearing the tales Shiva was telling her in private. Gunadhya thus hears the tales once in the immortal realm directly from Shiva and again, as if afresh, in the mortal realm from the goblin. In the introduction to her abridged 1994 translation of the *Katha Sarit Sagara*, Arshia Sattar notes that such an otherworldly claim raises particularly interesting issues of authorship: "While Somadeva may well be the 'author' outside the text, Shiva and Gunadhya are the authors inside the text."[47] Here we need to look carefully at the ways inside and outside are marked in our disciplined literary discussions of a text such as this, for the framing offers a more playful version of Eagleton's semiotic puzzle. Given that the *Katha Sarit Sagara* itself frames narrative within narrative within narrative, it is a lovely irony that those studying the text get lost trying to sort insides from outsides; the storytelling cycle embeds the riddling story of its own origins into a story that itself frames the embedded narratives in a seemingly endless series of loops.

Florida calls a similar move at the end of the framed narrative *Babad Jaka Tingkir* "a 'frame' turned inside-out."[48] Here in the *Katha Sarit Sagara*, however, nearly every "outside" is contained "inside" another narrative frame, so the storytelling cycle is comprised of an endlessly confusing web of insides-out (like the wikis of today).

Within the main frame of the *Katha Sarit Sagara*, the answer to the question of true origins—Who is the original composer of these tales?—leads us to an intimate scene in the heavenly realm, when the goddess Parvati asks her husband, Lord Shiva, to tell her stories no one else would have ever heard. According to this opening narrative, when blocked from entering this scene of intimate storytelling, Shiva's attendant cannot stanch his curiosity and uses his magical powers to slip past the doorkeeper to hear the tales. When Parvati discovers that these special stories have been heard by others, she curses those who had listened in, both the doorkeeper and Shiva's attendant, to be reborn on earth as mortals. At their pleading, Goddess Parvati specifies that the doorkeeper's curse will be lifted once he remembers his divine origins and tells the cycle of tales to a similarly cursed immortal named Kanabhuti who was reborn as a *paishach*, whose curse will in turn be lifted once he recounts the storytelling cycle to Shiva's former attendant Gunadhya, whose own curse will end once "he makes the story famous in the world" (or in Tawney's earlier, grander translation "when thou hast published it abroad").[49]

The frame story thus not only narrates self-reflexively its own translation between realms (celestial to mortal) and media (oral to written) but makes the storytelling cycle's further translation its express purpose: although Parvati became angry that this single oral performance was shared, now that it has been, she makes its transmission the condition of the lifting of the curse. One after another, we then watch each of these characters suddenly recognize himself in a story told about him in the third person when he is identified as the person able to lift his interlocutor's curse simply by recounting the tales Shiva told to Parvati, and at that moment—as in the case of the doorkeeper hearing about himself from Kanabhuti—he "remembered his origin, and exclaimed like one aroused from sleep, 'I am that very Pushpadanta, hear that tale from me.'"

Such an endlessly inside-out-turning web of displaced origins and retellings is especially meaningful given that the telling is said to originate with Lord Shiva, the god in the Hindu pantheon known as the Destroyer, for in story after story Shiva's destructive force is coupled with an opposite creative, even re-creative force. In this frame story we learn here, too, that for the story to be re-created, it must be destroyed—anticipating by nearly a millenium Eagleton's insight that laughter is "reconstructed by the very transgressive surge that deconstructs it."[50]

In order for this story to become famous in the world, these surging, transgressive, reconstructive energies must successfully negotiate not only the crossing of realms but hierarchical differences of birth and language that—in yet another playful inside-out flip—become the subject and then the medium of the stories. Kanabhuti, for instance, turns out to be a divine attendant cursed to take birth as a *paishach* for keeping company with his master's enemy—a lowly birth is the reward for consorting with one considered lowly.[51] Likewise, he is told he will be freed from his curse once he has passed along the story to Gunadhya who "has forsaken the use of Sanskrit, Prakrit, and his own language" and speaks instead in the *Paishachi* language.[52] Gunadhya had vowed to renounce all human languages while serving as a Brahmin minister in the court of King Satavahana if his rival could teach the king Sanskrit in six months rather than the six years Gunadhya had promised. Gunadhya later explains to Kanabhuti that the king had been laughed at by one of his queens for making a simple grammatical mistake and "pretending to be a scholar"; the king not only "is ashamed of his ignorance" but "craves knowledge."[53]

Gunadhya's rival does succeed through divine intervention in teaching the king Sanskrit in six months, and so Gunadhya leaves the court no longer able to speak in human languages. After meeting Kanabhuti and hearing him recount the storytelling cycle he once heard in another birth, he spends seven years writing down the version narrated to him in Paishachi rather than Sanskrit and ("afraid that the [learned] would steal his work") in his own blood.[54] Here interlingual translation issues become interchangeable with those of circulation: Gunadhya knows he must popularize the tale in order to be released from his curse, and sends his manuscript to King Satavahana since the king "is a learned man and he will spread the tale far and wide as the wind spreads the fragrance of flowers."[55] The king, however, still anxious about the status of his own learning, promptly rejects it for being written in the "crude" Paishachi language—and written in blood, at that. Gunadhya complies with the king's orders to destroy the manuscript and begins feeding the handwritten sheets to the fire one by one, reading them to a throng of attentive animals who cry as each page is swallowed by the flames. In the meantime, the king discovers Gunadhya's former status as divine attendant (*gana*) and begs him to save the manuscript; when Gunadhya stops, there are only one hundred thousand verses left of what will come to be known as the lost *Brhatkatha*. King Satavahana thus is credited with destroying as well as rescuing and passing on the tale written by Gunadhya after a tale told by the goblin

Kanabhuti after the version told by a fallen immortal doorkeeper after the version told by Lord Shiva.

Such a fantastic genealogy tells its own story about the value (and the precariousness) of texts passed along between oral and written forms, immortal and mortal realms. More than anything, this web of displaced origins and retellings describes not so much an easy equivalence as a tension—the text wobbling constantly between the opposing forces of destruction and recreation—and in the process offers a parable demonstrating validity for the widespread concern over the reliability of the written medium.[56]

Ironically, instead of playing along with such a delightfully transgressive, reconstructive framing device, scholars of Sanskrit literature since the early nineteenth century have become tangled up in trying to sort the fictional from the nonfictional, the playful from the serious, the written from the oral, in their quest for the grail of a tangible original text. M. Winternitz, for example, in the third volume of his exhaustive and authoritative *History of Indian Literature*, writes with a combination of consternation and longing (if not melancholy) of Gunadhya's much longer, lost *Brhatkatha*, which he says is mentioned with enthusiasm by Sanskrit writers of the sixth century such as Dandin, Subundhu, and Bāna.[57] He admits that besides stray references to the work, the only evidence of the text are what he calls the "derivative" versions: the two Kashmiri "versified versions"—the *Brhatkathāmañjari* of Ksemendra and the *Katha Sarit Sagara* of Somadeva—and a "free poetical redaction" called the *Brhatkatha-Slokasangraha* by the Nepali Buddhaswāmin, whose discovery was announced by the French scholar Felix Lacote in 1908. (Of the latter, Winternitz writes, "It is a matter of deep regret that we do not possess the complete works" of this Nepali writer, for "there are few books in Indian literature in which humour and mirth in life are so dominant."[58])

S. N. Dasgupta, in *A History of Sanskrit Literature*, engages in what in 1994 Sattar calls a "heated debate among scholars at the end of the nineteenth century about the literary merits of Ksemendra's version over those of Somadeva's collection."[59] Like us, their analyses focus on these texts to ask larger questions about what constitutes the literary. As if faithfully recycling a familiar narrative (albeit anachronistically, according to Sattar), Dasgupta complains that "The *Brhatkatha-mangari* of Ksemendra . . . seems to reproduce exactly the composition of the Kashmirian *Brhatkatha* with all its defects. When Ksemendra tries to hide the incoherence of the model, he does it by artifices of form while Somadeva tries to correct the plan."[60] More acutely, he complains that "Ksemendra's taste is undoubtedly inferior to that of Somadeva. He is verbose and full of mannerisms and has a tendency particularly to dilate upon erotic pictures."[61] Indeed, Sattar explains that the nineteenth-century debate would often degenerate into two opposing sides, with Ksemendra's champions calling Somadeva's version dull and dry (without literary artifice), and Somadeva's supporters charging that Ksemendra's version was overly adorned (lacking substance).[62] While she does not say so explicitly, Sattar's discussion of the issue of authorship calls into question the link scholars often make between formal virtuosity and an empirically provable textual pedigree. Instead, Sattar calls such a project into question, noting with wry humor:

> If we accept that Somadeva was a historical person who put the tales together from a larger collection, we still have to contend with the "authorship" of Gunadhya who is a celestial born as a human with the express purpose of spreading the tale that he overheard, the tale of which we now have but a part.[63]

I rehearse this debate here because it offers a more incisive critical language for discussing issues of fidelity, to wit: Dasgupta's discussion becomes especially interesting when he compares the creative decisions each of the Kashmiri authors make in their attempts to produce a version that is "loyal" (in Dasgupta's translation of Somadeva's line, "*yatha mulam tathaivatan*")[64] to the original before them. What precisely does he understand here by "loyalty"? On what basis does he propose we might ascertain said "loyalty" when we have little to no access to the text to which it is being compared? If we agree with contemporary literary theorists such as G. N. Devy, Meenakshi Mukherjee, and Harish Trivedi that India has had a long tradition of re-creation that has never called itself translation, then I would argue that these debates comparing the various versions of a lost *Brhatkatha* are an attempt to understand in Somadeva's announced terms what post-Renaissance English-literature scholarship would consider being "loyal" or "faithful" to an original; that is, a less rancorous reading of Dasgupta and others would say (with reference to the first section of this chapter) that they are interested in investigating the dialogic relationship being posited between one imagined composer and another.

How might we engage in such a comparative project without replicating the melancholic, wonder-that-was-India approach to textual criticism that was a signature of Orientalist scholarship, always searching for a lost glory?

To begin, we might understand the positing of a past glory in such fictions to be a fanciful conceit, one that allows the writer recounting such genealogies to announce his own greatness in ever-so-humble comparison. While the pre-nineteenth-century authors and critics cited by these scholars do not seem to have the same trouble reading the original composer of this story as partly or even wholly divine, these more empirically minded scholars (Winternitz and the like) find themselves caught by the distinction between the fictional and nonfictional and so are forced to conflate a story of creative gifts with a story of material production in a revealing misreading of what Somadeva announces as his own brand of genealogical truth. If we look more closely at Somadeva's Sanskrit lines, we see that the comparison between his source (*"mulam"*) and his own creation relies on a common rhyming relative-correlative construction (*"yatha . . . tatha"*) which does not so much answer interpretive questions as pose its own riddle about the nature of textual relation. This grammar of playful dialogism is difficult to translate into English because it challenges our very constructions of textual fidelity:

> *yatha mulam tathaivaitan na managapyatikramah* |
>
> (just as the source just so exactly this is not even a little bit out of order)
>
> *grantha-vistara-samksepa bhasa ca bhidyate* ||[65]
>
> ([except] the volume's breadth [becomes] summary and the language differs)

I draw attention to these lines specifically in order to argue that Somadeva's just-so-exactly (*"tathaiva"*) phrase doubles back on itself, for it means "just so exactly" and yet, in promising such an impossibility, at the same time laughs at our inability to ever know the source (*"mulam"*) with any certainty and even delights in the resulting confusion. This is no abject post-fall-of-the-Tower-of-Babel narrative that decries the chaos of so many languages, so many versions. Instead, the frame story introduces the fact of multiple versions in multiple languages as a blessing—a blessing in response to the destructive energy at its source that proves creative in turn. The *yatha-tatha* pairing claims the two texts to be alike because it is known that the two cannot be, but that striving to be alike in that difference is part of the creative tension necessary for such a story to carry on.

The versions of the frame story thus ask us to consider a series of riddles not unlike the riddles posed by the story of the switched heads: Do we prioritize turn of phrase or narrative structure when ascertaining a text's relation to other sources? (Should we determine a text's identity in comparison to a predecessor?) Do we determine a story's meaning by analyzing its formal features or by situating it in historical context? (Can formal features ever be studied in isolation?) Does the form govern the content or does the content govern the form? (What is the nature of such comparisons, especially in translation?)

Such riddles necessarily force us to interrogate our own disciplinary methods of comparison. How might we rework our own critical discourse to include flexible and self-reflexive inquiries into textual fidelity? We might begin approaching the issues raised by this particular text by emphasizing not just the relationality but the contingent import of the word *"iva"* as used in the crucial phrase of loyalty that Dasgupta highlights, *"yatha mulam tathaiva"*: while *"iva"* can be rendered "exactly" or "particularly," it might also be translated "as if." We thus see that the same doubled movement—is, not is—I assert was writ large in the story is here contained in a single, playful particle. This particular grammar of comparison is asking its readers to have faith in the contradictory nature of existence: just as we might have surmised already from watching the same interlocutor hear versions of the storytelling cycle in two different forms before telling it in turn, we must also acknowledge that none of us can verify an original version purported to have been recounted in the celestial realm. The text thus requires we approach it with a healthy reserve of playfulness. How else to read the journey of a story from the language of the gods to the language of goblins to the language of humans, but in a spirit that delights in such existential mischief?

In his six-hundred-page study of the cultural power of Sanskrit in premodern India, Sheldon Pollock lists Ksemendra's *Brhatkathamañjai* as an example of a text written in a "language of Place" (*deshabhāshā*) rather than one of the three languages (Sanskrit, Prakrit, Apabhramsha) deemed capable of literary production. Pollock notes that commentators in the day agreed there was something intrinsic to these languages that made possible literary devices such as "figuration, suggestion, aestheticized emotion, propriety," while the local speech forms were "to be used solely in a secondary, socially mimetic capacity and never as the primary language of composition."[66]

Pollock notes, however, that the seventh-century literary theorist Dandin includes a fourth language: Paishachi (goblin dialect), or Bhutabhasha (speech of the ghosts), which scholars through the ages have tried in vain to locate definitively (an eastern Middle-Indic dialect? an idiom spoken in the Vindhya Mountains? speech used by roaming gypsies? the language used in heaven by Lord Shiva's attendants?)[67]

Pollock gamely throws up his hands and decides that "there is little reason to bother to choose between science and tradition. Paishachi is the joker in the deck of South Asian discourses on language, having an exclusively legendary status, since it is associated with a single lost text, the *Bṛhatkathā* (The Great Tale)."[68] He reads the frame story of the *Bṛhatkathāmañjarī* and its supernatural genealogy as a subversive, albeit mirthful commentary on the literary taxonomies that would render its language of composition merely derivative of informal speech. He notes that "the logic of the narrative rests entirely on a cultural convention that renders the idea of literature not written in Sanskrit, Prakrit or Apabhramsha a bizarre, even demonic, anomaly."[69] Sattar, for her part, suggests that Paishachi was likely an everyday Prakrit ("natural") idiom spoken by the common people, in stark contrast to the highly refined Sanskrit ("artificial" or "well-wrought") language used in literary and philosophical discourse.[70]

Indeed, what seems to interest all the scholars writing on the *Katha Sarit Sagara*, from Winternitz to Dasgupta to Sattar, is precisely a vaguely conceived tension implicit in writing a coarse and chaotic oral-based storytelling cycle such as this in a more polished, literary form in Sanskrit, in such a way that it still retains an element of the natural or local.[71] (The argument is reminiscent of Bakhtin's regarding Rabelais, which I consider below). More provocatively, Sattar conjectures that the name Paishachi might be more than a neutral term for the common people of this region but might instead be exceedingly derogatory; historian Romila Thapar suggests that the Satavahan kings of the Deccan (the same line of kings as the one named in the frame story sketched above) were committed to replacing the local dialects they lumped under the category of Paishachi "with Sanskrit and related Prakrits as part of a larger project of Aryanization."[72] (Perhaps not coincidentally, such a narrative does echo the historical tension between Aryans and non-Aryans that Mahadevan writes about in regard to the story of the switched heads).

If we believe the story of such a genealogy, the question we are implicitly asking is why a writer such as Somadeva would translate from a common language with dubious and even despised origins into the elite and well-ordered language of Sanskrit, when the form as well as the content of the story seems to challenge the very orderliness of Sanskrit. Is this simply another story of an elite appropriating a folk form, as Sudhanva Deshpande, for example, charges of a modern playwright like Karnad? If we agree with Pollock that the language is the joker in the deck, then what of the writers who force us to rethink the relationship of this "goblin" or "ghost" language to Sanskrit?

Such a reappraisal is particularly important when so many of our narratives in English about the relationship of the "vernacular" to the "classical" are based on European examples, as Pollock in particular has noted. His recent articles on the historical relationship of the "Sanskrit cosmopolis" to the various local vernaculars offer daring observations on the dialectical relationship between languages and our understanding of it, especially relevant to our examination of translations from "language of Place" into a language necessarily displaced. Pollock contends that in the millennium of its ascendancy (300–1300 CE), Sanskrit as a language—unlike Latin—was not connected to any particular political regime and so offered "a new vision of power" that he considers an example of "voluntaristic" rather than "coercive" cosmopolitanism, based, as it was, not on military might or religious indoctrination but on the lure of a vision of globalized community articulated through poetry.[73]

Pollock suggests that Sanskrit, through a system he calls the "aestheti-zation of the political," offered polities across an amazing sweep of Asia—stretching from today's Afghanistan through Thailand and Cambodia to Indonesia, from Sri Lanka to Burma and Nepal—a literary and philosophical language through which to imitate and recreate imperial form "both horizontally across space . . . and vertically in time through historical imagination" but in a manner that accommodated the local.[74] In his telling of the history, the legendary exploits of Lord Rama in the past could be written as Kampuchea's unique present as much as Java's distinctive future, in a manner that connected the powerful elite across time and space. At its most ideal, this meant that Sanskrit's value lay precisely in its ability to offer a language of larger community to local leaders in a way that allowed each of them to cultivate what Pollock terms "its own distinctive cultural repertory."[75] He explains:

> In many of these cases, qualifying as an empire, whether imperial gover-
> nance was actually exercised or not, seems to have required a language of
> cosmopolitan character and transethnic attraction, transcending or arrest-
> ing any ethnoidentity the ruling elites themselves might possess. It had to be
> a language capable of making translocal claims—however imaginary these
> were—that defined the political imagination of this world. Moreover, it had
> to be a language whose power derived, not from sacral associations but from
> aesthetic capacities, its ability to make reality more real—more complex and
> more beautiful—as evinced by its literary idiom and style, and a literary his-
> tory embodying successful exemplars of such linguistic alchemy.[76]

In this optimistic version of an early-modern South and Southeast Asian cosmopolis, ambitious leaders happily channel a Sanskritic specter of comparison in order to secure a version of the otherworldly that could only be expressed in a language announcing itself as eternal. Madhav Deshpande shows that the very terms of this eternality were contentious, announcing themselves as timeless and immutable even as they varied tremendously.[77] Pollock contends that this operation of "a voluntaristic cosmopolitanism" offered very different relationships between local vernacular and classical language from those that theorists such as Bakhtin, Antonio Gramsci, Ernest Gellner, and others theorize when attending only to the European example of vernaculars challenging Latin, for Sanskrit offered the vernaculars in Asia "a new aesthetic value of being 'in place.'"[78]

Pollock contends that unlike the European example, the vernaculars did not feel compelled to displace the cosmopolitan classical language because the classical language offered possibilities for coexistence from the very start—a reading that is not so much contradicted as complicated by Thapar's description of the Aryanization of the Deccan. Pollock's primary concern is to propose a different model of territorialization from the one posited by Bakhtin (whom he singles out). For our purposes, the most important contribution is in rethinking the ways such an imagined community is figured locationally. Pollock points out:

> The creation of vernacular literature . . . was intimately related to new concep-
> tions of communities and places, which in turn correlated with a new kind of
> vernacular political order. And we can see that these were new because the

world of cosmopolitan language and literature had known very differently defined spaces, communities, and aspirations of rulership, little concerned with self-differentiation or self-limitation.[79]

Pollock maintains that since "no recognizable core-periphery conception ever prevailed in the Sanskrit cosmopolis," every use of Sanskrit offers its own example of instantiating the cosmopolis: "'regional' differences are part of the repertory of a global Sanskrit, the sign precisely of Sanskrit's transregionality."[80] Even in the example of the Sanskrit-Paishachi conflict that Thapar describes, we can see the possibility of such coexistence. After all, the implication of Pollock's work is that a writer working for the elite, such as Somadeva, could live in Kashmir and rewrite for his local queen a story that tells of a king ruling a kingdom on the banks of the Godavari River in the Deccan in such a way that readers would see that the analogy between King Satavahan and Queen Suryamati moves both ways at once: the Kashmiri queen is gratified to learn lessons of a legendary once-upon-a-time king, and the Deccan tradition, too, is strengthened to be compared to a contemporary, faraway kingdom in Kashmir. Each of the local dialects in these places can be called Paishachi only in relation to a cosmopolitan language like Sanskrit and thus the local dialect flows into Sanskrit even as it flows from Sanskrit. Pollock suggests that the relationships between these languages evidence an entirely different cultural economy from the one we usually theorize in English and thus suggests that our very reading strategies of literary texts are informed by our attitudes about the relationships between language systems.

As the debate over the goblin language indicates, these narratives about the relationship between languages is but one way we frame hierarchical relationships between speakers in a particular economy. Pollock mentions obliquely in his articles and more explicitly in his book that his argument applies almost entirely to the elite cultures of South and Southeast Asia. While certainly neither comprehensive nor definitive—he misses the *Katha Sarit Sagara* entirely, for example—his study does allow us to think more carefully about the ways Sanskrit derived power in the very practice of what he calls "repetition."[81] How might we compare Pollock's reading of repetition using classical examples from the Indian Ocean against Eagleton's "historical repetition" using modern examples from Europe? Pollock shows us that Lord Ram's legendary kingdom of Ayodhya existed once upon a time somewhere in northern India but also here and now once more in Siam, Kampuchea, Java. Sanskrit did not claim singular authority over its sources. Unlike the Latin of the Roman imperium, Pollock insists, "Sanskrit never sought to theorize its own universality," a tendency which he asserts is "consistent with its entire historical character as a cosmopolitan formation, an alternative form of cosmopolitanism in which 'here,' instead of being equated with 'everywhere,' is equated with 'nowhere in particular.'"[82]

If we doubted before whether Pollock was being overly utopic, he insists that he is offering a scholarly practice he calls "a tactical reversal of domination," since it allows us to see the ways "some people in the past have been able to be universal and particular, without making either their particularly [*sic*] ineluctable or their universalism compulsory."[83] At its best, his reading not only shifts the focus of the theoretical discussion away from Europe but offers an approach to the dialogic of translation that sees the flows between the languages as moving in multiple directions, relying on a mapping that requires we consider not only the temporal dimension but even the hierarchical. We see in the example of the translation from Paishachi to Sanskrit that the displacement would not—according to Pollock—be understood as a move from periphery to center and yet it still would be considered a move from low status to high. According to his theory, Sanskrit as a cosmopolitan discursive space would have offered to court writers like Somadeva and Ksemendra a means of stepping outside their familiar (and often narrow) ideological frame by transcending regional lines.

Claiming a lineage to this joker-in-the-deck goblin language thus challenges the nowhere-in-particular brand of cosmopolitanism that Pollock writes of. The frame narratives teach us that such hierarchical relationships were necessarily being negotiated in the very framing of the narrative as a location as much physical as political. They also teach us that we need to learn to read in a number of different directions at once.

Stallybrass and White's study of the poetics and politics of transgression in Renaissance England makes an observation quite relevant to our understanding of these premodern translations: that these compulsions to challenge the status quo, step outside the hierarchical order, and have contact with the Other (as someone from another class, or someone from another country) were exceedingly ambivalent and so necessarily moved in more than one direction at once.[84] They see such a theoretical tension represented most clearly in the image of the marketplace as "the epitome of local identity" and at the same time as "the unsettling of that identity by the trade and traffic of goods from elsewhere."[85] They describe the market-place—with captivating lyricism—as a dynamic, liminal space that recalls the communal body as not only transgressive but Tantric:

> As much a process of commercial convergence as an open space, the mar-ketplace gives the illusion of independent identity, of being a self-sustaining totality, and this illusion is one of separateness and enclosure. Thinking the marketplace is thus somewhat like thinking the body: adequate conception founders upon the problematic familiarity, the enfolding intimacy, of its domain. The tangibility of its boundaries implies a local closure and stability, even a unique sense of belonging, which obscure its structural dependence upon a "beyond" through which this "familiar" and "local" feeling is itself produced. Thus in the marketplace "inside" and "outside" (and hence identity itself) are persistently mystified. It is a place where limit, centre and boundary are confirmed and yet also put in jeopardy.[86]

Working from Bakhtin's analysis of Rabelais, they charge that Bakhtin is able to depict the marketplace as a "utopian . . . 'no-place' of collective hopes and desires" precisely because he reads it as "'outside' of the official local hierarchy and its languages and 'within' the popular festive body."[87] He thus reinscribes the very hierarchy we have called into question vis-à-vis Karnad's folkloric appropriations. In Bakhtin's schema, the laughing, plural body that expresses itself through the living vernacular is the center of local culture, resisting the humorless control of classical learning and imperial rule centered elsewhere.

We have already seen Pollock critique this static model of the vernac-ular-classical relationship in the case of the Sanskrit cosmopolis; he com-mends Bakhtin along with Gramsci for understanding the importance of the historical transformation that rendered vernaculars sites of power but contends they were "both wrong to believe that the vernaculars in Europe were upraised against a Mandarin Latinity and came to be written down only when 'the people' regained importance, or that the vernacular *tout court* represented a popular social force to be distinguished from and set against an 'official' Latin."[88]

When we consider Pollock's critique in addition to Stallybrass and White's, we see we are being called on to define "the people" more particu-larly in such vernacular-classical, oral-written exchanges. Each is calling on us to find a more dynamic, even fluid set of tropes for understanding these cultural economies. We might remember that rather than reading the local centers as a communal, utopic "no-place," Pollock's vision of the cosmopolis of vernacular-classical interaction instead sees them as performing "a new aesthetic value of being 'in place.'"[89] To understand the definition—and therefore the spatial boundaries—of this image of "the people," we might look more closely at the way their gatherings are figured. What is the value of the *place*—as marketplace, as common place—that Pollock and others refer to in our understanding of these transformations and reversals?

Stallybrass and White argue that a theorist such as Bakhtin could describe a European fair as a "discrete entity: local, festive, communal, unconnected to the 'real' world" because he ignores its commercial aspects.[90] Their historical description of fairs in England emphasizes instead a space that brings together "the exotic and the familiar, the villagers and the towns-man, the professional performer and the bourgeois observer" in a manner that both is unruly (and therefore resistant to dominant culture) and at the same time is put to use by that same dominant culture.[91] It was a place that represented both an "opposition to official ideologies" as well as "the means by which emergent mercantile interests could stimulate new desires."[92] For Stallybrass and White, languages are part of the mix of the objects (cloth, spices) and displays (animals, savages) from faraway lands that are part of the allure of the fair as "educative spectacle."[93] In direct disagreement with Bakhtin, they see the fair not so much as populist opposition to hierarchy but as "a relay for the diffusion of the cosmopolitan values of the 'centre' (particularly the capital and the new urban centres of production) through-out the provinces and the lower orders."[94] Rather than being satisfied in their local ways, they argue, local fairgoers are drawn to the possibilities of expanding their understanding of the world from beyond the familiar, so that the fair itself becomes "a museum in which the spoils from colonized cultures went on display."[95]

While Pollock argues that elite rulers throughout the South and South-east Asian cosmopolis were interested in repeating the glories of Sanskrit in their local center, here Stallybrass and White are suggesting that the provincial marketplace is interested in being connected to other provin-cial marketplaces, offering spectacles that transgress as well as reaffirm the boundaries between high and low, domestic and savage, vulgar and polite, in a gesture they refer to as "the double process of colonialism."[96] That is, rather than being a simple unidirectional movement from high to low that might be resisted in turn from low to high, the vectors of influence need also to be mapped laterally—from local center to local center across a range of cultural, linguistic, geographical borders in a complex network that must also figure the hierarchical structures in place in each of these locales. They observe, "The fair 'turned the world inside out' in its mercantilist aspect just as much, if not more, than it 'turned the world upside down' in its popular rituals."[97]

This is an understanding of the forces of cosmopolitanism that must be taken into account in our mapping of these cultural and linguistic transformations. Stallybrass and White assert that the limitations in our thinking on the subject are in large part institutional, since those studying economic history are primarily interested in marketplaces as sites of commercial distribution, and those engaged in cultural studies regard them in terms of popular revelry and political subversion.[98] They argue that as scholars we need to stop subscribing to those divides that approach the fair as "*either* a rational, commercial trading event *or* as a popular pleasure-ground" and instead understand it as the site of ambivalent transgression.[99] The fairgoer is drawn to the marketplace like a listener of a transgressive story is drawn to the storytelling circle, tempted and disgusted at the same time at the prospect of encountering someone of a different class or someone from a faraway place who dresses differently and speaks a different language.

With regard to class in particular, Stallybrass and White observe that "Repugnance and fascination are the twin poles of the process in which a *political* imperative to reject and eliminate the debasing 'low' conflicts powerfully and unpredictably with a desire for this Other."[100] We might generalize and note that the frames we use to demarcate inside and outside are guarded that much more fiercely when such dangers are heightened.

The storytelling cycle within a storytelling cycle that frames the story of the switched heads opens by situating us as readers formulaically in an imaginary time and place whose present tense is as much no-time as the place is "as if" somewhere particular: "The country of Pratisthana lies on the banks of the Godavari. In the old days, the famous King Vikrama lived there."[101] We are both there and yet not there, in a world that is real and yet completely imaginary. The rest of the narrative balances upon a similar liminality, following a well-meaning king as he negotiates a curious triangular relationship with a Tantric mendicant and a spirit-possessed corpse (a *vetala*) in a retelling of the Sanskrit epic that in its various translations throughout the Sanskrit cosmopolis offered lessons in proper kingly conduct.[102] Here we have an uncanny version of three-way relation, one that anticipates Freud's joking triangle; here, too, two of the figures are asked to make an alliance against the other. Most fundamentally, this frame narrative asks: What is the right path for the king to take? When it comes to matters of life and death, which of these characters should he trust?

Like the story of the switched heads that the narrative frames, these riddles of relation posed within the text point to metatextual riddles of relation outside the text: What are the bounds separating myself from another? The implication is that these networks bring us dangerously close to one another in cyclical, if not ritualized, repetition. How do we make sense of these fluid networks, especially those formed in readings of a story called "The Ocean of the Stream of Stories" (*Katha Sarit Sagara*)?

Uncommon Ground

The frame story of the *Vetalapanchavimshati* ("The Twenty-Five Tales of the Undead") itself riddles us with questions about the nature of transgression and our part in it. Among other lessons, we learn that once rules are transgressed and boundaries played with, more pressure is brought to bear on the spontaneous negotiation of individual relationships formed through these exchanges.[103]

We see this right away when our protagonist is faced with a question of duty: an ascetic comes to King Vikrama's court in Pratisthana—on the banks of the Godavari—and each day for ten years presents him with a piece of fruit. Only later by accident does the king discover that each piece of fruit contains a priceless jewel (just as King Satavahan overlooked the importance of the manuscript written in Paishachi in the opening frame story). The king demands the ascetic provide an answer to the riddle of why he is being offered such precious gifts, and in reply the ascetic explains that he needs a brave soul ("*vīrendra*") to perform a task for him. The king accepts the challenge, saying "*thatā*," "(thus) it shall be"; in this instance the relative pronoun "*yathā*" is not necessarily even implied but in any case describes a parallel sequence across time, just as we see above with Somadeva's *yathā-tathā* promise of loyalty to another's word. There, Somadeva promises to act according to Gunadhya's manuscript written in the narrative past. Here, King Vikrama promises to act in the future according to the ascetic's request stated in the narrative present.

As we see above, Pollock refers to such pairings across time as "repetition": in the scenarios he describes, the repetitions cannot be exact. Part of what made the Sanskrit cosmopolis successful—if you agree with his argument that such a system was successful—is that the uncentered, accommodating processes allowed and even encouraged precisely those differences borne of inexact repetition. How might we read such a pairing in this case?

We soon learn that the ascetic is interested in achieving as exact a repetition of pronouncement with action as possible.[104] Once he has the king's word, the ascetic articulates his requirements in great specificity: the king must meet him under the banyan or sheesham tree (depending on whose translation you read) at the cremation ground at midnight on the fourteenth day of the dark fortnight (*krishnapaksh*). Nirmal Trikha, in his study *Faiths and Beliefs in the Kathāsaritsāgara*, lists these details in particular— midnight on the fourteenth day of the dark fortnight, the ascetic sitting under a banyan tree—as evidence that the ascetic is engaging in a Tantric practice that would cast a spell to master a *vetala*, one of the powerful and mischievous spirits who temporarily possess corpses.[105] (Some translate this as vampire or zombie; irresistibly, Sudipta Kaviraj translates "*vetala*" as "the undead.")[106] Trikha notes that a Tantric practitioner might invite a *vetala* for noble or nefarious purposes—to cure disease, to vanquish a wicked enemy, to obtain lordship over one's competitors—and, regardless, needs the help of a brave man to carry the corpse the *vetala* possesses if he himself lacks the necessary courage;[107] overestimating one's powers could be a mortal mistake.

It is unclear in this story if the king knows the nature of the ascetic's plans: the narrator certainly does not explicitly describe the ascetic's intentions nor the king's internal reactions. The king is narrated entirely from the outside and looks to be a stock character who represents stereotypical ideals of courage and noble righteousness. As soon as the king takes up the Tantric ascetic's challenge, however, such pat categories are challenged: If the expectation is that the king must be faithful to his word, then what practical definition of fidelity do we endorse? The fictional quandary points to real-life questions of faith and alliance, ones that we could imagine being negotiated in Kashmir at the time this manuscript was written, but only if we acknowledge that this imaginary point of view is constructed in dia-logic relationship with our position here, now, at this shifting point in our continually repeated literary exchange: If the king strays from the path of righteousness, what price must he pay, and exacted by whom?

As Trikha and others note, it is no accident that the frame story begins with a tribute to Lord Shiva, given that Kashmiri Saivism, focused on Shiva, was in its ascendancy in this period, inspired as people were by, for exam-ple, the subtle writings of the greatly influential philosopher Abhinava-gupta, a contemporary of Somadeva.[108] Writing in the twentieth century, Trikha seems ambivalent about the status of Tantrism and its relationship to what he terms "the higher Hindu faiths" like Saivite worship—which he is careful to distinguish from "Tantrika Practices" as well as "The Bauddha Faith." A decade later Gavin Flood details a much more complex relation-ship between these various practices and belief systems: Flood cites Abhi-navagupta in particular, writing that one might outwardly be a follower of Vedic (that is, Brahminical) ritual while secretly practicing through Tantra a "disruption of the vedic body through ritual transgression of vedic norms and values."[109]

Flood acknowledges that fixed distinctions regarding Hinduism are com-mon in nineteenth- and twentieth-century scholarship, but he finds them anachronistic, for the designation "Hindu" is itself imprecise: the term was used by the Persians to refer to the many overlapping, warring, contradic-tory, and coexisting religious systems that were prevalent in the subconti-nent east of the Indus River. Practices that today might be separated into categories of High Hindu versus Tantric Hindu versus Tantric Buddhist, even Saivite versus Vaishnavite versus goddess worship, swirl in the ocean of the streams of this story like all the other uncategorizable belief systems and ethical dilemmas presented.

More than anything, a protagonist like King Vikrama (and like readers in turn) is being asked to solve real-life dilemmas presented by situations that blur neat boundaries. Our task as readers of this translation today is to note the particular transgressions that discomfit us so that we might ques-tion the usefulness of such frames in our own thinking, in response to those boundaries marked in these narratives. This might be our own version of dialogic engagement. After all, unlike Vedic practice, which encourages an adherence to purity laws as a way of maintaining social order, Tantric traditions contain the potential for what Flood calls "extreme, ecstatic, experience that shatters vedic, conformist structures."[110] We can see from this that the story invites readers—then as now—to wonder if this challenge to the Vedic order is one the king should endorse. To what order is the king being true?

The narrator tells us—in van Buitenen's vivid translation—that the "faithful king" (*mahāsattvo narpatih*) sets off from the palace on the specified night unobserved, "wrapped in a dark blue cloak and wearing on his face the marks that ward off evil spirits."[111] We likewise hear that he keeps his sword in hand, at the ready. Even the journey from palace to cremation ground signals a crossing into the dangerous world of the dead and undead, outside the healthy social order of Vedic control. Indeed, it is because cremation grounds are considered the most proscribed location in the Vedic order that Tantric practice locates their most powerful—and most transgressive—rituals there. The narrative only heightens the import of these perceived dangers, as we see (again in van Buitenen's translation):

> He entered the burning ground, which was enveloped by ghastly fog and smoke-filled darkness. The frightening flames of funeral pyres leered like ghostly eyes about him, and frenzied Ghosts and Vampires horrifyingly closed in around him as he stepped over the piles of bones, skulls, and skeletons of the innumerable dead. Yet this utterly frightful burning ground, resounding with piercing screams of ghoulish malice, like an apparition of the Dread God himself, could not perturb the king, and he traversed it swiftly. He looked about him and found the mendicant at the foot of the *vaṭa* tree where he was drawing a magic circle.[112]

Trikha explains that a magic circle (*maṇḍala*) in Tantric rites might be regarded as a representation of the circle of the horizon itself, marking off sacred space from the everyday world to create a symbolically charged site within which the worldly might communicate with the otherworldly. Trikha writes, "It is held up to be a potent centre of psychic energy," and as such "the evil spirits cannot break through it. The magician can force the evil power, captured in the magic circle, to obey him. The magic circle helps the magician to concentrate on his task. It also serves as a protective barrier to the dead."[113] The fear, of course, is that the king might not be included within the protection of such a framing device, and the force of it might be turned against him. In such a scenario, the worldly authority of the king must face off against the otherworldly influence of the ascetic.

The frame narrative thus invites us to consider in more detail in which power we have greater faith. The mandala is the ritual framing device by which Flood contends highly ritualized forms of worship contain divine power, just as a royal ceremony contains and redirects the often erratic forces of political alliance.[114] "The transgressive violence and eroticism of tantric deities," he writes, "becomes tapped and controlled by the institution of kingship."[115] We might assume, then, that the king ventures toward the ascetic's magic circle perhaps to ward off any threat of future evil intent toward himself or his kingdom or perhaps even to derive power from the Tantric ceremony. This ritual ground within the cremation ground is rendered a highly charged common ground between the king and this transgressive Tantric practitioner, a site where the various kinds of worldly and otherworldly power garnered between them might be renegotiated.

The ascetic orders the king to cross the cremation ground until he arrives at a sissoo tree (as it is called in van Buitenen's version) where he will find a corpse hanging on a rope; he must cut down this corpse and carry it back across the cremation ground to the mandala. The narrator offers little direct commentary. In terms of dialogue, all we see is that the king answers the ascetic's request by saying once more simply: "*thatā*." Thus it shall be. How do we read such an assurance? For now our primary interpretive clues must be seen in the nonverbal performances of the characters themselves, who have found common ground in the most uncommon of grounds: the ascetic sitting within the magic circle inside the cremation ground, the king crossing the cremation ground to carry a corpse back to this inner circle. In relation to one another, it is the ascetic who is now depicted as being centered and therefore—in this realm of reversals—sovereign. The scene presents a reversed mirroring of their initial exchange, when the ascetic came daily before the king at his audience hall humbly to present a single piece of fruit.

We might conclude, then, that their exchange is predicated on a constantly shifting balance of power between them, in a negotiation similar to the recentering that must necessarily have been part of the dialogic relationship between vernaculars and Sanskrit that Pollock describes. As I suggest above, such repetitions must be read in a manner attentive to their playful negotiations of attendant differences. Just as the complex relationship between ascetic and king becomes worked out in this fictional performance, so does the relationship between, say, Paishachi and Sanskrit. In either case, we miss the central tension at work if we assume a fixed, hierarchical basis of the exchange. How, then, might we learn to read the fluid shifts in balance more attentively?

If we understand their bodies to be "decentred sites of contradictions," as Eagleton suggests, then we must acknowledge that these sites perform their meaning in relation to one another: the ascetic might bow down before the king in the audience hall, but he issues commandments to him at the cremation ground. Of course, bodily relation is never expressed in a manner exclusively physical and—as we see in several of the stories contained within this very storytelling cycle (including the story of the switched heads)—relies on distinctions that can never be assumed to be neat and straightforward.[116] We see within the frame story of "The Twenty-Five Tales of the Undead," for example, that the sword-bearing king succeeds in finding the promised corpse hanging from the tree, but when he cuts it down, the corpse cries out. We might wonder (as the king seems to): Is this body alive? The boundary between the living and the dead, we discover, is not so very simple.

In this case, where an undead spirit has possessed a dead body and brought it back to life, it is not clear if it is the body or the spirit that has cried out. The English translators of this storytelling cycle add clues so that the reader unfamiliar with tales of the *vetala* will have a better idea about how to read this cry ("*chakranda*") by a character "as if alive" ("*jīvata iva*"). How do we understand this liminal scene, expressed by the same playful particle "*iva*" seen earlier, now this time in relation to a movement that countervails between the living and the dead? As we learn in Chapter 2, terms of possession are never as simple and straightforward as they pretend to be. Tawney writes the sentence in such a way as to emphasize the scream as an illusory effect created by a nonliving being: "And the moment it was flung down, it cried out, as if in pain."[117] Van Buitenen, however, plays up the ambiguity of wavering between feeling and nonfeeling, being alive and not alive, between illusion and reality: "the corpse struck the ground and screamed as if it had hurt itself."[118]

Such a transgressive story plays on our sympathy in contradictory ways. How should we identify with the pain of a body that has fallen from such a height, even if not fully human? Which is to ask: What rights do we ascribe to a being as much dead as undead? Such a line of inquiry might very well have us question ourselves for engaging in this literary exchange—that is, for being involved in a story about fictional characters like the king and the ascetic who themselves are "as if alive."

Such playful transgressions are important, since they lead us to ask: How are we to interact with characters different from us? Which are the differences that should matter to us and how? In Tawney's translation of this story, the king rushes to the corpse, and "supposing it was alive, came down and rubbed its body out of compassion."[119] Sattar's version reveals an even kinder side of the king: "The king hurriedly climbed down, thinking perhaps the body still held some life. He stretched out his hand and gently stroked the body to ease its pain."[120] Here the insistence on the word "body" depersonalizes it and separates it from the life or spirit that might otherwise serve to animate it. Conversely, the hand stroking the body is depicted as belonging to the king, the touch expressing his concern. In the case of the fallen body, however, there is a separation between the body and the spirit that cries out. How does any spirit claim to possess a body? As we have already seen in the case of Chapman and his metempsychotic claims of Homeric possession, such distinctions are intimately connected with the ethical and political projects we engage in during our literary exchanges. To which body do we imagine the spirit rightly belongs?

The narrator in Sattar's translation goes on to describe the events as if realistically: "As soon as he did that, the corpse quickly let out a chilling laugh that echoed all around." The narrator then adds, from a close third-person point of view of the king's, "The king quickly realized that the dead body had been taken over by a *vetāla*."[121] Such a conclusion is narrated as if this were common sense, even though we know such sense can be common only to those versed in the ongoing narratives of the *vetala*. The laughter of this liminal being thus plays along the line separating not just one being from another but the living from the dead, the real from the imaginary, even common sense and nonsense.

The scene introduces another set of questions of identity, perhaps more confounding than those we saw in the story of the switched heads. Who is laughing? Is the spirit laughing via this alien body? Is the body laughing at this spirit for giving it renewed life? Are the body and spirit now joined together in laughter? To entertain such a riddle, we must ask: To whom does the body belong—to the person who used to live in it, or to the *vetala* now possessing it? Might it be possible for a corpse (as corpus) to belong multiply?[122] Such an idea forces us to consider in even more (and admittedly uncanny) detail the grammar of possession discussed in the previous chapter. What does it mean to be in temporary possession of another's corpse? What are the bounds of such a relation?

Flood sees possession as a process of identifying closely with a received corpus—of texts both oral and written—in such a way that it allows the body of the practitioner to work toward divinization.[123] While he focuses on texts of revelation rather than literary works, his insights into the relationship of the reader to the textual tradition allow us to see how, for example, the writer of a storytelling cycle like the *Katha Sarit Sagara* might temporarily possess a text while at the same time allowing himself to be possessed by it (in a process similar to Eagleton's theory of language, that what I say to you somehow already includes what you say to me). Flood describes possession as a process of what he calls "entextualisation," a concept drawn from Michael Silverstein and Greg Urban's work in "The Natural History of Discourse," which opens by arguing that texts are not static objects that a scholar can analyze outside a particular context but are part of ongoing cultural processes that continually frame the text as such.[124] Silverstein and Urban emphasize that "the processes that result in phenomenal textuality . . . are the central and ongoing practices within cultural orders" that help define a culture to itself, and so the texts themselves are but one "phase in a broader conceptualization of cultural processes."[125] As their title suggests, they rely on life-and-death metaphors to describe the ways texts might be analyzed as, for example, "atoms of shared culture."[126]

My interest in such a question is both generalizable to our disciplined approaches to texts of world literature and quite specific to the tropes of this story in particular: How do we understand life as a common or shared possession? Seen in the context of possession, what exactly are the bounds of such a concept of life?

Flood makes clear that a body-identified tradition like Tantra cannot help but be aware of temporal limitations, since the body it uses to access and extend the tradition is born, ages, and dies. He sees such boundaries as an inherent narrative structure of life, one that Tantric traditions theorize in exceedingly complex, disciplined ways. He explains: "To speak of a body is to speak of temporality, and to speak of a body is to speak of narrative. Narrative and the living body are inseparable."[127] As such, he contends that the practitioner does not relate only to textual authorities but to all the other practitioners, past, present, and future: "The narrative structure of the body, being born and dying, therefore entails communities of other narrative bodies and the interrelation of bodies through time."[128] Like possession, the process of entextualization moves temporally in several directions at once: "in becoming the host for the deity or supernatural being external to the self," he writes, "the body becomes constructed in tradition and text-specific ways."[129] Because a reading or interpretation of a text becomes "communal and tradition-based, only taking shape within communities that have themselves been shaped by prior acts of reading of the same text or group of texts," a text can come to life—become possessed—only in the plural.[130]

Every text in the tradition, then, is necessarily a common or shared possession, one that negotiates—and teaches practitioners to negotiate—with power.[131] It is for this reason, Flood argues (citing Pollock), that these texts are located in "the Sanskrit cosmopolis," given that the process of entextualization requires that "the texts . . . be read and heard by those with the requisite authority, to be brought to life, and to be performed."[132] The power of the text derives from its life, which derives from the many lives of its practitioners, which in turn derive from the power they derive from the text. Writing in Sanskrit confers authority on the text not only because of Sanskrit's elite status but because it allows practitioners to connect across time and place. Moreover, Sanskrit's "aesthetization of the political" (in Pollock's handy phrase) enhances the power of the text, which in turn enhances its reach, which in turn enhances its power.

This is an aspect of the connection between the concepts of life and power via the textual tradition that often is overlooked. Because the tradition itself lives on through transmission ("by being received anew through the generations"), it demands a dialogic relationship with the text that forces the reader to attend to the very bounds of his or her own life in relation to the other: "the reader interprets and internalises the text in the act of understanding and in turn conforms himself in turn to the reader implied within the text."[133] Flood insists that such a reading is necessarily bodily: he sees the practice of inscribing oneself in tradition as an act of reading that defines a self that conforms to tradition and thus to the bounds of this self are defined by text and ritual.[134]

This paradoxical subjectivity can be best understood by paying close attention to pronominal usage. Flood explains that the everyday subject of the first-person predicate ("I") becomes subsumed by the otherworldly predicate set out within the text and thus becomes possessed, entextualized.[135]

The implication is that Tantra teaches its practitioners how they might perform bodily those subjectivities circumscribed by language:

> The specificity of the tantric tradition lies in the ways in which [practitioners] form a subjectivity, the ways in which the subject of first-person predicates, the "I," becomes an index of tradition and the way the body becomes entextualised. Patterns of texts are mapped on to the body in ways particular to Tantrism and in response to other ways of mapping texts on to the body, especially vedic ones.[136]

The very grammar a speaker relies on, then, frames personhood through such terms of possession. Urban draws attention to the flexibility with which the possessed speaker frames his utterance when speaking on behalf of a spirit.[137] He notes that the "I" that the possessed subject uses when describing walking down the street is different from the "I" used in this trancelike behavior of "carrying back" another's spirit into this body, since the "first-person usage may represent the speaker/narrator becoming an anaphoric substitute for a third person [*sic*] form."[138] Flood, however, notes that for the duration in which a body is possessed in these Tantric examples, the body and the spirit are treated as a single subject.

Indeed, we see in the frame story of "The Twenty-Five Tales of the Undead" that when the king responds to the *vetala*'s laughter, he asks in the second-person singular, *"katham hasasi? ehi, gacchāvaha"* ("Why do you laugh? Come, let us go").[139] He likewise bids him to come along in the first-person dual. From this, we can understand that our English-language traditions of literary interpretation are analogous to these Tantric textual traditions in Sanskrit: we have a series of interconnected triangular relationships that in each case discipline us to pretend to be dual. We can imagine that the king plays along with this grammar of possession the way we might refer to a man in drag as "she," signaling that we share the knowledge that these patterns are mapped onto the body in ways that are in response to other ways of mapping onto the body.

The *vetala* laughs within his narrative as Mr. Worth laughs within his: to remind us of these frames of transgression that we both must attend to and yet pretend do not exist. The king's response to the *vetala*'s laughter— "Why do you laugh? Come, let us go"—might thus be read as a subtle reassurance that he understands that this performance is a travesty and that he will play along.

As it happens, when the king speaks, the corpse magically and materially returns to its former position hanging from a high branch on the tree. The king must repeat the circuit of climbing up the tree, cutting down the rope, and shouldering the corpse to begin carrying the corpse across the cremation ground to the waiting mendicant; as he trudges along in silence, the *vetala* begins telling him stories "to beguile the way" (as he explains in Tawney's translation).[140] Each story he tells transgresses the bounds of the ordinary—be it the tale of the switched heads, the tale of a man who turns into a woman by day so he might be with his love at night and is then promised in marriage as both a man and a woman, or the tale of a clay figure brought to life by four men who all then want to marry her—so that every tale ends in a riddle challenging the king to ascertain proper conduct, to make sense of the nonsense: To whom does he or she belong?[141] Which rules of relation should we sanction?

Each time the *vetala* finishes a riddling story, he warns the king dramatically (as he does in van Buitenen's translation) that he must tell the answer: "Your head will burst asunder if you know it and fail to speak!"[142] And as soon as the king speaks, each time the corpse flies back to the tree, and the king must begin the circuit once more from the start. This repeats twenty-five times in nearly exactly the same way.

There is one significant change, however: with each round the narrative tension increases: Will the king have the patience and fortitude to fulfill his promise? Should the king stay true to his word? After the end of the first story, when the king answers the riddle and breaks the circle of silence, the narrator tells us that the *vetala* "immediately left his shoulder, and went somewhere unobserved by the force of his magic power" which the narrator explains (in Tawney's translation) was "in order to test his persistence"; at this point, early on in the exchange, being still full of energy, "the intrepid king at once determined to recover him."[143] The insistence on the king's determination indicates more of the struggle to come. After the king answers the second riddle and the corpse once more disappears from his shoulder, the narrator tells us:

> the king, who was bent on forwarding the object of the mendicant, made up his mind to fetch him again, for men of firm resolution do not desist from accomplishing a task they have promised to perform, even though they lose their lives in the attempt.[144]

After all, we know from the title that there will be twenty-five tales of the *vetala*, but the king does not, an ignorance the narrator seems to share.[145] How long is the king going to keep this up? Will his faith in doing his duty blindly be enough to carry him through the arduous revolutions that lie ahead? After telling an answer to the third riddling story, when the king goes to cut the *vetala* down from the tree, "it" utters "a horrible laugh" and then endeavors to plant a seed of doubt in the king's mind (and ours at the same time): "King, why do you take all this trouble for the sake of this wicked mendicant? In truth you show no discrimination in taking all this fruitless labour."[146] He thus establishes a relationship triangle whereby the king will be forced to choose between continuing to align himself with mendicant or switching allegiance to this unlikely travel companion who tells such engaging stories. The *vetala* does not belabor the point about the mendicant's potential untrustworthiness, he simply offers to tell another story "to amuse you on the way."[147]

It is not clear whom the king should side with. Is the *vetala* calling the mendicant wicked because the mendicant seeks control over him? Is he telling these riddling stories not to amuse the king so much as to trick him into talking so that the *vetala* might escape once more? Like the story of Chouboli, silence and speech are instrumental in maintaining and gaining power. Unlike in the story of Chouboli, however, it is not clear yet whose side we are meant to take, whom we would want to win.

After the telling of the fourth story, the king returns to the same tree and cuts the *vetala* down as before. This time, however, the narrator confides that the king, "after showing much displeasure with him, set out rapidly toward his goal."[148] We are not told exactly how he shows this displeasure, but the irritation reveals a vulnerability in the king that is as potentially dangerous as it is understandable. In response, the *vetala* tries even harder this time to charm him, announcing: "King, you have embarked on a toil-some undertaking, and I liked you from the moment I first saw you," before repeating a variation of the same formula, "so listen, I will tell you a tale to divert your mind."[149] Such attempts at manipulation endeavor to coax not just the king but us as readers to be patient with this endless circuit, to allow our own minds to be diverted. As such, the trick not only works to buy the trickster more time so that he might wear the king down, but gives him more of an opportunity to win the king over to his side.[150]

Outside the narrative frame an analogous procedure is taking place: as we become increasingly involved in these cycles of telling, we become closer and more receptive to our riddling storyteller—a tricksterish *vetala* whose stories are being recounted by a court minister named (confusingly enough) Vikramakesharin who—we are told—has learned the charm that allows him to master a *vetala* from an unnamed Brahmin who told him the story of King Vikrama (that is, "The twenty-five tales of the Undead") as proof that "you can obtain from a Vetála all you desire."[151]

Readers first see the storytelling Vikramakesharin from the point of view of his king, Mrigankadatta, who watched him "being carried through the air by a hideously deformed man" and when he dismounted from his shoulders, the minister ordered the deformed man to "come to me when I think of you."[152] Rather than carrying the possessed corpse as we have seen King Vikrama do, this minister is being carried by the *vetala*, in a mirrored reversal that is revealing. We learn that the Brahmin who told him the twenty-five tales of the *vetala* had in the process given the minister this "power" as a reward for the antidote to a snakebite so painful that he wanted to drown himself—thus suggesting that this narrative, too, situates itself on the edge between life and death.

Such a framing device alerts readers to the powers of this narrative, which they are now in temporary possession of, with the implication that they, too, might continue the exchange in the future. After all, Vikramakesharin tells the story in turn to Mrigankadatta while they are walking, and this exchange is being reported by a hermit, Pishangajata, to the lovesick king Naravahanadatta, in one of a series of tales about the exploits of Mrigankadatta, as a way of instructing Naravahanadatta on the ways of endurance, which is itself inside a frame story nested inside another frame story, and on and on until we find ourselves back at the manuscript being written in blood in the goblin language, or even further back in the heavens, when Shiva tells Parvati these tales that no one has ever heard. Each narrative frame relates to another narrative frame, which relates to another, in a circuit as seemingly endless as the king's riddled repetitions.

Our task is to ascertain the value of each particular telling. Is the lesson here that the king's persistence will win out and that in helping the mendicant, he himself will become empowered like Vikramakesharin? Or is the lesson that he should not trust the mendicant and should learn what he can directly from this otherworldly trickster? Each character in this curious triangle is instrumental for the other. What is the relation between the three? Another riddle is being asked implicitly through this embedded narrative, a riddle that our engagement with the telling implicates us in: What is the basis for the relationship in each frame between teller and listener?

The Specter of Comparison

Like "The Twenty-Five Tales of the Undead," Roland Barthes's *S/Z* stages its own narrative performance to think through issues of narrative performance and looks to ghosts to riddle the transgressive relationships we form through such texts. In turn, I put the *vetala* storytelling cycle in conversation with Barthes to create my own narrative performance, in order to respond to what Emily Apter has identified as the challenge of Comparative Literature, one that seeks "to balance the singularity of untranslatable alterity against the need to translate *quand même*," so that I might resist the pressure to accede too readily to what she terms "translation failure," the "all-purpose expedient" in her phrasing "for staying narrowly within one's own monolingual universe."[153] In so doing, I articulate an approach to the project of comparison through translation that might answer her call that we find a "corrective to the postmodern relativism besetting postcolonial studies" and "its fetishization of the politics of difference" including "a naive celebration of 'the local.'" In this case, rather than focusing melancholically on what we may have lost, I look to what we have found in such an exchange.

For Barthes, this literary act we engage in is a performance (even seduction) that is relational, playful. As in "The Twenty-Five Tales of the Undead," he proves through his own rhetorical performance that such an exchange moves in several directions at once; when he insists to us, the readers of *S/Z*, that this project "is not an *explication de texte*," he seems to be making fun in his own tricksterish way of the disciplinary conventions of reading that we have long been taking so seriously.[154] How else should we interpret the irony of a situation whereby a sophisticated literary critic such as Barthes introduces his reading by focusing on the most transgressive of rhetorical figures that creates and furthers a division between two entities (somewhat arbitrarily) marked as opposite—specifically between "inside" and "outside"—while adopting the conventionally authoritative, scholarly voice that positions itself as if outside the text?[155]

The further irony is that we often look for an answer to this question using reading conventions that his text calls into question—which would have us look toward his text and to the figure of the author (in this case, Barthes) to secure its meaning. We are thus compelled to engage in a revealing but perhaps infinitely self-reflexive and therefore maddening exercise when we read Barthes's riddle about Balzac's text against Barthes's own text: "Who is speaking?"[156] When Barthes, as engaged reader of Balzac's text, tells us that "it is impossible to attribute an origin, a point of view, to the statement" that announces "the appearance of a strange personage" of mysterious gender and insists that "the more indeterminate the origin of the statement, the more plural the text," then as engaged readers of Barthes's text, we find it equally impossible to attribute an origin, a point of view, to the statement that announces the appearance of a strange personage of mysterious gender and thus find the more indeterminate the origin of the statement that we cannot definitively apply to Barthes the author, the more plural the text.

Like the *Katha Sarit Sagara*, *S/Z* acts as stable and solid as water, slipping from our grasp anytime we reach out to contain it, fix it within neat, manageable borders. Our own fixation on securing meaning definitively—in the personage of the author—pulls us into the text's playful relationality. Here, as elsewhere, like Chouboli and like the king in turn, we are being seduced by an impossible, irresistible riddle that seems so specific to this narrative that we risk simplifying when we compare the framing device to other storytelling cycles.

Barthes, however, does not resist generalizing beyond storytelling cycles: he contends that every narrative exchange organizes itself around an enigma that the text formulates, delays answering, and finally endeavors to solve.[157] While I could readily apply such a description to "The Twenty-Five Tales of the Undead," he takes as his example the literary text *Sarrasine* by Honoré de Balzac, itself an embedded narrative that features the telling of a ghost story.[158] Like the *Katha Sarit Sagara*, spirits haunt every level of *S/Z*, frame within frame within frame. Barthes writes of Balzac writing of a narrator telling his readers the story of telling a woman he desires the story of a cadaver-like castrato in order that he might capture her attention. Here to ask "Who is speaking?" is to ask: How do we read these (gendered) narratives of possession?[159]

There is another question being asked, one that takes the entire book of *S/Z* to formulate, to delay answering, and finally to solve: What is the structure of the reader-writer relationship that leads us toward and around such an *abîme*? In French we might understand *abîme* to mean an abyss, a chasm, a depth, as in *"abîme de l'ocean"* (the depths of the ocean), but even more fortuitously we might also think of the narrative structure discussed in terms of *"mise en abîme"* to describe the enigma or riddle that storytelling cycles such as this frame for us.[160] We should see then that our own theoretical narratives frame images of the unfathomable: Paul de Man calls such *mise en abîme* "the kind of structure by means of which it is clear that the text becomes itself an example of what it exemplifies."[161] Reading *S/Z*, we participate in an elaborate joke on the project of meaning-making, a project that we thereby share. It is for this reason that I draw attention here to the formal characteristics of these interpretive conventions by which we navigate around these (seemingly fluid) *abîmes*.

To ask "Who is speaking?" is to ask if I (I who am writing this, you who may be reading this, Roland Barthes who was reading that) trust the narrative "I" in *Sarrasine*. (Just as we ask: Should the king trust the *vetala*? How has this "I" entextualized spirits of the past?) In both the essay "The Death of the Author" and in *S/Z*, Barthes positions himself as an engaged and intelligent reader of *Sarrasine*: his pronominal "I" does not comment explicitly on the relationship formed with us, his readers, via his own texts (for the text always exists for *the other*, from the other, kept by the other . . .), but, as in the *Katha Sarit Sagara*, the narrative performance cannot help but refract back on itself, occupy more than one figure simultaneously, past, present, and future. The text performs its own *mise en abîme*—instructing us how to read the Balzac text as a way of instructing us how to read any other text, which cannot help but include a reading of the text we are immediately engaged with. Barthes's performed reading frames *Sarrasine* just as surely as Balzac's story of the desirous narrator frames the embedded storytelling performance, leading us to circle around the *abîme* at the core of such an exchange like the king on the cremation ground with a possessed corpse on his back. We might pose a version of the riddle raised in the previous chapter: How does one possess a corpus?

Barthes figures the dynamic of textual relation in terms unromantically economic:

Since narrative is both merchandise and the relation of the contract of which it is the object, there can no longer be any question of setting up a rhetorical hierarchy between the two parts of the tale, as is common practice: . . . *Sarrasine* is not the story of a castrato, but of a contract; it is the story of a force (the narrative) and the action of this force on the very contract controlling it. Thus, the two parts of the text are not detached from one another according to the so-called principle of "nested narratives" (a narrative within the narrative). The nesting of the block of narrative is not (merely) ludic but (also) economic.[162]

The metaphor of the contract is not incidental; Barthes presents this analysis as if attention to economic forces might help us better understand the rules of the contract between reader and writer. The seriousness of tone should make us wonder, however, how such an analysis would play out if we were to investigate the relationship he posits through the ludic. Generally economic analysis promises to grant us access to unmediated, real, material truths but in the end opens up more enigmas than it solves; the ludic makes no such promise but in its playfulness gestures toward more complicated truths, even if indirectly. Given Eagleton's suggestive urgings, which open this chapter, about the importance of humor for understanding dialectic, I would have us consider the ludic and the economic as interrelated modes, so that we might approach these narratives productively by thinking of them as otherworldly examples of what I will call a ludic economy. Barthes contends that the narrative contract is predicated on a system of desire that assumes equivalence susceptible to change. Equivalence, as we have already seen in the opening chapter, is not so much a fixed aspect of relationality but a promise of a contract never to be fully realized. In this regard, Barthes gives as an example the figure of the Adonis in a painting in *Sarrasine* which the embedded narrator promises his listener access to in a triangle of displaced desire that the narrative facilitates, in a mirroring of our own triangular relationship with Barthes's text. (That is, just as the narrator of Balzac's story promises to solve the enigma of the painting for his interlocutor, so does the narrator of *S/Z* promise to solve the enigma of this enigma-driven narrative. This is what keeps us involved in the exchange.)

Barthes's insights into the triangular nature of this narratological relationship help us understand more specifically how the economic and ludic impinge upon one another—linking the facticity of bodily performance to the contradictory abstractions of metatextual relation.[163] Sexual exchange becomes merely one of the forms the fetishistic relationship might assume. Barthes equates narrative with "legal tender, subject to contract . . . in short, *merchandise* . . . represented *en abyme*, in the narrative."[164] Legal tender, like narrative, promises that it might be exchanged for the tangible object of our desire, which the *mise en abîme* structure holds out for us and withholds at the same time.

Barthes tells us that *Sarrasine* offers a generalized theory "as fable" to pose more difficult—and admittedly economic—questions: *"What should the narrative be exchanged for? What is the narrative 'worth'?"*[165] Here this worthy figure (the Adonis in the painting, the knowing Balzac, the knowing Barthes) is not laughing outright but might as well be, for this is the central riddle *S/Z* is organized around (and that scholars of both Area Studies and Comparative Literature have struggled to address in their evocation of translation). Barthes opens the book by asking how we might talk about "the value of a text" without reducing "all the world's stories" to "a single structure," a move that would render each example mere "Copy" and threaten the "difference which does not stop and which is articulated upon the infinity of texts, of languages, of system."[166] He does not overtly interrogate the original/copy binary such a system is predicated upon here.

Yet Barthes expresses a similar concern even more overtly in "The Death of the Author" (written contemporaneously with *S/Z*): that the mechanistic procedures of print culture will render writers "eternal copyists" fated to "imitate an ever anterior, never original gesture."[167] As we see above, Walter Benjamin names as great those writers (Cervantes and Sterne) who teach us to laugh at the "inauthentic," "counterfeit" aspects of a culture that must presumably be left behind in our search for dialectical justice. In Barthes's case as well, the humor here—if we can glean any at all—is embittered, guarded, stealing hope that we might discover together a more perfect world that leaves the counterfeit out. That world is the *abîme* that we are drawn to and circle around.

Like Benjamin, Barthes contrasts modern print-based rituals of literary performance with the storytelling traditions of premodern "ethnographic societies," which see the storyteller before them as "a mediator, shaman, or reciter" and thus do not expect him to release "a single 'theological' meaning (the 'message' of the Author-God)."[168] Like Michel Foucault in "What Is an Author?" Barthes focuses on the question of originality in order to examine the ways in which our modern literary institutions secure the value of a literary work (as "original") through the body of the author. While the text does not examine the metaphor explicitly, it makes clear that the concept of the "Copy" points to the paradox of narrative exchange in print culture that renders a text both singular and plural, both tangible and intangible: copyright, after all, posits a single text of "original" genius and plural mechanically reproduced derivatives; the legal language of the right to copy depends on the living body of the original author.[169]

Read conventionally, Barthes's texts participate in the same system, the same play: it is not the original text itself that we look to for meaning, but the figure of "Barthes." The author becomes fetishized. The ludic can be understood in economic terms when the origin you desire is rendered unattainable and instead you are handed an inferior copy as if it were the same: a contract that does not allow you to laugh along. In *S/Z* Barthes rails against "the pitiless divorce which the literary institution maintains between the producer of the text and its user, between its owner and its customer, between its author and its reader."[170] Read humorlessly, *S/Z* becomes an elaborate performance justifying the agency of the reader in the alienated circuit of literary exchange. Barthes asks how a "writerly" text might render the reader "no longer a consumer, but a producer of the text."[171]

Such a notion reformulates the inherent plurality in the literary contract. He examines a storytelling performance embedded in a literary text to rethink the relationship between an author and its reader to ask: What are the terms of this exchange? I turn this around to ask: How might we approach this riddle of literary exchange by reading *S/Z* humorously? After all, like the king and the *vetala*, we can address this plural text as if in the singular: Why do you laugh?

We soon see that for Barthes in *S/Z*, questions of possession do not break down neatly into binaries of oral and written, premodern and modern, precapitalist and capitalist, as we might expect; he looks to a high literary text (Balzac's) to reveal an underlying structure of narrative contract that might apply to a vast range of texts. He discusses the Balzac text in relation to literary exchanges that flirt instead with the distinction between "fiction" and "reality" and in so doing invokes more than one *mise en abîme* narrative featuring an oral storytelling performance:

> Here [in the case of *Sarrassine*], the narrative is exchanged for a body (a contract of prostitution); elsewhere it can purchase life itself (in *The Thousand and One Nights*, one story of Scheherazade equals one day of continued life);

and elsewhere, in Sade, the narrator systematically alternates, as in a gesture of purchase, an orgy for a dissertation, in other words, for meaning (philosophy *is equivalent* to sex, the boudoir): by a dizzying device, narrative becomes the representation of the contract upon which it is based: in these exemplary fictions, narrating is the (economic) theory of narration: one does not narrate to "amuse," to "instruct," or to satisfy a certain anthropological function of meaning; one narrates in order to obtain by exchanging; and it is this exchange that is narrated in the narrative itself: narrative is both product and production, merchandise and commerce, a stake and the bearer of that stake.[172]

Given that the text we are engaging with in this passage, Barthes's *S/Z*, also flirts with the distinction between fiction and reality to propose an exchange of narrative for a body, we might notice, too, how we participate in an economy that equates a story with a day of continued life. Indeed, it might seem distasteful and even cynical to discuss the value of narrative in terms of bodies, but our desires—to find a politically or sexually conceived union—cannot help but work themselves into our approach to the narrative. We take part in the exchange wanting to know, in part, how literature might help us negotiate exactly these kinds of real, life-and-death concerns. The economic and the ludic share common propositions: Shaharazad's "continued life" Barthes refers to can be read as a storyteller risking her body to trade story for safety, and can also be read as a playful move of resistance. As we see in Chapter 2, Foucault refers to the same embedded narrative Barthes refers to (*The Thousand and One Nights*) to think through the role of the author in extending the life of the community: How might Barthes or Foucault or any number of authors be performing for us a scholarly version of Shaharazad's role? If she relied on her powers to amuse in order to play with a system that said that one might either sacrifice or be sacrificed, then what aspect of this system might these metropolitan theorists be playing with?

For this exercise to be useful, we must notice what in our own conceptual frameworks is being prodded when I suggest that Barthes is laughing as he narrates. Such playful performances have precedent, after all, in postmodern theoretical circles: Jacques Derrida is said to have been so overcome with mirth during the oral performance of his paper "Différance" that he had to pause in the recitation to wipe away tears of laughter.[173] (There is, of course, a lovely irony here that a paper challenging the temporal relationship conventionally posited between speech [as anterior, signifying "presence"] and writing [as derivative, signifying "absence"] would gather paratextual legends about its own oral performance as originary.) And while the transcriber's notes to Paul de Man's orally performed reading of Walter Benjamin's essay "The Task of the Translator" emphasize more the transcriber's own serious-minded attempt at faithfully "foregrounding a gap between oral performance and printed text," his efforts at marking off such an *abîme* do indeed allow space for a reader to imagine the wry smiles, muffled chortles and sly winks being exchanged in the room that day.[174] Such an irony is even more charged when we keep in mind that in his reading, de Man delights in getting lost in a similar *mise en abîme* that he discovers in Benjamin's essay, a "text about translation [which] is itself a translation, and the untranslatability which it mentions about itself inhabits its own texture and will inhabit anybody who in his turn will try to translate it, as I am now trying, and failing, to do."[175]

Such a rhetorical stumble reveals the contradictions in the linear narrative of progress underlying so much history; it performs a slapstick reading of what de Man describes as Hegel's Christian understanding of spirit (*Geist*) as a phenomenon that "transcends the subjectivity of the ego, finds its true abode in the phenomenon of language"[176] as singular, harmonious unity, as opposed to the Benjaminian understanding of the "bottomless depth" that is "pure language."[177] The comparison between the Hegelian and Benjaminian understandings of language—whose ideological stakes are enormous—is sited very much in the body of the language speaker, as Eagleton has already suggested. How, then, do we choose to read these farcical repetitions? Later in the essay, de Man reads language in Benjamin's work as a broken vessel (*tikkun*) whose fragments "will never constitute a totality."[178] Thus de Man, in his own fragmented, untranslatable stutter, enacts the role of the very tricksterish spirit he postulates as an alternative to Hegel's *Geist*, one that does not try to control every facet of difference but endeavors to allow such contradictions to play. I look to these laughing figures (Derrida, de Man) in order to help us to understand the similarly tricksterish spirit of Barthes in *S/Z*.

After all, theorists cannot help but locate themselves inside such framed narratives, even as they (we) move toward the *abîme*. We could imagine ourselves as scholars repeating tales of the great theorists primarily to remind us melancholically of a time lost to us—when these great thinkers lived and conversed with (some of) us. I am suggesting instead that we have already

begun participating in an economy where such ludic antics enjoys a continued life through our own retellings (which, not incidentally, translate readily between forms oral and written; our own disciplinary practice provides
complex, provisional answers to the speech-versus-script riddles we repeat).
"Do we have any alternative to such play?" Michael Holquist asks—framing
Derrida's aporias alongside Bakhtin's internal loopholes.[179] Might we ever
work outside these *mises en abîme* constructed for us in our field?

Holquist summarily answers his own riddle with a succinct "no." He
explains in an engaging singsong: "Magritte is playing. Foucault is playing,
and . . . I, too, am playing. We are all playing—with language."[180] Holquist
draws our attention to the "surd," that "voiceless sound" heard in Derrida's
absurd performance of "différance" to highlight the absurdity of our own
disciplinary languages. Susan Stewart's work on play similarly highlights
the "absurdities" of absolute knowing that Edmund Husserl, for one, was
interested in interrogating. ("We are certain we are in possession of objective truth, based upon reliable methods of reaching [objective] reality. But
whenever we reflect we fall into errors and confusion. We become entan-
gled in patent difficulties and even self-contradictions.")[181] For Stewart, like
Derrida (who shares her interest in Husserl), such absurdities only serve to
make us aware of the arbitrary procedures underlying our attempts to create a coherent sense of the common and reasonable:

> There is no place in which one can escape metalanguage or framing. An
> activity that was not framed would be the completely natural, would be
> prelapsarian, a point that itself must of necessity act to frame "the unframed."
> This activity would be a purely natural gesture at the other end of the spec-
> trum of social process from the most impossibly social gesture—nonsense.
> The problematic nature of this "natural" gesture is foregrounded every time
> children play "copy cat." In this game one child will mime another child's
> gestures. If the victim crosses his legs, the copy cat crosses his legs; if the
> victim looks annoyed, the copy cat looked annoyed; if the victim says "stop
> it!" the copy cat says "stop it!" The victim becomes totally frustrated by
> the search for a completely natural gesture, a gesture outside of social life,
> outside of human communication and interaction—the gesture that is not
> socially adaptable. The "game" can only be ended arbitrarily. The social
> universe, the copy cat, always wins.[182]

Her analysis makes clear that the imaginary place (Stewart's "no place")
being framed in every language performance tells a version of the narrative

of our own history as languaged beings; implicitly such *mises en abîme* allow us to engage in an ongoing metatextual debate about whether this common ground we seek serves to replicate prelapsarian linguistic unity (before the Fall . . . of the Tower of Babel) or might anticipate a postlapsarian linguistic unity (Benjamin's *tikkun* that never arrives). Paradoxically, these playful performances help us arrive at a commonsensical understanding, recognizing that we can never arrive at this *abîme* together. We cannot help but participate in the ludic economy when we inhabit what Apter calls "the translation zone."

Yet Stewart's reading of nonsense makes clear that not all play is the same: winning a game of copycat is not the same as winning a hand of poker or winning a football game, for here the stakes of the play are intangible, even epistemological. In the ludic economy, achieving mastery in such an exchange does not confer power on the winner at the expense of the loser as much as create an experience of shared awareness. This, then, is a different order of knowledge as "mastery," not the winner-takes-all economy that R. Radhakrishnan in particular has urged us away from.[183] Like a child shouting in delight during a game of copycat, we might imagine an undead figure like a *vetala*, a Barthes or a Derrida, laughing at the repetition of his own playful performance because he knows the impossibility of achieving the desires these exchanges promise will be fulfilled—of total unity, of complete union. Such a promise simply tricks us into engaging in the exchange. In *S/Z*, as in "The Twenty-Five Tales of the Undead," we come to the end of the riddling engagement with the text and realize that all along it has been the exchange itself that has been our secret goal.

The Ludic Economy

Barthes suggests overtly that we see the growing awareness of the value of the exchange in the storytelling relationship that has developed between the narrator and his love interest in the frame story of *Sarrasine*; of course, the implication is that we, too, have grown similarly close to the figure of Barthes, with whom we have been in narrative relation. In "The Twenty-Five Tales of the Undead," such an insight is performed without being stated explicitly. By the twentieth round, the king seems more interested in answering the *vetala*'s riddles than in reaching his original goal and does not seem to mind at all when the *vetala* leaves his shoulder and returns to the tree. We no longer hear descriptions of his irritation but we do notice that the *vetala*'s chiding is even more pointed: "King, what is the meaning of this persistency of yours? Go, enjoy the good of the night; it is not fitting that you should carry me to that wicked mendicant."[184] The choice of alliance becomes even starker: Is the *vetala* wicked, or the mendicant?

The *vetala* does not argue further but goes on to tell the king the story of "The Boy Who Sacrificed Himself" (in van Buitenen's translation), which Tawney—more descriptively—calls the "Story of the Brahman Boy, Who Offered Himself up to Save the Life of the King."[185] Here we see performed conversations across the framing device. For the story features a protagonist who also happens to be a trustworthy king, one who has inadvertently incurred the wrath of a powerful "demon of Brahmin caste, black with soot and lightning bristling in his hair" (according to van Buitenen's translation) for trespassing on his haunt. The demon threatens to tear out the king's heart and drink his blood and finally, after much persuasion, agrees to forgive the king his "crimes" if "on the seventh day from today you shall sacrifice, with your own sword, a seven-year-old boy, the son of a Brahmin, who has offered himself voluntarily to take your place."[186] Such an outrageous display within this embedded story allows the *vetala* to issue King Vikrama a warning within the frame of the story to think carefully about the threat the mendicant might pose once he gets what he is after—since the Tantric rituals will only make the mendicant that much more powerful, that much more able to defend his ground from intruders. The *vetala* tells the story in such a way that the king in "The Boy Who Sacrificed Himself" seems not only well-meaning and sympathetic but blameless, a victim of circumstances beyond his control.

Within that embedded narrative, when word goes out throughout the kingdom, miraculously a seven-year-old Brahmin boy decides that he wants to "surrender this perishable body for the good of mankind."[187] His parents are horrified, but he insists that "this body, loathsome from the moment of birth . . . will surely perish soon. Yet the merit which one may acquire through his body is called by the wise the essence of existence."[188] The irony is that such syrupy formulas are purportedly being repeated by a spirit who has temporarily taken possession of a rotting corpse. And indeed, the story comes to no easy conclusions; we are told that seven days after encountering the demon, the king and his retinue return for the sacrifice to the same

haunted spot with the boy and his parents; as the king's house-priest prepares for the rite by drawing a mandala, offering oblations to the fire:

> with a roaring laugh, Spitflame the Demon of Brahmin caste appeared, recit-
> ing the Veda. Drunk with the thick red spirits of blood, he yawned and belched
> continually, rolling his bloodshot eyes, and his horrifying shape caste a dark-
> ening shadow over them.[189]

Here, laughter is but one indication of the demon's terrifying, greedy
intent.

As the *vetala* continues narrating, we realize that perhaps the analogy
might work the other way: that the vetala might share more with the wise
seven-year-old boy who wishes to shed his loathsome body and acquire
merit for the good of all, and that the mendicant he calls wicked has more in
common with the Veda-reciting demon. We see at the moment of sacrifice
that the boy's laughter might signal not malevolence but deep awareness:

> the boy was fetched before the Demon, and the mother took hold of his hands
> and the father gripped his feet. And as the king drew his sword to slaughter
> him, the boy began to laugh. And all who were there, even the Demon, in
> amazement stopped what they were doing, folded their hands, and, staring at
> his face, prostrated themselves before him.[190]

The *vetala* finishes his story by demanding of the king the question we,
too, must ponder as readers:

> Tell me now, O king, for what reason did that boy laugh under those cir-
> cumstances, at the very moment of death? The question intrigues me, and
> if you do not reply though you know the answer, your head shall burst in a
> hundred pieces![191]

He thus repeats the king's own riddle—Why do you laugh?—back to
him, this time adding specifications ("under those circumstances, at the
very moment of death") that distinguish this scenario from his own. The
exchange makes clear how much more they understand each other than
when they first met—due in no small part to the riddling storytelling
exchange they have both taken part in.

The king's answer to this laughing riddle applies not only to this story
within this frame but to the other laughing riddles we have considered so
far, including the one that commenced the exchange between the *vetala* and

the king. Here, too, the question of power is being negotiated, for the king tells the *vetala*:

> A weak creature, as soon as he is threatened by danger, begins to cry for his father and mother. When the parents have died, it is the king who takes their place as the guardian of the oppressed. And if there is no king, any available deity is implored. The boy had all of these at hand, but in a rather different fashion. His father and mother held him by hands and feet because they were greedy for money. The king was about to slaughter him in order to save himself. The deity was the Demon of Brahmin caste who was about to devour him. What mockery of people befooled by a body which is transitory, intrinsically unessential, and tortured by pain and sorrow![192]

By the king's logic, the humor thus revolves around a central riddle of bodily existence, one that he then connects to questions of faith:

> Where even Brahma, Indra, Visnu, and Siva, and all the lesser gods must die irrevocably, there *they* exhibited such an illusion of the permanence of their bodies! And witnessing their incredible self-deception and knowing his own ends secure, the Brahmin boy laughed from amazement and joy.[193]

The story urges its audience to ask whether such a sacrifice would ever be worthy and then to analogize the example: If the mendicant is planning to use the *vetala* in a ritual to gain power for himself, will such domination be just? If the mendicant is planning to sacrifice the king, will such a sacrifice be worthwhile? If the king has a responsibility to care for those in his kingdom who are weak, then who is more deserving of such protection—the mendicant or the *vetala*? And by the king's own logic, do either of them qualify as deity and thus reign above the king in the hierarchy he himself has set out?

Lee Siegel opens his chapter on social satire with this story as an example of what he calls "The Laughter of the Child," a child whose innocence grants him special insight into the proper—and improper—workings of power. While in Siegel's view, humor prompts us to laugh at ourselves, satire—in his words—"laughs when concealments fall away" and thus exhibits a tension between "the amusing literary creation and a grim literal reality."[194] As we see in the previous chapter, even power can understand the value of such satire. Siegel explains, "The satirist, like the child, sees the folly and vice that others cannot see, the degradations of understanding and virtue to which both the holders of power and the masses, who have allowed them that power, have become inured or blind."[195]

Here we might recall, too, Walter Benjamin's insight that "the critique of spiritual realities . . . isn't something that language can achieve other than by the detour of a deep disguise: humour." Siegel reads the child's laughter in this story as a victory, for "he subdued his elders by manifesting the very virtue—selflessness—which each of them . . . was ideally supposed to display."[196] Like Stewart's reading of play in terms of the copycat game, this is a victory that can be potentially inclusive, a reading strategy that, I would argue, the king's response to the *vetala* demonstrates for us. As we have already seen, Hutcheon, too, argues that irony can be used as a dynamic strategy of inclusion.

Siegel suggests that these insider territories of inclusiveness are marked out through play, one whose rituals correspond uncannily to those we have already seen the mendicant engaging in through Tantric ritual:

> Satire draws a magic circle, an area set apart from the degenerate society that it depicts, a place in which one has both protection from, and a clearer panoramic view of, the world of folly and vice. To laugh is to enter the circle, to join the satirist against the world. . . . One function of social satire is the establishment of . . . secret groups, such refuges in which both hostility and despair are aligned with pleasure. But the pleasure cannot hold. The refusal to suffer cannot last. Satire is painful comedy. There is a sadness intrinsic to it, the sorrow of all transience. When the laughter ceases, as it must, the circle disappears and those who have laughed realize that they are inextricably a part of the decaying world at which they have looked in amused indignation, a world that will devour them and absorb their laughter.[197]

We can thus imagine that the *vetala* is drawing the king into a kind of mandala ("magic circle") through this playful, riddling storytelling exchange different from the mandala the mendicant has already drawn through Tantric ritual—the circle the king ostensibly endeavors to return to. While ideally in Tantric ritual, such a secret circle uses bodily performance to help practitioners understand the transient nature of all aspects of the world (including pleasure), in playful exchange bodily pleasure (including laughter) allows practitioners temporary release from such awareness—even while reminding practitioners of the existence of such "grim literal reality" (in Siegel's phrase) in the very gesture of concealing it. In each case, power is seen to reside in the one marking out that magic circle—the Tantric mendicant, the riddling joker. In each case, power derives from controlling access to well-guarded secrets that the language marks off from its speakers, circling around it as surely as de Man circles around his untranslatable *mise en abîme*.

How do we approach such concealments? As we see in Chapter 1, Ranjana Khanna's project to understand, in her words, "the basis for an ethico-political understanding of colonial pasts, postcolonial presents, and utopian futures" is figured as a specter constantly riding us—although hers elicits more a melancholic response than one engaged in playful esprit.[198] Khanna relies on the work of Nicolas Abraham and Maria Torok to understand the ways a traumatic "secret" begins to haunt language and is passed down generation to generation as the inability to assimilate a collective loss. She notes, "The phantom of the secret manifests itself in language as symptom [of melancholy] when the secret is in danger of being revealed."[199] Reading the *vetala* stories against such postcolonial riddles, I am suggesting that we find a new way to frame these "demetaphorizations" by playing instead with their potential revelations in a manner that acknowledges our own positionality.[200] Freud observes that the joking mechanism is designed to keep knowledge of both the source of the pleasure as well as the purpose of its technique out of our consciousness, which means, he says, that "strictly speaking, we do not know what we are laughing at."[201] The secret, then, in some way remains a secret, even as we stand inside the magic circle, framing ourselves as if (*tathaiva*) outside the frame.

Like the mendicant's magic incantation, the power of a joke can always turn on its teller. It is this dangerous flexibility, contends Jerry Aline Flieger, that makes a joke by someone like Freud comparable to a literary text like Edgar Allan Poe's "The Purloined Letter," in that both are premised on a lost original. Flieger maintains that the main insight of psychoanalysis à la Lacan, "the discovery that everything human is textual, caught in an intersubjective narrative web, has been purloined from Freud," and that we are all caught in this ludic web of language.[202] She reads Freud's joking triangle against literary enterprises such as our institutional practice of arguing over the interpretation of "The Purloined Letter" as a "joking chain," one that is inherently dynamic:[203]

the joking triangle is always a quadrilateral of sorts, a social chain in which the imaginary capture of both the joke's object (pole two) and its listener (pole three) is perpetuated with a changing cast of players. Even though the joke *seems* to function as a tool for establishing community (between one and three) and for allowing the ego of the victorious joker to triumph over adversity by circumventing obstacles to satisfaction, the joking process nonetheless turns out to be as double-edged as its punchline. For the joking process is a circuit in which no one's identity remains uncontaminated by exposure to the Other's desire.[204]

She thus reads Freud's joking triangle as an ongoing network of exchanges. Rather than assuming the three roles of the joking triangle to be fixed, based on essential bodily identities, she sees them as provisional, positional, a set of relations renegotiated in each performance of the joke as part of an ongoing joking chain. Like the translational storytelling exchange I describe above, listener becomes teller becomes listener in an ongoing game that keeps the circuit alive and therefore the network constantly extending.

The stakes of this comparison between joke and literary text become more provocative when she compares this narrative to another famous triangle, the story of Oedipus, which she reads as a bad joke pulled on the subject by "the Father/Fate, who reveals the punchline—'your girl is your mother'—too late to allow Oedipus to avert the tragic short-circuit, the incestuous bond."[205] Like the riddles in the *vetala* storytelling cycle, such readings force us to rethink the terms of our own relation—as much in real life as in this imaginary exchange. Like Freud, Flieger reads the joking as a response more generally to that which is not supposed to be spoken about. She argues that such a joke—as a sudden revealing of a secret—is not only on Oedipus but on Freud, "the master-storyteller" himself, because in such situations there is no neutral position.[206]

In a move that should be familiar from Barthes's *S/Z*, Flieger compares the joking triangle to the writing triangle formed between writer and reader, the writer staging "a tasteful strip tease, consummating his own pleasure by establishing a bond with the reader."[207] Unlike Barthes, however, she compares work on creativity—in her case, Freud's on writing and on joking—to point to the importance of child's play—as a source of pleasure in rebelling against "logic and propriety" and as "the initial process by which the child gains mastery over reality" by repeating upsetting scenes with a different outcome. Flieger does not employ the magic phrase "what is lost" that so interests scholars of colonial melancholia such as Khanna, but she does take as her example the game a child plays substituting a toy for the "real object" (such as the Mother) "taken out" (ostensibly by the Father). Flieger explains:

> Like the writer or the joker, the desiring child comes to terms with privation or frustration with a creative solution which affords him a compensation for the satisfaction denied by the interference of the third party (the Father who initiates him into the social contract or comic bond to which all human beings are subject).[208]

She then adds that it is through *play* ("only in the repeat performance") that the powerless child can move "from the passive to the active role," which results in "mastering reality," a mechanism that Flieger describes as "strikingly similar to that by which the joke's hearer gains vengeance on the teller by repeating the joke to the next victim."[209] Thus these hierarchical roles associated with joking triangles and other such play are constantly shifting, being negotiated and exchanged in repetition, because, she insists:

> each player is active *and* passive, desiring *and* desired, giver *and* receiver, not only successively but simultaneously. Since one only receives the punch line (like the purloined letter) in order to give it away, the notions of "active" and "passive" lose their specificity, as do the corollary notions of "male" and "female" gender.[210]

In any given performance, we might play at being on one side or the other of these binary distinctions—dead versus alive, male versus female, teller versus listener—but such complicity only threatens to disrupt the system. Flieger's witty essay itself shows that wit might force the terms of such triangular relations to renegotiate and that the "enigma" in *S/Z*, like the riddle in the *Vetalapanchavimshati*, is organized around a truth, a secret, that the narrative exchange helps us move toward and away from at the same time.

The storytelling cycle ends with a riddle the king cannot answer. The story revolves around a case of mistaken footprints: a king and prince see two pairs of feminine footprints tracking through jungle terrain and agree that the father will marry the woman who belongs to the larger prints, the son to the daintier. As it turns out, the queen has the smaller feet and the princess the larger, so the father marries the daughter and the son marries the mother. The riddle the *vetala* asks the king is: How are their offspring related? The king walks on in silence, unable to untangle this relational web in which everybody could be called by multiple (seemingly contradictory) terms. In the narration, too, our relation to the spirited-possessed corpse of a storyteller suddenly riddles us in a different way, moving as it does inside his head to a first-person point of view:

> the *vetala* in the dead man's body, perched on the top of his shoulder, laughed to himself and reflected, "Ha! Ha! the king does not know how to answer this puzzling question, so he is glad and silently goes on his way with very nimble feet. Now I cannot manage to deceive this treasurehouse of valor any further, and this is not enough to make that mendicant stop playing tricks with me, so I will now deceive that villain, and by an artifice bestow the success, which he has earned, upon this king, whom a glorious future awaits.[211]

We are assured that the battle of wits has been between the *vetala* and the mendicant all along—the king has been the tool by which each might gain power over the other. At this point in the narrative the *vetala*'s laughter is inclusive and comprehensible—compare this with the terrifying peal that animated the corpse when we first encountered him. Now it seems inevitable that the king should side with the *vetala* against the mendicant.

Indeed, we cannot help but be drawn into this circle of deceit that the *vetala* has drawn through his storytelling. We might even go so far as to believe the work of divine justice has ensured that the *vetala* will be successful in his effort to make the mendicant "stop playing tricks." How else to explain the precision with which the *vetala* can forecast the events about to unfold? As we see here in van Buitenen's English version:

> The monk for whom you are carrying this corpse will soon conjure me up and worship me. Then the scoundrel will try to sacrifice you, and he will ask you: "Prostrate yourself so that all eight limbs touch the ground." You must answer: "Show me first so that I can do it like you." When he throws himself on the ground to demonstrate the position, you must cut off his head with your sword.[212]

If threat of death were not enough, he then adds extra incentive. You follow my orders, he explains, "So you yourself will accomplish the end which he sought to achieve, the sovereignty over the Spirits of the Air."[213] Given that in Sanskrit *vidyadhara* ("spirits of the air") are liminal creatures neither of the earth nor of the heavens, those "preservers or possessors of knowledge" (to translate literally) who inhabit not so much an external, physical realm but an internal one, to have dominion over the *vidyadhara* is to achieve a subtle power that would, for example, allow the spells you cast to come true.[214] In this story, then, sovereignty is ephemeral and can be located here, there, or in–between; it is figured as a kind of self-discovery, as knowledge of the world—not a definitive, single Truth but instead something more subtle.

And the final encounter unfolds just as the *vetala* predicted. When the king carrying the corpse (now empty of the storytelling spirit) arrives where the mendicant is waiting, he finds himself walking into a site prepared for Tantric ritual:

> On the ground, which was soaked with blood, the sorcerer had traced a magic circle with the white powder of ground bone and placed pitchers with blood on the cardinal points. The circle was brightly illumined by lamps that burned on human fat, and beside it blazed a fire in which an oblation had been poured. All the necessary gifts for the ritual worship of a special deity were assembled.[215]

Both the mendicant and the king now stand in terrifying, transgressive territory where life and death commingle; they stand at a ritual precipice, one foot in each world, and one of them must fall (or rather, be felled). We know from the previous dialogue that this liminality is not purely ritualistic but is also pivotal in terms of the narrative: all along we have feared that the king's life (and therefore the life of the narrative itself) has been threatened; here is the moment when that truth will be realized: one of these characters—we have been cued—will die. And the story, too, will soon come to an end. The telling and the told begin to merge.

When the mendicant sees the king arrive with the corpse on his shoulder, he exclaims:

> Maharaja! You have done me a favor which was well-nigh impossible. What has a mighty prince like you in common with these doings here, this hour or night, this grisly place? Indeed, they call you the greatest of emperors because of the unalterable trustworthiness of your given word—and justly so, for you have accomplished a fellow man's purpose with utter disregard for yourself! This is what the sages have called the true great of the great: not to waver once a promise is made, even when life itself is at stake.[216]

Of course, the mendicant's gushing praise of the king's unwavering "trustworthiness" now seems ironic given that the king suspects the mendicant of plotting to kill him and also because we know the *vetala* has instructed him to kill the mendicant first. A link is made between the king's "given word" and his life, but because of the way the text is constructed, we also know that this same link could apply to the mendicant himself to justify his being killed: because he goes back on his word (i.e., betrays the king), he deserves to die. How can justice best be served here?

Only our own faith can assure us definitively that the *vetala*'s charges against the mendicant are true. As in real life, we cannot know ahead of time whether the mendicant is really going to try to kill the king or not. The narration moves to the mendicant's point of view but is vague about what he believes his "ends" to be:

> While he was talking, the monk, who now thought his ends achieved, lowered the corpse from the king's shoulder. He washed the body, anointed it with unguents, and garlanded it with flowers; then he placed it within the circle. For a brief while he stood there, his body smeared with white ashes, wearing a Brahmin's thread of human hair, cloaked in the dead man's shroud, and sunk in deep concentration.[217]

The ritualized mingling of life and death becomes more dramatic, intratextually as well as metatextually. We do not know if the mendicant wears the dead man's shroud because he is going to kill or because he is going to be killed. The king delivers the corpse and stands back to let the mendicant take over, acting as if the mendicant is entirely in possession of the corpse. Ignorant of this new-formed alliance between king and corpse, the mendicant concentrates on his own ritual:

> And by the power of his wizardry he conjured up the good Vampire and forced it to enter the corpse. Thereupon he began his worship: first he proffered the guest-gifts, which were contained in a skull with immaculate teeth, then a flower and fragrant ointment, two human eyes for incense, and an oblation of human flesh.[218]

The mendicant goes on to bid the king to prostrate himself with "all eight limbs touching the ground," just as the *vetala* predicted he would. Now we have arrived at the critical juncture: Is the king going to believe the *vetala*'s warning and kill the mendicant first? Or if he refuses to kill first, will he really be killed?

At the beginning, the king was a dutiful, brave, and (it must be admitted) fairly unimaginative bearer who was simply following orders. He seemed as expendable as the *vetala* seemed horrifying and dangerous. But in the exchanges with the *vetala*, the king (and in turn, the silent, invisible readers) was forced to speak about situations that seemed unspeakable, to solve paradoxes that seemed unsolvable; in the process of these linguistic, even *spirituel* transgressions, he was forced to consider the world anew. By listening to the spirit that animated the corpse he carried, he was forced to recognize the spirit animating his own body. And so the king became riddled (with, among others things, doubt). When he last left the mendicant, he was just a body carrying another body (and this is what the mendicant thinks he sees and praises when the two arrive) but over the course of the journey he has become alive to himself. The result is that the king switches alliances, and to follow the *vetala*'s orders, he must become duplicitous:

> Remembering the Vampire's warning, the king replied: "I do not know
> how to perform it. Show it to me first, and I shall do it in the same fashion,
> Revered Sir." And when the mendicant knelt on the ground to show how it
> was done, the king struck out with his sword and cut off his head with one
> blow. He tore the broken heart-lotus from his chest and offered heart and
> head to the Vampire.[219]

Next, "invisible crowds of Ghosts cheered excitedly," as if not just the plurality of the text but a whole literary tradition or two welcomes the sacrifice. The *vetala*, too, offers the king a boon. And after the requisite remonstrances, the king chooses a boon in the fine tradition of storytelling, a formulaic closing affirming that the life of the story is of much greater importance than the lives of the individual tellers and listeners who took part in this particular performance, in a variation of the "age after age" blessing that opens "Chouboli": "may your twenty-four ravishing, wonderful tales and this last concluding tale forever be famous on earth and forever be cherished!"[220]

In a twist of convention, the listener within the frame story now is the one to frame the performance he or she has just experienced as a storytelling cycle and thus shows how these tales might "forever be cherished"—by each listener telling the stories in turn, in an ongoing chain of similar such exchanges. In so doing, the listener-turned-storyteller comments metatextually on the very narrative device that locates this telling in the past and yet also in the present (even future), thus mapping a laughing dialogic that is both displaced and yet very much in place.

FOUR

A Divided Sense

The Displaced No-Place of Vernacular-English Exchange

How do we map those acts of literary exchange that take place across languages? Pollock might champion the idea that in the Sanskrit cosmopolis the site of power was "nowhere in particular," but in the world where we live today, if the mother tongue you write in is Rajasthani or Gĩkũyũ, having your work sited "nowhere in particular" might not necessarily represent the triumphant challenge to global center-periphery binaries that Pollock imagines for world literature circa 300 to 1300 CE.[1]

If, like Vijay Dan Detha or Ngũgĩ wa Thiong'o, your Rajasthani or Gĩkũyũ writing is celebrated in English on the Web, translated and published in the online journal *Words Without Borders*, for example, or on the Commonwealth Foundation's official page announcing the short list for the 2007 Booker Prize, someone could well argue that your literary work can no longer claim to be sited at the periphery.[2] And this may be so, but I would want to point out that Detha and Ngũgĩ are both identified in English on those particular Web sites (*Words Without Borders*, Commonwealth Foundation) by the country where they grew up (India and Kenya, respectively) and so, in the utopic (no-place) imaginary of the Web, are very much locally *placed*. Even if the issue of the source languages they wrote in is given scant attention by readers, and even if a writer like Ngũgĩ is forced to write his work in exile from the country he calls home, these writers working in non-European, non-English vernaculars are sited as peripheral. To ask how we map these translated texts is to ask how we identify and make sense of crucial differences in this nowhere-in-particular, home-(page-)away-from home that is the community of world literature in translation.

David Damrosch worries that in this "postcanonical, hypercanonical age," we pretend to have moved beyond the two-tiered system of major and minor canonical authors which we judge based on gradients of perceived mastery ("Western masterpieces") to a system so market-driven that it treats world literature as "some literary Miss Universe competition, an entire nation . . . represented by a single author," with the result that formerly celebrated but "minor" authors such as Premchand and Ghalib (his examples) are now neglected by world literature scholars.[3] Damrosch implies that the former expertise of what he calls "the home-country and area-specialist audiences" is now considered so parochial as to be perceived as dowdy, an attitude that helps establish the cultural capital of postcolonial cosmopolitanisms in the name of a vague postnationalism.[4] Given that much of the work of these neglected minor authors is more critical of nationalist projects (and in much more specific detail) than much of the work of professedly postnationalist cosmopolitan writers like Salman Rushdie, it might help to ask more specifically: What is the place of vernacular literature in the world today?

Salman Rushdie himself tries answering this question in his introduction to *The Vintage Book of Indian Writing 1947–1997* by focusing more on the question of the literary and less on vernacularity. Given that the anthology promises to celebrate fifty years of Indian nationhood, his assumption that the literary and the vernacular are mutually exclusive categories caused quite some controversy when it was published. Since his map of world literature seems to make clear where he locates vernacular literature (that is, at the periphery), I would rephrase the above question to ask instead: How might we value vernacular literature in translation?

Since the days of the fatwa following the publication of *The Satanic Verses*, we are no doubt used to Rushdie provoking us. Here, too, in the introduction to this anthology, he cannot seem to resist playing up his own ambivalences about the country of his birth in such a way that resonates both home and abroad (however one maps those terms): he describes the diversity of the Indian experience in terms of the country's vast size ("Put India in the Atlantic Ocean and it would reach from Europe to America; put India and China together and you've got almost half the population of the world") and its teeming culture ("that vast, metaphoric, continent-sized culture that feels, to Indians and visitors alike, like a non-stop assault on the senses, the emotions, the imagination and the spirit") and concludes that "It's high time Indian literature got itself noticed, and it's started happening."[5] Happening, that is, on the world stage, where Rushdie performs regularly as "celebrity author" (in David Damrosch's apt phrase).[6] More than anything, Rushdie's defiantly upbeat tone makes him sound like a frustrated tourism minister. There is no obvious logical link, after all, between geographic mass and cultural complexity. What exactly is being touted in his selling of Indian literature to world markets? That size (of potential Indian markets) matters? That he is no longer "there" but "here"?

Whether here or there, few would take issue with him only for trying to sell Indian writing to the world market. What makes this introduction so very controversial is his emphatic claim that:

> the prose writing . . . created in this period by Indian writers [and this he underscores] *working in English*, is proving to be a stronger and more important body of work than most of what has been produced in the 16 "official languages" of India, the so-called "vernacular languages," during the same time; and, indeed, this new, and still burgeoning, "Indo-Anglian" literature represents perhaps the most valuable contribution India has yet made to the world of books.[7]

And this from someone who once embraced so euphorically his position as "translated man"![8] The long-standing divide in South Asia between those working in the "*bhasha*," or vernacular literatures, and those working in English had never been articulated so publicly or so provocatively.[9] The irony that has surfaced since Rushdie's comments in 1997 is that postcolonial critics in the West in our contemporary era have inadvertently participated in reinforcing the disdain for *bhasha* literature that nationalists of the colonial and postcolonial eras have historically worked against.

During the century since the Bengali writer Rabindranath Tagore received the Nobel Prize for literature while fully engaged in the struggle to achieve freedom from British rule, each side has seemed to be reacting against the other in an endless play of authenticity one-upmanship.[10] To make matters worse, today "the home-country and area-specialist audiences" are put in the impossible position of having to prove the value of these literary texts to the world community in nationalist-as-transnationalist terms that they know many of the texts themselves work to complicate.

S. Shankar articulates this irony most pointedly, zeroing in on Rushdie's virulently parochial antiparochialism to interrogate the distinction that critics in the North American academy in particular automatically make between what he calls a "vernacular postcolonialism" and a "transnational postcolonialism." Shankar frames brief but complex analyses of three works of Tamil literature (a poem by K. N. Subramanyam, a play by Komal Swaminathan, a short story by Ambai) with a discussion of Rushdie's Anglo-writing claims in order to demonstrate how often vernacular texts represent to the critic in the West a position of the local and the indigenous as (falsely) authentic and nationalistic. Shankar charges that the "influential forms of postcolonial criticism and theory have generally been suspicious of any robust idea of the local or the vernacular, when these terms mark hostility to the hybridizing force of transnational cultural flows."[11] Postcolonial criticism, in his view, participates in exactly the kind of fixing we accuse the nationalists themselves of engaging in.

Shankar demonstrates through close readings of the three Tamil works that vernacular writing itself often works across national borders, even if postcolonial theory has no vocabulary for understanding such vernacular forms that move in multiple directions at once, ironizing "the notion that mimicry is disruptive of the authority of colonial discourse."[12] He thus takes elegant but direct aim at Homi Bhabha's effort to equate the vernacular with a minority perspective as something of value, to the exclusion of the "local," the "traditional," and other such terms that fix our critical attention. Shankar's criticism is that the latter category comes to represent an authentic culture inevitably defined by what Bhabha calls "the driving cataract of history, flowing relentlessly in the direction of the global."[13] In such a scenario, the local cannot but be fixed and then appropriated by the transnational forces of capitalism.

Bhabha, too, is looking for alternative narratives of translation. His 1997 introduction to a special issue of *Critical Inquiry* on "minority maneuvers" calls for a politics of freedom and hope attentive to the minoritarian perspectives often left out of the homogeneous empty time of nationalist discourse. The move is not only laudable but important; Bhabha is interested in articulating what he calls the "double reflexivity of the middle voice" that might turn an anxious, melancholic attachment to "the trap of identity" into a more flexible "dialectic of difference," one that does not "represent the numerical measure of majority and minority" as much as open up, "within a political movement, a form of social agency."[14]

Such a strategy might remind us of the discussion of dialectical humor in the previous chapter, for it forces us to recognize these forces as dynamic and to see that finding true equilibrium in such an exchange depends on the individual contributions of the performers at any given time. In his 2000 article "The Aura of Authenticity," Aamir Mufti makes the call for the inclusion of minoritarian voices in our theorizing even more trenchant: he works from Bhabha's articulation of "minority maneuvers" to point more specifically to what he calls the "double movement" of cultural critique, charging that "The task of criticism with respect to the struggles for authentic forms of selfhood in the postcolonial world is not to authenticate the violent attempts to restore aura to culture that these struggles often produce. It is rather to make visible the workings of this aura and the social costs of these attempts at its restoration."[15] Even if he does not address explicitly the hierarchical relationship between English and vernacular that underwrites such an exchange, his approach helps us to articulate a transnational version of the argument by Stallybrass and White discussed in the previous chapter: that it is less productive to label any of these cultural expressions we study as inherently conservative or progressive; rather, our task is to identify the epistemological divisions these cultural artifacts help institute.

Mufti makes clear in this case that we are to be suspicious of our own reliance on nationalist rhetoric in postcolonial criticism, but he still leaves open the nagging question: How specifically are we to read the "double movement" he points to in the vernacular?[16] My suggestion from the previous chapter is that we understand these modes of exchange as moving in more than one direction at once, across space, time, language, medium, as flexible, dynamic dialectics of difference not fixed in any set nationalist or postnationalist narratives. How might we incorporate an awareness of language hierarchies into our discussions of these ongoing literary relationships?

Irresistibly, Bhabha discusses this dialectic relying on the trope of translation, one he describes as a poetics of liminality. He announces that "The
critical edge of minority writing is born of this tangential temporality
that resignifies or translates the discourse of the majority in terms of the
minoritarian tradition determined by its point of tangential departure,"
and goes on to cite Alasdair MacIntyre's notion of translation at the end
of *Whose Justice? Which Rationality?* which, he says, "suggests that, where
difference exists not only as incompatibility but as incommensurability, we
must learn the poetic art of knowing how to go on by going through the
disjunction of the untranslatable, itself a liminal breach in the object."[17] In
Bhabha's writing, such a breach is figured not only spatially but temporally,
allowing our critical response to move to a future that "in the midst of the
translation of theory and politics, or anxiety and emergence, . . . brings the
past nearer, too."[18] And yet, whether spatial or temporal, the movement of
"going through" figures itself in his work in unidirectional terms.

In his 2004 article "Midnight's Orphans," Shankar joins Bhabha in sounding a similarly hopeful note but refines Bhabha's articulation of social agency
by complicating the terms of vernacular translation. He asks skeptically: "is
not the notion that the driving cataract of history moves relentlessly in the
direction of the global a form of metanarrative needing careful elucidation?"[19]
For Shankar, the careful elucidation he proposes is done most effectively by
creating a critical language that links "translation as practice and as trope in
the postcolonial context," a project I have endeavored to take up in my own
writing.[20] Shankar contends that such an approach should allow "the felicities
and fallibilities of comparativism as a methodology capable of drawing into
critical light hitherto ignored aspects of the postcolonial," which he sees specifically as "the place of the vernacular within the national imaginary," not as
a fixed, stable site of authenticity as terminus but as one of many fraught loci
actively participating in these ongoing (and historically unequal) globalwide
exchanges.[21] Here, then, we are presented with a practical instantiation of the
network of translation that I discuss in the previous chapter as an ongoing
chain of playfully positional triangular relationships. What part do we each
play in managing the endless supply chain of *Weltliteratur-as-Weltmarkt*?
The choice to sell or not to sell vernacular literature in translation to the
world market—and if so, how—offers an exceedingly material if not crass
example of what Bhabha sees as "the possibility of choice—ethical, aesthetic,
political—in those negotiations of culture and identity," even if it does not

manifest in quite the sublime form of incommensurability that Bhabha might have imagined.[22]

Rushdie's introduction to *The Vintage Book of Indian Writing 1947–1997* attends more directly to the inequalities of the world market: besides Rabindranath Tagore winning the Nobel Prize for literature earlier in the century, he offers, no translated work from Indian languages has "ever made much of an impact on world literature."[23] For him, the category of "world literature" is one that is obvious and would necessarily drive not only his but any criteria of literary evaluation. What might this be when it comes to translated work? He tells us that he and his coeditor, Elizabeth West (I'll draw our attention only this once to the inadvertent symbolism of the name West), tried not to be prejudiced, tried simply "to make the best possible selection from what is presently available in the English language, including, obviously, work in translation."[24] The result, in this particular case, was that "to our considerable astonishment, only one translated text—S. H. Manto's masterpiece, the short story, *Toba Tek Singh*—made the final cut."[25]

It is perhaps not surprising that they would choose a text that darkly ironizes the nationalist categories that not only Bhabha and Mufti but many of us hold in such suspicion. What is surprising, however, is that such a literary critique would work so well in English translation and that we as postcolonial critics have so little critical language for reading the link between translation as practice and as trope in this particular postcolonial context which is both vernacular and transnational in addition to being postcolonial. Here in this chapter, I apply such an approach to the practice of comparing multiple translations of "Toba Tek Singh," a modern literary text that itself plays self-consciously and ironically with the very idea of a fixed versus fluid mapping of these dialects of difference in order to ask how attention to the details of vernacular work in translation might offer an opportunity for us to approach the gaps of untranslatability in our own transnational, transcultural, translingual, and therefore hierarchical exchanges with more complexity.

Common Ground

Aamir Mufti devotes an entire chapter of *Enlightenment in the Colony* to the short stories of Saadat Hasan Manto so that he may think critically about what he calls "the relationship of Urdu literature in the two decades before the Partition of India to the canonical forms of nationalism."[26] The project of his monograph more generally, he writes, is to address "the problematic of secularization and minority in post-liberal culture as a whole."[27] In *Limiting Secularism: The Ethics of Coexistence in Indian Literature and Film*, Priya Kumar likewise focuses on Partition and post-Partition texts, including the stories of Manto, to offer what she calls "a fundamental rethinking of the very origins of the Indian nation-state," which she considers premised on the Muslims of India being *"contained* in the role of the minority" in "ambivalently coded anomalous citizenship."[28] For Kumar, a thoughtful engagement with these literary texts offers the opportunity to explore "the ethics of coexistence" of her title, an ethics that is neither complacent nor patronizing but reworks this shattered sense of provisional unity that we have all inherited, through what she, too, refers to as a strategic "double movement":[29]

> On the one hand, at the macro level of nation and state, we must work toward the creation of alternate public spheres that can recognize and acknowledge the suffering of victims of mass violence or genocide; on the other, at the micro level, we must also allow for the rebuilding of interpersonal relationships and the establishment of new ways of inhabiting the world together for communities and survivors.[30]

As above, but here more pointedly, I suggest that this double movement will be more productive if we become aware of the hidden third term of translation necessarily involved when a fluid multilingual, multiethnic environment is divided along fixed categories.

Treating these exchanges (whether at the national level or the interpersonal) as sites of translation forces us to recognize the ways we, as English speakers, are implicated in the complicated history of the vernaculars being used in relation to English to draw dividing lines from above, as if the distinction between "Hindi" and "Urdu," for example, were natural and inevitable.[31] Both Mufti and Kumar grapple with the complicated limits of the secularist project in postcolonial India as it relates to the minority figure in nationalist discourse and make a compelling case that these crucial conversations must involve literature scholars.[32] But in making translational "fidelity" the unexamined goal without recognizing the implicit faith-based categories employed in reading literary texts across languages, they run the same risk so many have spoken of in treating the discourse of secularism itself as neutral.[33] How, then, do we read a postcolonial, vernacular story in English that itself questions the identity-based, nationalist categories on which so much world literature unconsciously depends?

"Toba Tek Singh" narrates the unresolvable quest of an insane asylum inmate named Bishan Singh who is trying to make sense of the violent partition of the former colony of India into the two separate, independent nations of India and Pakistan in 1947. Singh is scheduled to be transferred across the new border from Pakistan into India because, being Sikh, he is a minority in this newly formed Muslim nation, and the story recounts his befuddlement that he could suddenly not belong to the place that has been his home for most of his life and the home of generations of family members before him. The riddle of belonging that we see in the previous two chapters here assumes a version referring to real-life, concrete incidents of irreversible but abstract division: How can one have faith in the social fabric once it has been torn in two?

"Toba Tek Singh" articulates these questions so powerfully that it is included in numerous English-language historical accounts and literary anthologies that self-consciously cross boundaries of language, culture, and nation but also of discipline.[34] The historians Sugata Bose and Ayesha Jalal, for example, end an agonized description of the violent division of Partition by admitting, "The colossal human tragedy of the partition and its aftermath has been better conveyed by sensitive creative writers and artists—for example in Saadat Hasan Manto's short stories and Ritwik Ghatak's films—than by historians."[35] Gyanendra Pandey, too, while laying out the ground, as it were, of the events surrounding "the three Partitions of 1947," asks meaningfully: "Where would, or could, Toba Tek Singh 'go,' in Manto's justly famous query?"[36]

Historian Mushirul Hasan, in his introduction to the first of several books devoted entirely to the issue of Partition, sets the names of creative writers such as Mir Taqi Mir, Qurat-ul-ayan Hyder, Faiz Ahmed Faiz, and Saadat Hasan Manto alongside political figures such as Jawaharlal Nehru and Mohammed Al Jinnah (nationalist leaders and the first prime ministers of India and Pakistan respectively) when trying to understand how such an event could have ever been conceived of—before, during, and after the fact.[37] His book is remarkable in that he includes Manto's short story "Toba Tek Singh" (in an English translation by Khalid Hasan) alongside documents from the day such as Jinnah's pivotal two-nation theory speech delivered in Lahore in 1940, excerpts from Gandhi's collected works, and Nehru's *Discovery of India*, as well as historical interpretations by contemporary scholars such as Partha Chatterjee and Lance Brennan. (Notably, most of the contributions were written originally in English, including Jinnah's divisive speech and Nehru's nationalist odyssey.)

Hasan went on to edit a companion volume, *India Partitioned: The Other Face of Freedom*, which he introduces by explaining, "The first volume encapsulated three overarching themes: the Muslim League's mobilization campaigns, the meanings attached to the 'two-nation' theory, the bloody legacy of Partition and the nightmare of millions uprooted from their homes and separated from family and friends. They bore the brunt of their country's Partition."[38] He then observes with moving simplicity, "Official records do not reflect their pain and agony, their fear and afflictions, and their sense of dismay and disillusionment. Creative writing does."[39] I write this chapter in the belief that we, as literary scholars, have an ethical responsibility to respond seriously to such quests for meaning, noting most particularly the use of English to render these accounts comparable, translatable. What critical vocabulary might we use to attend to the details of narrative construction that made a story such as "Toba Tek Singh" so imminently repeatable across multiple languages?

We cannot ignore the brutal facts of the violent events leading up to and following Partition that have made the story so meaningful to people half a century later. At the same time, we must acknowledge that it is not entirely the real-life situation referenced but the way these experiences have been translated that has so captured people's imaginations. What does this literary text accomplish that so many historical texts could not? In 1961, when he was called upon to write a history of modern India, Percival Spear's otherwise objective language turned florid and figurative as he struggled to describe the violence that accompanied Partition:

> From the day of independence the Panjab was in turmoil. Broadly speaking, Sikhs and Hindu Jats fell on the Muslims of the east Panjab and Muslims on the Sikhs and Hindus of the west Panjab. Communal fury mounted to frenzy and was fed on reports of what the other side had done elsewhere. Whole villages were exterminated and trainloads of migrants butchered as they huddled in the coaches. The administration was paralyzed, and the Boundary Force was helpless because its sympathies were too sharply divided. Soon the massacres

resolved into two lines of migration which piled up into convoys 30,000 to 40,000 strong. As refugees arrived in Delhi at the end of August, the same frenzy overtook the capital. . . . By mid-1948 it was estimated that five and one-half million refugees had been moved *each way* between West Pakistan and the western border of India, with another million and one-quarter moving from East Pakistan into West Bengal. Later, 400,000 Hindus left Sind in Pakistan for India. The exact number of casualties is unknown, but the dead are thought to have approached the million mark. The horrors of the episode and the size of the migrations embittered the relations of the two countries and left a deep scar on the consciousness of both.[40]

Such a rhetorical strategy acts as if assuming the role of the seemingly impartial Boundary Force trying to restore order somehow. This seemingly nonpartisan, distant perspective on the numbers of dead and displaced depicts more than anything the mirroring of the violence that took place on each side of the new border, as members of each community took revenge for wrongs done to their people. The final image in Spear's description of the "deep scar" left on the two populations underscores this unnerving symmetry, inviting us to regard the scene as we would two twins left wounded after a fight. The image recalls René Girard's discussion in *Violence and the Sacred* of mimetic doubles whose similarities compel them to fight to the death. Such a comparison makes even more sense in a colonial and then postcolonial context, as Partha Chatterjee has described it, each nationalist narrative so worried that it be seen as "derivative discourse" that it must "relentlessly . . . demarcate itself from the discourse of colonialism."[41] In such a schema, each side would be anxiously imitating the same imagined origin, struggling first to differentiate themselves from it and then from each other in mirrored gestures of violence.[42]

In their more recent history of South Asia, Sugata Bose and Ayesha Jalal figure the land not as twins but as one anguished individual, abject in its suffering: "The dawn of independence came littered with the severed limbs and blood-drenched bodies of innocent men, women and children: this is the nightmare from which the subcontinent has never fully recovered."[43] This description of collective pain metaphorizes even more explicitly the image of the subcontinent as a single, wounded body divided against itself. In this version, what residents of the subcontinent have in common across the national borders is a "wounded attachment"—in Wendy

Brown's phrasing—to these fixed communal identities as forever separate and painful.[44] The attempt to create a common narrative across the contentious communal borders of South Asia makes more explicit the inherent contradictions that arise trying to work from a provisional notion of "community"—imagined or otherwise. The puzzle over the dialectic of difference that I show Shankar, Bhabha, and Mufti worrying at in the previous section assumes an even more intricate form in reference to the literature of Partition, when the attempt to find commonality across these borders or identify within strengthens the very tropes that led to the violence in the first place. The question we are faced with is a version of the riddle Bishan Singh must solve: Is there an ethically (and even ethnically) neutral space in which we might locate ourselves vis-à-vis these partitioned narratives?

Postcolonial critics have asked a specific version of this riddle in response to Benedict Anderson's work on the nation as "imagined community": What are the grounds on which we might compare one nation to another?[45] Partha Chatterjee objects to Anderson's characterization of the politics of nationalism as inclusive in contradistinction to the politics of ethnicity as exclusive, divisive: "Such a conception of politics requires an understanding of the world as *one*, so that a common activity called politics can be seen to be going on *everywhere*."[46] This leads Chatterjee to conclude pessimistically that "Politics, in this sense, inhabits the empty homogeneous time of modernity."[47]

To find a more flexible and heterogeneous rubric for understanding these translations in postcolonial politics, we might look to Shankar's distinction between a vernacular and a transnational postcolonialism so that we might begin interrogating the assumption that such translations must be understood in the modern, nationalist terms that can only read multiplicity as exemplary of a postlapsarian, post-fall-of-the-Tower-of-Babel narrative of chaotic destruction. Pheng Cheah notes in the introduction to *Grounds of Comparison* that "the nation is also imagined in spatial coordinates and its boundaries bring to mind contiguity to *other* national bodies, but within the *same* world. This makes comparison an inevitable component of nationalism."[48] Given the specters of comparison that we consider in the previous chapter, we know it does not necessarily follow that the work of comparison—including translation and historiography—relies on a nationalist framework and is therefore bound in what Anderson refers to as "homogenous, empty time."[49]

Naoki Sakai observes that "the putative unities of national languages" are constituted precisely through the operation of translation, which is "represented as a form of communication between two fully formed, different but *comparable* language communities."[50] If such representation is a historical construct, he continues hopefully, then "there should be many different ways to apprehend translation in which the subjectivity of a community does not necessarily constitute itself in terms of language unity or the homogeneous sphere of ethnic or national culture."[51] This is one of the challenges, I would argue, that the history of Partition in general and translations of "Toba Tek Singh" in particular urge us to address.

Pandey, for one, devotes an entire book to investigating "what that moment of rupture, and the violent founding of new states claiming the legitimacy of nation-statehood, tells us about the procedures of nationhood, history and particular forms of sociality."[52] He argues that "in the history of any society, narratives of particular experiences of violence go towards making the 'community'—and the subject of history."[53] In his view, it is not the narratives per se but our inflexible relationship to them that maps a troublesome terrain.[54] By way of example, he compares accounts of a single incident that took place in Garhmukhteshwar in November 1946, "the site of a massacre of Muslims on the occasion of an annual fair," in order to understand better the relationship between the "local" and the "global" in producing narratives of violence.[55] After all, one of his aims in writing the book "is to underscore . . . how different the history of Partition appears from different perspectives."[56] By reading the colonial administrator's disdainful accounts of the "savagery" alongside vaguely triumphant reports by National Congress sources ("the violence, which was already spiralling, had quickly been stopped")[57] as well as outraged responses by the Muslim League representatives ("The houses of [the] minority community were singled out, marked with chalk and shown to the marauders by the villagers of the majority community"),[58] he shows that some local stories "cannot—apparently—be narrativised."[59]

They cannot be narrativized because they do not fit neatly into the "beginning, middle, and end" narrative of global progress (as Chatterjee also argues). From the perspective of the colonialists, most specifically, the narratives create an impression that such incidents of disorder are seen to be there, waiting on the margins, "self-evident, one-dimensional and unchanging."[60] Like the unruly lower-class "other" whom, Stallybrass and

White argue, the elite depended on to construct their provisional sense of order amidst the liveliness of carnival, here we see that the performance of nonsensical violence helps the colonialists—and transnational scholars in turn—mark out a common sense they might affirm across borders.

Pandey's critique of the (colonialist) narrative framework recalls the charges in Edward Said's influential polemic *Orientalism* that "Orientalism depends for its strategy on this flexible *positional* authority, which puts the Westerner in a whole series of possible relationships with the Orient without ever losing him the relative upper hand."[61] And more important for this study, Pandey's critique recalls Said's charge that Orientalism was based on "a proclivity to divide, subdivide, and redivide its subject matter without ever changing its mind about the Orient as being always the same, unchanging, uniform."[62]

In *Siting Translation*, Tejaswini Niranjana applies this Saidian critique to the issue of translation most particularly to suggest that "translation participates—across a range of discourses—in the *fixing* of colonized cultures, making them seem static and unchanging rather than historically constructed."[63] She then adds a provocative statement that, as in Pandey's work, points to a potential site of agency: "Translation functions as a transparent presentation of something that already exists, although the 'original' is actually brought into being through translation."[64] The task that I have set here in this chapter is to think more carefully about what kind of "original" is actually brought into being through the eleven different translations of "Toba Tek Singh" that I have chosen to analyze—which is to inquire, after Pandey: What different perspectives do these versions offer across a range of categorical differences?

We know that "Toba Tek Singh" was written by Manto in Urdu not long after Independence, just after he had made the considerably anguished—and, many conjecture, quite impulsive—decision to leave his home in Bombay, India, and establish a new base for himself in Lahore, Pakistan, in a new nation where Muslims such as himself would be in the majority and Urdu was the official language of the state. These biographical details—a Muslim living in Pakistan and writing in Urdu—might seem to paint the portrait of somebody who has placed himself very squarely on one decidedly polarized side of the communal borderline. After all, one of the most tragic outcomes of Partition was that it forced stark divisions in so many facets of life—as members of villages, families, language groups, cultures, histories—that before had offered a sense of association and identification that was fairly flexible and heterogeneous. But we can see from reading both his fiction and his nonfiction that Manto was extremely suspicious of such clear-cut divisions.

He began his writing career as a translator, bringing Victor Hugo's *The Last Days of a Condemned Man* and Oscar Wilde's *Vera* into Urdu before going on to pen his own fairly transgressive prose.[65] While his writings do not hint at a romantic longing for a precolonial time when there was no distinction between Hindi and Urdu—as, for example, the titles of Amrit Rai's book *A House Divided* and Christopher King's *One Language, Two Scripts* would imply—it becomes clear from his fiction and nonfiction alike that he was no nationalist.[66] Work like "Toba Tek Singh" suggests that he felt himself caught in the contradiction so many translators find themselves caught in, yearning for a single, transcendent language to unify all humankind, all expression, and at the same time reveling in and even feeling protective of the differences between the individual languages.

The story "Toba Tek Singh" has become allegorical in our day in the same way the tale of the Tower of Babel has articulated in the Judeo-Christian tradition a kind of confusion that finds expression no other way. Each of the stories helps us understand the ways our narratives about multilinguality try to solve the puzzle over the dialectic of difference. Writing about the Babel myth in his essay "Des Tours de Babel," Jacques Derrida explains, "This story recounts, among other things, the origin of the confusion of tongues, the irreducible multiplicity of idioms, the necessary and impossible task of translations, its necessity *as* impossibility."[67] And while the builders of the Tower of Babel worked in the plural to "make [them] selves a name, that [they] not be scattered over the face of all the earth,"[68] the protagonist in Manto's story begins the solitary search for his place on this earth babbling a nonsensical mishmash of languages and taking the name of his hometown "Toba Tek Singh" (a signifier without signified, it would seem) during an era when a Babel-like scattering has already occurred. Implicitly "Toba Tek Singh," like the tale of the Tower of Babel, asks us to consider a more general metatextual riddle: On what basis do we find language in common when telling the story of language(s) dividing us against one another?

Such a riddle requires us to map our differences in world community neither in "homogeneous, empty time" nor in homogenous, empty space.

As we see in the previous chapter, India's contentious multilingual history in particular demands a new approach to mapping imagined community that allows overlaps and gaps, contradictions and conflations. The approach I am advocating necessarily complicates Anderson's much-quoted line that "imagined communities" are not defined strictly by the limits of physical territory, nor will their members ever "know most of their fellow-members, meet them, or even hear of them," especially in an age where various media can carry news around the world, yet somehow "in the minds of each lives the image of their communities."[69] Here the image of the community in the singular becomes divided against itself. All over the world, as Anderson details, these "imagined communities" have come to define themselves both through and in terms of language; in South Asia, such distinctions became one of the images of that division.

It should be understood that one of the most incendiary issues raised during the nationalist movement to oust the British was which "vernacular" should replace English as the language of rule; in the case of Hindi versus Urdu versus Hindustani, linguistic identity was represented by script—with Hindi as Hindu in the same script as Sanskrit, Urdu as Muslim in the script of Persian and Arabic, and Hindustani written variously, including in roman letters.[70] At certain points, nationalists such as Gandhi tried to argue that roman letters would be the least divisive, but it was difficult to shake the association with English as the language of the colonizer. Then, as now, speakers of Indian languages were still living with the institutional effects of Thomas Macaulay's explicit comparison in his 1835 Minute on Indian Education, in which he claims to have endeavored to "form a correct estimate of the value" of indigenous languages such as Sanskrit and Arabic by appealing to the "valuation of the Orientalists themselves," and "never found one of them who could deny that a single shelf of a good European library was worth the whole native literature of India and Arabia."[71]

At Macaulay's urging, a system of English education was adopted in India that would, as he said, "form a class who may be interpreters between us and the millions whom we govern; a class of persons, Indian in blood and colour, but English in taste, in opinions, in morals, and in intellect."[72] So a century later, when nationalists worked to assume governance, English was the language Nehru used to write *The Discovery of India*; English was the language Jinnah used to write and deliver his "two-nation" speech, English was the language used by the activists in London who penned the manifesto for the

All India Progressive Writers Union in 1935 (as I discuss in more detail in the following chapter). Their manifesto was later translated into various indigenous languages, but its genealogy shows that the imaginary territory of this nation's common ground was imagined as being charted largely in English. I would even suggest that the violence that accompanied Independence testified in part to the overlapping and contradictory forms that nationalism assumed, as nationalists advocated a unified community of language speakers that was next to impossible in a multilingual country such as India.

Sumathi Ramaswamy has shown most persuasively how the pressures to counter the colonial-era movement in the north to make Hindi the national language resulted in Tamil speakers rallying around their mother tongue as a mother goddess to be venerated in absolute terms. She begins her study with a scene of a series of sacrifices taking place in 1964 and 1965 that were widely reported by newspapers to be in the name of "Death to Hindi" and "life for Tamil" (*"inti olika!" "uyir tamilukku"*).[73] She is justifiably reluctant to adopt the narratives of "fanaticism" that are often used to describe such events and instead asks:

> How do I, a late-twentieth-century historian, make sense of these deaths? Disciplined by history, I would naturally demand, What is it that led so many men and women to proclaim that they would live and die for their language? Why did they so passionately confess that a life without Tamil is not worth living?[74]

This she announces as her effort to ask "the language question" (Gramsci's *"questione della lingua"*) in such a way that includes "the 'unassimilable,' the 'untranslatable,' the 'different'—. . . the stuff of histories written in a post-colonial moment."[75] Rather than assuming the isomorphic one-language-equals-one-nation formula, she investigates the *"parru"* (the structure of affect and sentiment) that accrues around Tamil so that speakers are urged "to cultivate *tamilpparru*" and "not to sacrifice *tamilpparru* for worldly gains."[76] In the end, however, she is forced to conclude that the narratives of the devout Tamil speakers demand such sacrifices in the very ways they rely on the modern grammar of (language) possession:

> In order to enable Tamil to live and flourish, *tamilpparru* transforms its speakers, who ought to have been masters of the language, into its subjects, a critical reversal of the patrimonial imagination it inherited from European modernity. Their dearest possession, their language, ends up by possessing its devotees, compelling them to sacrifice to it their body, life and spirit.[77]

Pheng Cheah could very well read Ramaswamy's study as an example of the "vitalist imagery" that he argues haunts the modern nation. Such an interpretation—in which the life-and-death tropes of language narratives are seen as a modern phenomenon positing a many-to-one relationship between citizen and nationalized body—is underscored by Sheldon Pollock's insistent observation that "Prior to Europeanization, no southern Asian writer ever biologized the relationship to the vernacular as one of maternal generation."[78] Yet such a reading does not explain why the maternal body would have to be figured in the singular—especially in cultures where the mother goddess herself is depicted as having many forms. Ramaswamy ponders the riddle that is—as the title of her second chapter has it—"one language, many imaginings": she notes that in the anti-Hindi Dravidianist regime, "descent is reckoned solely from Tamil, which is not merely one among a 'family' of languages *in* a putative Indian nation . . . but is *the* language *of* the nation."[79]

In many of her examples, as in the passage noted above, Ramaswamy makes clear that Tamil is necessarily figured in opposition to the other primary modern vernacular of the nation (Hindi) or the other primary classical language (Sanskrit) that it must displace for precedence. This is a winner-takes-all contest. Like Girard's mimetic double, it is believed that to survive, the language must kill its chief competitor. Sakai would have us understand instead that its survival defines itself in terms of an other language—Tamil against Hindi, for example, Hindi against Urdu, or Telugu against Tamil (as Lisa Mitchell shows). In Jean-Luc Nancy's phrase, we can only be "singular plural," that is, we cannot be singular except in comparison to others. The case of India is an important example, since these relationships between singular-plural languages form not just transnationally but within the nation. A story such a "Toba Tek Singh" is popular precisely because it forces us to rethink the Tower-of-Babel narratives that teach us that multilinguality is dangerous. How might we read the ironies of this story so as to challenge our own monolingual expectations in English?

Tower of Babble

How do we read a translated text multilingually? I will answer the question with a practical demonstration of a critical reading practice, taking as an example not only Khalid Hasan's 1987 translation of "Toba Tek Singh," which was anthologized by Mushirul Hasan in 1993 and Rushdie and West in 1997, but ten other versions of greater and lesser renown that have appeared in forms oral and written, actual and virtual, in America, England, Pakistan, India, and elsewhere from 1970: Robert Haldane's version appeared in an American academic journal in 1970; Tahira Naqvi's version was published in Pakistan in 1985 in a volume of Manto's work; Jai Ratan's version was published in India in 1987 in a collection of Urdu writing; Harish Trivedi's version was published in India in 1993 in an anthology of Hindu and Urdu short stories; Madan Gupta's version was published in India in 1997 in a collection of Manto's writing; G. A. Chaussée read his version at a book festival in the United States in 2000; M. Asaduddin's translation was published in India in 2001 in an anthology on Partition; Sundeep Dougal's version (which he—with self-effacing humor—calls "hurried, pathetic") was also published in 2001 in a current events magazine in India; Richard McGill Murphy's version was published in an online literary journal; and Frances Pritchett's version published on an academic Web site for South Asian literature in 2005.

What grounds of comparison might we rely on to compare these translations? The traditional reaction would be to line up each of the English versions side-by-side with Manto's Urdu text and comb through them line by line, pointing out where each of the translations (as copy, imitation) falls short of the original. This approach, of course, would take advantage of the specialized knowledge of the bilingual reader (which for professional and personal reasons I am loathe to discount) but then leaves us with the same problem: How do we critique the bilingual reader's construction of that original, especially if it is inaccessible to the English reader (who, we might note after looking at the publication details listed above, is just as likely to live in South Asia as anywhere else in the world)?

In any case, such a schema assumes a pristine separation between the world of the Urdu text and the world of the English, which I am arguing against. Even if a bilingual reader could cleanly divide her Urdu consciousness from her English, there would still exist a translation problem, in that she would then need to render her thoughts and impressions of her Urdu reading experience into English. Do we disregard the rhetoric of her critical expressions in English, assuming Urdu and English to be exactly equivalent, the second language a perfectly transparent conduit of her Urdu-inspired thoughts?[80] And even if this were possible, it does not allow us to take into greater account the ways these English translations have served to construct the original, as per Niranjana's suggestion. My aim, then, is to compare these eleven different English versions of "Toba Tek Singh" as a way of setting out a reading practice of translated work that might then be used by a reader not necessarily conversant with Urdu to assess other translations—of "Toba Tek Singh" or other pieces of prose—in a manner that helps us see the "double movement" Mufti describes, making visible both the workings of nationalist aura and the social costs of these attempts at its restoration. Take, for example, the first few sentences of Hasan's translation that so caught Rushdie's and West's eyes:

> A couple of years after the Partition of the country, it occurred to the respective governments of India and Pakistan that inmates of lunatic asylums, like prisoners, should also be exchanged. Muslim lunatics in India should be transferred to Pakistan and Hindu and Sikh lunatics in Pakistani asylums should be sent to India.[81]

The authoritativeness of the narrator's voice assumes a knowledge of the time and place of Partition, even a memory of the "country" (note the use of this term establishing commonality beyond ethnic, linguistic, and national distinctions) before it was divided into two nations. Like Bose and Jalal's description of the violence of Partition, the rhetoric here strives to be evenhanded in apportioning blame to the Indian and Pakistani sides. But unlike the historical accounts, this translation makes an implicit distinction between the state—actually, the two governments—and the ethnically branded citizens who are moved across these national borders, all in a bureaucrat's day's work.

Hasan's translation, however, does not exaggerate the soul-numbing functionality of these bureaucratic transfers as much as I do in the sentence above. To find that, we would need to look at the (purposefully?) awkward formulation in Naqvi's translation, which—as it happens—declines to maintain (as most of the other translations do) the exact grammatical symmetry in describing the conditions of transfer from Pakistan to India and India to Pakistan:

> Two or three years after the Partition, it occurred to the governments of India and Pakistan that along with the transfer of the civilian prisoners, a transfer of the inmates of the lunatic asylums should also be made. In other words, Muslim

lunatics from Indian institutions should be sent over to Pakistan, and Hindu and Sikh lunatics from Pakistani asylums should be allowed to go to India.[82]

In this and all of the translations, attention is drawn to the inmates' ethnic markers, but in a way that makes it clear that this is a state-mandated designation, not the personal classificatory system of the narrator, which makes the classification system appear somewhat ridiculous—which, in turn, gives the story its humor. This is a different ironic effect from the one we encounter in Detha's storytellerish prose in the first chapter. How can we explain the sly effect of this particular translation?

Writing not on translated work but on irony in fiction more generally, Wayne Booth suggests that every act of reading offers an exercise in ideological contention. Ironic cues signal the reader that she will have to make a choice, he explains, between siding with the worldview implicit in the narrative or against it. "All authors . . . invite us to construct some sort of picture of their views and to judge them as in some sense coherent or plausible or challenging." Booth suggests that:

> ironic authors obviously offer that invitation more aggressively, and we must answer it more actively: since the reader has in a sense put the final position together for himself, he can scarcely resist moving immediately to the . . . judgment: "Not only do I see it for what it is, but it must be sound since it is my own."[83]

Elsewhere Booth compares these moments of textual irony to joking situations that take place in person.[84] As with the triangular joking relationship that Freud outlines, the reader is put in a position where she must choose sides: Will she laugh with the implied author at the situation (which could quite possibly mean laughing at the narrator), or will she refuse to participate in this dangerous moment of intimacy?[85] Booth describes these moments of ironic recognition as those of "joining, of finding and communing with kindred spirits,"[86] and elsewhere—most crucially for this particular example—of finding "common ground." Booth explains:

> From Aristotle until the nineteenth century, treatises on rhetoric as the art of persuasion always included an account of the intellectual "locations" that could provide such points of agreement. Once found, these locations—what the Greeks call *topoi*, the Latins *loci*, and the English *places*—were used almost literally as platforms on which speaker and listener could securely stand while

conducting an argument; there were, of course *"common* places," yielding points useful in arguments on any and every subject, and "special places" useful only for certain subjects or kinds of arguments.[87]

He goes on to explain that the pleasure in irony results from the movement from one "common" place—the ground where we imagine the narrator standing—to another—the common ground we share with a projected authority (which Booth terms the "implied author"). For example, in Naqvi's translation, we read "Muslim lunatics" and "Hindu and Sikh lunatics" and are forced to decide: do we value these ethnic distinctions or imagine we're joining the author and his ilk in making fun of people who parrot such distinctions?[88] In the case of translated work, I suggest that the translator becomes part of the plural construct that we might call, along with Booth, an "implied author." It is the translator with whom we share a language and therefore a judgment about the value of these ethnic distinctions; the resulting judgment we imagine more trustworthy when we can imagine the translator herself a reader in turn similarly engaged with the author in an ongoing chain of triangular exchanges—as we see in the previous chapter.

To map our interactions with these texts more accurately, we need to note the fact of these exchanges as ongoing triangular networks in such a manner that we may learn to measure the spaces between the points in these imaginary triangles as they connect four-dimensionally through time and space—the relative positions figured laterally in terms of political geography or linguistic geography or even vertically in terms of class hierarchy. M. Asaduddin's translation, for example, plays up the differences between everyday colloquial speech low to the ground and a more formal, written bureaucratese rendered as if floating above:

> Two or three years after the Partition, it occurred to the governments of
> Hindustan and Pakistan that, just as they had exchanged civilian prisoners,
> they should exchange the lunatics confined in the asylums as well. In other
> words, Muslim lunatics interred in the asylums of Hindustan should be sent to
> Pakistan, and the Hindu and Sikh lunatics confined in the asylums of Pakistan
> should be handed over to Hindustan.[89]

The narrative reveals through syntactic mimesis that it is as wryly skeptical of the stiff grammar of this impersonal state-sponsored exchange ("it occurred to the governments of Hindustan and Pakistan") as it is sympathetic to the straightforward bafflement of inmates suddenly treated as so much bureaucratic baggage ("Muslim lunatics . . . should be sent to Pakistan, and the Hindu and Sikh lunatics . . . should be handed over to Hindustan"). If we agree with Mufti that the task of criticism is "to make visible the workings of this aura [of authentic culture] and the social costs of these attempts at its restoration,"[90] then how might we read the double movement of this text between these poles of government functionality and an alienated citizenry? M. Asaduddin's translation of these opening lines makes clear that neither the government nor the citizenry perfectly represents the idea of the nation being claimed here in this description. What tools of literary analysis might help us map the complexity of the text's conceptual terrain?

Simplistic and binaristic definitions of irony—that the text says the opposite of what it means—fail to capture the dynamism suggested by Mufti's concept of "double movement" nor the conceptual agility implied by Bhabha's notion of "double reflexivity," which we notice in evidence in this translation. Instead, its irony might be understood more productively in the sense Hutcheon describes: as "an oscillating yet simultaneous perception of plural and different meanings."[91] Rather than positing a pair of contrasting points from which to view nationalist discourse (as authentic and original, for example, versus counterfeit and derivative), the story calls into question the very system of authenticity and originality that nationalist discourse often relies upon. We intuit that even the governmental syntax which seems to float above the citizenry, classifying them and translating them from one domain to the other (from "ours" to "theirs" and vice versa), can survive only if it has living, breathing, speaking citizens to classify and translate (as "ours" versus "theirs" and vice versa).

The story thus offers another version of the riddle of belonging discussed in previous chapters: that the nationalist narrative I rely on to identify (and thus draw boundaries around) you already includes the nationalist narrative you have relied on to identify (and thus draw boundaries around) me. Hutcheon's reading strategy helps us understand the dynamic loop we are already involved in, for she has us focus less on "the two 'poles' themselves" so that we might see instead that it is the "rapid perceptual or hermeneutic *movement between* them that makes this image a possibly suggestive and productive one for thinking about irony."[92] Such an image allows us to read, as she suggests, "ironic meaning as something in flux, and not fixed. It also implies a kind of simultaneous perception of more than one meaning . . . in order to create a third composite (ironic) one."[93] Treating the resulting meaning as a dynamic synthesis of an ongoing dialectic, she argues, should lead readers to take responsibility for the 'evaluative edge' they bring to a text and see that it is they, the interpreters, not the texts themselves, that create irony.[94]

To map such a dialectical engagement using the tropes developed in the previous chapters, we might see that the activity of interpretation (like translation and telling in turn) involves playing the part of audience (listener, reader) in one triangle in the chain of repetitions and turning around to play the part of performer (teller, writer) in the next. Where exactly "next" might be figured (performed afterwards in time? across a linguistic, cultural, national, regional border? up or down a range of audiences perhaps unfamiliar with the literary, unfamiliar with theoretical debates, unfamiliar with the historical issues of South Asia being addressed here, unfamiliar with on-the-ground realities of the people referenced in the story) reveals the ideologies framing our own metanarratives. As interpreter of Asaduddin's translation, for example, I might notice the distinctions in the narration between high-level government decisions and the people on the ground whose daily lives are affected by these decisions, so that when I recount this story (as I have done here), my interpretation maps the highs and lows of bureaucratic hierarchy rather than, for example, the distinctions of "Hindustan" versus "Pakistan" or "Muslim" versus "Hindu or Sikh." After all, writes Hutcheon:

> We all belong to many overlapping (and sometimes even conflicting) communities or collectives. . . . This overlapping is the condition that makes irony possible, even though the sharing will inevitably always be partial, incomplete, fragmentary; nevertheless, something does manage to get shared—enough, that is, to make irony happen.[95]

Moreover, she contends that "ironic discourse . . . is . . . *made possible by* . . . those different worlds to which each of us differently belongs."[96] Hutcheon's vision of the common ground that ironic literary texts establish recalls more than anything Benjamin's image of translation as a broken vessel (*tikkun*) whose fragments, de Man reminds us (once more) "will never constitute a totality."[97] James Boyd White contends that it is not only literary texts that play along the borders between languages and cultures (as the title of the volume to which he contributes terms it), but that any literary exchange should necessarily be regarded as partial, fragmentary, an exercise not so much of total understanding but of "not understanding,"[98] one "reminding the reader that one is always at the edge of what can be done" and what can be articulated in any given language.[99] White works from bell hooks's suggestion that we see "*not understanding* [my emphasis] as a space for learning" from each other.[100] I would like to argue that this space is exactly the place (that is, actually "no-place") we might imagine ourselves moving into in the future of criticism, one that understands that we can ground our own subject position only in relation to others.

We might notice, for example, that whether the translations refer to the inmates as "lunatics," "crazies" (in Chaussée's), or "madmen" (in Trivedi's), it does not become clear that the narrator is parodying government speak until the next few lines; this can be seen quite clearly in Haldane's version:

> Perhaps it was a good idea, perhaps not, but at any rate, wise heads had decided and so there were high level conferences on both ends. A date was even fixed for the exchange. There was a thorough investigation to determine which Muslims still had families in India. Those would remain there; the others would be taken to the border. Here in Pakistan, as almost all of the Hindus and Sikhs had left, there was no question of keeping any of them. All those remaining would be carried, in police custody, to the border.[101]

In this version, the more pronounced the bureaucratic disregard is for the inmates, the more sympathetic the inmates become. In Gupta's version, however, there is so much focus on the indelicacies of the governmental procedure in carrying these men across that the space in the reader's mind that might be reserved for the inmates' experiences drops away almost entirely:

> One doesn't know whether there was no sense in this but high-level conferences were held to implement this exchange. The matter was gone into in great detail. Muslim lunatics whose guardians were still in India were allowed to remain in India. The others were to be dispatched to the border. Practically all the Hindus and Sikhs had left Pakistan. Therefore the question of retaining any Hindu or Sikh lunatics there did not arise. All the Hindus and Sikhs were sent to the border under police protection.[102]

It is much harder to argue for an ironic reading of the story in this translation; with so much emphasis on one perspective, it is not clear if the narrator is imitating government speak with the aim of perhaps ridiculing it; nor is it clear between what two places we might imagine ourselves caught (in both the literal and the figurative sense). In each of the versions, the translator must decide whether to locate the narrator-reader pair ("us") "here in Pakistan"—as do Haldane, Trivedi, Chaussée, and Murphy—or to leave such imagined distinctions vague—as do Gupta and the rest. The choice says less about the translator's patriotic loyalties (of the eleven, only Tahira Naqvi and Khalid Hasan claim Pakistani citizenship and neither of them include the "here in Pakistan" phrase) and more about their efforts to create a sense of common ground. We need to consider instead whether these attempts to erase or even transcend the limits of nationalist-minded difference open up the "space of learning" that White urges us toward, or if a reader of a translated text needs these lines of imagined community mapped out more definitively so that she can better visualize the loci between which she is being urged to be moved (in multiple senses of the phrase).

No-Man's-Land

As the story progresses, we are introduced to the cast of characters who populate the insane asylum and then finally to the man whose fate we will follow most closely for the remainder of the story, a Sikh man named Bishan Singh who asks over and over again where his home town of Toba Tek Singh is—In India or in Pakistan? The various answers he receives to this simple question of belonging seem nonsensical, as we see in Ratan's translation:

> But nobody seemed to know where it was, much less whether it was in Hindustan or in Pakistan. Those who tried to explain, themselves got bogged down in another enigma. Sialkot which was in Hindustan now happened to be in Pakistan. At this rate, Lahore which was now in Pakistan may go over to Hindustan. For that matter, the whole of Hindustan may become Pakistan. It was all so confusing. For all he knew, one day both Hindustan and Pakistan may disappear from the face of the Earth.[103]

As readers, we begin to wonder if perhaps everyone in this historical moment has become mad even while these few individuals are conveniently separated from society. The narrator makes no explicit comment on such a possibility but simply explains flatly that Singh refuses to sit or lie and that he repeats nothing but an unintelligible mishmash of words when given a chance to speak. The string of words he repeats confounds any attempt to maintain strict borders between English and Urdu, Hindi, Hindustani, and Panjabi and so poses riddles of belonging in the realm of language that are similar to those he asks outright in the story in terms of geography. How are readers to make sense of such nonsensical babble as it is translated into English?

As we see in Chapter 3, Stewart contends that "Nonsense is the realization of the possibility that the discourse of everyday life could become totally conscious of its own procedures: it is . . . a halt to the ongoing nature of social discourse, and an extreme movement away from any conception of such discourse as natural."[104] These moments of nonsense catch us in that liminal zone between languages and cultures we move across, freezing the frame we were not necessarily aware was even there in such a way that suddenly we cannot ignore it. Not just as translators but as interpreters of these English-language versions, we suddenly feel the "evaluative edge" Hutcheon refers to cutting into our approach. Stewart tell us, "To engage in nonsense is not only to engage in a state of transition, it is also to engage in an exploration of the nature of the transition."[105]

We might notice that the "transition" Stewart refers to is not a point further along a linear narrative of progress, as Dipesh Chakrabarty and others critique, but a more complex, more literary understanding of a text that forces us to reckon with our own unconscious ideological mapping.[106] Suddenly we become aware of the sequence we provide for such a transition: Do we imagine the movement taking place afterwards in time? Across a linguistic, cultural, national, regional border? Up or down a range of audiences—those unfamiliar with the literary, unfamiliar with theoretical debates, unfamiliar with the historical issues of South Asia being addressed here, unfamiliar with on-the-ground realities of the people referenced in the story? These answers reveal much about the ideologies framing our own metanarratives. What do we imagine to be within the bounds of common sense and what do we exclude as nonsense?

A successful translation should allow us as readers to feel the evaluative edge we apply to the text and can do that only if it allows the prose to move beyond the confines of a neatly defined, homogeneous linguistic space and allows the lexicon and even the syntax to scatter beyond the ordinary boundaries, as we see in Haldane's version: "Upar di gar gar di anks di unawareness di mung di dal of the lantern."[107] The concern is that the reader will not trust that such a move is purposeful and will assume the translator was not in complete control of his own reading or writing. Notice, for example, the endearingly defensive endnote that Haldane adds: "Not only the statement as a whole but most of the words are meaningless gibberish." It seems Haldane is not comfortable enough with the shifting ground of the literary terrain he works on to play with it. And if he were, could his readers play along?

Similarly wary, Gupta refers to the "unintelligible reply" only indirectly, leaving out the nonsensical string of words altogether. Murphy, like Asaduddin, Dougal, and Pritchett, decides to transliterate the syllables directly: "*Upri gur gur di annexe di be-dhiyana di mung di daal of di laaltein.*" However, Dougal then provides a footnote that makes an attempt to provide a literal rendering of what he calls this "nonsensical phrase": "The lack of contemplation and lentils of the annexe of the above raw sugar of the lantern." As with the literal translation of the *chougou* presented in Chapter 2, the attempt to provide a word-for-word translation only shows how much we rely on syntax to find meaning in common. We can imagine that with two languages such as Urdu and English, which have so few grammatical structures in common, a word-for-word translation would turn even a straightforward commonsensical sentence into nonsense. How much should we, then, expect a translator to mediate? It is because of this very ambiguity that translators are often reluctant to risk letting their translations stray too far from the range of acceptability in the target language, even if they enjoy such transgressions (of "not understanding") in their reading of the source.

Trivedi, for example, supplies a partial literal rendering of these "strange words"—"opar di rumble-tumble di annexe of the thoughtless of the green lentils of the lantern"—and in the process leads his readers further into the terrain of the "Hindi" (for he claims to have translated the story not from Urdu but from the "original Hindi," on the basis of the script in which he read the story).[108] Those familiar with the languages he's mixing are invited to get involved in the game and try to parse the string of letters to form recognizable words like "annexe" versus "di axe" (as "the axe"), "good" or "gur" (as in jaggery), or "*di bay dhaniya*" ("the bay coriander") versus "*be-dhyaanaa,*" ("without concentration") in a game similar to the one we play reading Rushdie's *chamcha* prose.[109]

The string of syllables offers multilingual sound puzzles and in the process challenges the ethnically conceived boundaries associated with various scripts (as we shall discuss in more detail in the next chapter) and in its own playful way suggests that perhaps English's roman letters do end up appearing more neutral than the Hindi and the Urdu with their historical links to Hindu and Muslim religious texts written in Sanskrit and Arabic, respectively. In some way, the multilinguality of the humor cuts even more surely when framed as an English translation for the ways it cannot be located definitively in a single place on the (linguistic, national) map.

Chaussée's translation offers a particularly insightful example of this, not only because it was written to be performed orally in a diasporic, multilingual environment in the United States. The roman letters used in his personal copy were not meant to be published but instead were meant to cue him to read vowels long or short, consonants retroflex or dental, as if this were a storyteller's prompt book or even a musical score: "*OpaR dii guR guR dii aneks dii be-dhyaanaa dii mung dii daal aaf dii laalTen.*"[110] Because many in the audience were Indian-Americans studying with him, they knew some rudimentary Hindi or Urdu. The way his reading of the babble skirted between languages without making straightforward sense—especially from someone who was ordinarily so strict about making them follow the rules of grammar—made people laugh out loud in happy surprise. The technique should forces us to wonder what the difference is between nonsense and sense spoken in a foreign tongue and simply repeated without any mediation. How much "sense" do we have to have in a translation in order for it to be considered a translation?

Such a riddle forces us to ask larger questions about the role we expect the translator to play in framing sense for us. We might notice that Trivedi's self-conscious explanation of the meaning of "*tek*" in Hindi that he embeds in the narrative not only opens up the possibility of understanding this story in more than one language but also indicates another happy transgression, in that he's offering himself up not only as a writer of the text we're reading but as a critically engaged reader of the "Hindi" text before that:

> There was a Sikh who had been in the madhouse now for some fifteen years. Strange words were to be heard rolling off his tongue all the time: "Opar di rumble-tumble di annexe of the thoughtless of the green lentils of the lantern." He slept neither day nor night. The guards said he had not slept a wink all

these fifteen years. He never even lay down. All he might do sometimes was to take a "*tek*" or lean his back against a wall. Because he stood all the time his feet were swollen and his calves were distended but in spite of the physical discomfort he never lay down to rest. He listened attentively whenever there was a discussion among the madmen on Hindustan, Pakistan, and their own transfer from the one to the other. Whenever anyone asked him for his opinion he replied with utmost seriousness: "Opar di rumble-tumble di annexe of the thoughtless of the green lentils of the Government of Pakistan."[111]

In one swift move Trivedi has established multiple sets of common ground that work both in contention and in collusion through his text—those who understand the meaning of "*tek*" in context, those who would need the word to be translated into English ("lean his back against a wall"), those who, like Bishan Singh, can think across these languages and thus have a more complex reading of what it might mean to take a *tek* in "Toba *Tek* Singh." While ordinarily "Toba Tek Singh" is simply a proper name without greater meaning, Trivedi's translation turns the seeming telos of the story into a riddle: Can we find support in something when the sound of a word becomes separated from its meaning, when a name no longer designates the place where one belongs?

The story plays along the boundaries not only between languages but between speech and silence (as we saw in Chapter 2), between what one is able to say and what one cannot. In one especially moving scene, we see one of Bishan Singh's friends visit him in the asylum. In Dougal's translation, the syntactic coherence of this ostensibly sane man begins to break down as he tries to reassure Bishan Singh that he has been a reliable friend and neighbor amidst all the divisiveness:

> Fazal Din stepped forward and put his hands on Bishen Singh's shoulders. "I had been thinking of meeting you for many days, but remained caught up. Didn't get free . . . all your folks left for India safely . . . I helped all I could . . . your daughter Roop Kaur . . ." He paused mid-sentence.[112]

Suddenly the point of view shifts, and we see that "Bishen Singh strained his memory," repeating the words to himself, "Daughter Roop Kaur. . . ." It is clear from his friend's response—"Yeah, yeah . . . she too is safe . . . went with them only"—that the friend might be trying to conceal an unpleasant truth from Bishan Singh, one that Bishan Singh might very well be aware of. Perhaps the daughter was raped or even murdered, as she had to flee a home where she was no longer safe to find refuge in a new land that was now supposed to be where she belonged.[113]

Jai Ratan's translation shows the dialogue between the two being interrupted first when Fazal Din falls silent at the mention of Roop Kaur's name and soon thereafter when Bishan Singh "kept silent" at the assurances that "Yes, yes, she's all right. She too accompanied them."[114] Gupta's translation, however, does not insinuate as forcefully as the others that Fazal Din is trying to hide an awful truth about the daughter:

> Fazal Din came forward, put his hand on Bishan Singh's shoulder and said, "I was thinking of coming and seeing you for a long time but work kept me busy. All your relations have gone safely to Hindustan. Whatever help I could give, I gave. Your daughter Roop Kaur. . . ." He interrupted himself. Bishan Singh started thinking . . ."Daughter Roop Kaur. . . ." Fazal Din said haltingly, "She is alright. . . . She has also gone away with the rest." Bishan Singh was quiet. Fazal Din began again, "They had asked me to visit you and enquire about your welfare."[115]

Even though in this version Fazal Din's syntax seems less awkward and his narrative sequence less jumpy, the sudden reference to the daughter cannot help but raise a question the text does not answer. In every version, this ancillary enigma feels purposeful and thus related to the larger enigma driving the story.

Hasan's version has the friend putting his hand on Bishan Singh's shoulder as he reassures him, "All your family is well and has gone to India safely. I did what I could to help."[116] At that, he makes special mention of the daughter, hesitates, and adds, "She is safe too . . . in India." When the reader is wondering what the unspoken story of the daughter is, whether she is dead or alive, whether the journey across the border was arduous or noneventful, the choice of words used to describe these awkward pauses—as hesitations, interruptions, silences—becomes exceedingly significant.

The narrator in Dougal's translation, for example, tells us pointedly that in the face of Fazal Din's assurances, "Bishen Singh was silent."[117] Even more telling, Fazal Din begins sputtering uncomfortably in response to this silence—"They asked me to enquire after you . . . to see to your welfare . . . now I have heard you are going to India"—but we see that Bishan Singh is not distracted by this. He understands that this new divide between them is as arbitrary as it is dangerous. He repeats the question he has been repeating as often as the babble, this time with renewed significance: "Where is Toba Tek Singh?" Pritchett's version shows the humor of trying to answer such an impossible question with a simplicity that does not take into account the new realities of postcolonial, Partition logic:

> Fazal Din said with some astonishment, "Where is it? Right there where it was!"
>   Bishan Singh asked, "In Pakistan, or in Hindustan?"
>   "In Hindustan—no, no, in Pakistan." Fazal Din was thrown into confusion.[118]

The scene ends with Bishan Singh wandering off, muttering a slightly modified version of the string of syllables he usually repeats. Murphy, for example, writes: "Upar di gur gur di annexe di dhiyana di mung di daal of di Pakistan and Hindustan of di dar fatay mun!" The choice of how to render these last few syllables becomes significant. Only two render an English approximation: Pritchett has Bishan Singh mutter, "Upar di gur gur di annex di be dhyana di mung di dal of the Pakistan and Hindustan of the get out, loudmouth!" while Trivedi has him end with "shame on the lot of you!"[119] Hasan's transliteration, *"dur fittey moun"* (which I would render "distant broken silence") suggests a reading of the Urdu vowels closer to these interpretations. We see in Chapter 2 that Rajasthani storytellers invite readers into these interpretive puzzles that the nonsensical narratives offer by making a game out of them: "What is the sense? What does it mean?" Likewise in this story, the nonsense the protagonist repeats offers its own interpretive puzzle to readers of this translated text (for these syllables are always—always already—displaced) that allows it to serve as a playful, fictional version of the nonsensical violence many have had to suffer through in real life. It allows readers a playful attempt to make sense of what makes no sense.

Even if we were unfamiliar with the historical narratives, it would still be clear that all along the narrative has been leading inexorably to the final scene in which the inmates are brought to the border to be exchanged. The ending of the story shows dramatically how Bishan Singh's attempt to locate the place where he feels at home introduces the larger riddle at the core of the story: What are the metanarratives we rely on to create a common sense of belonging? Is it possible to create community that does not violently divide neighbor against neighbor, friend against friend? We arrive at the border crossing hoping to discover a more complicated answer to his question—Where is Toba Tek Singh?—so that he can belong multiply to the various communities he identifies with and not have to make such a stark and reductive choice based on ethnically conceived mappings of territory. We see in Ratan's translation that the various ways of mapping his home begin colliding with one another until he feels at home only where he stands:

> When Bishan Singh's turn came an officer proceeded to jot down his personal details in a register. "Where is Toba Tek Singh?" Bishan Singh asked. "In Pakistan or in Hindustan?"
>
> The officer laughed. "In Pakistan, of course," he said.
>
> Hearing that Bishan Singh jumped with excitement and ran back to join his remaining companions. The Pakistani guards caught hold of him and dragged him to the other side. But he refused to go. "Toba Tek Singh is here! Right here where I'm standing!" he cried. *"O pardi girgir di axe di bedheniana di moong di Dal of Toba Tek Singh and Pakistan."*
>
> They tried to get his thinking straight, "Look, Toba Tek Singh has gone to Hindustan," one of the guards tried to humour him. "If it is not there we will see to it that it is despatched there at once."
>
> But Bishan Singh was adamant. When they tried to drag him to the other side he stood firmly on his swollen leg in the middle of the road as if no power on earth could dislodge him from there.[120]

Here the officer's laughter and the guard's unsuccessful attempts at humor only serve to illustrate how alienated Bishan Singh is by the governmental discourse which tries to cajole him into complying with its classificatory system. Like the storytelling exchange between the laughing *vetala* and the taciturn king in Chapter 3, such a performance allows us as readers to imagine extending the triangles frame after metatextual frame to notice our own response to these foiled attempts at relational alliance. Even though the guard's attempts at humor seem friendly and more than anything illustrate that they, too, are victims of a system beyond their control, to laugh along with the guard is to side with government functionality against this alienated figure who has become our unlikely protagonist.

It is at this moment that we see that the ironic edge introduced at the beginning of the text has framed our interpretation of this joking triangle we engage with in displacement. Suddenly, the zone of translation, whose boundaries we are usually scarcely aware of, makes us aware of how dismal these utopias are, for the story is asking what it means to belong to no-place. Bishan Singh becomes Toba Tek Singh, as a repetition of his question rather than an answer to it. The joke the guards make becomes even more complex in translation, since "Toba Tek Singh" is figured alternately as the man lost in this liminal zone and as the zone where he loses himself. What Ratan translates as "Look, Toba Tek Singh has gone to Hindustan. . . . If it is not there we will see to it that it is despatched there at once" Naqvi renders, "Look, Toba Tek Singh is in Hindustan now—and if he's not there yet, we'll send him there immediately."[121] Each of the translators must make a distinction in English—"it" or "he"—that in Urdu may remain ambiguous—as the (gendered) person and the (neutral) place. Such a play reveals the impossibility of remaining neutral when narrating a scene where the guards try to make this Singh character see some sense—a project we now cannot help but react to ambivalently.

The story ends with a dramatic fall, an image that lingers beyond the confines of the story and suggests in its very telling that we should question these nationalist narratives that promise the community's members that it will live on beyond them, as we see in Hasan's translation:

> Just before sunrise, Bishan Singh, the man who had stood on his legs for fifteen years, screamed and as officials from the two sides rushed towards him, he collapsed on the ground.
>
> There, behind barbed wire, on one side, lay India and behind more barbed wire, on the other side, lay Pakistan. In between, on a bit of earth which had no name, lay Toba Tek Singh.[122]

Readers of this story do not know with any certainty whether Bishan Singh actually dies at this moment or collapses in a state of acute paralysis. Regardless, the image of suspension helps us understand the literary tools at our disposal for making sense of Partition more generally: the irony in this story when figured spatially becomes static but figured temporally is dynamic. How might we analyze the temporal figurations of such irony in translation?

The question might be rephrased: How might we narrate the complexities of transnational displacement? The subject is especially difficult—and especially crucial—to address when analyzing a narrative that questions the very tropes of national origin and cultural authenticity on which our analytic vocabulary depends. In the previous chapters, I suggest we read translated narratives as necessarily repetitive, self-consciously derivative performances. In this chapter I am suggesting more particularly how attention to the literary aspects of such translational performances might help us make sense of the events of our day that otherwise make no sense to us. The translator, I have argued, is the storyteller of world literature, who—in Walter Benjamin's words—"takes what he tells from experience—his own or that reported by others" and then "in turn makes it the experience of those who are listening to his tale."[123] The authority from which the storyteller speaks, Benjamin asserts again and again throughout the essay, is his experience as a mortal human being, a "tiny, fragile human body" caught in "a field of force of destructive torrents and explosions" in this age of mechanical warfare.[124] How can one make sense of such an experience when language itself (as both singular and plural) is fragmented?

"Toba Tek Singh" might have been singled out by Rushdie and West as one of the great works of modern literature from India, but I would argue that its many translations testify to the power of the story in repetition, as storytelling performance. It is because the story has continued to be exchanged so many times in so many places by so many writers in the decades following Partition—by people who have had to contend with the daily realities of these divisions—that the questions being asked accrue greater meaning. Benjamin observes that "Death is the sanction of everything that the storyteller can tell. He has borrowed his authority from death."[125] If such translations worry at the question of fidelity, we should notice that the word "death" here is in the singular because it is a collective noun, one that subsumes the many deaths of the plural members of the community, including that of the storyteller. The story of "Toba Tek Singh" teaches us that the elusive unity we move toward and from as a community is one that has that knowledge in common. It is not the ground itself that divides us against one another but narratives which demand to be read as belonging exclusively to one community or another.

I offer this comparison of eleven different translations of "Toba Tek Singh" in order to argue against reading the final image of the prone, silent body of Bishan Singh as an allegory for translational exchange. The image can only be read as a fixed, static figure of paralysis if we refuse to see the different versions in dynamic relation with one another, if we refuse to take seriously our own agency as interpreters passing these stories along in turn, engaging in a version of the riddle of belonging that Bishan Singh's interlocutors within the story puzzle over. ("Those who tried to explain, themselves got bogged down in another enigma. Sialkot which was in Hindustan now happened to be in Pakistan. At this rate, Lahore which was now in Pakistan may go over to Hindustan. For that matter, the whole of Hindustan may become Pakistan. It was all so confusing.") Otherwise we are indeed doomed to repeat, as Ahmad phrases it, "the same allegory, the nationalist one, rewritten, over and over again, until the end of time,"[126] and are thus doomed to be stuck in a no-man's-land of what Jameson calls "Repetition with Difference." Instead, by taking seriously the "evaluative edge" we use to frame these narratives, we might begin articulating a more powerful critical language for describing what Bhabha has called a "poetics of liminality," one that would identify our own part in engaging in this "dialectic of difference" through but not stuck in nationalist, linguistic, class, and other ideologically driven frames. I am suggesting instead that we use the *mise en abîme* techniques of storytelling cycles and map these nationalist narratives in the singular-plural, as temporarily useful fictions that we can be both inside of and outside of at once.

If we agree with Jean-Luc Nancy's simple but powerful observation in *Dis-enclosure* that "There is no sense that is not shared," we must see that these networks of exchange we participate in connect us across not only space but across time, negotiating a value system moral even while it announces itself as monetary, a part as much of our past as of our future, one that makes us as much as we make it.[127] Here we find a more specific version of the riddle of belonging—one that thinks self-consciously of the ways we make sense with and against others. Nancy writes that the monetary economy "seems to regulate today the horizon of sense and its sharing" and in the process leads to a tension that threatens to tear us apart, one that "distends within itself the equivalency of these absolute values that human beings are supposed to be."[128] The ethos we seek as a community would have us maintain a sense neither fixed and full nor unlocatable and emptied. While Walter Benjamin figures this always-already-displaced utopic space of community as *tikkun*, Nancy otherwise engages with Christian imagery, but here looks to the work of Roland Barthes to find an "exempting of sense" that "always ends up postponing ultimate sense, placing it outside language, in the ineffable."[129] Nancy posits "the apogee of sense" in the unnameable, the unsayable, a project that must be given up in order for us to go on speaking.[130] Here we find Nancy suggesting that sense is an ongoing relationship not only with others but with the word itself imagined as eternal—a triangle of meaning-making secured not beyond itself but in the details of the exchange.

Nancy insists that "There is no sense just for one. . . . What makes sense is what does not cease circulating and being exchanged, like coins in fact, but coins whose currency is incommensurable with any possible equivalent."[131] As I argue in the opening chapter in regard to Gandhi's ludic exchange, we make meaning in incommensurability. Nancy rejects understanding this relationship to sense as either "excavation" of meaning or as "'*mise en abîme*' of a sense whose negativity . . . keeps on reiterating, always a little further on," and yet he goes on to describe the very act of meaning-making as "feeling itself going from one to the other (from one person to the other as well as from one sense to the other)" and thus as "the movement to and fro"[132]— as if to suggest that faith in this ongoing enterprise of interpretation might be found in such moments of suspension in the shattered Tower-of-Babel unity of a multilingual world, as we see in "Toba Tek Singh," as if the no-place of world literature might provide provisional common sense, even if divided, because we could both be there and not there at once.

Passing On

Spectral Justice

We could address the riddles raised in the previous chapter a little differently and ask: If we are interested in articulating a more complex "dialectic of difference" in our reading of world literature, which differences should we decide to address (and even redress) in our evaluations of a text? What value system should we rely on to frame our literary historiographies? Here we need to acknowledge the multiple *values*—moral, political, economic, aesthetic—that are put into play in this ongoing, collective enterprise of literary *evalu*ation.[1] Ultimately, it will not be productive to dismiss summarily the frames of nationalism usually organizing our interpretive practices (as would be the first reaction to reading a story like "Toba Tek Singh"), for without a dynamic, self-reflexive awareness of the framing tendencies themselves, another framing device will simply replace the nationalist narratives that similarly fix the text in time and place. We will still be left unaware of our own ideological position in relationship to the text. To begin understanding how these framing devices negotiate an intersection of colliding values, we need to look more closely at the relationship we assert exists between one corpus and another in our own literary historiographies. What is the basis of such a comparison?

The stories of a Rajasthani writer such as Vijay Dan Detha, for example, cannot read be exclusively alongside other writers in his language (whether you categorize that as Rajasthani or Hindi), other writers of his nation, or even of his era, but should read transtemporally, transspatially, translingually. We might locate his work in comparison to the writers he names as his major influences: a social-realist Hindi writer such as Premchand, German folklorists such as the Brothers Grimm, a Russian fabulist such as Anton Chekhov. We might even read him in comparison to a writer like Ngũgĩ wa Thiong'o, whose work I contend raises similar issues about the relationship of language to nationalism in a postcolonial context. I am suggesting here that part of the task of formulating a critical practice of reading translated work is to take into account the fact that these literary exchanges go beyond tidy national, cultural, temporal, and linguistic boundaries. Part of the task is to understand that even a work read directly in Hindi or in Rajasthani is already a translation. And thus part of our task here is to formulate a critical reading practice that accounts for what Benedict Anderson, in a nationalist context of political performance, has called "the specter of comparison" haunting all our literary endeavors. Not just translators and literary critics but all writers and readers participate in a network in which we interpret a text and pass it along. What values do we assume we have in common?

We already know from the example of Salman Rushdie in the previous chapter that not only do contemporary writers of world literature participate actively in such transnational projects of comparison—holding forth on the writers they deem part of the world literary club or not—but we as the audience of such pronouncements respond to them in our own production of literary scholarship in an ongoing chain of triangular relation. In the early nineties, the Nobel Prize winner Saul Bellow purportedly declared, "Show me the Zulu Tolstoy and I will read him!" thus setting off a storm of controversy.[2] Put crudely, such an ejaculation assumes we agree that Tolstoy's contribution to the world of letters is valuable whereas nothing in the Zulu tradition is worth talking about. The truth Bellow touches on indirectly is that the majority of readers do know the name of Tolstoy and do indeed have trouble naming a single Zulu writer. We ourselves are part of an economy of world literature that participates in exactly the kinds of inequalities we find so reprehensible. These are not the values we would wish to subscribe to, and yet we cannot help but notice that we not only subscribe to them but reinscribe them in our own exchanges over topics literary.

Bellow's crass remark should be interesting to us not just because of the questions it raises about our unconscious habit of creating hierarchies in our evaluations of world literature but also because it makes us aware of the rhetorical strategies we use to negotiate the bounds of community in our discussions of world literature. After all, the genealogy of Bellow's Zulu Tolstoy remark is as vague as Gandhi's civilization quip we started the book with, and thus illustrates that the joke had sting precisely because it was attributed to a Nobel Prize winner. Like Gandhi's quip, Bellow's remark has moved from oral to written, gaining currency in our ludic economy precisely because it points to an imbalance we would otherwise not be able to acknowledge.

The remark—as phrased this way—first appeared in print in Edward Said's tract *Culture and Imperialism* and was attributed vaguely to "an American intellectual."[3] Bellow in turn wrote an op-ed piece for the *New York Times* a year later insisting that this characterization attributed to him had appeared "nowhere in print" and was instead made as an offhand remark in an interview he no longer even remembered clearly, part of a point he was making about the differences between what he termed "literate and preliterate societies."[4] However offended we might be by such a simplistic distinction, we should notice that it does ask larger questions about the ways our systems of evaluating literature depend on a notional equality our daily realities do not seem to bear out. If we are at all piqued, instead of being angry at Bellow for pointing out the hierarchy at work, we might ask ourselves how the enterprise of literature has helped us relate in specific instances to issues of social justice. If we believe that a work of literature might lead to social change, then who exactly defines what that change might be, and how does it then become realized in people's daily lives?

The debate over Bellow's remarks, like the retellings of Gandhi's quip, reminds us that we need to protect a space where we might allow the thornier sides of these issues to be discussed in such a way that takes care to distinguish the reversible (here, the literary) and the nonreversible (as the real). On a fundamental level we are, of course, aware that making a distinction, for example, between "literate and preliterate societies" does not necessarily cause the imbalance Bellow points to; the concern, however, is that such remarks might indeed serve to perpetuate the very inequalities being named. The debate then asks us to think about a basic riddle: How might we answer the need for open scrutiny of the daily practices of injustice in such a way that makes good on our collective commitment to work against those unjust practices? Here, two different value systems (one imagined as strictly political, another as strictly aesthetic) are being addressed. Bellow, for one, contends that those criticizing him have conflated the two. He asks facetiously:

> Now why did my remarks, off the cuff obviously and pedantic certainly, throw so many people into fits of righteousness and ecstasies of rage? France gave us one Proust and only one. There is no Bulgarian Proust. Have I offended the Bulgarians too? We, for that matter, have no Proust either: should the White House issue a fatwa and set a price on my head for blaspheming against American high culture?[5]

Rather than piqued, we should be thankful for this bit of cantankerous jocularity, not only because it has allowed a range of public intellectuals in America—Edward Said, Martha Nussbaum, Charles Taylor, Alfred Kazin—to comment on issues of power connected to the evaluation of literary texts, but also because it has asked us to think more generally about the ways we evaluate literary texts. In this case most particularly, it allows us to think self-reflexively about the *values* underpinning this ongoing, collective enterprise of literary e*valu*ation we engage in.

Bellow, for one, announces that he is interested in guarding against the "righteousness and rage [that] threaten the independence of our souls," which he compares to "the official falsehood machine" of Soviet Russia and its veneration of a particular humorless brand of social realism. Here he casts the real as the false and the humorous as the true:

> In the days of Mark Twain, of Mr. Dooley and H. L. Mencken, we were still able to kid ourselves. Mencken's wicked jokes on Boobus Americanus—his term for the average man—had a salutary influence on the discussion of public questions and on public behavior. Sometimes crude, openly prejudiced but often very funny, he banged away at the professors, the politicians and the Jim Crow South. But fanatics and demagogues had far less influence in those presensitive days. Child gangsters did not then kill the kids who "dissed" them.[6]

Whatever I think of the political sensibilities driving Bellow's comments, I do share with him a concern for protecting the rights of an author to speak out—humorously, provocatively, perhaps even unjustly—against all manner of perceived falseness. If not, we risk participating in the scapegoating that Benjamin, Barthes, Foucault, and others have warned us of—foretelling the death not only of the author but of the jokester and therefore of the storyteller as well. I like to think of this controversial Zulu Tolstoy Bellow refers to as a tricksterish specter of comparison that has something to teach us about our critical reading practices today. It is for this reason I have decided to focus this chapter on the work of not a Zulu Tolstoy but a Hindi Tolstoy. The celebrated early-twentieth-century Progressive Indian writer Munshi Premchand is of interest not only because a number of respected readers of world literature—including Vijay Dan Detha—hold him in such high regard. He is of interest because part of Premchand's appeal is precisely the deftness with which he is able to unite his political commitments with a concern for the aesthetic. I would like to ask how we account for such engagements in the ways we frame our comparisons—especially when the value system at work is unfamiliar or even antithetical to our own. How do these values (political, economic, moral, aesthetic) translate?

Given that Premchand translated Tolstoy's moral tales into Hindi, calling Premchand a Hindi Tolstoy is a bit of a play on words. He was a Hindi Tolstoy in the way we might understand Chapman to have been an English Homer, except that Premchand did not seem haunted by such a specter of comparison. Like M. K. Gandhi, Premchand was deeply influenced—politically, creatively, even spiritually—by the writing and thinking of Leo Tolstoy and believed that his own work translating Tolstoy's moral tales was part of a larger, necessary project working for social change. I look to his work for what it may teach us more generally about the trope of translation and for its usefulness in cultural and literary theory engaged in articulating a dialectics of difference. After all, Premchand saw in translation a very pragmatic means for uniting people in a common movement for justice. Rather than depicting the source language as something to move past and leave behind, he chose work to translate that would enlarge the worldview of the Hindi reader and thus inspire him to effect revolutionary change.

Unlike many writers working today, Premchand did not seem anxious to avoid the charge of his work being read as "Repetition with Difference; the same allegory, the nationalist one, rewritten, over and over again, until the

end of time."[7] He read avidly the news of the Bolshevik revolution, writes his
son Amrit Rai, and yearned, like others in that hopeful age, for "a similar
conflagration, a similar earthquake" in his own country.[8] He was committed
to conjuring a comparable phenomenon in India and did not seem concerned
that such a project might be considered derivative. What might we learn
from this example about the ways we frame such comparisons? What value
system do we uphold in our approaches to the very subject of translation?

However general such a question may be, it is formulated to engage
with scholars in the American academy who have responded to disciplinary crises in established fields such as Comparative Literature and Area
Studies—whereby expertise in local languages and cultures must explain
itself in the general, even universal terms that English-speaking students
and colleagues will readily apprehend—with studies that use the trope of
translation to look closely at our own critical engagements with institutions
of knowledge and power.

David L. Szanton opens a 2004 volume on the disciplinary crisis of Area
Studies in the United States, *The Politics of Knowledge: Area Studies and the
Disciplines*, by announcing, "'To know, analyze, and interpret' another culture . . . is inevitably an act of translation. It is primarily an effort to make
the assumptions, meaning, structures, and dynamics of another society
and culture comprehensible to an outsider."[9] In defense of Area Studies, he
argues—in a manner recalling Lawrence Venuti—that "a fundamental role
of Area Studies in the United States has been—and continues to be—to
deparochialize US- and Euro-centric visions of the world in the core social
science and humanities disciplines, among policy makers, and in the public at large."[10] And while Szanton admits that conventional boundaries of
"nation" and "language" around which Area Studies fields are usually organized have been as generative as they have been limited, his focus inevitably
is on that "something" that "is almost always lost in translation."[11] He concludes that "rough or partial translations are the best we can expect," and
leaves it to another contributor to the same volume, Alan Tansman (from
whom he borrows the trope), to argue for reading Japanese Studies through
what Tansman calls "the Intangible Act of Translation."[12] I am interested in
bringing together discussions of the "tangible" and "intangible" aspects of
translation by an Area Studies scholar in order to understand not only how
we might locate this Hindi Tolstoy but also where. Could this translated
text be read in a Hindi literature class, for instance? Why or why not?

Tansman identifies a "push-and-pull" in Area Studies between scholars working on "tangibles" (which he speaks of in terms of detailed archival work) and those working on "intangibles" (in which broader, theoretical concerns are addressed) and suggests that such tensions are reconciled most productively in the work of translation, which combines readings of the archive that are as "careful and close" as they are "deep and wide."[13] To "grapple with foreign materials in their own terms and strive to render clear what seemed opaque," he suggests, should lead to a version of Asian Studies (he specifies Japanese Studies) "grounded in politics, not in the narrow sense of tendentious arguments, but in its self-awareness as an epistemological arrangement of disciplines and geographic areas responding to a complex world and its cultures."[14] The disciplined double movement he advocates for approaching the translated text on both the micro- and macrolevel at once might very well reassure the wary World Literature scholar that the purview of "the home-country and area-specialist audiences" need not be so strangulatingly narrow and fixed.[15]

In fact, if Area Studies scholars could identify reading strategies for evaluating the translated text in languages other than English, this would go even further toward complicating our institutional assumptions equating "the home-country and area-specialist audiences" with perceived sites of original cultural production. This would in turn teach us to read the trope of translation itself in response to the complexity of the multilingual, multicultural world we live and work in. Translation as a critical trope should not be conceptualized only as a unidirectional movement into English.

Specialists of world literature such as Damrosch and others in the Comparative Literature field have for decades looked to translation to negotiate the same micro-macro epistemological divides that Tansman mentions, albeit from the other side of the exchange. How might we enable members of the two different approaches to work together toward the goal of promoting a greater complexity and attentiveness in our approaches to these literary texts?

In 1993 in his report to the American Comparative Literature Association on the state of the discipline, Charles Bernheimer stressed the reading of translation as one of the main points of departure from previous generations of scholars. He writes that historically, "comparative literature studies tended to reinforce an identification of nation-states as imagined communities with national languages as their natural bases," which then emphasizes "the reading and teaching of foreign language works in the original" as "the very basis of comparative literature's elite image."[16] Previous reports (in 1965 and 1975 by Harry Levin and Thomas Greene respectively) railed against the increasing use of translated material in world literature classes by scholars without access to the original languages as a slip in "professional standards," but admitted that "it would be unduly puristic to exclude some reading from more remote languages in translation."[17] Bernheimer points out that such an approach encourages an elitist-minded, two-tier system whereby "Europe is the home of the canonical originals, the proper object of comparative study; so-called remote cultures are peripheral to the discipline and thence can be studied in translation."[18]

Interestingly, the assumption made in the Greene report is that this elitist attitude, demanding that scholars read the originals, was cast in terms of "standards" and "values" that applied as much to Comparative Literature as to Area Studies and so aimed to strengthen both disciplines. In 1975, Greene and his committee insist: "Courses in translation are potentially of great value to the student, but if no one in the classroom, including the instructors, is in touch with the original language, then something precious has been lost to the learning experience, and something also of our Comparatist integrity."[19] They worry about "the erosion, if not the withering, of the strength of foreign language departments" that might be due in part to the growing popularity of Comparative Literature courses in English, even though they insist that "Comparative Literature can only exist if it enjoys the support of neighboring disciplines and depends on a continuing intimate relationship with them."[20] They suggest that "this ideal [of high standards based on foreign language expertise] which seemed so desirable and feasible ten years ago has been challenged . . . by rapid historical change," and warn that, "The slippage of standards, once allowed to accelerate, would be difficult to arrest."[21]

Bernheimer and his committee urge a reworking of these standards by mitigating "the old hostilities toward translation."[22] They argue that translation might help us work out the ethical component of the project of Comparative Literature more generally, for it "can well be seen as a paradigm for larger problems of understanding and interpretation across different discursive traditions" that they insinuate might have been overlooked with so much focus on mastering foreign languages.[23] Rather than focusing melancholically on the loss of unity and peace before the harrowing events of

World War II that so many scholars have identified as central to the development of the discipline,[24] they are more interested in "what is gained in translations between the distinct value systems of different cultures, media, disciplines, and institutions."[25] They, too, urge us to map this translation network in terms of relative positionality:

> the comparatist should accept the responsibility of locating the particular time and place at which he or she studies these practices: Where do I speak from, and from what tradition(s), or countertraditions? How do I translate Europe or South America or Africa into a North American cultural reality, or indeed, North America into another cultural context?[26]

In this chapter I am interested in pursuing such a recommendation by asking how we might discuss a translation not as a carrying across but as a telling in turn, one that "speaks from" Russian in Hindi via English. How might we locate this multilingual, multicultural common ground in the shifting network that is the web of world literature in translation? On what basis might we evaluate the terms of the resulting exchanges?

I am interested here in pursuing Gayatri Spivak's 2003 suggestion in response to the Bernheimer report that those of us in Comparative Literature work to "collaborate and transform Area Studies" by "approaching the language of the other not only as a 'field' language" and the resulting texts as "active cultural media rather than as objects of cultural study by the sanctioned ignorance of the metropolitan migrant."[27] What would such an engagement with active cultural media entail? Such disciplinary activism might require, to start, that those of us in Area Studies work to collaborate with and transform Comparative Literature in turn so that the positionality of our own intangible acts of translation might be more meaningfully located through tangible texts that challenge our conventional disciplinary mappings. Moreover, if we are to pursue meaningfully Spivak's proposal that we interrogate "the performative of the other" by taking up the task of translation "not from language to language but from body to ethical semiosis," then we need a complex critical language for understanding our own part in constructing that utopic no-place that is the site of translation, even as we deconstruct it.[28]

In earlier chapters, I ask how we might reconcile the calls by Homi Bhabha and Judith Butler for the salve of translation with the lessons of colonialism Lydia Liu, Tejaswini Niranjana, and others have cautioned us to be wary of when trying to formulate a critical vocabulary for human rights. The example of Premchand's optimistic translation of the Russian Revolution is instructive in this regard because its promise to work toward an uncompromising equality is one we might endorse even though we know, given our historical vantage point, that the day-to-day realities of such projects were ultimately ill-conceived. Such a perspective makes clear how much these two divergent approaches to the trope of translation in the American academy depend on the historical position of the translated figure himself in relation to the translating agent—as either triumphing in the face of discrimination (at some moment in the future) or succumbing to the self-serving pressures of power (in the past). Thus, rather than conceiving of the network of translation exclusively in spatial terms, we must also consider the temporal. I would like to suggest that the example of a Hindi Tolstoy asks us to formulate an approach to translation that complicates the neat linear narrative underwriting most of our evaluations, whether housed (spatially) in a Comparative Literature or an Area Studies department (be it Slavic, Asian, or English).

I focus particularly on an oral-based story Tolstoy wrote in Russian that Premchand then read in English translation and rendered in Hindi as "*Bhoot aur Roti*" ("The Ghost and the Bread").[29] I ask how we might read not just the genealogy of this tale but also its humor so that we see that these spirits of hoped-for progress haunting our narratives need not always be fixed in relation to ourselves across a chasm of irreconcilable difference—located helplessly in another time, another place, another language, another class. More specific than "human rights" as a broad category, the story offers a funny twist on the project of social realism by narrating the plight of a poor peasant seduced by an enterprising spirit. In the reality of this story, our trusty narrator solves the mystery of a purloined piece of bread by telling us simply:

vastava main ek bhoot ne ootha li thi[30]

[In reality a ghost lifted that bread]

Whether you render "*vastava main*" as "in reality" or "in fact," you are still asked to understand the ways of the supernatural ("*bhoot*") within a conventional frame of seemingly objective narrative authority whose playful reference to a social reality undoes the very categories that traditional Marxist analysis might insist are stable. Here the real is presented as fantastic and the humorous as true. What kind of social reality is this? What *vastava* is assumed in which present—where and when? What kind of *bhoot kaal* (past tense, or literally "ghost time") is thus being constructed that a Hindi-speaking audience is being asked to move away from in this translation? I analyze this oral-based Russian folktale in Hindi translation through a discussion in English in order to complicate the institutionalized framework of Area Studies, which would fix this text neatly in a single time and place.[31] Instead of this fixity, we need to develop a critical idiom for discussing the promises and paradoxes of these literary translation networks across institutional categories.

The fact that the story is attributed to Tolstoy, a nineteenth-century author now considered an iconic example of social realism, so much so that Vladimir Lenin, of all people, once called him "the mirror of the Russian revolution," makes the international implications of this example even richer.[32] The question opens up issues not only of genre but once more of possession (as we see in trying to evaluate "Chouboli"): How might we understand the reality of a ghost in an English version written from a Hindi version written from a Russian story that itself is said to have been translated from an oral version? Whose realities—be they literate or preliterate—do we then imagine we are engaging with? I have chosen this example in particular because it encourages us to make better use of the literary tools available to us to understand the complex narrative relationships between texts that purport to translate "social realism." Such projects pose a riddle as much alive today as it was then: Is a writer such as Tolstoy or Premchand a recorder of a reality that has already taken place or someone who writes a reality that is yet to come? Whose past and whose future? How do we draw the line between these possessives?

Our Haunted Realities

Most grand, sweeping literary histories seeking to understand social change—like those written by M. M. Bakhtin, Fredric Jameson, Georg Lukács, Franco Moretti, Ian Watt, and others—assume at the outset that the realities of the people are represented most faithfully by that modern fictional form, the novel.[33] Meenakshi Mukherjee, for example, in *Realism and Reality* follows such conventions of thought, by investigating the links between the literary form of the novel and the social and political situations that gave rise to it and asks how such a history might be written of the novel in India most particularly. She compares the novel to storytelling cycles such as *Kadambari* and *Panchatantra*, which she calls "pre-novel narratives," and suggests that the difference between the two forms can be found in the ways the reality of time and space are apprehended:

> The pre-novel tales have a "once-upon-a-time" ambience where the tensions of time past and time present are absent. . . . Instead of dealing with the unchanging moral verities of life in the abstract, the novelist depicts situations on spatial and temporal axes, employing realism as one of the viable modes of viewing this concrete human reality.[34]

As should already be clear from my readings of the storytelling cycles "Chouboli" and "The Twenty-Five Tales of the Undead," I do not agree entirely with the linear narrative underwriting this characterization of prenovel tales; I would amend her distinction to suggest instead that these playful narrative modes do not ignore the tensions of time past and time present but instead use the "'once-upon-a-time' ambience" to allow a chain of interpreters to negotiate concrete human reality age after age—as a moral schema that is necessarily changing because it responds to the verities of life time and time again. This requires us to ascribe agency to the ongoing generations of interpreters rather than the single writer of a literary text, as Linda Hutcheon argues.[35] Mukherjee's emphasis, however, on developing a critical reading practice that attends closely to "the spatial and temporal axes" of a literary text is worth pursuing, especially if we are able to find more complex ways of reading the temporal axes of a storytelling cycle through the conventionalized realities of the novel and the novel as seen in the once-upon-a-time playfulness of a storytelling cycle.

Mukherjee opens her chapter on Premchand's novel *Godaan* by situating his work in historical context, telling us that the year Premchand died (1936) was also "the most important year in his literary career" since the novel was published that year, as well as his most memorable short story "*Kafan*."[36] Not only that, but in April he presided over the first session of the All-India Progressive Writers' Association (AIPWA) held in Lucknow and he was able to articulate what she calls his "sharpest indictment of the capitalistic system of values" in a brief essay entitled "*Mahajani Sabhyata*" ("The Community of Great People"). Amrit Rai's biography creates a similarly dramatic narrative arc in laying out the convergence of Premchand's political and literary interests in this year, and comes to similar conclusions.

Other critics look at Premchand's corpus to investigate more specifically what the relationship might be between literature and politics. K. P. Singh, for example, uses Premchand's later work to make an argument tracing Premchand's gradual disillusionment with Gandhian ideals, starting in the 1930s. Singh begins by noting Premchand's trouble with Gandhi's identification with Hinduism, for one: "In a religion in which one cannot drink the water touched by others," Premchand wrote, "there is no room for me."[37] Singh also points to Premchand's increasing distaste for the capitalist underpinnings of the nationalist movement and the bourgeois character of the Congress Party in particular.[38]

Singh notes Premchand's chagrin over Gandhi's advice that the peasants continue to work within the feudal system and points out that in Premchand's last novel, *Godaan*, one of his characters exclaims, "Nobody has a right to fatten upon the labour of others."[39] This for Singh is evidence that "Each and every work of Premchand enshrines an intention to undo the injustice and exploitation and to bridge the gap between the haves and havenots"; he adds reverentially, "Premchand is an authentic writer of the masses before whom the liberation of the people is the foremost aim."[40] Singh's aim is clearly to convince the doctrinaire Marxists of his day that Premchand did indeed endorse the Communist Party line: he admits that Premchand never called himself a Marxist but points out that Premchand railed against *"Mahajani Sabhyata"* (which he renders "Bourgeois Culture"), predicting—in Singh's translation, presumably—that:

> The sun of the new culture is rising from the remote corner of the west (Soviet Union) which has uprooted this capitalism. No doubt, this new culture has broken the paws, nails and teeth of individualism. Now, in that state, a capitalist cannot flourish at the cost of others by exploitation. Many many thanks to the culture which is undermining private property, [*sic*] The rest of the world will follow it sooner or later.[41]

In attempting to understand Premchand's work, we must be able to ask how, in this post-Soviet age of globalized exchange, we are to understand the call to be an "authentic writer of the masses" that in 1980 a historian such as K. P. Singh could believe in so fervently. If we do believe that "the liberation of the people is the foremost aim" of writers, then how do masterful works of fiction which are still being read, admired, and debated these many decades later help translate this project into voices for a new age? Singh, for one, seems reassured that terms such as "bourgeois culture" are rendered so faithfully, even piously, in Premchand's Hindi, but I would argue that we should be looking instead at those points in Premchand's language that signal a less certain translatability, for these are the moments that put pressure in the opposite direction, challenging the universalizing gestures upon which these exchanges are based. To learn to read Premchand critically in more detail is to learn to articulate issues of justice across borders of language and nation in a manner that does not homogenize the competing needs and interests of "the people" whose voices Premchand translates so deftly.

In the chapter of her book devoted to Premchand's work, Mukherjee is less interested in considering translation issues (which she takes up later in her career) but in establishing, as she says, "a link connecting the short story, the presidential address and the essay" in order to understand why the novel *Godaan* "eludes a neat schematic correlation with any ideology" such as thirties-style Marxism.[42] Most discomfiting, the novel asks the reader not to align with the rebellious character named Gobar but instead with "his patient and fatalistic father Hori to whom change or progress is inconceivable."[43] While in the mid-nineties in America Saul Bellow was railing against Soviet-style social realism, a decade earlier in India Mukherjee wondered why this novel was one of the few of Premchand's works that does not "prescribe a remedy for specific social problems."[44] After all, in his inaugural speech at the AIPWA conference, Premchand had stressed the need for socially purposeful writing, literature that would generate what he calls "*gati, sangharsha aur bechaini*" (which Mukherjee renders "dynamism, struggle and uneasiness").[45]

This imaginary future, which he calls his audience to join him in working toward, is very much situated rhetorically on specific spatial and temporal axes: "By 'progress' we refer to that condition which creates in us strength and vigour, which makes us aware of our misery, which enables us to analyse the internal and external factors that have reduced us to the present state of inertia, and which attempts to remedy them."[46] Mukherjee thus uses this historically situated performance to frame her own engagement with his fictional work to pose similar questions of the present state in which she works and lives: If there is misery and inertia, how might we remedy the situation? While she does not address such questions explicitly, she does note that Premchand's fictional work, such as the novel *Godaan* and the short story "*Kafan*," are so successful as literary works precisely because they leave behind what she calls the "tendentious . . . problem-solving approach" of most socialist realism.[47] In this evaluation she shares something with Bellow. She calls "*Kafan*" in particular "the almost perfect distillation of a situation that disturbs the reader with intense but understated horror."[48] We might note that the story's irony defies any attempts to locate it definitively on one side or another of a series of neat borders and thus demands our agential engagement with the text as readers age after age.

In the first scene of "*Kafan*," the narrator describes a poor father named Ghisu and his son Madhav sitting before a weak fire one winter night, waiting, while inside the hut Madhav's wife, Budhiya, shrieks in agonies of difficult labor. Madhav asks flatly why she doesn't just get it over with and die.[49] When she does so within a few short paragraphs, the father seems equally uncaring. As a reader, it is easy to find yourself having trouble sympathizing with such a seemingly heartless pair but then hating yourself for hating them. You cannot help but notice that there is a judgment implicit in the manner in which the narrator introduces the two to us—in a stiff, circumspect manner bordering on old-style ethnography: "The two came from a family of Chamars and were infamous throughout the village."[50] You find yourself unsure whether Premchand's story means to ridicule these two Chamars (because, being from the caste of leatherworkers, they are marked as "untouchable"), to make us feel sorry for Madhav and Ghisu and angry at the system that compels them to act this way, or something else entirely.

Such scenes have raised contentious questions within India about the value systems we endorse in evaluating literary work featuring characters identified as "untouchable" (now called "Dalit"), analogous to the questions we have seen in the American context with Bellow's Zulu Tolstoy comment. For example, in a 2003 interview, in response to publisher S. Anand's question about "nondalits" writing about "dalit" experience, the writer and editor Sivakami discusses Premchand's "*Kafan*" (as a Tamil writer, Sivakami specifies that he read the story in English translation):

> What the author wanted to portray was a simple reality, which has no past and possibly no future. Not only are the conversations between the father and son imaginary (showing them in a very poor light) but also their silence has been interpreted to the advantage of the author for his reader-oriented aesthetics.[51]

In his introduction to the volume where this interview appears, *Touchable Tales*, S. Anand offers an outline of the history and debates of the Dalit literary movement and assumes at the outset that the work of translation has laid the groundwork for the Dalit movement.[52] Similarly, Sivakami does not apologize for engaging in this critical discussion of Premchand's short story through a translated text; in his response to Anand's question about his "impressions of the literature produced by nondalits on dalits," he is more interested in engaging in the complicated question of the relationship of literature to "reality" as it relates to one's identity:[53] "I hold that nondalit writers emerge as self-styled autocrats passing adverse judgements on dalit life, or that they use dalits as toys to tickle a few strange nerves of their regular readers. Else, they like to play the role of saviors, though in reality they are not."[54]

Laura R. Brueck has likewise shown that members of the Bharatiya Dalit Sahitya Akademi (BDSA; the Indian Dalit Literary Academy) have publicly attacked Premchand's works for their unsympathetic characterization of Dalits; in July 2004 members of the BDSA burned copies of Premchand's novel *Rangbhoomi*, and in 2005 the BDSA president, Sohanpal Sumanakshar asked in an essay whose responsibility ("*zimmedar kaun?*") such interpretations should be:

> Why would Premchand make such a characterization of [Dalits] in "Kafan"? Only so that he could win the praises of the upper caste brahmins and have them call his work "literature." Premchand indeed won the praise of the brahmins and was bestowed with the rank of emperor for his literature which displays dalits as loveless, soulless, base characters.[55]

Sumanakshar criticizes Premchand's work for simply not being "realistic." His critique raises a more interesting question for us as scholars of world literature today: How do the demands for realism challenge the limits of our conception of the literary? Brueck argues that his intervention in literary historiography is a necessary step in the project to create a "growing Dalit literary critical lexicon" and for "claiming space in the public discursive sphere." Most basically, we should understand that such a space is created precisely because Premchand is such a celebrated author in Hindi—just as Bellow's Zulu Tolstoy comment has more heft because Bellow is a Nobel Prize winner and Tolstoy is recognized as one of the world's great writers. Sumanakshar's evaluation seems as formulaic in its own way as K. P Singh's: Sumanakshar does not seem to read Premchand's prose with the kind of agential, "evaluative edge" that Hutcheon, for one, argues that irony invites.

I rehearse this controversy in order to ask how we decide who in the community of literary critics is to arbitrate such a debate. Who is to argue that the portrayal of these Dalit characters be understood as ironic, and what do we understand the underlying value judgment of that irony to be? If you agree with my argument in Chapter 3 that the political effect of a literary text's humorous critique is one that gets negotiated over various generations of repetition, then here a more specific version of that question is raised: What political and aesthetic framing devices do we rely on to evaluate the terms of a text's irony?

Just as we notice the wry, affectionate manner in which the narrator of "Chouboli" narrated the grim realities of spouse abuse in Chapter 2, here we realize we cannot help but get pulled into a narrative alliance that is as intimate in its humor as it is discomforting. Like Mukherjee, Singh, or Sumanakshar, we struggle to make comparisons drawn as much from real-life situations as from literary predecessors to help give meaning to the questions the story raises. Just as in the story "*Toba Tek Singh,*" analyzed in Chapter 4, we find ourselves asking: How do we together make sense of such nonsense?

We follow the two characters through the rest of "*Kafan*" as they go to various people in the town begging for money for a *kafan* (a type of shroud) for their recently deceased wife and daughter-in-law. It is easy to see the townspeople's disgust but also what in the pair is worthy of disgust. We come to understand that they have begged for money before this, ostensibly for medicine that might have helped the young daughter-in-law, for food that would have kept her strong. It seems unlikely that the money was then used for anything but alcohol. More than anything, the outrage we begin to feel is for the most vulnerable member of the town, the one who has recently passed away. It is the memory of her impossibly difficult straits that haunts the story. This time, too, the townspeople begrudgingly hand over money in the name of the daughter-in-law, which the pair proceeds to squander on drink rather than wrapping her in a decent *kafan*, taking her to a priest for last rites, and cremating her properly. The Chamars end up in a tavern (as more than one person has translated the *madhushala* of many a verse) and drink to the memory of the deceased woman they ironically call the queen of Vishnu's paradise.[56] The story ends with the two singing and dancing, drunkenly falling over each other while the other patrons look on at the spectacle; finally the two pass out in a pathetic heap.

It is not clear if perhaps the two are acting out of grief—at the loss of this family member, at the state of their lives that makes them unable to keep her alive—or out of habitual dereliction. How are we to judge what ghosts haunt them? One worry is that we are being invited to participate in the familiar triangle of judgment that Spivak characterizes as "white men saving brown women from brown men."[57] What kind of evaluative edge are we employing in our engagement with this text? If we agree that the fault for Budhiya's mistreatment up to and even following her death lies only partially on the shoulders of Madhav or Ghisu but equally on the townspeople and maybe even on those further away who rely on a system that necessarily marginalizes a segment of the population, then a seemingly realistic and certainly complicated story such as "*Kafan*" really does demand something extraordinary of its readers to make judgments about the rights Budhiya might have as a Dalit woman, even at the expense of her Dalit husband and father-in-law or her fellow townspeople. How wide do we decide to map these responsibilities across bounds of time, place, language, nation, class?

Sara Rai compares "*Kafan*" to Premchand's previous (and less celebrated) story "*Poos ki Raat*," a story of a farmer named Halku that ends with the protagonist in penury, his fields destroyed, grateful nonetheless that he has work as a wage laborer and so will not have to sleep in the cold.[58] Compared to this story of "desperate poverty," in which the protagonist "can envisage no further depth to his misery," Rai finds, "In *Kafan*, Ghisu and Madhav are shorn even of the sentimentalization of Halku's 'pure and noble spirit.'"[59] She takes note in particular of "The desperate greed with which Ghisu and Madhav sit eating potatoes outside the dying woman's hut, neither agreeing to go in and attend to the woman, not trusting the other with the potatoes," and suggests this "is testimony enough that at that level of poverty emotional and familial ties become mere will-o'-the-wisp when the horror of hunger and misery looms large."[60] Rather than blame the two characters for the degradations of poverty, in her reading, the story more than anything blames the society they are part of that reduces them to such a state.

We might very well wonder what the limits are of social responsibility in this globalized age. To whom do we ascribe the right to identify the values at work in such a story, and how does this right then translate across borders of time, nation, language, class, and culture? A translator herself, Sara Rai claims in English that the story highlights "the irony of the ritual ridden social system" that has a character such as Ghisu exclaiming, "What a rotten custom it is that somebody who didn't even have rags to cover herself while she was alive, has to have a new shroud when she dies!"[61] If we agree with Rai that such an ironic social indictment does indeed incite us to act, we need to look more closely at details of the exchange in order to understand what we are called on to do, where, when, by whom, and on behalf of whom.

Given Sumanakshar's indictment, we might very well wonder if such literature marks out a space in which imaginary figures like Ghisu and Madhav become agents of a democratic system or if it merely perpetuates a system that makes them subjects of it. When I quote Sara Rai quoting David Rubin's translation of Premchand's story in which a fictional character named Ghisu comments on the irony of buying a dead woman a new shroud that is only destined to burn like her, the danger is that in each repetition this literary representation does not give poor Dalits a voice in the new nation but merely ensures that they will continue to be spoken about in the third person, then as now. (We have heard the question before: Can the subaltern speak? Elsewhere in her essay, Spivak worries about "the first-world intellectual masquerading as the absent nonpresenter who lets the oppressed speak for themselves."[62])

Focusing on translation as a trope of telling in turn asks us to address the issue at stake here in more complex terms so that the exchanges themselves comment on the terms of the exchange and in the process rework their very frames of reference as they get passed along. As we see in Chapter 3, we cannot assume that Hindi is a homogeneous whole: we need to look instead at Premchand's role as translator of "the people" with as much scrutiny as so many theorists have used to examine colonial-era crossings along divisions of race, language, and nation. Sumanakshar's castigation of Premchand's gesture of representing, even appropriating, the Dalit experience reminds us that the irony of this critique of the system as expressed through a translated voice of the Chamar subject might comment on our own reading practices in translation so that we can learn how to read the ironies of history in translation, age after age, and use these insights to effect a more self-reflexive, dynamic, and therefore responsible mechanism for social change.

Such a moment of literary historiography speaks to broader, more general concerns, ones that Dipesh Chakrabarty identifies as pointing to "a key question in the world of postcolonial scholarship," a question that understands that "The problem of capitalist modernity cannot any longer be seen simply as a sociological problem of historical transition (as in the famous 'transition debates' in European history) but as a problem of translation, as well."[63] I take up such a challenge with regards to the work of Premchand in this chapter to ask how we might read the trope of translation against that of transition. Indeed, Chakrabarty is not the first prominent scholar to turn to the trope of translation as a conceptual tool for understanding the dialectic of difference that we consider in the preceding chapters. In a manner echoing Homi Bhabha, Robert Young, and Judith Butler, Chakrabarty announces that he looks to the work of scholars who have "demonstrated that what translation produces out of seeming 'incommensurabilities' is neither an absence of relationship between dominant and dominating forms of knowledge nor equivalents that successfully mediate between differences, but precisely the partly opaque relationship we call 'difference.'"[64]

Here "difference" is understood relationally, as the lines that divide and separate and thus frame the very narratives that create provisional common ground (as if past, present, and future). Ironically, in the 1920s and thirties Premchand seemed to see translation as an instrument of the kind of progress (as transition) he was working for: his writing urges toward a better future even in the name of being attentive to the details of the past and present. In this light, Sumanakshar's critique of Premchand raises larger disciplinary questions about the ways we frame the ideologies of agency. We might ask how we might move away from the literary-historiography version of the great-men-of-history narrative. How, for example, should we narrate the relationship of a celebrated individual such as Premchand, Tolstoy, or Gandhi to the mass movements they comment on and many times inspire? This is a different version of a *mise en abîme* in the narrative, one that allows these agents to be narrated as both inside and outside a people.

We know from historical accounts that both Gandhi and Premchand considered Tolstoy their teacher, a thinker who formulated a philosophy of nonviolence that was an implicit critique of a singular modernity.[65] Both Premchand and Gandhi translated Tolstoy's prose (into Hindi and Gujarati, respectively), for they felt that the realities of the Russian people as described by Tolstoy had particular relevance to the Indian people in a time of great transformation. It is important to look carefully at these exchanges to see that simplistic notions of translation—as static original to mindless copy—do not apply, for Premchand and Gandhi were each attentive mediators and saw to it that the ideas in the source text would be adapted to the needs of the target culture as much as they worked to see that the target culture might adapt to the ideas in the source text. Just as important, they understood that they were not the masters of the languages they were writing in nor of the ideas they were conveying, but were servants of the people they wrote to and for.

We need to diagram these triangles of translational exchange to capture their enduring complexities. How, for example, might we account for Sumanakshar's position in these ongoing triangles of relation as someone who takes part in this ongoing dialogue in part because he is in conversation (however negatively) with Premchand? We can see what possibilities the figure of Premchand creates in Sumanakshar's alliance with readers of world literature, but it is less clear what possibilities Sumanakshar creates retrospectively for a Hindi Tolstoy or a Russian Dalit. How do we frame these tales of revolution as they translate across time?

Tolstoy's "A Letter to a Hindu" is an exemplary document of translation in the way critics have been theorizing it most hopefully. Here we have a nonfiction text written by Tolstoy in Russian to a formerly colonized Indian subject turned nationalist living in Vancouver, drawing on American sources that contemplate the movement against slavery, a discussion Tolstoy draws on to argue against fighting the violence of a colonial regime with violence, a call that another colonized subject (Gandhi) took up first from his vantage point in South Africa.[66] The very rhetoric of the document reverses some of the hierarchical propositions underlying the commonly narrativized relationship of civilized to primitive, modern to premodern, violent to nonviolent (which drives, for example, Bellow's system of evaluation).

While Akeel Bilgrami and Robert Young have recently looked to Gandhi's writing to rethink colonial critiques of modernity, here I am particularly interested in his critique of colonialism for the way it complicates the easy binaries and linear sequences we usually rely on in our thinking on revolution.[67] Javed Majeed argues that Gandhi's complex construction of truth stems precisely from his work as a translator, as an acknowledgment of his inability to "master" languages such as Gujarati and Hindi.[68]

Framed this way, these translations offer yet another version of the riddle of belonging that we have been pursuing: the tales of revolution they wrote belonged as much to them as to the people they were writing to and from, past, present, and future. Sumanakshar can possess Premchand's corpus many decades later because in Premchand's corpus he is already—always already—displaced.

We know now from our historical vantage point that Gandhi was extremely effective at translating his critique of mastery into a viable nationalist movement in India; what is perhaps more instructive for amending our understanding of translation is to see that for Gandhi this *satyagraha* movement started in response to a question posed by Tolstoy, who pointed to the contradictions of a civilized modernity that relied on violence to conserve its power. Such a critique was based on a notion of truth not as singular and timeless but instead as historically contingent. If the insights were to be translated effectively, they had to be adapted to each particular time and place, in a strategy that depended on the enfranchisement of the many. How do we explain the multiple displacements at work in such translations?

Gandhi introduces the English translation of Tolstoy's "A Letter to a Hindu" by commending Tolstoy as someone who might inspire a colonized "us" in our own struggle. Rather than calling for a simplistically divisive solidarity against the colonizing West, Gandhi appeals to the "best instincts" of individual members in our greater human family to distinguish our own version of the false from the true. He writes:

> When a man like Tolstoy, one of the clearest thinkers in the western world, one of the greatest writers, one who as a soldier has known what violence is and what it can do, condemns Japan for having blindly followed the law of modern science, falsely so-called, and fears for that country "the greatest calamities," it is for us to pause and consider whether, in our impatience of English rule, we do not want to replace one evil by another and worse. India, which is the nursery of the great faiths of the world, will cease to be nationalist India, whatever else she may become, when she goes through the process of civilization in the shape of reproduction on that sacred soil of gun factories and the hateful industrialism which has reduced the people of Europe to a state of slavery, and all but stifled among them the best instincts which are the heritage of the human family.[69]

Gandhi's characterizations of Japanese appropriations of "modern science" call into question the very life-and-death metaphors of nationalism that

Pheng Cheah will critique these many decades later; Gandhi's distinction between lifeless, hateful (what Benjamin calls mechanical) reproduction and a healthier, more instinct-based passing on offers us a new approach to the impasse we have reached in our thinking on translation today. Instead of concerning ourselves with distinctions between original and derivative, Gandhi's writing calls on us to theorize translation—and thus revolution—with a more complex understanding of its potential afterlife. This understanding of the afterlife participates, like Premchand's translation of Tolstoy's moral tale, in ongoing conversations distinctly spiritual—here understood as ephemeral (*dharmik*), as ghostly (*bhoot*-like), and as humorous (*spirituel*) all at once.

In this and other writings Gandhi, like Tolstoy and Premchand, calls his reader to rethink the ways "dharma" and "truth" might be conceived; here I read Gandhi as using English words such as "evil" and "faith" politically to underscore the ethical contradictions at the heart of the British colonial enterprise. Such critiques have a renewed relevance for us today, in an age when we talk hopefully about the possibilities of translation as a site of equality without reconciling such projects with the violent history of unequal exchange. Here we must ask once more: According to what faith do we judge fidelity in a literary translation? The possibility I see here in Gandhi's introduction to Tolstoy is one that posits a narrative of multiple faiths and thus implicitly challenges the image of, say, a Hegelian *Geist* as the spirit (in the singular) governing narratives of liberation. These translations show that the realities they narrate in the past and present as a way of theorizing the future do not necessarily need to be written in terms of a singular, Christian modernity.

How then might we apply this riddle of the afterlife of translation to the ethical but specifically textual questions of revolution? If we want work to be relevant, then we need to articulate how we might judge such genres of realism and reality in translation today. How are we to describe the truth of a conflagration that was and yet was not to be?

Reading the Future Perfect against the Past Progressive

The question becomes even more complex when we consider the prose Premchand used to translate not oral-based Russian fiction but the 1936 manifesto of the All-India Progressive Writers' Association (AIPWA), written collectively in English by a group temporarily in London. This

was in the era after Gandhi's nonviolent *satyagraha* movement had succeeded in making the Indian National Congress a viable political force
in favor of home rule, and thus at a time when divisions between various
factions within the nationalist movement vied for power with increased
intensity. Who would represent the people of the nation? Which people,
defined how?

Not unlike the Négritude movement of disaffected students from the
French colonies in Paris (whose movement is said to begin with their own
manifesto, *Légitime défense*, in 1932),[70] the AIPWA was a group of well-
meaning Indian elite from Lahore, Bombay, and Calcutta who were studying at places such as Oxford and the University of London and had gathered
together at a Chinese restaurant in London determined to effect solid
change.[71] Movingly, Carlo Coppola describes them as disheartened by the
rise of Nazism and inspired enough by the work of the British communist
Ralph Fox to draft a document in the only language they shared between
them: English.[72] He quotes a letter in which Sajjad Zaheer writes eloquently
of "the painful darkness which, spreading from the bright world of art and
learning that was Germany was throwing its fearful shadow on Europe—
all this had shattered the inner tranquility of our hearts and minds."[73]

The manifesto was published first in the *Left Review* in the February
issue of 1935 and only later mimeographed and sent back to the colony to
be translated into the important vernaculars. Members of the group obviously had some misgivings about this choice of language, for they close the
manifesto by declaring—in English—that Indian writers should "strive for
the acceptance of a common language (Hindustani) and a common script
(Indo-Roman) for India."[74] The document articulates a forward-looking
vision of "the lives of the people" that both ignores and refuses to ignore
the very divisions that would prove so disastrous to the country. When we
look at Coppola's 1974 comparative reading of the collectively written English and Premchand's Hindi versions of the AIPWA manifesto, we see that
these sites of translation have much to teach us about the ways we might
understand the spirit of those past progressives and the ways we might want
them to continue haunting us today in the present progressive tense.[75]

I draw attention to the present progressive tense in order to formulate
a way that discussions of translation and postcoloniality might play on the
border separating "us" from "them," the present from the past, the living from the dead. Such a strategy is inspired in part by Wendy Brown's

performance in *Politics Out of History*, in which she conjures Derrida's spirit conjuring the spirit of Marx in conversation with Walter Benjamin's angel of history to suggest ways of thinking about our own agency as ethical subjects in the world after the end of Soviet-style communism.[76] For her, Derrida offers what she calls "the tentative beginning of a historiography for historical-political consciousness in the time after progress," that is, when the Marxist historical narrative no longer seems tenable.[77] Her lyrical description of the historical moment we are in today makes fully palpable both the fearful and the hopeful aspects of this time that rushes by so ferociously, rendering each of us a version of Benjamin's storyteller, a "tiny, fragile human body" caught in "a field of force of destructive torrents and explosions" in the age of mechanical (or even nuclear, chemical, and biological) warfare. The comparison between Brown's ethical subject and Benjamin's storyteller makes clear that each of us is a storyteller trying to share our wisdom and insights with a larger world community in order to make sense of the past, present, and future:

> On a daily basis we live the paradox that the most rapid-paced epoch in human history harbors a future that is both radically uncertain and profoundly beyond the grasp of the inhabitants present. Moving at such speed without any sense of control or predictability, we greet both past and future with bewilderment and anxiety. As a consequence, we inheritors of a radically disenchanted universe feel a greater political impotence than humans may have ever felt before, even as we occupy a global order more saturated by human power than ever before.[78]

Like Chakrabarty, Brown seems interested in understanding the present globalized world as an enchanted place, but while Chakrabarty asks how we might incorporate the supernatural, enchanted stories of the subaltern into the grand narratives of history we write, Brown does that by writing about the specters and angels that are part of our narratives today and offer "strategies for conceiving our relation to past and future that coin responsibility and possibilities for action out of indeterminacy."[79] Such an approach helps us ask what our mandate is as we consider a writer such as Premchand, who died in India in 1936 with dreams of a more equal world in some near-distant future. I would like to suggest that this future that did not come to be is also part of the past we must account for when we discuss a writer like Premchand.

The example helps us pursue the suggestion in Chapter 1 that we think of our ongoing networks of translation as a fragmented unity (one "that does not involve the retrieval of the past, but a futural projection") "always—always already—displaced."[80] Brown contends that Derrida's

> is a permanently contestable historiography, one that makes contestable histories an overt feature of our political life as it encourages us to struggle for and against particular conjurations of the past. It never claims to exhaust or settle historical questions. History becomes less what we dwell in, are propelled by, or are determined by than what we fight over, fight for, and aspire to honor in our practices of justice.[81]

I read Premchand's translations in order to think more carefully about the rhetoric we use to write contestable histories of world literature, just as I would argue Premchand's reading of the Tolstoy tale or the AIPWA manifesto in his day shows what he aspired to honor in his own practice of justice. How do we read these idealistic attempts to write a literature of social realism working toward a vision of equality and justice when it is the very histories of those specifics that we not only contest but have trouble accepting in this day and age? Scholars today such as Pheng Cheah suggest that our efforts to realize a more equitable cosmopolitan unity are hampered by the specter of nationalism still haunting our literary exchanges. He warns grimly, "The common association of nationalism and the desire for the archaic suggests that nationalism destroys human life and whatever future we may have because its gaze is fixed on the frozen past."[82] Marx and Engels, of course, have a solution for this: in the *Communist Manifesto* they suggest beguilingly that in the epoch of the bourgeoisie, "national one-sidedness and narrow-mindedness become more and more impossible," until "from the numerous national and local literatures, there arises a world literature."[83] Such a proposition should be of particular interest to us today, when global capitalism has made some national identifications superfluous but not in the ways perhaps imagined by Marx and Engels.[84] Symptomatically, Marx and Engels never investigate specifically how such an undifferentiated construct as "world literature" might come into being and thus seem in the *Manifesto* to dismiss the annoying demands of linguistic difference and therefore the ongoing necessity of translation.

I suggest in Chapter 1 that rendering the process and project of translation invisible only serves to keep the specter of difference haunting us as we engage in literary exchange today. I argue that we need instead to recognize that translation has become a site where we might learn to better negotiate the terms of this worldwide community that we are already taking part in. Here I focus on the temporal figuring of such fixations to look more closely at how the critical use of our own literary tools shapes them in the present progressive.

Coppola's 1974 analysis of the translation dilemmas faced by the members of the AIPWA in the 1930s makes clear that the contentious history of multilinguality in South Asia offers particularly instructive examples to investigate. For example, Coppola's discussion of the decision to call for the "acceptance of a common language (Hindustani) and a common script (Indo-Roman) for India" points out the irony but also the necessity of the manifesto being written in English by the group in London, then in Devanagari script in Premchand's Hindi version, before being taken out of the Lucknow manifesto altogether in order to ease sensitivities and—in Coppola's words—"accommodate dissident groups."[85]

The details of such exchanges make clear the amount of delicate, attentive work involved in finding provisional common ground across a range of potential divisions; the important work of achieving community—whether within a nationalist movement in the 1930s or a transnational project post-9/11—requires we have a critical vocabulary for understanding the larger import of the smallest details of translation. Whatever unity in this construct called "world literature" we might work for does not exist primarily in some dreamy future or soft-focus past but right here, now, in the ways we engage with each other, past, present, and future, through these texts. I would argue that reading Coppola's work on the AIPWA manifesto now offers us strategies for conceiving our relation to these spirits of progress past and future in such a way that coins responsibility and possibilities for action out of translation. Here I wish to address Sivakami's charge that what Premchand "wanted to portray was a simple reality, which has no past and possibly no future."[86] How do we rely on translation to write the past and future of these simple realities together?

Relevant here is Douglas Robinson's observation that in Marx's writing, translation becomes a metaphor for the relationship of the past to the present and on into the future. In *Who Translates?* Robinson contends that in *The Eighteenth Brumaire*, Marx looks unfavorably on language-learning, for example, comparing it to moments when wannabe revolutionaries think they are "creating something previously non-existent" when really they are "anxiously summon[ing] up the spirits of the past to their aid."[87] Marx writes:

> Just so does the beginner, having learnt a new language, always re-translates it into his mother tongue; he has not assimilated the spirit of the new language, nor learnt to manipulate it freely, until he uses it without reference to the old and forgets his native tongue in using the new one.

This is the passage that interests Derrida in *Specters of Marx* for its paradoxical appropriations of time: "the more the new erupts . . . the more one has to convoke the old,"[88] Derrida writes. I would argue, however, that Premchand's translation of the AIPWA manifesto into Hindi (especially in Coppola's reading) complicates the easy binaries of new and old, past and present, original and copy that so much of the rhetoric Derrida critiques has relied on. That is, Premchand's work succeeds in assimilating the spirit of a collective vision because he has learnt to manipulate it freely without reference to old and new. In Marx's scenario, Robinson argues, such transparent translation is seen as a bad thing, for it is "a bridge back to the past, to the native language and in Marx's spectral logic to the spirits of the dead, to ghosts. The true revolutionary must cut the ties that bind him to the past, to the spirits of dead ancestors, to the mother tongue."[89] Derrida calls this a forgetting without forgetting, an aporia Robinson renders a "translating without translating."[90] I have identified this as the central riddle of translation Sivakami and others grapple with today: How might we take possession of such spirits temporarily without allowing them to possess us completely?

In the days of the Progressives, every translation decision—to call for the establishment of which national language, if at all—raised larger questions about the very future they were writing into being: Who would represent the people of the nation? Which people, defined how?

Coppola calls the AIPWA manifesto "the most basic document in the development of Socialist Realism in India" and notes in particular the discrepancies between the English and Hindi versions which to him are symptomatic of (what he delicately calls) "certain problems which the group would have to face when it took the Movement to India the following year."[91] (These contradictions, I suggest, resonate uncannily with those pointed to decades later by Derrida and Robinson). The manifesto starts by announcing with much bravado in a charged-up present progressive,

"Radical changes are taking place in Indian society," and that "It is the duty of Indian writers to give expression to the changes taking place in Indian life and assist the spirit of progress in the country." Coppola is particularly interested in showing that the more doctrinaire elements of what he calls "the leftist-liberal criticism of the period"—phrases such as "spirits of progress" and "spirits of reaction"—are left out of Premchand's Hindi version entirely.[92]

In *Poetry of the Revolution*, Martin Puchner calls the genre of manifestos a literary genre that is performative, creating a space in the future for those in the present to step into, and that, in his words, "uniquely represents and produces the fantasies, hopes, aspirations, and shortcomings of modernity."[93] He sees the cracks of this modernity performed in the very rhetoric of the manifesto—in German, English, and French in his examples. Puchner writes that the *Communist Manifesto* in particular breaks "the conjunction of authority, speech and action on which" conventions of the old type of the manifesto rest, and instead creates "a genre that must usurp an authority that it does not yet possess, a genre that is more insecure and therefore more aggressive in its attempts to turn words into actions and demands into reality."[94] Drawing predominantly from European examples that have a fairly stable sense of nationalized language in place at the point when he examines them, he does not have the opportunity to investigate how these translations into actions and reality might be affected by the very language politics at work in the rhetoric of the manifestos he analyzes.

We see, for example, in Premchand's translation of the opening lines of the AIPWA manifesto an attempt to temper some of the top-down elitism of the English-language document ("social and political institutions are being challenged") with a reliance on more immediate metaphors of tree-felling and childbirth: *"Bharatiya samaj main bare-bare parivartan ho rahe hain. Purane vicharon aur vishvason ki jare hilti ja rahi hain aur ek naye samaj ka janam ho raha hai."* [Very big transformations are happening in Indian society. The roots of old ideas and beliefs are being shaken and the birth of a new society is taking place.] Such a reading would resonate well with, for example, Amrit Rai's celebrated biography of his father, which sees Premchand as a populist who worked tirelessly not to allow the house to be divided (as the title another of his books on this period calls it), not to let the one language be divided along two scripts (as Christopher King's monograph charges).[95]

Not just Coppola, but Vasudha Dalmia, Francesco Orsini, Gyanendra Pandey, and Alok Rai have all written persuasively of the pressures on writers of this period to conform to the newly emerging rules of a partitioned, ethnic-identity-based language and culture.[96] Robert King goes so far as to read the history of the language politics of postcolonial India as a "nonlinguistic" use of language identity whereby the language instead is treated "as icon" and thus serves either "as a badge of membership in the community or as a means of exclusion and exile."[97] King's account, that of a linguist, looks critically at the imperative that one language equals one nation equals one language (a formulation he calls "isomorphic"). While King does not overtly attend to the Babelian imagery that is often evoked when describing the fear of a multilingual state, he does recount that Jawaharlal Nehru himself (the first prime minister of the nation and the subject of King's book) was significantly influenced by works he read in jail in 1935, such as C. K. Ogden's *Basic English* and *Debabelization*, works that influenced Nehru's support of Gandhi's move to have a single language called Hindustani be adopted as the national language of an independent India.[98]

It is significant that Nehru wrote nationalist essays in English—because he did not feel comfortable expressing himself in the national language he proposed (be it called Hindi, Urdu, or Hindustani)—and that his conversations and correspondence with Gandhi on issues of national strategy and interest were conveyed in English, even though Gandhi claimed to be a native Gujarati speaker and proponent of Hindustani. Their communications demonstrate the critique by so many elite members of the proposal for a national language of the people called Hindustani: that the definition of the proposed national language was based not so much on literary conventions but on oral, on-the-street formulations, and that such a basic language could not support the substantially intricate work of the state. These critics felt that the requirement to express more complex issues would force a speaker to choose partisan vocabulary (of Sanskritic, Perso-Arabic, or English roots) and therefore be completely partisan in the end.

We can see fault lines similar to the ones Puchner reads in the project of the manifesto in the very language used by a Progressive like Premchand in his translation of the manifesto: the inclusion of an abstract Sanskritic word such as "*parivartan*" (changes, transformations) and the very gesture of naming the nation "Bharatiya" (rather than "Hindustani") can be read as a bow toward Hindu elitist Nagari Pracharani's pressure to Hinduize, even

Brahminize, this newly forming national language. It is clear from reading this document closely that the very concept of Indianness as a monolingual category does not translate easily into the newly conceived language of a Hinduized Hindi nor even the nonsectarian Hindustani that the writers of the AIPWA manifesto were hoping to write into being. I would suggest that this example forces us to articulate in this day and age an approach to translation that understands the contentiousness of the linguistic-as-national categories upon which our very enterprise depends.

Nehru and Gandhi both agreed with the Progressive agenda of the day that no one was more qualified to enunciate the complex wishes of the people and therefore to found a truly representative national language than the creative writers (Premchand translates "*sahityakar*"). Premchand was not the only writer of his day to take this responsibility seriously; but in the subsequent decades he in particular has become emblematic of the ways prose might become partisan despite the intentions of a "soldier of the pen" such as himself. In this chapter I argue that we must first learn to read such literary historiography attentively so as to complicate the assumptions of multilinguality (that is, Babel) as unruly and backwards.[99]

I suggest that we do a disservice to Premchand's interventions in the political landscape of pre-Independence India if we do not have a critical language for discussing his work as a translator—in multiple senses of the term. In the biography of his father, Amrit Rai tells us that Premchand began his career in 1903 publishing in Urdu (a designation presumably signaled not only by his use of Perso-Arabic vocabulary but also by his use of the Persian script) and that he studied both Persian and English in school (significantly, both were officially administrative languages of the subcontinent in the nineteenth century) and began publishing simultaneously in Hindi and in Urdu in 1913, when the Hindi-Urdu language camps were consolidating their respective bases.[100] He had a brief flirtation in the 1920s with the proposal for an oral-based Hindustani written in Roman letters but toward the end of his life embraced Hindustani as a language of the people, written in either Devanagari or Persian script.[101]

These details tell an emblematic and complex story of the ways common ground becomes established through the writings of a nationalist litterateur such as Premchand. To tell this story in English without being aware of our own Babelian narratives that are implicitly privileged in such a gesture is to reinstitute a teleological narrative that equates monolingual English examples with modern (and perhaps globalizing) structures of power, the space of progress democratic nations must struggle to work toward. I ask, then, a more particular version of the riddle Wendy Brown raises: How might we create a space of optimism that lives up to the hopes of justice and equality that the writer and colonized citizen Premchand worked for, one that enables us to take into account the disappointments of the communist legacy these many decades later? My contention is that each of us writing on Premchand—Vijay Dan Detha, Amrit Rai, Ram Vilas Sharma, Meenakshi Mukherjee, Harish Trivedi, and others—is participating in an exchange across time and space that works out present-day issues through an engagement with the past.[102]

While Niranjana and Liu use the trope of translation to show how "effective histories" must contend with these temporal and spatial dislocations, I would point out that the metaphorization of translation as crossing temporal and spatial boundaries institutes precisely the one-nation-equals-one-language formulation so many of us have learned to be wary of.[103] The historiography of the corpus of Premchand suggests a way for us to think more critically about the task literary criticism might engage in when presenting literary texts that work at the borders of a cluster of official languages and thus comment in their very textual strategies on the premises of linguistic nationalism.

In Reality a Ghost

While Wendy Brown's description of our haunted contested histories as sites of struggle might as easily apply to Bhabha's "dialectics of difference" as to Benjamin's trope of the broken vessel as *tikkun*, it is the concept of the joking triangle which might help us identify in more detail the relationality of the enterprise Brown describes, but here as a struggle that links us together across differences of time, place, nation, language, gender, and class in our ongoing practices of collective justice. I would offer that learning to read these triangles of joking relation across a range of differences will help us formulate a critical reading practice that does not claim to exhaust or settle these historical questions but articulates instead the complex relationality involved in such appropriations. We need a critical practice that might do justice to Premchand's translation of one of Tolstoy's moral tales, for example, in such a way that would make clear to readers today what he aspired to honor then in his own daily practices of justice, so that readers might be encouraged to think in turn about what we fight over, fight for, and aspire to honor in our practices of justice.

Premchand's version of *"Bhoot aur Roti"* ("The Ghost and the Bread") inherently challenges the linear-development model that Bellow's literate/preliterate distinctions are based on. In the preceding chapters I argue against applying such linear notions of temporality to literature in translation and use as my example a range of literature that moves back and forth between oral and written forms—as do the Zulu Tolstoy debates on multiculturalism and world literature. Here it is important to consider the value system at work that commits scholars to assuming Tolstoy's novels as more valuable than his oral-based stories, for example. John Burt Foster Jr. asks why a Russian novelist like Tolstoy has become one of the representative figures of a certain brand of generic realism, observing that the novels represent only a small proportion of Tolstoy's output, one that came early in his career and which he foreswore in favor of what Foster calls "narrative forms that were much closer to traditional storytelling forms."[104] Tolstoy's moral tales do not fit in the familiar schema of literary progress that we ascribe to as we write histories of world literature. How might we rework our own categories to account for such expression—when a great novelist begins to write in the voice of the people later in his career?

In *Culture and Imperialism*, Said sees in Bellow's Zulu-Tolstoy remark an argument that "allows the old imperial enterprise full scope to play itself out conventionally," an attitude that says "Westerners may have physically left their old colonies in Africa and Asia, but they retained them not only as markers but as locales on the ideological map over which they continued to rule morally and intellectually."[105] We might well wonder: Are all East-West, North-South exchanges doomed to be similarly haunted? Said allows that there is a less objectionable way of reading into this "heart of darkness": to see a narrative such as Conrad writes as "local to a time and place, neither unconditionally true nor unqualifiedly certain."[106] And as if unconsciously in conversation with Marx, Said compares the historical context of imperialism to "speech itself" which "would have its moment, then . . . would have to pass."[107] Conrad's more welcome contribution to the ongoing conversation of world literature, according to Said, was to *date* such a passing. The question of translation that we need to address once more is: How do we account for not just the *passing* but the attendant *passing on* of literary vocabularies across bounds of time, place, language, culture, class?

Georg Lukács makes an argument similar to Said's about the importance of Tolstoy's novels in documenting the passing of bourgeois culture in nineteenth-century Russia. It seems to matter little that Tolstoy himself was a landowner or that his novels focused on the lives of the elite; Lukács classifies him as one of the "great realists" who "always regard society from the viewpoint of a living and moving centre and this centre is present, visibly or invisibly, in every phenomenon."[108] What is of interest here is the way Lukács theorizes the relationship of "reality" to artistic representation; that is, he asks versions of what I might like to think of as one of the questions propelling this chapter: How does a writer like Tolstoy translate the realities of nineteenth-century Russia into literary form in such a way that allows them to be repeated by others in different times and languages, in such a way that each assumes renewed relevance? (Note the use here of the present tense to indicate such regenerations as temporary possessions). How do we write literary histories that account for the relationship of a writer to the historical moment he lives in and still take into account our own position in this triangle of relation?

Lukács insists that when he talks of "realism" he is not urging "the exact copying of reality by a mere onlooker" but that "The true artistic totality of a literary work depends on the completeness of the picture it presents of the essential social factors that determine the world depicted."[109] For Lukács, such a picture is a relationship between the writer and the realities of his time, for "it can be based only on the author's own intensive experience of the social process."[110] Lukács does not comment self-reflexively on his own position in this triangle but simply goes on to call the resulting representations "a heroic struggle against the banality, the aridity and emptiness of the prosaic nature of our bourgeois life."[111] Lukács's construction of the first-person plural ("we") here is worth noting, for it assumes we understand Tolstoy's corpus, and therefore the historical moment as well, through an individual subjectivity even though we are reading across languages and through multiple subjectivities. Engaging with Lukács engaging with Tolstoy forces me to ask another version of the question of this chapter: Who do we imagine is framing whose reality when we are reading a fictional text of "social realism" in translation?

If we look closely at the opening lines of my English translation of Premchand's Hindi translation of *"Bhoot aur Roti,"* we readily see that it does not conform to our usual understanding of realism. It assumes a simple style of narration that reminded me so much of other folktales I had read in Hindi (especially Detha's) that I wondered which had influenced which:

> One morning a poor farmer tied up two rounds of bread from home in his scarf and harnessed up the plow. When he arrived at his field he set the bread underneath a bush and began plowing the field himself. As the afternoon began to set in he let the bullocks off to graze and when he got there to pick up the bread it had disappeared. He looked here, looked there, not a trace, nor any sign of someone going from there. So who had taken the bread?

Of course, being a folktale, the riddle asks a specific, tangible question on the surface that implies a broader, intangible question: Who has the right to bread? What rules of (temporary) possession do we wish to live by? We might assume, somewhat facilely, that everyone should have bread. Like most calls to equality, this is easier to claim in theory than in practice. If there is a limited amount of bread, if one is in possession of it, another is not. This is exactly the basic dilemma being addressed in the story, for the narrator then goes on to tell us, "In reality a ghost had taken that bread. He was sitting behind the bush hiding." The riddle this leads us to ask next is not explicitly announced—Why would a ghost want to steal the farmer's bread?—but still has us ponder the broader, ethical questions about the distribution of wealth. The story needs to signal itself as a folktale precisely so that its generic vocabulary might adapt itself to other specific times, places, and dialects. Such a generic framing of time (its "'once-upon-a-time' ambience," to quote Mukherjee once more) allows new readers and writers to negotiate the concrete realities of human existence age after age.

We might notice that the formal issues of generic expectation as they translate across the borders of language and culture convey an ethical framework that brings together the political and the aesthetic. Within the frame of the story, the farmer shrugs good-naturedly and decides that someone must have taken the bread who needed it more than he and it will not hurt him to miss a meal. He takes rest in the shade before returning to plow his fields. The narration soon makes clear that the ghost has been sent down to torment the farmer by a no-good character Premchand dubs "Adharma" in order to provoke the farmer into choosing the wrong path in life. The riddle of the story then becomes: What is the wrong path, and how do we recognize it?

This riddle assumes an even more interesting avatar in Premchand's Hindi translation; "Adharma" is a curious and noteworthy word choice, for it is a Sanskrit-root word that usually refers to an abstraction: not according to dharma, and therefore not right, not lawful, irreligious. (For Gandhi, as I intimate above, "dharma" is linked with truth and therefore supports a different belief system from the ordinary understanding of faith as religion). The uncharacteristically high Hindi associations of the word might seem at odds in nowadays with the ideals of a committed secularist such as Premchand, who in his lifetime worked to close the divide between an increasingly Hindu-oriented Hindi and a Muslim-oriented Urdu. In his version of the story, the narrator does not specify overtly which "dharma" Adharma is at odds with; the philological associations are the only hints we get. In the English translation of the Russian by Louise and Aylmer Maude that Premchand was presumably working from, the bread thief is called an "imp" and his boss is called the "devil." Premchand manages to work these overtly Christian associations with the devil out of his version and he renders "imp" as "*bhoot*," a Sanskrit-based word used by grammarians to talk about the past tense. *Bhoot* is a ghost but it is also the past. In Hindi, then, I cannot resist noting the double meaning in the line: "In reality a *bhoot*." How do we understand the reality of a ghost as a past? Whose ghost? Whose past? Can it be both local and universal? How do the rules of possession work formally and ethically in translation?

Even though a theorist such as Lukács does not look to Tolstoy's moral tales to comment on the relationship of reality to artistic representation, we can see contemporaries of his, such as Premchand and Gandhi, using this story to think through ethical questions of the day. How do we read these riddles of revolution they are posing a language away and nearly a century later? We soon realize that Adharma is dismayed by the farmer's nonplussed reaction. But the ghost tells Adharma not to worry, he'll sort the farmer out. So the ghost goes to the farmer in the guise of a servant and gives him misleading advice. The first year he talks the farmer into planting his grain in the marsh; then there's a drought, and his crop is saved. And the next year, when he advises him to plant on high ground, record rains come and his is the only crop that does not drown. It seems as though the ghost and Adharma have been foiled. But the farmer has so much extra

grain that the ghost is able to convince him to make liquor from it, and
that leads to his eventual ruin—he no longer works hard and even chases
some Hindu ascetics (needy *sadhus!*) out of his house in his miserliness. He
becomes as abject as Ghisu and Madhav in "*Kafan.*" Adharma Maharaj is so
pleased with the ghost that the story ends with him awarding the ghost a
prize.[112] Who do we imagine offering the moral of this tale to whom as we
read it across languages and historical periods in multiple translation?

After all, one might very well imagine Tolstoy passing this tale on as
the voice of the Russian people, and Premchand passing this tale on as the
voice of Tolstoy capturing the voice of the Russian people, which I, too,
have passed along in turn. Understanding the complex ethical framework
being constructed in so many reiterations requires a reader such as yourself
to identify each of the iterations in the telling chain as historically localized
and therefore as both passed and past. You might be able to gather from my
English translation of the Hindi that the narrator is reliable to the extent
that he reports what he thinks he sees—that is, a ghost hiding behind a
bush—but that he does not convey his own moral judgment of this ghost or
of the ghost's master, Adharma. That he sees these supernatural figures and
overhears their conversation is considered perfectly realistic. This is part of
the playfulness of the story, a playfulness that could be read as ironic, but
only if we understand it in the more open-ended sense of the term laid out
in the work of Linda Hutcheon, for example.

I argue in earlier chapters that such playfulness is an ongoing, plural
enterprise that builds community in successive generations and successive
iterations across languages, cultures, and time periods, but only if each
act is local, temporary, and gives way to another local, temporary itera-
tion. The narrator does not express a judgment directly in order to create an opportunity for the reader to articulate and answer the questions
suggested by the narrative in seeming conversation with the figure of the
author beyond death: for example, convention would have us imagine Tolstoy's aim in writing the story this way. We read my English translation
of Premchand's Hindi translation of Tolstoy's Russian translation of this
oral-based tale and attribute to it a "moving centre," as Lukács describes
it, just as surely as that narrator saw the ghost take that bread. This figure
animating the piece, like speech, would necessarily have to pass away, and
like speech might also rejuvenate itself in another place and time. This is
how Wendy Brown's reading of Derrida's reading of the specters of Marx

applies to translation: the different versions of these stories—including our readings of them—are "a permanently contestable historiography, one that makes contestable histories an overt feature of our political life as it encourages us to struggle for and against particular conjurations of the past."

While Cheah might urge us to be wary of such vitalist imagery, my suggestion is that instead we become more critically aware of the ways we participate in promoting the afterlife of such discourse. For example, we need to notice the kind of ethical imperative we ascribe to a tale such as "*Bhoot aur Roti*" and how we think that differs from the one Premchand might have tried to convey, or Tolstoy. This is my spooky solution to a question about how to read translated literature beyond binaristic linear temporalities—of original to derivative, of past to present. The relationship of the past to the present, the living to the dead, even the local to the universal is much more complicated than that. My argument in the book more generally is that as literary scholars we are always telling ghost stories but we pretend we do not believe in ghosts.

Like the Zulu-Tolstoy debates sparked by Bellow's remark, I suggest that discussions about reading and writing (in short, translating) world literature across borders introduce other debates about what the world might become. Lukács, for example, reads Tolstoy spectrally, calling him "the poet of the peasant revolt that lasted from 1861 to 1905," for in Tolstoy's lifework, he argues, "the exploited peasant is . . . never absent from the consciousness of the characters themselves."[113] We might assume that the peasant consciousness he looks for is even more obvious in a tale such as "*Bhoot aur Roti*," especially in the ways it attempts to channel a voice of the people not bounded by time; but Lukács (like Bakhtin, for example) focuses his analysis on a bourgeois genre like the novel, where a single genius of an author always speaks for the anonymous collective in his age (whether that is the age of a Rabelais or a Tolstoy). The novel is easier to analyze than a moral tale, in that its form organizes the peasants as a peripheral consciousness even while—at least, according to Lukács—announcing their primacy in the abstract. While it would be interesting to analyze in more detail the formal relationship of the individual subject to the collective in the critical writings of a range of Marxist theorists (my hunch is that some of the contradictions of the Marxist political program get played out in their writing), in this chapter I am interested in introducing a broader question: How do we bring together the political and the aesthetic (or the ethical and the formal) components of our engagements with literature when we practice criticism of oral-based tales such as this?

In Chapter 2, I introduce the question of generic expectations by asking how we end up framing the questions we think are worth addressing "age after age" (as the opening line of Detha's "Chouboli" has it). I would like to suggest here that the concerns of these fantastic moral tales such as the one written by Tolstoy and translated by Premchand are not so very different from those conveyed in novels and even theoretical tracts and therefore give us some insight into reading each of these genres in relation to the other. Lukács insists that "what is important in Tolstoy is the putting of the question and not the answer given to it."[114] The "correct question" he identifies in Tolstoy's novels is the "inexorable division between the 'two nations' in Russia, the peasants and the landowners."[115] Lukács cites Chekhov, agreeing that "putting a question correctly is one thing and finding the answer to it is something quite different; the artist absolutely needs to do only the first."[116] The implication, of course (a sentiment articulated by Lenin), is that Tolstoy asked the question so well that he managed to inspire Russian readers to a world-changing answer: in a word, revolution. Seen in this regard, Lukács's assessments of "realism" have a very specific ethical imperative that does not translate easily into the literary debates of today.

A student of South Asian history today, for example, would likely not immediately think of class divides when hearing the phrase "two nations" but would instead think of the tensions between the Hindu and Muslim communities involved in the nationalist movement, tensions that—as we see in Chapter 4—eventually led to the partition of the colony into India and Pakistan in 1947, eleven years after Premchand's death. Likewise, Lukács is reading back into history, seeing evidence for the Russian Revolution in Tolstoy's vivid prose. But in the process, I would like to suggest, he is also arguing for the direction the revolution should take in his own time, just as Amrit Rai is making an argument about communalism in the way he writes the biography of his father, Premchand, or just as I might use Lukács to make an argument about the ways theorists can be so convinced of the rightness of their own perspectives that they do not see that their speech, too, is passing.

My suggestion here and elsewhere in this book is that we take cues from historiographers such as Dipesh Chakrabarty who are increasingly relying on literary texts and tropes of translation—rather than transition—to work out the contradictions of such teleological narratives, especially when trying to include the voices of people who are regularly left out of historical accounts. My suggestion is that Chakrabarty is pointing us in an interesting direction and that such a project—what he calls "provincializing Europe"—can best be undertaken by scrutinizing our own critical methodologies in reading these novels and especially moral tales as translations. It is literary theorists, not historians, who might most effectively use the critical tools of literary analysis to ask more specifically what we can learn from a narrator who takes seriously and playfully at the same time the moral lessons learned by attending to the reality of a ghost.

To ask what question is being asked by a translator and theorist in this age in response to Premchand in his age in response to Tolstoy in his age is to begin attending to the ways our own speech is itself passing, as a site where various conjured specters and spirits are in conversation. This is a different site of meaning-making as *mise en abîme* from the one ordinarily theorized. My suggestion is that such a course forces us to formulate a methodology that negotiates extreme relativism and absolutism (which Bakhtin warns us away from, as we see in Chapter 2) to read such rhetorical positions in a way that takes into account not only the mixture of realism and idealism at any given point in time but also our own mixture now, reading those moments. Here and in Chapter 6 I ask us to look more closely at our ghost stories to ask self-reflexively and dynamically how we might more productively read such *bhoot* in translation. After all, it is this forgetting that is not forgetting, translating that is not translating that haunts the enterprise of "world literature" and forgets itself as an exchange distinctly spiritual.

Narration in Ghost Time

Framing the Politics of Translation

If we decide to read these playful, oral-based ghost stories about injustice as stories not of transition but instead of translation (following Chakrabarty's suggestion in *Provincializing Europe*), then how do we understand the narrative relationship of these spirits and specters to one another as they are told in turn, if not in linear sequence?[1] This is an especially confounding riddle to ponder when we recognize that the tongues in which these translations take place belong as much to the tellers as to the listeners. How do we apply the lessons of the previous chapters and frame the temporal, ethical, and spatial bases of these differences we assert (dialectically, dialogically) in sites of ongoing playful exchange in such a way that is neither forbiddingly absolute nor exasperatingly relativistic? In this chapter I would have us pursue this question by returning to the work of Vijay Dan Detha, comparing his written version of *"Thakur rau Bhoot"* ("The *Thakur*'s Ghost") with the oral version that Detha's childhood friend Bhola Ram told to me one sunny winter day in the courtyard of his home, in a triangle of ongoing exchange as curious as it is revealing.

Detha and I had gone together to hear Bhola Ram's version because Detha had told me he had heard from Bhola Ram the original version of the tale that he reworked to become *"Thakur rau Bhoot."* Both Detha's and Bhola Ram's versions satirize a landlord's foiled greed even into death and a helpless farmer's inability to refuse such unfair treatment by the landlord's ghost. Both versions ask us to think about the ways we might avoid such disparities and the resulting injustices. Even in Bhola Ram's impromptu, therefore somewhat abbreviated, and necessarily contrived performance, the narrative style he adopted made it seem ridiculous that the farmer would be so frightened of the *thakur* and his feudal sense of entitlement that he would agree to let the *thakur*'s ghost take charge of the land. When the ghost appears to the farmer in his dream, telling him not to do his own farming (*"to kai kheti mat karjai!"*) he asks why, and is told simply, "You are like my brother. I am going to bring you lots of grain" (*"ke thoon mhaarou dharam-bhai hai. Mhain thaarai anaaj I thooni bahut laay deoola"*). That is, the ghost will do the farmer's work in his stead. The farmer thinks to himself, "What a great thing!" (*"ghani acchi baat hai"*), and proceeds to sit there, Bhola Ram told us with understated but wry drama, doing nothing. As the monsoon rains come, he still sits. As his neighbors sow and reap, he still sits, doing nothing. He keeps hearing the assurances of the ghost, who assures him, "I will do it in a day" (*"ek din mai i kar devai"*). That day, of course, never comes.

More explicitly than the dream of revolution we saw in the last chapter, Bhola Ram's version asks us to be skeptical of the terms offered in such a dream.[2] If we agree with Walter Benjamin when he reads Marx as urging people not just to possess "the dream of the thing" but "to possess the consciousness of the thing in order to really possess it," then here it seemed Bhola Ram's wry skepticism was offering me the chance to participate in a narrative exchange that would challenge and refine such a general notion of agential possession.[3] (Once more: Can the subaltern joke?) The tale asks us as English speakers to explain in more detail the narrative relationship formed in another tongue between ourselves and the spirit of disenchantment introduced through the *bhoot kaal*—here understood as both ghost time and past tense. How might we narrate the relationship of the individual tellers (Bhola Ram, Detha, myself) to these *bhoot* and to each other in such a way that might allow the individuals to take possession of the thing on their own behalf and still be in dialogue with the others who have preceded them and will follow them? The tale offers an example of the narrative strategies we rely on to understand our own *bhoot kaal* that haunts the community of world literature.

We might notice that Detha's version of the tale is likewise set in a vaguely remote past not historically locatable. It asks us to devise a more complex way of mapping the relations and judgments of the narration than a standard, binaristic narrative of good guys (the revolutionaries, for instance) against the bad guys (the entrenched order). The story opens in a once-upon-a-time fairy-tale era of feudal cruelty whose past-tense lessons might apply as much to the present as to the future. Even in (my) English translation of the written Rajasthani, the narration does not specify exactly whose *bhoot kaal* this is:

> Once there was a *thakur* of a petty feudal territory somewhere whose preten-sions were as grand as his estate modest. His subjects nearly killed themselves working to keep up the standards of a big *thikana*. Land tariffs and taxes, coer-cion and co-option, so fierce it made you weep. His subjects suffered horribly. And yet they had neither the courage nor the means to leave this place where their families had lived for so many generations.

I argue in Chapter 5 that these playful narrative modes do not ignore the tensions of time past and time present but instead use the "'once-upon-a-time' ambience" (as Mukherjee calls it) to allow a chain of interpreters to negotiate their versions of concrete human reality age after age—as a moral schema that is necessarily changing because it allows storytellers and listen-ers to respond to the verities of life time and time again in each telling. We see in this tale that some kind of change does inevitably come, but not one that gives any kind of agency to the subjects who have suffered so:

> The *thakur* kept up his nasty habits and the people in the *basti* went on suffer-ing in silence. But no one's status can help them face down mortality, so how could the *thakur*'s? He put up a good fight but soon his resources were sapped and he headed straight down the road of death at an early age. His body had finished. His spirit was released. But it would not leave the confines of that *thikana*. The *thakur*'s spirit would circle around from *ker* bush to *khejari* tree, from Banyan tree to ficus tree, from drinking well to step well. Before too long

people in the area realized the *thakur* had become a ghost and was appearing at different places around the edge of the *thikana*.

Just as the narrator of "Chouboli" makes fun of the *thakur* in that story for his compulsive habits of cruelty (shooting an arrow through his wife's nose ring one hundred and eight times), so does the narrator here ridicule the *thakur* for his own "nasty habits." This story also comments teasingly on the downtrodden subjects' unwitting complicity in such cycles of injustice, especially when these entrenched habits threaten to continue even after the *thakur*'s death. It is not clear how he can continue to tyrannize the people when his power is entirely spiritual and immaterial. Rather than asking simply whether this is a good ghost or a bad ghost, the story thinks through the ways people give power to such spirits when there is no material reason to do so. In both Bhola Ram's and Detha's versions, the humor of the tale asks us to consider how we understand the relationship of these afterlives of past injustices to our present realities. Here I am asking in turn what critical tools we have for explaining the complex temporalities of such translations.

As discussed in Chapter 5, the spirits inciting us toward a better, more equal future are not so distinct from the ghosts of the past (as *bhoot*) that we are urged to distance ourselves from. We might even imagine that these ghosts and specters might be enticing us, riding us (as the *vetala* rode the king), laughing at us in an ongoing exchange as lively as it is . . . spirited. If Brecht via Eagleton tells us "I have never found anybody without a sense of humour who could understand dialectics," we might notice similarly that Marx opens *The Eighteenth Brumaire of Louis Bonaparte* by noting wryly: "Hegel remarks somewhere that all facts and personages of great importance in world history occur, as it were, twice. He forgot to add: the first time as tragedy, the second as farce."[4] The one-two rhythm of such a quip could just as likely be heard coming from the affable, cigar-chomping mouth of a Groucho Marx as from an enraged and engaged Karl. We might go so far as to read the line as a conjuring of a Karl channeling a Groucho, one that urges us to outwit dialectical materialism by playing along with the big joke that history tries to play on us. As shown in Chapter 5, Derrida understands such confusing and even contradictory temporal narratives to be a forgetting without forgetting, or what Douglas Robinson sees as a translating without translating.

Robinson observes, "In wanting to 're-discover' the spirit/*Geist* of revolution *as opposed to* summoning up its *ghost/Gespenst*, Marx is very close to calling for ghosts without ghosts."[5] As opposed to the spirits (*Geister*) of the revolution to come and the ghosts (*Gespenst*) of the past, the *Geist* of Hegel that appears so regularly in Marx's writing is "both a spirit and a ghost," Robinson observes, and thus can signify a range of "other 'spiritual' things . . . like mind, culture, mood."[6] My suggestion is that we understand these inevitable spiritual displacements precisely in terms of humor, for a playful mien allows the flexible networks of plural relation such a situation requires. The trick is to learn to play with them in a way that allows a range of people to take possession of such *Geist* in turn according to the curious temporalities implied in the riddle of belonging—that what I say already includes what you say to me.

How else to understand the specter of Marx except as temporarily possessed? After all, Marx himself likens the revolutions he urges toward not just to translation (as Robinson discusses) but also to parody:

> The raising of the dead in those [truly revolutionary] revolutions, therefore, served to glorify the new struggles, not to *parody* the old; it fostered in imagination an aggrandizement of the set task, not flight from its actual solution, a rediscovery of the spirit of the revolution rather than a summoning up of its ghost.[7]

The specter of Marx I conjure here is alive to the productive contradictions implicit in the turns of speech he adopts as so much derivative discourse. Such a reading allows his use of the verb "parody" here (in Robinson's English) to be nearly synonymous with "re-translate" in the way he uses it elsewhere in *The Eighteenth Brumaire of Louis Bonaparte*—"Just so does the beginner, having learnt a new language, always re-translate it into his mother tongue; he has not assimilated the spirit of the new language"—as re-presenting someone else's speech in such a way that you do not make it your own.[8] We might worry that such an approach to translation and parody alike assumes there is a clear, fixed line separating the past from the present, one's mother tongue from another, mindless repetition from the more spirited modes of possession that he advocates. Unlike Partha Chatterjee and Aijaz Ahmad, however, I do not see him dismissing such repetitions out of hand but asking readers to distinguish the false copy from the real, to recognize the difference between the ghosts of the old order and the spirits of true revolution.

Here, then, we find ourselves asking another version of the riddle that has perplexed Chouboli and Gandhi alike (as shown in chapters 2 and 4): Which one is true? I suggest in previous chapters that the conscious effort to distance oneself from a fixed notion of the past only succeeds in engaging oneself further in ongoing fetishistic relationship to it as one tries to release oneself from the pull of a secret awareness nearly within one's apprehension and yet always—always already—displaced. Marx dismisses the possibilities of parody, like translation, as the wrong sort of repetition; I would argue that these framing devices he employs so ambivalently and even contradictorily are the very heuristic that might help us play along with the complex temporal workings of such revolutions.

Throughout the *Brumaire* Marx implies that history might very well be playing a big joke on us that we are not allowing ourselves to play along with. In the preface to the 1869 edition, for instance, Marx tells us he writes this tract in order to argue against representing Napoleon Bonaparte's 1851 coup d'état as "only the violent act of a single individual" (a faulty perspective he attributes to "bitter and witty invective") or "as the result of an antecedent historical development" ("the error of so-called *objective* historians"); he endeavors to demonstrate instead "how the *class struggle* in France created circumstances and relationships that made it possible for a grotesque mediocrity to play a hero's part."[9] His own spirited analysis combines bitter and witty invective with objective historical research to offer new techniques for framing the relationship of past event to future potential.

If, as we see in Chapter 5, Martin Puchner argues that the manifesto as a genre created new possibilities for understanding the narrative relationship of past to future, I would argue that Marx's writing in the *Brumaire* offers a new discursive mode—one whose very spiritedness is a crucial component of his critical project. I am interested here in identifying critical tools that might help us understand the relationship of past to future as spirited exchange. Marx observes that in the years between 1852 (when the *Brumaire* was first published in America) and 1869 (when he wrote this preface for publication in Germany), "French literature made an end of the Napoleon legend with the weapons of historical research, criticism, of satire and of wit," but that this "violent breach with traditional popular belief," which he calls a "tremendous mental revolution," had until that point not been taken up outside France.[10] We might, then, understand Marx's project as bringing the weapons of historical research, criticism, satire, and wit across the bounds of the French language. Approaching his tract as a style of thinking allows us to understand better the play between the ghosts of past injustice and the specter of revolution as it appears not only in Marx's writing but in other work concerned with issues of justice—like the two versions of the tale of the *thakur*'s ghost riddling this chapter.

In *The Eighteenth Brumaire of Louis Bonaparte*, Marx assumes a clear distinction between the kind of conjuring he champions as the right kind of revolution and the type of summoning of ghosts he eschews as parody. In the process, however, he performs in his prose a kind of parody that might very well lead to the revolutions he writes of so approvingly. For such a reading to make sense, we must understand parody in the historical sense Margaret Rose writes about "singing after the style of an original but with a difference," a gambit that allows this act of repetition to communicate both "nearness and opposition" in the same rhetorical gesture.[11] By such logic, a parodic text allows the ghosts of the past to be in conversation with the specters of the future within a single narrative frame, if the reader is attentive to the complexity of these performative relationships. The very metaphors of "embedding" and "continued form of existence" that Rose employs to discuss the workings of parody should recall the triangular relationship established between *vetala*, corpse, and king and thus should remind us that the riddles we seek to answer often lead us to trust different spirits from those we imagined at first.

The narrative structure of "The Twenty-Five Tales of the Undead" teaches us that an entire journey can take place within a single frame, one that ends in discovering a most curious and hard-won version of truth that necessarily refracts back on our past assumptions but also conditions our future projections. Rose likewise figures parody in such a way that it confines itself to a single narrative frame connecting past, present, and future simultaneously: she notes that parody necessarily contains two texts within one—the parody and the parodied—and that "the embedding of the parodied text within the text of the parody both contributes to the ambivalence of the parody," an ambivalence that "derives from its ability to criticise and renew its target as part of its own structure," whose integrity of form "ensures some continued form of existence for the parodied work."[12] Just as Benjamin's afterlives renew the spirits of the original text through translation, so does Rose argue for the continued life of these texts through parodic repetition. Such a reading is possible only if we understand these spirits of past, present, and future to engage in ongoing and even conten-tious exchange through such textual encounters. That is, we must under-stand, *pace* Marx, that parody, like translation, allows a speaker to borrow someone else's speech in such a way that it can be read as neither strictly (and mindlessly) derivative nor an absolute appropriation of someone else's words. We might in turn see agential possibilities in Marx's own riddling declaration on repetition when he writes: "The riddle is not solved by such turns of speech, but merely formulated differently."[13]

Here we have a slight adjustment to the order of temporary possession from that shown in previous chapters: parody, like translation, invites read-ers to engage with these texts as passing performances in such a way that they move us in endless interpretive loops, enacting another version of the riddle of belonging that we have seen before—that what I say to you already includes what you say to me. If irony has its readers oscillating between more than one ideological location within a single temporal frame, parody's dynamism moves readers temporally but within a single imagined spatial frame. For Rose, the difference between irony and parody revolves around a similar riddle of belonging: "the parodied text generally . . . remains in the ambivalent position of belonging both to the work of the parodist and to the author and reading public attacked by the parodist."[14]

Unlike translation, successful parody deftly copies the rhetorical devices used conventionally within a single language domain to create an impression of normativity and yet at the same time suggests an ideologi-cal perspective at odds with such framing and so calls into question its very basis.[15] Current examples of popular political humor in the United States function similarly—from the startling and hilarious headlines and leads of *The Onion* ("U.S. Finishes 'A Strong Second' in Iraq War" and "A field study released Monday by the University of North Carolina School of Public Health suggests that Iraqi citizens experience sadness and a sense of loss when relatives, spouses, and even friends perish, emotions that have until recently been identified almost exclusively with Westerners"),[16] the trenchant mock–news analyses of *The Daily Show* (Bush "takes the subtext of a speech and makes it his speech. . . . When he's giving speeches, it's like he's reading the stage directions. . . . He's our first meta-president"),[17] the clever bumper-sticker campaigns of Billionaires for Bush ("SMALL GOVERN-MENT BIG WARS"),[18] or the outrageous tactical media stunts of the Yes Men ("Dow Releases 'Acceptable Risk' Program at Banking Conference.

'Risk Calculator' Helps Ensure Sound Business Practice," and "Find out whether *your* business project will result in 'golden skeletons,' or just regular ones—try out the Acceptable Risk Calculator™ *free!*").[19] In each case, the medium they use to channel these figures of injustice must pass at first glance as real; it is only when the audience notices something out of the ordinary (an exaggeration, perhaps, that reveals an implicit incongruity) that they realize these injustices are being addressed in some measure, which then causes them to begin scrutinizing both the content and the framing devices themselves.

As Susan Stewart argues, playful nonsense calls into question the framing device that distinguishes commonsense from nonsense and thus "always refers back to a sense that itself cannot be assumed." Similarly, parody reveals the falsity of these forms of discourse that claim to be real and authentic. Rose observes that parody does not only reveal that these discourses are false but shows how—not by setting up a straightforward, binaristic contrast to a utopic ideal but "by showing a variety of conflicting ideals or representations of reality."[20]

Joanne Richardson similarly identifies such ideological agility as a feature of what has recently been called "tactical media": "In contrast to mainstream media," she explains, "tactical interventions don't occupy a stable ideological place from which they put forward counter-arguments; they speak in tongues, offering temporary revelations."[21] We might very well read Gandhi's quip that I open the book with as engaging in tactical media in an age before it was so named. In her article "The Language of Tactical Media," Richardson works from a distinction between strategies ("which belong to states, economic power, and scientific rationality" and thus "are formed around a clear sense of boundary, a separation between the proper place of the self and an outside defined as an enemy") and tactics (which "insinuate themselves into the other's place without the privilege of separation; they are not a frontal assault on an external power, but makeshift, temporary infiltrations from the inside through actions of thefts, hijacks, tricks and pranks") to ask a version of the same question a range of thinkers address: How to relate to these ghosts of the past and specters of the future in a manner we might find ethically tenable?

Richardson opens her article with a lyrical meditation on the impossible temporalities of our critical moment ("The future is a series of small steps leading away from the wreckage of the past, sometimes its actors walk face forward, blind to the history played out behind their backs, other times, they walk backwards, seeing only the unfulfilled destiny of a vanished time") that recalls more than anything Benjamin's own melancholic "angel of history" discourse. She ends, however, with the fiercely hopeful yet cheeky suggestion that the way out of such an impasse is to reframe the rules of the game as it is commonly played:

> As wars rage around us—wars that rationalize the trafficking in merchandise under the shadow of sublime principles, wars against terrorism, wars against drugs, wars of information against information—maybe what we need least is to advertise our practice as an extension of one or another principle of warfare. When asked to take sides, for or against, siding with one army or the other, sometimes the only real answer is not to play the game. This refusal should not be confused with an exodus, a silent passivity, or a patient resignation. It is the vigilance of continuing to think, beyond the obvious—of a third, a fourth, or fifth alternative to the apocalyptic or utopian sense of the media.

Just as Gandhi shifts the rules of the game of colonialism by refusing to be complicit in the cruel habits of the "civilizing power" and with a single mischievous reply turns the grammar of possession against itself, so, too, do the actors in the ongoing joking chains that Richardson describes question the very framing devices that ask us to take sides in an apocalypse-versus-utopia game not of our own choosing. In this case, the actors play along as if in earnest, but copycatting to such a degree of fidelity that the very game itself is revealed to be absurd. In conjuring such a spirit of playfulness, the copycat establishes a ground of "makeshift commensurability" to work from that allows the speaker to highlight what Lydia Liu calls the "relative absence of hypothetical equivalence between" guest and host languages in translating a term such as "universal human rights."[22] Such translations are as "proleptic and performative" as Judith Butler and others could ever suggest they be, for they create the rhetorical possibility for "the consciousness of the thing" (as Benjamin terms it), even if in play (or, using Susan Stewart's logic, especially because in play).[23] If we agree that such acts of parody, like translation, render the material copied the possession of the copier as much as the copied, then these afterlives affect our understanding of the potentials of the past as much as the present and future. Such tactics offer a different way of framing these tales of possession to show how they connect us.

It is in this way that we might compare the Yes Men's fake "Dow Representative" Erastus Hamm, for example, to the *vetala*: the Yes Men insist that they engage not in "identity theft" but in "identity correction," taking possession temporarily and purposefully of a common type precisely to trick their audience into questioning the underlying logics of relationships that we ordinarily assume to be trustworthy and natural.[24] That such a maneuver (as "tactic") can carry on infinitely is a sign of optimism for someone like Richardson, and not of despair, for it ensures that no one can claim to have formulated the "true, genuine, democratic form of representation" just because they have opposed "the false media shell with counter-statements made from a counter-perspective."[25] She argues that such strict oppositional thinking is a feature of the strategies of state-sponsored warfare, one that assumes the enemy is clearly on that side of the line, over there. Instead, we might extrapolate and conclude that tactical media and other forms of parody would have us understand that the spirits inciting us toward a better, more equal future are not so distinct from the ghosts of the past that we would like to distance ourselves from; it is not the people themselves but the tactics that help us negotiate in a world where such boundaries of belonging are not so very distinct.

After all, we know that any of us can move from being listeners to being tellers and listeners again in turn; we know that the words we read in the present belong to writers long since dead; and we likewise recognize that the voices we imagine we hear could be channeling ghosts from a past we would like to leave behind or might be conjuring specters of the kind of future we would want to work toward. Calling such spirits "afterlives" does not, then, necessarily imply a strict linear sequence, as we see in my reading of Karl Marx's history-as-farce quip as if performed by Groucho Marx or in the networks of interpretations that accrue as we read my English version of Detha's Rajasthani version of an oral version of "The *Thakur* and the Ghost" that Bhola Ram told once upon a time in comparison to my written English translation of the oral version Bhola Ram told to me with Detha looking on. Benjamin argues that these translations ensure the "continued life" of the original; likewise, Butler argues that parody brings into relief the utterly constructed status of the so-called original.[26] In each case, the relationship of these versions to one another does not articulate a stable ideological place from which they put forward counterarguments but instead shows that the versions necessarily speak in tongues, offering temporary revelations that are relational and dynamic because they are always—always already—displaced. What critical tools are required to read the temporalities of these relationships with the flexibility they deserve?

To Play the Game

When Gyan Prakash heard similar oral narratives of what he terms "the relation between the living and the dead" in his work on *Bonded Histories*, he noted that "spirit-cult practices . . . provided a critique of social relations founded on private property in land" but he ultimately concluded that "the notion of regeneration made time cyclical" and so "individual biographies and change were denied and social order became eternal."[27] His characterization of such tales and practices seems far more ambivalent than James Scott's description of the "cynical and mocking" taunting that tenants employ behind their landlord's back, a tactic James Scott has celebrated as one of the "weapons of the weak."[28] I would have liked to have read "*Thakur rau Bhoot*" as M. M. Bakhtin read the marketplace humor in Rabelais's fiction—as "gay, triumphant, and at the same time mocking, deriding."[29] In this case, neither Prakash's pessimism seemed justified, nor Scott's and Bakhtin's exuberance. How might one read the effect of the humor in "*Thakur rau Bhoot*"?

One afternoon, sitting out on string cots in Bhola Ram's courtyard, Ram agreed that the story made him laugh, so I earnestly inquired, "What makes it funny?" He explained with a warm, delighted chuckle: "If someone deceives you, they can deceive you anytime" ("*dhoka devan walou to kadai hi bhi dhoka dey sakai!*").[30] In a single statement, Prakash's eternal social order had met Scott's everyday resistance in an ongoing present tense decidedly not progressive. Bhola Ram's clever remarks relied on a different grammar of social change.

Bhola Ram then gestured to Detha, the famous author and landowner who also happened to be his lifelong friend whom he called Bijji, and added, "We're not supposed to see that today Bijji could deceive me just this way" ("*yah nahi dekhna ki mujhe bijji aaj ij dhoka dey sakai*"). He related the possibility to me as earnestly as I had just asked him about the story, as if we shared a universal understanding of our own collective blindness, as if there were no differences of age and class and education and language fluency.

Bhola Ram made me inadvertently complicit in teasing Detha, someone many years my senior. By using the relationship between the two of them as a particular example, he turned the parley into a joking triangle that I could not help but be part of, a triangle whose good-natured mischievousness I might even pass on in turn (as I have done here). In the process, I have thus been compelled to renegotiate the various incommensurabilities inherent in the relationships connecting us over time, using the tellings to create a ground in common of makeshift translatability. Because Bhola Ram's comment on Bijji's potential deceptions was not just conditional but playful, it allowed each of us to wonder what conditions there could be that might allow us to play along with such an injustice. It did not assume there were clear, stable domains demarcating the good and the bad but instead that these were processes any of us could become complicit in. We see a similar process of recognition at work in Detha's written version of the tale (here in my English version):

> Once on the festival of *Akhateej*, the *chaudhuri* [farmer] of the village put his
> hoe on his shoulder and headed out to clear his fields, as a farmer ought that
> holiday season. He carried a basket on his head packed with millet *roti*, *saag*
> of green beans, *galvani* sweets, and cooled water. He had just arrived at the
> edge of his field when a partridge called, warning him off. A very inauspicious
> omen. He paused for a moment, looked around, then went on. This time the
> partridge didn't coo.[31]

Soon enough, however, we read that the farmer "saw a man in sparkling white clothes standing before him under the *khejari* tree." The narrator has already told us, his readers, who this is. The farmer, however, "walked closer and still he had trouble recognizing who this was. He greeted him and then asked, 'Who's that?'"

In the frame of this story the ghost (as *bhoot*) is not confined to the past (as *bhoot*), for we can see his expression and hear the spirit speak directly in a manner that lords his superiority over the farmer:

> The man in white smiled, "Chaudhuri! You've garnered so much pride in so
> little time. I never would have imagined you would have forgotten the lord of
> the village this quickly. Two moons have hardly gone by since I died."

His attempts at gentle scolding through charming repartee are directed at the farmer but indirectly speak to us, the invisible audience, also trying to figure out how to place him. We might not even be conscious of the irony here: How many stories have a character speaking of his own death in the recent past? What kind of *bhoot kaal* is this? It is one that clearly sees how much the past threatens to be part of the present, for the ghost tries to claim his former status in relation to the farmer.

We watch to see if the farmer will comply. The narrator does not tell us explicitly that this is the struggle going on via such dialogue; the narrator describes the truth dawning on the farmer in close third person as a way of introducing the farmer's understanding of the situation and thus his internal struggles to us, his invisible audience:

> When he heard this the *chaudhuri* suddenly understood that this was the *thakur*'s ghost. But now there was no need to be afraid. He gathered his courage and said, "Graingiver, this was my first thought. But then I realized you must already be ruling up in heaven. I assumed it was only us lowly types who turned into ghosts and phantoms and roamed around from bush to bush."

Such a narrative strategy is important to note, because it establishes a difference between what the farmer thinks in the privacy of his own mind and what he says out loud to the ghost in the formal feudal language of entrenched hierarchy (which the narrator also abides by in addressing him courteously as "Chaudhuri" and the ghost as "Thakur"). He tells himself he need not be afraid but still acts courteously toward the ghost (addressing him conventionally as *"Annadatta"* [Graingiver], even though he is the one who harvests the grain given by the Creator) and thus participates in exactly the kinds of hierarchical injustices sanctioned by tradition.

If we were ignorant of the history of such forms of address in feudal relation, we might turn to the story of a surprise encounter between a *kisan* (a peasant rather than a *chaudhuri*/farmer) and a *thakur* that Ranajit Guha writes about in his study on the *Elementary Aspects of Peasant Insurgency in Colonial India*. Guha's tale is based on a historical record of a notorious farmer turned outlaw from Bihar at the beginning of the nineteenth century who, surprised by a villager asking him to identify himself, answered with an abuse: simply "your father" (which Guha glosses as "you bastard!"). Guha is interested in investigating the possibilities of insurgency through transgressions more criminal than playful and notes in this case that the switch in hierarchy was punished with irreversible physical violence. ("He had his forearms chopped off and bled to death.")[32] Guha writes approvingly of the ways these bandits "combined a cool disregard for the authorities with humour, hospitality and even chivalry to impose the rhetoric of combat between equals."[33]

I would go even further with this point and suggest that the true heroics are not in the criminal performances whereby these bandits lost their limbs or even lives but in the rhetorical performances that established an alternate basis for equality—not so much a hierarchical inversion (as Guha reads these stories) of a strictly dual system of dominant and dominated but a provisional triangularity where such hierarchies are played with—a version of makeshift commensurability. Guha's reading of history recovers moments of humorous subversion that are more tactical in Richardson's sense than strategic, for they make clear that the real answer to such a question— Who's that?—is not to play the hierarchical game of deference.

While Guha insists there must be "two different and contradictory ways of looking at the violence of peasant rebellions—the rebel's and his enemy's, giving rise to two different and irreconcilable ways of interpreting and generalizing the experience of that violence," we can see how necessary it is in reading a story such as "The *Thakur*'s Ghost" to allow the power relations to sound beyond such binaries. In the space of this fiction that is negotiating real-life questions, rather than judging the basis of such narratives as rational or irrational, we need to look more carefully at the relational nature of these powers the ghost claims to possess, to understand the ways that power might very well be dangerous to the farmer— whether we imagine such a force to originate with the farmer's frame of mind or with the circumstantial privileges of the landlord.[34] Unlike historical narratives of rebellion, the story does not fall easily into ready categories of siding with the rebel or siding with enemy state. The narrator, for instance, seems as worried about appeasing the *thakur*—ghost or no—as the farmer does:

> Hearing the *chaudhuri*'s gentle words made the ghost's temper cool. He thought for a moment and then said, "Chaudhuri, when I was alive I ruled for all I was worth. But now I have no wish at all to rule. If I tell you the truth you're not going to believe it: I have made a choice not to establish my *raj* up in heaven so that I may stay down here on earth and look after you farmers. When I was alive I made my subjects suffer terribly. Now that I've become a ghost I will help you watch over your fields. I would like to compensate you somehow."

We see that the *thakur* plays the part perfectly of the pathetic, remorseful landowner. At this point the narrator does not flit omnisciently inside the *thakur*'s head as he does with the farmer to tell us what he is thinking, and so is nearly complicit in this act of duplicity. We register his reactions and speech only from the perspective of someone standing across from him, like the farmer. Do we trust the *thakur*'s sweet, guilt-soaked offer? Should the farmer? In the triangle with the *vetala* we learned to trust the tricksterish spirit speaking to us.

The *chaudhuri* tries to summon the same polite, formal language the *thakur* has used to turn down the *thakur*'s offer, but we find that such borrowed speech only works to preference the *thakur*'s wishes. The *thakur* snaps, "Burdens aren't lifted just with words. I really want to do something for you people" and goes on to demand, "Tell me, Chaudhuri, how many maunds of grain do you reap every year?"[35]

The *chaudhuri* answers obsequiously, "Graingiver, this isn't something that's hidden from you. In a good year it has never been below a thousand maunds." More and more we notice that the relation being negotiated between them is that of a relation between the (omnipotent) lord and his faithful devotee. Nothing is hidden from him? We are then treated to the (former) lord's song of regret, which we might be tempted to trust:

> The ghost said, "And out of that you wouldn't even get a hundred. Today my
> soul writhes to think of the crimes I committed against you people. Listen
> to me, there's no need for you to plough a single furrow. You go back home
> the way you came. I'll make it my responsibility to see you get two thousands
> maunds of millet in the autumn harvest. And you're not to give a single grain
> to the *thikana*. Those people don't deserve it."

Here an attentive and suspicious reader gets a brief glimpse of a possible motive besides regret for the *thakur*'s insistence that the farmer not plow his field: he is angry at his relatives for doing rituals that keep him from returning to his old haunts and he wants to seek revenge by keeping them from getting a share of their tenants' crops. We are not told if the farmer is on to the *thakur*'s deviousness, however; we only see him answering, as if earnestly:

> The *chaudhuri* shook his head, "No, Graingiver, Lord Ram protect us from
> such ill-gotten gains. Beasts of burden like us can't compare to big people
> like you. Hearing such nectar-filled words from your noble mouth, it's as

if I've been blessed with not just a thousand maunds but a harvest a *lakh* [100,000] strong instead. But Graingiver, lowly folk such as ourselves after this many generations have gotten used to eating the fruits of our own labor, so are unable to digest anything else. We'd rather die than sit around not doing any work."

The phrase *bina kamaairou dhaan* ("ill-gotten gains") appears again and again in the story as the situation the farmer claims to be truly scared of: that he would have to live off someone else's labor. The phrase does not appear in the abbreviated version of the story that Bhola Ram narrated to me when I asked him. In Detha's version, however, the humor turns on the phrase, for it uses the postfeudal rhetoric of the nobility of labor against the *thakur*.

The ghost is quick, however, to turn such rhetoric back against the farmer once more. Now suddenly the narrator dips into the ghost's point of view to tell us what he is thinking:

The *thakur*'s ghost didn't at all like what the *chaudhuri* said. But he held his anger in check as he said, "What, you wish to say that all of us *thakurs* eat the fruits of others' labor? That we gulp down ill-gotten gains?"

Where before we saw the farmer thinking to himself that he need not be afraid of the *thakur*—because he is a ghost of himself, because the feudal system he relies on to sustain himself is now in the past, in *bhoot kal*—we see that these traditions die hard. The *chaudhuri* suddenly reverts to the old hierarchical ways:

The *chaudhuri* clasped his hands right up to his elbows and folded in on himself, pleading, "Graingiver, such a statement would never have come out of these lips of mine. It's not as if this mouth is borrowed from somewhere, why would I use it to defame my lord? The work you big people have to do is taking it easy, as a result of the karma you've done in your past birth. According to our karma, we have to labor and toil. That such grace has come from your royal mouth is more than enough."

The *chaudhuri* uses the formal word of pleading from the feudal past, "*pharamaavanou*," twice in his effort to argue for a different present: first to insist that the *thakur*'s karma (*karmaan*) is to enjoy rest, to take it easy ("*aaraam pharamaavanou*"), and then to suggest that such grace from "your royal mouth" is enough ("*aap srii mukh soon pharmaayou, vaa ii mayaa kisii kama hai*"). The genealogical substance of the farmer's low-caste mouth is compared with the high-caste landowner's in a manner that renders such borrowed speech parodic. At first glance, this repetition is parodic in exactly the way Marx warned us away from.

Here, after all, we have a well-intentioned feudal subject using the vocabulary from the past in an effort to argue for a different present, but in the performance of it he is trapped by the hierarchical vocabulary into repeating the very same injustices of the past; in such discourse, his mouth will always be rated as inferior. I would argue, however, that in the context of this story, the decorous use of the word "*pharamaavanou*" seems as ridiculous as the idiomatic expression "*moondou bhaadai thodou ii laayou*" (lit: "it's not as if I took my mouth out on loan," which I translated: "it's not as if this mouth is borrowed from somewhere"). Marx might have railed against borrowed speech, but here the character of the farmer suggests through borrowed speech that words are less trustworthy when spoken through a borrowed mouth.

I would like to think that such a comment calls into question the whole system of ownership upon which the characters' relationship is based, as Prakash suggested with the stories he heard of *bhoots*. After all, what would it mean to own one's mouth? To own one's tongue? Can one ever truly be self-possessed? The irony, of course, is that everyone is on borrowed time, and no one knows this better than the *thakur*, whose time (*kaal*) is up. He can claim sovereignty now only insofar as he can manipulate the living. And perhaps this is the sly witticism the story is suggesting we see: that when living, the *thakur* could claim sovereignty only insofar as he could manipulate the living, dance them like puppets with their hands clasped right up to their elbows, folded in on themselves as they repeat phrases like "*aaraam pharamaavanou.*"

It is important for us to be aware that the *thakur* does not take possession of the farmer, making him repeat these outrageous feudal rhetorical gestures; the storyteller, the *vaatpos*, parodies both of them, takes possession of this borrowed speech that renders the *chaudhuri* abject and the *thakur* vindictive. I would suggest that the narrative has us laughing not at the farmer exactly, but at a rhetoric that has him repeating such absurdly feudal gestures—a rhetoric we recognize, one that is common to us as well, even in English translation. And because we have common ground in this makeshift translatability where the rhetoric of rights is as questionable as these gestures of injustice, we have hereby formed an imagined community haunted by feudal iniquities, one that a storyteller like Bhola Ram is alert to.

We might conjecture that the scene is funny because the farmer is innocently describing all the inequalities that are supposed to remain unspoken. His obsequiousness reveals the historic cruelty of the *thakur*'s behavior. Ironically, the farmer is pointing to the discrepancy between the formal discourse that pretends to be so gracious and the actual practice that is so violent and unjust, a discrepancy he pretends to be oblivious to just as the narrator pretends to be oblivious to his own double-voicedness. The reader thus needs to be able to imagine that the farmer is being *naïve* or is pretending to be naïve in order to outmanipulate the *thakur* and that she will never know for sure which it is. Thus each of the tellers representing this scene in turn needs to be able to count on the paradox of the borrowed mouth: that speech must be borrowed, must move from mouth to mouth, and can never be owned by one person in perpetuity for all time.

Serve Yourself

People often told me that the stories Detha wrote were read and even retold in various settings—formal and informal, rural and urban, to audiences literary and nonliterate—but when I actually had the chance to witness such a performance myself, the locale and the context were such a surprise that I didn't recognize the performance as a retelling at first. I had gone with friends to hear a talk by two activists from Mazdoor-Kisan Shakti Sangathna (MKSS; the Worker-Farmer Strength Association) in Rajasthan who were touring America to talk about communal violence in terms of the Hindu right-wing, anti-Muslim violence that had taken place recently in Gujarat.

The MKSS had begun as a grassroots organization in Rajasthan to help the poor. MKSS members went to villagers asking what could be done to help alleviate poverty; in response to suggestions, they started organizing individual complainants to come together and speak out against systematic mid-level corruption which discriminated against the poorest and the most disenfranchised. This show of force not only shamed exploitative agents of government but sparked a larger movement that successfully agitated for legislation requiring transparency between the state and its people—a necessary legal tool for rooting out corruption. I had heard about the MKSS not only through friends in Rajasthan but through the media. One night, for instance, I turned on my local NPR radio station in Ann Arbor to hear their work being extolled on the BBC World Service.[36]

The MKSS had decided that while its work was local, the perspective needed to be global. That afternoon in Ann Arbor, Aruna Roy spoke eloquently about what she and the others of the MKSS were doing to work against the political divisions that had led to recent atrocities of communal violence; she spoke with respectfulness, evenhanded clarity, and good-natured humor that made everyone in the room feel not only the urgency of the problem but the practical possibility of change that we could be part of. This wasn't a plea for money; this was a call to think about the ways we are implicated in such atrocities even on the other side of the world. Roy was giving us critical tools for thinking about the ways we might work against the right-wing Hindu nationalist backlash that was sweeping India, and one of those critical tools was humor—not as a weapon of the weak but as a deliberate, well-aimed use of insight that claimed its strength by narrating a different version of the world that revealed the kinds of truth the powerful did not want us to name or recognize. She was reframing the issues using rhetoric that worked both to include us and to show the daily, practical ways we on this side of the globe should hold ourselves accountable for the everyday life on that side of the globe where she lived and worked.

Shankar Singh spoke next in Hindi about the anticorruption campaign and the work of going town to town providing a public platform where the citizens of Rajasthan testified publicly to incidents of being cheated out of government funding owed them or being forced to offer bribes. The power of these public statements had forced corrupt officials to return the money they had stolen, and others had been drummed out of town. "This is called a democracy," Singh called out with cheerful optimism tinged with wry wariness. I could see why the MKSS campaigns had been so effective—Singh's patter was so fun and energetic and inclusive that it made you want to be a part of whatever they were creating. And before I knew it, he was telling a story I recognized, the story of a man accused of a crime who is asked to choose his own punishment.

I had translated a version of the story years before with Kailash Kabir from a version he had translated into Hindi from a version Detha had written in Rajasthani. Kabir called his version *"Riayat"* ("Freedom"), and Detha called his *"Uchal Panthi"* ("Weigh Your Options"). The convict in the story had the freedom (*riayat*) to deliberate between two options (*uchal panthi*): he must either eat one hundred raw onions or submit to one hundred lashings of the shoe.[37] When I translated the story, I could not make the humor work. Lashings of the shoe? I understood the story was making fun of the king for thinking he was being generous to his subjects in allowing them freedom of choice, but the punishments were so preposterous, even comical, that they seemed to misdirect the target of the humor. I had decided not to include my version of the story in the collection of English translations I was preparing. But there I sat listening to Singh tell a version in a way that made the dilemma seem both comical and important. He fluttered his hands in exasperation and shook his head in chagrin as he described the criminal, so flummoxed by the choice that he goes back and forth, first this, then that, until he ends up serving double the sentence.[38] Shankar paused and looked up with such a mischievous look that we all seemed to understand the irony of it at the same moment and laughed out loud, slapping our thighs in recognition. Then he concluded dramatically: "And that's how our democracy in India works today."

I made a mental note to think of this version and see if I could draw out what worked in Singh's telling as I made another attempt at translating the story into English. I realized I should not worry if an American audience had never heard of shoe lashings as a punishment; I should focus on the ridiculousness of such a choice calling itself freedom (a humor not so much strategic as tactical). Of course, I assumed that Singh had heard the story from somewhere in the swirl of oral tradition, like Detha, once upon a time. But when Roy retold the story in English on the spot, she added: "Then Shankar-ji told a story by the esteemed Rajasthani writer Vijay Dan Detha." I was astounded, elated, and surprised to see the storytelling tradition moving from oral to written and back to oral again—not in some quaint, defanged setting with a bunch of conservative locals sitting around talking wistfully about days gone by but in a setting with smart, caring activists in the United States using storytelling to change the world.

Afterwards I talked to Shankar Singh; he perked up when he heard me mention Detha's name and told me that he had read through all the volumes of *Baatan ri Phulwari* and used the stories all the time to make his points at rallies just like this one. It made no difference to him if he was in Ann Arbor talking to Indians abroad and Hindi-speaking foreigners like me, or in Bhilara speaking to Rajasthani locals—as I would soon witness for myself.

A few months later, when I was back in Rajasthan, Detha told me he had heard the story of the convict and his punishment not from a nearby villager but in Jaipur, Rajasthan's capital, from a politician named Kumbha Ram-ji, who used it in his own speech as he was urging his fellow citizens to wake up and realize that now the people were the rulers. A few weeks later, when I met up with Singh and Roy in Tilonia, one of the villages in Rajasthan where they worked, the genealogy of the story, made them laugh to hear me tell it; they seemed not only amused but reassured to know that this leader whom they held in such esteem used exactly the same tools as they were using to remind people that in democracy the people were the rulers, that leaders were meant to be servants of the people. Each of them in turn had repeated the feudal rhetoric in such a way that turned it around.

I began to wonder what the role was of a storyteller such as Singh or a writer like Detha in promulgating what MKSS literature calls "Social Change with a Difference."[39] I learned that year that Singh had gone to training sessions at the Rupayan Samsthan founded by Detha and Kothari and had participated in folktale workshops to learn how to be a more effective storyteller. At what point did people like Shankar and Detha stop being considered part of the people and start becoming leaders or mouthpieces? Progressive writers such as Premchand or Saadat Hasan Manto were also interested in releasing the people's hidden potential for initiating broad-based social change. They, too, wanted to find ways of allowing people to speak in ways that would be institutionally recognized. In phrases that echo Wendy Brown's and Joanne Richardson's, the MKSS pamphleteers write earnestly of "a time of increasing skepticism about the possibilities of broad-based social change," and suggest that the MKSS has helped foster "a strong feeling of solidarity, of a sharing of joys and sufferings, of a community determined to change their world for the better by standing up with courage and patience to secure justice."[40]

To ask how a writer such as Detha or Premchand might help in this effort to build a more just community is to pay attention to the details of our own practices in this globalized community of world literature. If these versions speak in tongues, offering temporary revelations that are relational and dynamic because they are always—always already—displaced, then how do we approach a narrative frame that works best when it undoes itself?

After all, it is not clear within Detha's version of the story whether the *thakur* and the farmer believe they themselves are being straightforward and earnest when speaking of leisure as hardship, whether they are playing along with this game to trick the other, or if they both know they are playing a game and each one is seeing if he can keep it up longer than the other. For in a curious turn, the *thakur* begins arguing vehemently for the importance of practice over empty discourse:

> The ghost stepped close. He said through gnashed teeth, "Nothing happens through mere words, it's all in the doing. There's no need for you to step a single foot in these fields after this. You don't have to do anything but sit there and two thousand maunds of millet will appear. Then you will be able to judge for yourself how true these words of mine are. It will be good for you peasant types to suffer a little by taking it easy. After all, we've had to endure such suffering for generations."

The rhetoric flips so many times it's unclear just who means what by words such as "suffering" (*dukh jhelanou*). Does the ghost really believe he has suffered by having others to do work for him? Does the farmer truly believe he is going to suffer by not working or is he simply using this rhetoric in a foiled attempt to dissuade the *thakur* from going through with his plan? The story makes us call into question our attempts to rely on such discourse as real and true.

While at first the farmer claims not to be afraid of the dead *thakur*, not more than three pages later the narrator tells us:

> The *chaudhuri* was stuck. He didn't want to take the millet without earning it and he also didn't want to argue with the ghost. This wasn't just any ghost but the *thakur*'s. Displease him, and he would go after everyone in the farmer's home.

The story thus ascribes a new source of power to the *thakur*, one that comes from "traditional popular belief" (as Marx phrases it).[41] The story teaches us that our own stories have the power to make us fight or fold to these *bhoot*. The farmer tries pleading, "Graingiver, if you'll let me, I'd like to sow a good auspice on this day of *Akhateej*." But the ghost bellows, "I've appeared to you after death, what better auspice do you need than this?" The farmer realizes there's no arguing with the *bhoot*. Just like in the old days:

> The *thakur*'s ghost wouldn't listen no matter what he said, so the *chaudhuri* had to walk back home without having luffed up a single *chigdo* [clod] of dirt with

his hoe. He had heard plenty of stories about the marvelous feats of ghost and phantoms. Nothing was beyond their powers. If the ghost was promising to produce two thousand maunds of millet then surely he'd be good at his word. But in spite of this the *chaudhuri* wasn't very happy. How could he agree to profit from a harvest that he hadn't grown himself?

This passed-down story itself is warning us to be alert to haunted speech: the farmer had heard of the feats of ghosts and so will trust that the *thakur*'s ghost can make similar miracles happen or can bring destruction upon his family. It does not even seem to occur to the innocent farmer that the *thakur* will not keep his promise. He seems so concerned about avoiding the specter of ill-gotten gains that he does not take due precautions against the spirits that have been haunting him all along.

The narrator describes him telling his wife his story and shows that she, too, reacts with alarm at the thought of eating ill-gotten gains; she becomes "as livid as a cobra whose tail has been stepped on." She exclaims, "If we haven't earned it ourselves we don't need a single speck of that ill-gotten grain. Such indolence won't be erased for seven generations. Better we should die of hunger." The next several scenes show the farmer's mounting frustration as he watches his neighbors plow their fields and then mopes even more as the rains come, but every time he tries to go near his fields, there the *thakur*'s ghost would be, standing under the *khejari* tree waiting for him. The narrator admits in close third person:

> The *chaudhuri* couldn't do anything with this ghost staring him down except swallow the proverbial rancid *daal* and go back the way he came. The ghost wouldn't let him pull a single weed or plow a single furrow. All the other fields in the area had been plowed and the soil looked as soft and light and pretty as sweet *magad*, while the village *chaudhuri*'s field was packed down solid and ugly like a *talra* scab on the earth. The village *chaudhuri* didn't say anything to anyone. He wandered around gazing at everyone else's fields. Here and there people asked why he hadn't worked his fields, but he'd just become vague and evade their questions. When he saw the green shoots of millet unfurling in the other fields, the image of his gray, colorless fields bothered him like a splinter in the eye. Now what was he to do? He wandered around and finally arrived back at his fields. That donkey of a ghost hadn't left his place under the *khejari* tree. As soon as the *chaudhuri*'s eyes fell on him he started pleading, "Grain-giver, green shoots of millet have begun unfurling in all the area, except in my colorless fields. How are we to reap a harvest that hasn't yet begun to sprout?"

The use of vocabulary specific to farming—*chigdo, magad, talra*—speaks to a kind of practical expertise the *thakur* (like this reader) is undoubtedly ignorant of. These are, to him, just "empty words" and so their repetition becomes tactical.[42] Even if you believe the *thakur* intends to work the *chaudhuri*'s fields, you begin to wonder if he could follow through with his plan. What kinds of powers does a ghost have? Is he capable of what he promises?

The reader is in a curious situation: she wants the *chaudhuri*'s hopeful trust—not so much in the *thakur* but in the ways of farming and thus in justice—to be rewarded. But the story has made that trust complicated, because if the *thakur* does come through with what he is promising, he is teaching the farmer (and thus us, the audience of this story) that leisure is more valuable than labor. The *thakur* responds to the *chaudhuri*'s query

> with a sharp laugh, "Reaping grain, that's the human way of working. All we godly types have to do is make a wish and take in a *lakh* maunds of grain. Are you only going to turn this over to me when a sudden drought or an early flood wipes out your crops? I told you so many times and still you haven't given up your ways?"

Now he claims to be more than an ordinary Rajput: in this new form he is *devjoon*—born of a godly womb. Not only is he claiming divine powers for himself but he is insisting that the farmer's reward will come from submitting to the hierarchy of the social system rather than recognizing the value of one's own labor within a more complex system of creativity and reproduction. The *thakur* is asking the farmer to put his trust in powerful social forces that he claims are godly types rather than the forces of nature that good sense would consider truly reproductive. If the story advocated an old-fashioned kind of justice, the joke would be on the character (be he dead or alive) who fails to recognize the truly creative forces in this world.

Tools of the Trade

To understand the context of such riddles, let us focus for a moment on a practical scene of translation that takes place one sunny day in Jaipur at not quite 11:00 in the morning on a weekday in November 2002. Kailash Kabir and I have been at work in my rented flat in the C-Scheme neighborhood.

He has his reading glasses on and has been sitting on the couch skimming more of *Baatan ri Phulwari*, combing through the collection yet again to see if he might find a story he had not noticed the last time he read through all the volumes. He is passing time, really, while I am seated at the desk reading line after line of "*Thakur rau Bhoot*" and squeezing out inside my head an approximate English version which I then type into the laptop computer before me. When we are called upon to address each other, he calls me *bahin-ji* ("respected sister") and I call him *bhai sahib* (literally "brother boss," as in "revered older brother"), but despite the familial-seeming relationship, we are worried about how seemly it is for the two of us to work together so closely in an office that also serves as my bedroom.

The last time we worked together at length was in the summer of 1989. Then I made arrangements to stay at a hotel in Jodhpur not far from where Kabir lived with his wife and children, and we would meet every afternoon at the Jodhpur offices of the folklore institute, Rupayan Samsthan. Thirteen years later, when we decide to work in Jaipur, Detha arranges for Kabir to stay at a government hostel two miles away because it is cheap, clean, and not fussy. Kabir arrives in the morning freshly bathed between nine and ten o'clock and we work until seven, sometimes eight or nine o'clock in the evening, when he goes back to the hostel; the day is spent with me reading and writing, conferring, him reading over what I have written, then me rewriting.

I have been awarded a literature fellowship from the National Endowment for the Arts that I combine with a grant I received from the university to pay our expenses. His cousin told me that Kabir would be grateful for the work, but we both hate that I am in the role of disbursing the funds. It is not just that he is a man in a patriarchal society, or that he is the one who is older and more experienced, or that he is from the land of the rupee and I am from the land of the dollar. Every day we are forced in our daily lives together to make conversions; we can look on the Web to see that we will receive 49.20 rupees for every dollar from the research funds, but that does not help me decide whether it is worth the expense of having a hot-water geyser in each of our rooms for our baths (we each express guilt at such an extravagance but then are disgruntled on mornings when the geyser does not work), or whether it is worth my taking the time to cook a meal during the middle of the day because I get sick from the food outside and he is my guest. Then again, am I serving him food each day because I am a woman and he is my *bhai sahib?*[43] Each day he critiques the food I have prepared as assiduously as he critiques the passages I have written; with the food I expect him to be uncritically grateful for whatever I serve, even though I am grateful for his criticisms of the translated work.

We share an ambition for the stories but have trouble working out the means of attaining the goals in our own practical day-to-day lives together. I suspect that he suspects that I am not sharing the award money equally with him, that I allow myself luxuries I begrudge him, and I suspect that he will spend all the money I have been awarded for this project and more. He has a nearly grown family to take care of, with children in and out of college, and nearly as many loans to repay as I do. I call him *bhai sahib* but know I cannot expect him to help me with my financial responsibilities; he calls me *bahin-ji* but wheedles and pleads with me subtly as if I am the *sahib*, the boss of a factory while he is the worker, as if I am the head of a house and he is the servant. It is embarrassing for us both that I have not just this grant for the year but a regular job at the university to return to when this project is over, and Kabir does not, that he has a family to be responsible for, and I do not. Sometimes these various differences between us are articulated; some just float in the air, making us act alternately ashamed, stressed, elated, accusatory, these hierarchical postures and failed expectations working their way into every sentence we write.[44]

This is the ground we work together, that of makeshift translatability.

I read over the story and ask Kabir questions as I convert the prose into English. Sometimes the questions seem simple (What does this word *"argata"* mean?) and sometimes they are more complicated (In this instance is the story in the present to mean the narrative past's future or its present?) I have learned the rules for converting sequence of tenses from Hindi into English, but when it comes to translating an actual piece of literature, the rules often do not apply as neatly as the grammar books promise. These critical tools are, after all, just critical tools. This is both the fun and the frustrating agony of the work we do; we are, after all, not simply translation machines. Sometimes we react to the uncertainty by laughing together, and sometimes by quarrelling. At first the convention of addressing each other as *bahin-ji* and *bhai sahib* seemed quaint, but now that a working relationship has developed between us, I really feel he might be like an older brother—it helps to know we can laugh together and it helps to know we can argue, and still neither of us has walked away from the project. This is how trust builds gradually between us—not exactly unconditionally, but something tentatively approaching this. What binds us together, I realize, is a faith in these stories to mean something to future readers besides ourselves.

Kabir is Vijay Dan Detha's primary Hindi translator and he is also his son. I started working with him in the late 1980s at Detha's urging; this was more than a decade after the first two collections of Kabir's translations had been published in Delhi to much acclaim but a decade before his translation work would be recognized formally by the Sahitya Akademi. That summer of 1989 I was a few years out of college, had already studied Hindi for several years, and decided to take a few months off from my freelance writing work to finish a collection of English translations of Detha's stories. This was before I had started graduate school, before I started learning about translation theory and postcoloniality as a field of study, and also before I started learning Rajasthani formally. That would all come later, when the work would start to make me ask questions I was not able to answer on my own.

In the 1980s Ruth Vanita had already started translating some of Detha's overtly feminist stories for the magazine *Manushi*, so I concentrated on others that were concerned with broader issues of justice and human rights.[45] Like Vanita, I worked from Kabir's Hindi translations, which I sensed were well done, but I could not say exactly why the prose felt both pleasing and challenging as I read along silently in my head. I understand now that Kabir has a gift for making the Hindi sound like Rajasthani while still communicating to a monolingual Hindi reader (if such a thing can be said to exist). And he has a gift for making Detha's prose style sound in all its complexity in Hindi. When I started translating, I tried to convey in English the relationship I sensed Kabir expressed in Hindi for Rajasthani and for his father's prose. This was as much of a struggle, I soon discovered, as creating a voice in English for myself. I seemed to have found something that worked, but I could never be sure. Whom to ask? Like Detha, Kabir can read English but does not feel comfortable expressing himself in it, whether writing or speaking. When Detha arranged for me to work with Kabir, he explained that his son understood his stories better than he did and could explain their nuances in more detail. This I found to be true. But I also found that when we came to an impasse, we never knew if the misunderstanding was due to my nonnative understanding of Hindi, his nonnative understanding of English, or a more basic miscommunication.[46] We had nothing but these two different languages in which to argue over these differences in understanding. Hence we joked and we quarreled. In 2002, as the pressures to finish became more intense, we seemed to joke less and quarrel more. We were scheduled to complete a first draft of the whole book by the end of November.

That morning I called over to him, What is *"argata"*?

He put down the book he was reading, shaking his head. He had me read out the whole sentence: *"Logaan rai khetaan argata vhai jaidi sittiyaan loomai."*[47] I understood everything but that one word: "The heads of millet in people's fields were swaying like . . . *argata*."

He made a face. Then he put down his book, came over to the desk to read the sentence himself. *"Argata?"* he repeated. It was not just my American pronunciation. He did not know what it was either.

I had already looked in Sakariya and Sakariya's Rajasthani-Hindi dictionary and found something for the feminine *argati* (a kind of tool used to plane or peel) but nothing for the masculine plural *argata*. When Kabir looked to see how he had translated the sentence in a recent collection on ghost stories, he started to laugh as he read the sentence out loud: *"Logaan ki kheton main argata jaisi sittiyaan loom rahi thi."*[48] Like me, he had translated everything into standard Hindi but the word *argata*. If, as Susan Stewart argues, dead metaphors are emptied of meaning from overfamiliarity,[49] then this was the opposite—a metaphor not so much dead as spectral, waiting for a moment to rise up and be useful again. Could we believe such a thing would happen—in Hindi or in English? In Rajasthani even? Such a question struck at the very basis of Detha's writing.

I had heard from Kabir, from Kothari, and from Detha himself that when Detha wrote a story told by a potter or an ironworker, he would sit with the man's family for hours talking, taking notes of the specific phrases they used to describe the everyday details of their trade, and then work that specific metaphorical landscape into the language of the story—so much so that once or twice, when I read out a random line to a friend from the region, she immediately recognized that this was a story told from the point of view of a barber or a farmer. In *"Thakur rau Bhoot"* this strategy was especially important, since the dramatic tension of the story centered around the tangible question of working the land: Should the farmer protagonist trust the *thakur*'s ghost to do all the planting and sowing, as the ghost insisted, or be insubordinate and do the work himself, as the farmer felt was right according to not just custom but karma? The everyday details of farming were the basis of the story, and the specialized vocabulary supplied the rhetorical tools the Rajasthani version relied on to make the dilemma come alive. Detha and after him Kabir eschewed the use of standard equivalents in their prose, specifically to make the point that these tools of local Rajasthani knowledge were not equivalent to those in hegemonic languages like Hindi.

Such methods, I knew, had some precedent in English translation studies circles. Critics such as Lawrence Venuti or Tejaswini Niranjana, for instance, argue in different contexts that when translating into a hegemonic language, we should import a word such as *"argata"* wholesale, since it would offer a "foreignizing" or "disruptive" moment that should make a Hindi or English speaker aware of the difference between their experience of the world and the real material life of Rajasthani speakers.[50] And yet, as Tarek Shamma astutely points out, Orientalist translator Richard Burton can be said to be employing a "foreignizing" translation strategy in his *Thousand and One Nights* in his insistence that certain Persian words are untranslatable.[51] Vicente Rafael argues that in the next generation the colonized might succeed in subverting the master/slave logic of such translations and that keeping certain words untranslated and therefore untranslatable has been a strategic manner of domination the missionaries or colonialists have historically employed, which formerly colonized peoples have subverted in turn by insisting on their own untranslatability.[52] Rafael argues that such tactics are parodic.

By including a word like *argata*, was Detha likewise reinforcing a hegemonic version of the Rajasthani people, exoticizing these farmers and iron-workers? My worry was that he was inadvertently employing a manner of re-presenting (as making present once more) this borrowed speech that fell prey to colonial-era "strategies of containment"—as Tejaswini Niranjana has phrased it—that turn the translations into "objects without history."[53] Niranjana's suggestion is that the power is not in the writing but in the interpretation of such words, and that we learn to read these translations with an awareness of these contentious historical relationships implicit in the choice of a single word choice—like *argata*. We need to see these various translational exchanges in relationship to one another, to read these words across multiple historical frames.

Indira Karamcheti argues similarly that in *Notebook of a Return to the Native Land* the postcolonial writer Aimé Césaire succeeds in removing "the false glamour of the exotic" as a commodity in the exchange circuit of literary tourism and "simultaneously reglamorizes the landscape with symbolic, spiritual content."[54] Such a tactic does not call for a return to a paradisiacal time before colonial conquest and capitalist exchange, Karam-cheti argues, but is rather a refusal to do obeisance to an understanding of "reproductions" as mechanical, derivative, inferior because part of a history of objects narrated in homogeneous, linear time. Instead, she suggests that the reproductions of Césaire's "subjective geographies" can be construed as sacred in their very temporariness and plurality. Hence the English versions of *Notebook of a Return to the Native Land* and "The *Thakur*'s Ghost," like *Cahier de la retour au pays natal* and "*Thakur rau Bhoot*" in French and Rajasthani before them, insist in their very rhetoric that such reproductions be thought of in agricultural terms, as a constantly recurring cycle of life and death. Such an attitude takes seriously Detha's platitude that to write well, one must honor the seed of the story. As I argue above, such an attitude forces us not to approach a translation in the binaristic terms that regard such reproductions as property but to interpret these re-created texts in their networks of production. Kabir and I talked at length about such theories, but on that November afternoon we still did not know in practical terms how to work "*argata*" into an English-language version of the story in such a way that would avoid the object-without-history trap. We wanted the term to be meaningful in multiple ways, but we did not even know what "*argata*" was in Rajasthani.

Kabir decided we should call his father in Borunda. We used my cell phone, gesturing wordlessly toward the recurring joke between us on the marvel that is technology.

"*Kai?*" His father asked in Rajasthani, confused: "What?" Once again I read the sentence out loud. Then I handed the phone to Kabir and he tried reading the sentence to his father.

Kabir listened for a moment, grunted "*hun*" in agreement, and then hung up.

"He's going to go and ask someone who might know," Kabir explained.

That someone, it turned out, was Detha's childhood friend, Bhola Ram, who lived on the other side of the village. That day Kabir explained to me that Bhola Ram was a farmer and would no doubt recognize the everyday details of the work of farming that are so integral to the story, given that he had worked as a farmer nearly all his life and was probably the one Detha had heard use the word in the first place.

Kabir went back to reading his book on the couch while I wrote a little note to myself—"Bhola Ram's rare word"—in the text waiting on my computer and then plowed on with the first draft. I could not help but wonder what a farmer like Bhola Ram or any of his fellow villagers would think when they heard the story being read to them full of references to objects and processes that were part of their everyday life—*argata, sud karno, deni deno.*[55] I knew that there were periodic performances of Detha's versions and had been told that people appreciated hearing the phrases they used in everyday life given a certain recognition by being included in a real, published book—a book that garnered awards in Delhi and abroad and made people realize that Rajasthani was a real language with a rich culture. Did having these spoken words printed in a book make them more real, more viable? To whom did they belong? For instance, I knew from talking to Detha that part of his aim was to preserve the collective knowledge contained in a simple phrase like *"deni deno."* Kabir grew animated as he explained the specificities of that and related verbs to me:

> The first part of the process of harvesting grain is when the bullocks tamp on it to separate the kernels and chaff [*gahno*], the second when they pour the two from a bit of a height so that the chaff gets blown away from the (heavier) millet grains [*uphanano*], and then they mark the piles in special designs with ash so they know if anyone has touched them in the night [*deni deno*]. *Deni deno* is a form of protection from theft.[56]

I thought of the elaborate discussions the three of us had already had about copyright, the letters and contracts we composed and agreed on were our own writerly version of a *deni deno* ritual.[57] What part of a story in English, say, were we claiming was whose property? I had read that when a writer sends out a manuscript, she should send herself a copy of a text in the mail and not open it; in the case of a copyright dispute she could dangle in front of the judge this date-stamped envelope with a document inside that proved this text was hers, word for word. I also knew that encyclopedia editors include fake entries so they can catch someone copying their work.[58] I knew from friends that in American legal courts these matters of intellectual property come down to percentages of the work one could claim to have created. But in matters of translation it was harder. If I imported *"deni deno"* into the English text, was the phrase mine for writing it in this text, Kabir's for explaining it to me, Detha's for seeing its literary potential and including it in his story in the first place, or someone like Bhola Ram's for using the phrase in front of Detha in the first place? And how do we even know if Detha first heard it from Bhola Ram or perhaps heard it from someone else before? Or made it up entirely?

The paradox is that such a phrase—like the story more generally—would not pulse with such vitality if it did not refer to the practical, daily realities of the farmers who kept the phrase in circulation but that they are not the ones who would be given credit for framing this vital expressive force. When Bakhtin wrote his celebratory tract on Rabelais's work and its ability to incorporate the exuberant, marketplace language of the people, he never stopped to ask about questions of ownership. If Rabelais were writing today in India, I could imagine him being accused of stealing the local people's carnivalesque culture to make a name for himself. If we are to work against such unproductive accusations, we need to attend to Bakhtin's suggestion that appreciating the popular, democratic, rhetorical gestures in Rabelais's work "requires an essential reconstruction of many deeply rooted demands of literary taste, and the revision of many concepts. Above all . . . the tradition of folk humor."[59]

The example of the multiple translations of Kumbha Ram-ji's wry story of freedom of choice in a democracy makes clear that the very distinction between "folk humor" and elite literary taste in Bakhtin's discussion must be complicated if we are to understand the means by which a story enjoys continued life in parody and translation and if we are to understand the relationship between these various versions. Richardson's discussion of tactical media similarly shows that the tool of parodic repetition can be employed by anyone who recognizes enough of the code to play with it in dialogic relationship with an interlocutor who shares a similar level of understanding. In such a schema, differences of language, class, gender, and nation are not reinscribed but ridiculed and thus are turned into a source of humor that members of the triangle are invited to share. It is in this way that a story such as *"Thakur rau Bhoot"* might come alive in succession generations, each one asserting its own investments in certain ideological frames. These shifts in meaning help encourage the life force we want to honor when we ask a text to come alive generation after generation. This is the logic of reproduction whose temporalities defy the mindless and the mechanical.

Less than an hour later, Kabir called his father back. As it happened, Detha had sent a car for Bhola Ram, and the two of them were sitting in Detha's study together, gossiping and reminiscing. Kabir listened for a moment then started laughing uproariously, his body pitching forward, the arm holding the cell phone held high. Finally, he announced to me: "Bhola Ram doesn't remember either. He thinks it might be some tool, like a *reti*." Later, I wrote down a note to myself: "This is a tool like a *reti* (chisel?) only bigger, and curved, but still for planing wood." Detha concluded it was the handle of the tool he was trying to compare, and we decided it did not really matter what an *argata* was, as long as readers got the idea that it was a local farm implement. We got off the phone to leave Detha to talk with Bhola Ram, and I wrote: "The heads of millet in people's fields were as round and strong as the handles of *argata*."

I had to admit that these reproductive metaphors did not work perfectly, for in the case of *argata*, it wasn't clear what was the tool and what was the seed. And when it came to matters of planting, anyone looking at our gestures from a distance would not know the difference between planting and burying, between an organic and inorganic object. Even we would not know—intention counted for little here—until we saw evidence of the seed sprouting up from the newly worked ground. But in this case the ground would be the imaginative landscapes inside our readers' minds—a place we could not see or touch but had to have faith would come into existence through and for the story. We wrote knowing that the value of the work we did would be determined by some imagined community in the future.

Objects of Possession

On that bright winter January morning when Detha takes me to meet his friend Bhola Ram, he promises to help translate if I have any trouble with Bhola Ram's Rajasthani or if he has trouble understanding my Hindi. At first, Bhola Ram seems baffled by my questions and more than once turns to Detha and speaks about me in the third person, "*e kaain poochhnou chaavai?*" ("What does she want to ask?"). In one instance Detha, too, is baffled, and repeats Bhola Ram's question back to me (in the familiar form of you, "*tum*"): "*kyaa poochhna chaahti ho?*" ("What do you want to ask?"). Triangles do not always connect through humor.

I fumble around to rephrase my convoluted question, trying to under-stand what Bhola Ram thinks about seeing the tale he told his friend transformed into a written story in a book. My attempt to be sensitive to the fact that Bhola Ram cannot read or write have made me incomprehensible, apparently. Both men are looking at me quizzically, and so finally I ask simply: *"is kaa sabak kyaa hai?"* ("What is its lesson?").

Bhola Ram responds just as simply: "The story was what I just told you. Then he added the spices and made it what it is." He nods his head towards Detha, his friend.

They begin working off one another in a routine that in retrospect seems comedic. Detha begins explaining the metaphor to me, "You add spices to vegetables, no?"

Bhola Ram joins in, "You add spices to make a dish, no? So these spices that have been added are all his."

I had not expected to be broaching the question of story ownership so soon into our impromptu interview but am happy to see that our foundering conversation has taken such an interesting turn. Back in Jaipur, Kailash had told me stories of Bhola Ram's smarts—perhaps to reassure me after the *argata* incident. Back in the early 1970s, when Mani Kaul was filming his art-house version of Detha's story "Duvidha" in Borunda, time after time Bhola Ram was able to solve practical problems no one else was able to figure out. In one memorable story, Bhola Ram trapped a fox they needed for a sequence, and when they needed to film it sleeping, he picked it up by its tail, whirled it around his head until it wanted to pass out, and then laid it down in the chosen spot, where it lay quietly trying to compose itself, eyes closed. During the winter when Kabir and I were working together on the collection of translations, Kabir was also waiting to hear about the fate of a revised screenplay of his translation of the story of "Duvidha" that would later become a high-budget Bollywood production starring Shah Rukh Khan called *Paheli* ("The Riddle.") We laughed together trying to imagine an actor like Shah Rukh Khan or a director like Amol Palekar waiting while Bhola Ram spun a fox over his head. I was quite eager to meet this resourceful man I had heard so much about.

That afternoon in January, however, my video camera and prepared abstract questions in Hindi seem to make Bhola Ram nervous. Once more he insists that the story belongs to Detha, the author, "My part is just providing the vegetables. All the spices which make the dish, that's his part."

I could not help but think of Gandhi's economic critique of the British relationship with the colony of India: that the British extracted raw materials such as cotton and salt, refined them in Britain, and then sold the processed goods for much more money in the colony. I wondered if Bhola Ram might have said something different if Detha were not sitting there or if he were talking to someone besides me.

A few minutes later I ask more explicitly, "Do you have any objection to your name not being given in the published version of the story?"

He insists, "No objection at all," and explains, "I wasn't the one to make this story that I could place such a *charge* [he uses the English word]. I heard the story told and I told it in turn. He has certainly become the *malik* of the story, because he is the one who added all the spices." Detha, the *malik?*

Malik means lord, and therefore owner. Detha had told me Bhola Ram had worked his whole life as a farmer and after Independence was able to buy his own land. His use of the word *malik* surprised me, for it invoked feudal associations at odds with the defiantly democratic ideals featured in the story or the confidence with which he could trap a fox or expertly needle his friend in conversation.

A month later when I was in Tilonia, Rajasthan, interviewing Shankar Singh and the others in the group of storytelling performers associated with the MKSS, they became just as baffled as Bhola Ram when I went through the formal routine the Institutional Review Board at my university demanded regarding their rights to the stories they were recounting. If published, did they want their names to appear connected to the stories they were recounting? Would they prefer these stories not to be published at all? They demanded, "Why would you ask such a thing?" They were incredulous when I repeated Bhola Ram's modest admission that he was not the *malik* of the story. These stories have flowed on for generations, Shankar Singh teased.[60] No one person has a right over them. He began to laugh as he explained—fondly, indulgently, as one would to a misguided child—that this was the same kind of thinking that allowed rivers to be sold to multinational corporations at the expense of the people who lived there. His manner was in stark contrast to Bhola Ram's, but he, too, used metaphors of raw materials. But in this case Singh openly challenged a system that would treat stories as property to be owned and teased me for playing along with its logic.

In the version of the story that Bhola Ram told me on that bright day in January with my videotape running, the farmer is gullible and believes the *thakur*'s talk of camaraderie, believes the dead *thakur* wants to do something for the farmer because they are *"dharam-bhai"* (like brothers). In Detha's version, the same ironic lesson is communicated, but in his tale, the farmer is helpless to avoid being deceived. He cannot risk the displeasure of this ghost, so instead pleads, "Graingiver, it's not too late, allow me to start plowing my fields. I feel like I'm going crazy sitting around doing nothing." Once again, it is the ghost who is shown to be dominant, laughing, but in such an exaggerated way that we cannot help but see his character, too, as an empty puppet being played by the storyteller:

> The ghost laughed a belly-rolling laugh and said, "Now you understand, don't you, that in this world there's nothing more difficult than taking it easy. But you people used to see us and feel jealous. Chaudhuri, there's no greater happiness than that gained from labor."

Rather than trying to understand who "owns" these lines—where they might ever be true and univocal—the story is teaching us to read them as temporarily possessed and thus to read them as skeptically as we would read anything else, because their meaning depends on shifting and complex sets of relations. For in the end, the narrator tells us, the ghost "wouldn't let that *chaudhuri* plow a single furrow." The irony, of course, is that the cruel *thakur* is the one repeating these simple words of wisdom, "There's no greater happiness than that gained from labor." This is parody, perhaps not in the way Marx used the term, but one that is no doubt dangerous for the revolution—to have those in power using the rhetoric of empowerment to disempower factory workers and farmers. Here the specter of communism is being eradicated by a ghost of the feudal order. The story makes it clear how crucial it is to understand who is saying what, how, and in what context. The moral of the story depends on the complicated level of parody that your reading of this line constructs; it depends on your interpretation. There cannot be a single owner of this story for all time. The story thus teaches that the "once" of the English translation is as arbitrary and temporary as the "once" of the story's opening in any language.

We cannot know with certainty in any of the versions if it is gullibility or helplessness that leads the farmer to put his trust in the *thakur*. The narrator in Detha's version that Kabir and I worked on announces, "On the fourth day he went once again to that khejari tree. The noonday sun was high overhead." We know from the present-tense narration—"The *thakur* hasn't moved from that spot"—that we are seeing the ghost from the farmer's point of view. At the same time, we also see that the farmer is trying still to play according to the old rules of etiquette:

> The *chaudhuri* greeted him and immediately announced, "Graingiver, if you don't honor my request I am ready to commit suicide. Everyone else has exhausted himself hauling away carts full of millet. What a year it's been, as if it were raining down sweet pearls of millet. Please, if you would, just clap your hands right here and make the piles of millet appear. Then at least I'll get to do the work of carting it away.

That his threat of suicide might be simply rhetorical is very relevant to a story such as this, especially one that was written in an era when—as Vandana Shiva, Akhil Gupta, and others have pointed out—the incidence of suicide among farmers unable to repay loans taken out on seed, tools, and land has actually gone up.[61] We know generally that rhetoric can become a crucial issue, one with real-life, reversible consequences, but here the details are specific: the *thakur*'s empty words have not translated into tangible results in the field. It is not as if the farmer and his wife can eat the *thakur*'s words. Why are the words of loan and ownership any less empty? When the story repeats the phrase "ill-gotten gains," it teaches us the importance of taking practical possession of these tangible objects.

Now that it is too late for the crops to be planted and harvested, we see that the *thakur*'s laughter is not so much wise and compassionate as cruel and vindictive:

> The *thakur*'s ghost heard the *chaudhuri* and began snorting with laughter on and on without stopping. Still chuckling, he said, "Chaudhuri, I've seen many lunatics in this world, but none to match you. You really believed that I was going to make good on my promise and see that you received all that millet? You *kala*, I devoted so much of my time alive to making sure you suffer, if I were to start ensuring you were happy, it would be hell for me. You would never have obeyed my words if I hadn't given you that promise. The harvest would have been the best in the region and I wouldn't have been able to tolerate that. You two will just have to just enjoy millet in your dreams."

If the reader is surprised by the *thakur*'s sudden turn to transparent cruelty, the farmer does not seem to be. The final few paragraphs of Detha's version reframe the terms under which a character such as the farmer might "enjoy millet in [his] dreams."

That morning, hearing Bhola Ram's version, I learned that his tale starts with a bad dream that soon comes true (of the farmer's lord betraying him), while Detha's version ends with the farmer satisfied that he could recognize what was important (honest labor) and what was not (hierarchical obeisance), what was true (practice) and what was not (empty words). In Detha's version, the narrator reveals:

> the *chaudhuri* was happy to hear what the *thakur*'s ghost said. He responded,
> "You've bestowed the greatest contentment of all upon us, Graingiver, in lift-
> ing this burden off our brows. It doesn't bother me a bit that you didn't bestow
> grain upon our waiting hands. If you had filled our idle hands with grain, then
> I would have been upset. There is a deep bond between the earth and our
> sweat. We'll be raising millet as long as we're standing. I'm going to distribute
> twenty-five *ser* of raw cane sugar in my gratitude for being saved the ignominy
> of receiving ill-gotten grain."

The image of the future that he points to with this active participial con-struction ("*ghani ii baajariyaa nipjaavaalaa*" "we will be raising millet") is predicated on his own mortality ("*jivta rahyaa tou*" "As long as we're stand-ing/living"). There is an awareness of the double-voicedness of this par-ticular *bhoot kaal*, one that uses borrowed speech, a borrowed mouth, even a borrowed tongue, to speak to a relationship between past, present, and future in dynamic relationship to one another. The *thakur*'s ghost (as past) might appear to them as a dream (therefore future), if they can insist on framing the narrative relationship that way in their tellings. Detha's version of the story ends with a seemingly mythical image that romanticizes the rewards of labor in a past tense that could be any time at all:

> For the first time in days the *chaudhuri* slipped into a deep, carefree sleep.
> He had the loveliest, sweetest dreams. In his dreams he worked and labored,
> labored and toiled. And all that toil brought a sheen of sweat to his skin. And
> from that sweat they were able to reap countless, priceless pearls.

While Bhola Ram's story begins with a dream that his version warns us not to trust, Detha's version seems to suggest that we must hold onto our dreams—dreams understood here not as premonition but in the sense of a collective hope, as Susan Buck-Morss's "dreamworld" might convey. Buck-Morss spends the course of her book *Dreamworld and Catastrophe* trying to understand how we might rekindle hope for the future with the crumbling of the Soviet dream. She turns to Benjamin and insists:

> When an era crumbles, "History breaks down into images, not into stories." Without the narration of continuous progress, the images of the past resemble night dreams, the "first mark" of which, Freud tells us, is their emancipation from the "spatial and temporal order of events." Such images, as dream images, are complex webs of memory and desire wherein past experience is rescued and, perhaps, redeemed.[62]

In earlier chapters I suggest that unlike the response of dreaming, humor offers a means for expressing unnameable loss from the past in such a way that brings individuals into provisional, playful relation with one another in the present continuous—a shifting positionality whereby any speaker can be alternately the one joking, the one being joked about, or the one laughing along. Every version of the story (just as every telling of a joke) becomes a parody of "borrowed speech" because it is never clear who owns what in which context. The very rhetoric of ownership and borrowing is thus called into question: in a world where possession is said to be nine tenths of the game, you must learn to keep your wits about you. This is what we learn by approaching these versions through the trope of translation rather than transition.

As it turned out, I discovered that my conversation with Bhola Ram was haunted by a different ghost from what I had imagined. In explaining the meaning of the story, he insisted that a *thakur*, or anyone from the *rajput* caste, for that matter, could deceive someone after death. After we had spent more time talking, he began telling me details of his mother's life, the woman he called Jiji who happened to be the storyteller from whom he had heard the story of "*Thakur rau Bhoot*" that had him laughing so hard. She had had a difficult life, he told me, but lived to the age of 105. She had been born in Shekhavati, the daughter of a concubine and her lord, a *thakur*, and so belonged to that *thikana*. Bhola Ram did not explicitly question an institution that rendered his mother both property and propertyless, but when I asked how she came to Borunda, the town where he was born and grew up, he clarified, "*Matlab, dulhan ke dahej main diyaa*"[63] ("I mean, she was given in the bride's dowry").

It is I who am haunted by yet another image of translation with irreversible consequences: this was a story of a young woman carried across from one part of Rajasthan to another. That morning he told me that she was born into a situation where she had no right to decide whom she slept with, whom she married, where she lived, what would happen to her children; she just had to obey. She watched her son go off to fight in Bhutan for the British army, then watched the feudal system be dismantled, watched her son buy land and start to farm it for the family, like the farmer in the story. As he talked excitedly of his mother, the formality between us gone, he jumped up suddenly and retrieved a photo album that showed the crowds carrying the decorated bier at her funeral procession. This was one of the ghost stories he was telling me: that there had been change during her lifetime. And the other ghost story he was telling me was that nothing changes. A complicated understanding of literature in translation should allow both perspectives to sound.

So I end this final chapter by suggesting that we learn to read stories such as these to understand someone else's dream in a way that accounts for the differences from our own. Re-presenting versions of the story from oral to written form, from a nonstandardized language like Rajasthani into a globalizing language like English, allows us to talk about that *thakur* and that farmer as if they are them, not us, as a way of positing fictional distance that allows us a gap for reflection. This is what all the various listeners and tellers of this tale have in common: that we can take temporary possession of it without entirely owning it. A story that begins in *bhoot kaal* with *"ek ha thakur"* ("once there was a *thakur*") should make us see that the *"ha"* refers to a *bhoot kaal* that not only existed once in a simple past but is part of a recurring present that includes us. A transition narrative would have us insist on a separation between the two—between us and them as between present and past—and would refuse to take account of the ways such distinctions are created in our own framing gestures. A transition narrative would refuse to see that by assuming that a translated story exists only over there, in the past, its knowledge and insights belong only to them. Framing such narratives in terms of transition, we are refusing to take part in re-presenting more complicated versions of the world—refusing to acknowledge the *mise en abîme* that is part of our daily lives. In the process, we cannot imagine that the *bhoot kaal* can be as double-voiced as the *bhoot*.

A Double Hearing (to close)

If I started the book with a real-life tale of triangular, spirited exchange, I end with another, one that I admit riddles me even more than the first. It is February 11, 2003, and I have come to a town in Rajasthan named Beawar at Shankar Singh's invitation to witness for myself one of the public hearings regularly sponsored by Mazdoor-Kisan Shakti Sangathna (MKSS; the Worker-Farmer Strength Association). During the previous summer in Ann Arbor, I had seen footage of these events, a moveable forum in which the most oppressed members of the local community speak out against the injustices they have suffered and in the process collectivize to take action.

Incongruously, I have been told the all-day affair will begin with a *ratha yatra* (palanquin journey), a ceremony I know to be anything but neutral. Traditionally, a *ratha yatra* is a public ceremony that involves carrying a consecrated image of one or more of the Hindu gods to a place of ceremonial importance—to a holy river for bathing, for example. These public translations often involve great numbers of the local community spilling out of their houses to join in festive parade.[1]

More than a decade earlier, L. K. Advani, one of the leaders of the Hindu fundamentalist Bharatiya Janta Party (BJP; the Indian People's Party), had appropriated the ritual for a specific purpose, traveling from town to town across India in a much-publicized *ratha yatra* to Ayodhya in an incendiary demand that the Muslim mosque he claimed had been built on the exact birthplace of Lord Rama be converted back to a Hindu temple.[2] In official court hearings, archaeologists and other state witnesses were called upon to examine pillar structures and government property records underneath the Babri Mosque to determine unequivocally whether the original structure on this site might have belonged to Hindu priests designated to look after the site of Lord Rama's birth; in the lanes of Ayodhya, busloads of agitated supporters from across India overwhelmed police barricades and succeeded in razing the contested mosque to the ground brick by brick. In the process, voters were so stirred up by the powerful rhetoric of original rights that representatives of the BJP were elected to form a national government on their promise to bring back *"Rama rajya"* (the rule of Rama). Here the once-upon-a-time ambience of these narratives claimed historical veracity in a move whose consequences, not just to the mosque building but to quite a few random individuals, turned out to be irreversible.

Privately MKSS members told me they worried that further support of the BJP in Rajasthan could lead to more such incidences of communal violence. That morning in February, however, their *ratha yatra* parodied the details of Advani's performance as assiduously as Advani had conjured the traditional *ratha yatra* of a mythic yesteryear: Singh, dressed in the white *khadi* (homespun) outfit and Gandhi cap associated with the stereotypical nationalist politician, was carried along on a modestly decorated *ratha*, while ceremonial umbrellas twirled around him and a pious-looking devotee led the gathering crowds in a call-and-response Hindu chant over a crackling rented green loudspeaker advertising *"payal redioj"* (anklet radios, as shown in my picture of Singh on the cover of this book; the saffron-colored banner over his head clearly reads *"ratha yatra"* in red letters). As they paraded down the narrow thoroughfare, members of the town came forward to garland Singh with marigold wreaths, which he accepted with stiff, dutiful (and seemingly feigned) humility. Shopkeepers came to their stoops and residents to their balconies to watch the spectacle, smiling to each other as they commented on the parade passing by, some of them stepping down to join in.

I could not help but notice that a few of the spectators seemed more interested in watching me, the foreign woman taking videotape of the occasion, than they were in following the antics of the man sitting on the *ratha* uttering the same well-worn phrases they must have heard so many times in these lanes—"I am only your servant come before you to do your bidding." I wanted them to look at Singh and not at me, wanted them to understand that he was making a joke of this rhetoric of democracy and that he was making a mockery of the kind of divisive politics the BJP took advantage of in the name of Hindu-style democracy. I tried to catch their eye in a quick, conspiratorial smile. They laughed along with me at what I took to be the absurdity of the whole event, but I could not be sure exactly what part of it they found absurd, if they did, and whether they imagined they were laughing along with Singh or thought they were laughing at him.

Suddenly a tough-looking woman in her fifties planted herself in front of me, studying me with great focus through the other end of the video camera. Finally, unable to ignore her nor divert her attention, I asked her in Hindi, "What do you think of this politician's promises?" I called Singh "*neta-ji*" (esteemed leader), just as I had heard the MKSS workers refer to him facetiously. I was not sure she understood my scholarly, urbanized Hindi, much less my ironic framing gestures. Could she hear the quotation marks around "*neta-ji*"?

She shrugged, and responded in the local Rajasthani dialect, "All these *neta-jis*, they always promise the same thing. All empty words."

I was about to ask her another question when she turned from me and joined the parade as it funneled down the lane toward the tent where the public hearing would take place. I wondered later what she thought to see Singh strip off his *neta-ji* costume with little fanfare and step to the microphone to lead the hearing against corrupt politicians. But I was unable to find her in the crowd.

A week later, in Tilonia, Singh laughed when I told him of the incident. "She took the duplicate to be real, and the real to be a duplicate!" ("*Sahi dooplikat samjhi aur dooplikat sahi samjhi!*"). We were speaking in Hindi, but he used the English word "duplicate," as if referring to a pamphlet we might reproduce mechanically at the photocopy shop. He did not say this in a way that scorned her intelligence but instead credited her with a deeper understanding of the political situation. He added, musing delight-edly almost to himself, "*Dooplicat kyaa hai, sahi kyaa?*" (What is a duplicate? What is real?).

The comment made me realize he was able to trust his framing device as a political tool because he trusted this woman in the crowd and her ability to make sense of his performance as absurd—regardless of whether she read his particular version of a *neta-ji* as duplicate or real. In his parody he was not primarily interested in making alliance with her but in creating a space of inquiry that could be replicated beyond his individual performance. In all my conversations with members of the MKSS and in their brochures they invariably emphasized the same thing: this was a system for making change that could be replicated. In retrospect, I could see that the wom-an's spirited response to the mock(ing) conjuring of this Advani-like leader revealed a skepticism that the tactical interventions of the MKSS counted on. They were most interested in creating a common space where she and her neighbors could tell stories in turn that would arbitrate—dynamically and responsively—a collective vision of right and wrong. The political power they helped people realize day after day, age after age, provided a different makeshift answer to the riddle of belonging from the one a *neta-ji* like Advani was working from. He was whipping up nationalist Hindu sentiment in order to conserve his own power, while they were trying to enfranchise people to create a more equitable political system for all that any of them could take up and pass on.

Such a tactic dictated the way someone like Singh approached a *ratha yatra* as a performer as well as the way he approached a story by Detha as a reader looking to perform it. If we agree that what I say already includes what you say to me, then we can see that playful possession of the rhetoric of power reminds us that no one's position of superiority is fixed but is always—always already—displaced. I might interpret the dismissive shrug of a nameless subaltern as playful, but such a reading had no more basis in verifiable reality than the claim that the site in Ayodhya originally housed a temple to Lord Rama. My interpretation of events would always necessar-ily be beholden to future readers as much as to those of the past, whether that interpretation was performed in an oral medium or a written one. As each of us takes our turn telling our own version of the story, we take part in a network of exchange premised on such temporal and spatial displace-ments of meaning. In these pages I argue that the closest we can come to understanding the provisional truth of such an economy is to attend to the framing devices we rely on to establish rhetorical ground in common across a range of uncomfortable and even dangerous differences. Singh's reading of the nameless woman's comment on the duplicitous nature of politicians reminds us that every text has the potential for enfranchisement of both parties involved, if only we can learn to engage with an equally spirited sense of mirth at the inherent duplicity. The alliance we make in each triangular exchange riddles each of us in turn because of this ongoing work of displacement, a movement that both binds us to one another and alienates us at the same time.

Our response to such displacements not only defines our interpretive approach to literature but reveals the ethical stance we assume when negotiating differences with others more generally. To understand how such a process works, we might take note of our response to a last and final example, this one another playful, oral-based tale written in Rajasthani by Vijay Dan Detha. This one tells the scandalous story of same-sex love. The title itself plays with the interpretive frame we use to understand the terms of the scandal: Detha mischievously titled the story *"Dovari Joon"* in Rajasthani, Kailash Kabir called it *"Dohari Zindagi"* in Hindi, and I rendered it as "A Double Life" in English. In all three languages, the title makes fun of the discrepancy between outward appearance and the secret life one leads. Here we have announced explicitly the fronting or even *mise en abîme* gesture that we see in the triangular relationship with Chouboli, the niece, and the *thakur* of Chapter 2.

In this story, it is only when we try to understand the judgment being made on such duplicities as they perform within the story that the double entendre in the various versions of the title begins to hint at the inherent duplicities that sound in our own translational exchanges. For in more than one sense the story does offer a double hearing: it laughs across languages at these riddles of belonging that pretend we have an idiom in common when clearly we do not, and in the process it makes us wonder how it is we use these examples of world literature to hold forth on the failure of this or that society to adhere to a universal code of human rights. We could ask simplistically: How do we parse right from wrong in a language and a culture to which we only provisionally belong? This story makes us ask how we can ever claim to belong to a language and a culture—however provisionally—that might allow us to make such a judgment for ourselves and others. The answer given within the frame of the story by those conserving the status quo is that we can claim to belong only if we pretend to play along with the mainstream set of rules, even if they are at odds with our own reality. This story, more than Shankar Singh's playful performance, makes us question: What is a duplicate? What is real? How do we distinguish between the two in a way that is faithful to our own version of reality and yet to others' as well in this ocean of the stream of story that is our imagination of the world?

Like so many of Detha's stories, *"Dovari Joon"* achieves greater complexity precisely because it repeats a story that has been repeated in various forms over the generations, and thus it invites its audience to take active part in a system of collective meaning-making whose spirited transgressions have been going on for generations. The tale is most familiar to people from its zesty but admittedly cursory appearance in the *Mahabharata*, which tells of a girl—Sikhandin in the *Mahabharata*, Beeja in Detha's tale—raised as a boy so that her family may receive instead of pay a huge dowry for her/his wedding. She grows up wearing boys' clothing, speaking in a first-person pronoun that is masculine, not feminine, and acting the part of a young boy in society as she has been taught. The trick her parents have played is discovered only after the two girls are married, and in most versions tragedy is then averted when some beneficent being (god, saint, or otherwise, depending on whom you wish to exalt) bestows a blessing that changes the she into a bona fide he. In Detha's version, however, the implied criticism of entrenched gender roles become much more explicit: after the switch, the groom is suddenly and inexplicably riled by the egalitarian arrangement they had been living by previously as same-sex partners and becomes increasingly belligerent (even violent), until at last, in a moment of rain-soaked crisis, he realizes that life was much happier when he was a woman. He makes a wish to reverse the sex switch, which is granted immediately. The couple, we are then told in seemingly conventional storytelling method, lives happily ever after.

In this version, tragedy is not the fact of same-sex union but of a patriarchal system that renders women property and men property owners. When the men in the town insist the two women cannot stay married, the two lovers exile themselves and find refuge in an old ruin inhabited—serendipitously enough—by ghosts who take their side against the conservative townspeople. This version thus appropriates traditional storytelling techniques to challenge traditional unexamined notions of right and wrong, and in the process challenges us to rethink our relationship to past, present, and future. The story suggests that it is not easy to recognize which *bhoot* (figure of the past) we trust enough to lead us into the future. We are thus presented with another version of the question of effect examined in Chapter 3 with the story of the switched heads: When considering the riddles raised by stories of unbelievable transformation, what real-world beliefs do we hope to reconsider and even transform in the process of passing on these riddling stories?

In the story of "A Double Life," we are asked how we might translate the fictional awareness brought by a fantastical (double sex) change in the realm of the playful into actual, irreversible social change in the real world. I suggest in the preceding chapters that we should understand these translations as an ongoing, collective, and exceedingly dynamic negotiation that keeps in sight the dreams of a more equal world (as Bhabha, Butler, Clifford, and Young understand "cultural translation") while still attending to the false promises and duplicities of the practical dimensions of such uneven exchange (as Asad, Cheyfitz, Kothari, Liu, Niranjana, and Rafael argue in the colonial context most particularly).[3] Singh's reading of that nameless subaltern's skeptical comment suggests that we do not necessarily need to fix on a single interpretation, do not need to locate a third person's stance in relation to ours once and for all, but need to trust that these tales might have a continued life, a life that might very well go past what we thought imaginable or believable to serve a different justice from the one whose bounds we currently apprehend. Individual instances of universal human rights (to use the examples Butler and Liu each write on) are worked out in just these kinds of performances, age after age, as generations of tellers and listeners negotiate real-life riddles of right and wrong in turn. Detha's story of "A Double Life," like Singh's play on the duplicity of democracy, invites us to reconsider the ways we understand such a hearing, understood doubly in the sense of listening (Can the subaltern speak?) and in the sense of having one's day in court.

Such examples of double entendre might allow us to account for the complex investments we have in these tales of injustice to speak for those we understand to be otherwise silenced and disempowered; such examples might allow us to acknowledge the inherent duplicity at the core of any enterprise of representation that performs in the present voices of the past to be passed into the future and thus relies on the tongue of one to speak the truth of another in an interlinking network of displaced, triangular exchange connecting past, present, and future.

The rhetoric of fidelity is not entirely misplaced here, for we need to have faith that we are performing a valuable service by attending more closely to the unexpected insights offered by those with whom we engage in these acts of individual exchange across lines of difference. Otherwise, why undertake such challenges to our old way of thinking? We need to imagine that the ethical ground we have in common with those we are engaging across time and space in these provisional narrative communities is vouchsafed by some transcendent figure of justice, and goodness, and greater hope, even if the skeptical part of us knows that the ideals we seek might never be perfectly achieved. Rather than reacting melancholically to that inevitable distance between the ideal and the reality, my argument in this book is that we learn instead to laugh together at our ongoing efforts and in the process negotiate these translations of ideal to real by using the process to forge a bond that in the end is more reliable because it is dynamic, flexible, and responsive.

We might notice in this regard that Kabir's Hindi translation of *"Dohari Zindagi"* opens by invoking a local Rajasthani goddess—*"adehi anang tushtaman ho kar harek ko do-do jivan bakhshe ki"* ("May the Bodiless One, the Formless One grant each and everyone two lives to live")—as if each of us (*"harek"*) believed the same thing, as if this bodiless narrative voice were inviting us to take part in an oral storytelling performance set in a village in Rajasthan.[4] The technique immediately invites each of us as a reader to play along with the illusion that she is just one of many sitting in the audience, listening to this narrator telling a story; at the same time, we find ourselves sharing an implicit awareness with someone—to us bodiless, formless—that such a hearing is always—always already—displaced.

The Hindi reader has already been alerted to this delightful duplicity by the title, for *dohari* is a doubling, a duplication, a folding together, and *zindagi* is a Persian-root word for "life" (as in lifetime, but with a connotation of liveliness). Detha's Rajasthani title (*Dovari Joon*) makes a similar "double life" pun but takes the double entendre even further, since *joon*, besides meaning life because it means birth, also—to recall its own Sanskrit origins—means yoni, the female genital organs. Over the course of these different tellings, we learn that the continued life of this particular story offers an indictment of a system that would treat the *dovari joon* of these two women as dangerous if not circulating inside the economy of patriarchal ownership, and in the process readers become aware of how very "two-faced" (*dohari zindagi*) and even "doubly lacking" (*dovari joon*) such demands can be. Thus it is not just the text itself but the translational context that has a double life we need to be attentive to, for it offers a double hearing that signals ways of negotiating these lines separating the duplicate from the original, the real from the ideal, in ways we otherwise might not have considered before.

In this version of the story, the happily-ever-after ending ends with a self-conscious performance that thinks about issues of fidelity that have particular relevance for the ongoing questions of translation. The formless, bodiless narrator announces that not too long ago he was a listener invited to the couple's palace in the wilds outside town, where ordinarily "no male of any species—even a bird—is allowed for miles . . . except me," who "saw it with my own eyes." He makes the even more fantastic claim that the story we have just read was dictated to him by Teeja, the bride of the happily-ever-after couple (*"ar jyun tija mhanai a bat likhai, mhain likhi"*) even though he does not make clear exactly which part of the narrative is hers and which is his. In this playful negotiation of fictional and nonfictional worlds, oral and written story conventions, male versus female visions, he character-izes his role as one of faithful (male) scribe, writing down Teeja's story so critical of the patriarchy without "adding a single syllable" (*"un parbarau ek akhar"*) for fear of being persecuted by the head spirit that protects the couple in the story. And yet even his appeal to this powerful higher author-ity in the fiction (*"i bhelyan bhutan rau sirdar mhanai kad chortau!"*; "Who knows when the Head Spirit would let me be!") skirts the line between the serious and the playful, the believable and the unbelievable, and therefore between belief and nonbelief. This is a different notion of fidelity from the one that translators in the West are often urged toward. Such a telling assures the reader as much as the writer that this version of the story will need to be read, like the other versions before this, as if real and yet not real, believable and yet unbelievable, in a mode whose singular-plural duplicities I play with in my version:

> And the Head Spirit's miracles never cease. . . . After that no male of any species—even a bird—could go near the Wondrous Mahal for twelve and twelve makes twenty-four miles around. Except once when Teeja invited the author there. He saw the Wondrous Mahal with his own eyes and wrote what

Teeja told him to write word for word, and I have passed the tale on in my own language just as faithfully. If he or I have added even a single word to her tale, who knows when the Head Spirit would let us be!

Here the narrative relation is established across time, language, culture, media, not as an abstract engagement but a playful, rigorous questioning, one that does not need to be vouchsafed by any workable notion of ultimate meaning or eternal unity. The joking triangle, then, is also a translation triangle, one that does not fix another unidirectionally but interrogates multidirectionally—as a form of agency that invites another to take part in its play of translation, generation after generation. It is in this way we see that a text's "continued life" is not to be found in the single lost original of the past but in an uncanny present necessarily temporary and plural, one whose to and fro we rely on to make commonsense both individually and collectively.

CAN THE SUBALTERN JOKE? (TO OPEN)

1. While this is an oft-repeated exchange attributed to Gandhi and a British reporter, it is difficult to find evidence of it in available documents. What is more, "British civilization" (or its British spelling, "civilisation") is cited on the Web nearly as often as "Western civilization."

2. The list is long, but most noteworthy are the accusations the Dalit leader B. R. Ambedkar made at the time: that the very caste-based Gandhism gaining popularity amounted to "the doom of the Untouchables." Ambedkar, "Gandhism: The Doom of the Untouchables," in *Essential Writings*, 149; excerpted from *Mr. Gandhi and the Emancipation of the Untouchables*, 274. Madhu Kishwar argues that Gandhi's treatment of women was similarly patronizing: he emphasized their "non-violent temperament" and capacity for self-sacrifice, which resulted in women being cast in roles almost entirely "auxiliary and supportive" in the nationalist movement; Kishwar, "Gandhi on Women," 54.

3. See, e.g., Leela Gandhi, *Postcolonial Theory*, 17–22; and Young, *Postcolonialism*, 337–59.

4. Freud, *Jokes and Their Relation to the Unconscious*, 118–21. Relevant here is Eve Kosofsky Sedgwick's discussion of "Gender Asymmetry and Erotic Triangles" in *Between Men*, 21–27.

5. Freud, *Jokes*, 118–19.

6. Friedrich A. Kittler, *Discourse Networks 1800/1900*, 36.

7. Marcel O'Gorman, *E-Crit: Digital Media, Critical Theory, and the Humanities*, 22 and 23.

8. Ibid., 5 and 4.

9. Thanks go to Deirdre de la Cruz for her insights into Kittler's work for my project, especially her whimsical, provocative suggestion that I think about what it might mean to "surf" the ocean of the streams of stories.

10. Tufte, *Visual Explanations*, 121.

11. For a helpful introduction on authorship, the creative commons, and the contradictions of current reinterpretations of intellectual property rights,

see Nimus, "Copyright, Copyleft and the Creative Anti-Commons." More basically, see the Creative Commons Web site at http://creativecommons.org, as well as the post, "CC in Review: Lawrence Lessig on Compatibility," at http://creativecommons.org/weblog/entry/5709. Lessig has also written a helpful post, "Commons Misunderstandings" on his own blog: http://lessig.org/blog/2007/12/commons_misunderstandings_asca.html. To think about the creative commons as a dynamic, fluid network, see also Lessig, *The Future of Ideas*; as well as his own experiments with the creative commons, as seen in the wiki version, "Code v2" (http://www.socialtext.net/codev2/index.cgi), which in his Preface to the 2nd ed. he calls "a translation of an old book," *Code: And Other Laws of Cyberspace.*

12. Mehta, *Liberalism and Empire*, explores this inherent contradiction with particular elegance.

13. "Sly Civility," in Bhabha, *Location of Culture*, 93–101.

14. Here I am drawing on Jean-Luc Nancy's recent insistence that we include the sensuality of collective meaning-making in our understanding of "sense." See "An Exempting from Sense," in Nancy, *Dis-enclosure*, 121–28. Nancy writes of *"sense* as signifying, sense as in the five senses, and sense as direction"; ibid., 123. My thanks to Helen Tartar for pointing me to this reference.

15. Bhabha, *Location of Culture*, 93. Bhabha, following Jacques Derrida, describes such a colonial encounter as being waged between the forces of writing and the forces of speech; this example should persuade us to distinguish more particularly between performances that are fixed and those that are flexible. Mayaram, *Against History, Against State*, 4–6, makes a similar argument with regard to Rajasthani historical accounts.

16. See, e.g., Shaikh, "Interview with Amartya Sen"; and Guha, "Using and Abusing Gandhi."

17. While the work of Lydia Liu and Gayatri Spivak has been particularly influential, Melas, *All the Difference in the World*, xii, offers a succinct and extremely relevant formulation that draws attention to the paradoxical advancement of the figure of common ground: "comparison, under these conditions, involves a very particular form of incommensurability: space offers a ground of comparison, but no basis of equivalence."

18. Liu, *Translingual Practice*, 20.

19. For the connection between Freud's own critical practice and institutions of colonialism, I work from the argument of Khanna, *Dark Continents.* She does not, however, address the question of humor. I should add that while Freud does not mention race, nationality, or ethnicity in his discussion of the joking triangle, besides gender, his analysis does include distinctions based on class.

20. The figure of "Mother India" becomes the site first of nationalist-minded veneration in the early decades of the twentieth century, then international contestation in the 1920s with the publication of the American journalist

Katherine Mayo's exposé of the degraded conditions of women in India, as Sinha shows in *Specters of Mother India*.

21. Rao, "Texture and Authority," 204 and 205.

22. M. K. Gandhi, *Evil Wrought by the English Medium*. I would like to thank William Baxter for—quite literally—providing me this reference.

23. For an insightful analysis of Gandhi as a translator and its impact on his political style, see Javed Majeed, "Gandhi, 'Truth' and Translatability," 303–32. The issue of Hindustani as an Indian national language is addressed more fully in Chapter 5.

24. Ngũgĩ wa Thiong'o, *Decolonising the Mind*, 9, writes that "language was the most important vehicle through which that [colonial] power fascinated and held the soul prisoner. The bullet was the means of the physical subjugation. Language was the means of spiritual subjugation." It is in this essay that he announces he will no longer write in the colonial language of English but in his mother tongue, Gĩkũyũ.

25. See, e.g., the work of the Sahitya Akademi, Katha, Bhasha, the Central Institute of Indian Languages, or the collaborative project, Anukriti, described on their Web sites: http://www.sahitya-akademi.org/sahitya-akademi/prj3 .htm; http://katha.org/WhoWeAre/default.htm; http://www.bhasharesearch .org.in/Site.html; and http://www.ciil.org/; http://www.anukriti.net/.

26. G. N. Devy, *In Another Tongue*, 135.

27. Prins, *Victorian Sappho*, 25. She asks: "How can any song be reclaimed from the tatters of such texts, torn out of context and riddled with gaps? How are these scattered letters 'voiced'?" She goes on to suggest that ongoing generations of "scholarly speculation and conjecture are necessary to reconstruct a singing voice for Sappho," and thus that "Reading Sappho is a form of riddling."

28. Relevant here is Haun Saussy's recent discussion of such a "space of comparison" as a zone of untranslatability; Saussy, "Exquisite Cadavers," 27. Note, too, that I use the phrase "uneven world" to reference the work of R. Radhakrishnan.

29. Such an idea was inspired not only by my own browsing habits but by the explicit invitation made by Ajay Skaria to indulge them in his own nonlinear monograph that itself is likewise concerned with the tension between oral and written sources in oppositional discourse: Skaria, *Hybrid Histories*, 17–18.

I. HUMORING THE MELANCHOLIC READER OF WORLD LITERATURE

1. In the story I refer to by Borges, Pierre Menard sets out to compose not "another *Quixote*—which is easy—but *the Quixote itself*"; Borges, "Pierre Menard, Author of the *Quixote*," 39. To complete this task, he sets out to become Cervantes in every way and thus to recreate the *Quixote* without reference to the original. In closing, the narrator tells us that only another Menard

could possibly understand all the scribblings but that in any case the work is brilliant because it has "enriched, by means of a new technique, the halting and rudimentary art of reading; this new technique is that of the deliberate anachronism and the erroneous attribution" (44).

2. Freud, *Jokes*, 36. Freud's discussion of the humor of this pun reveals his assumption that a translator's activity is always and necessarily criminal: "The similarity, amounting almost to identity, of the two words represents most impressively the necessity which forces a translator into crimes against his original." When you try translating this mischievous Italian adage into English, you unwittingly prove his point: translator—traitor?

3. While the fictional author of this letter might not have realized it, I discovered he was quoting Richard Howard verbatim, quoting Roland Barthes in French; Barthes, "Death of the Author," 49.

4. In their entry for *"dieu/*god" they write: "Voltaire himself said: 'If God did not exist, it would be necessary to invent him'"; Flaubert, *Bouvard et Pécuchet*, 308.

5. Venuti, *Scandals of Translation*; Felman, *Scandal of the Speaking Body*.

6. Felman, *Scandal of the Speaking Body*, 14.

7. I have posed a similar riddle to the English translation of Roland Barthes's essay, "Death of the Author," an essay which itself pursues a related inquiry. See Merrill, "Death of the Authors a.k.a. Twilight of the Translators."

8. For her biography, see the 1975 edition of the *New Columbia Encyclopedia*. It says she lived from 1942 to 1973 and was a U.S. fountain designer and photographer best-known for her collection of photos of rural American mailboxes, *Flags Up!* She was born in Bangs, Ohio, and died in an explosion while on assignment for *Combustibles* magazine. The entry makes no mention, however, of her more literary work, such as this story. Permission, however difficult, has been obtained from the author for this use of her story. See also "Lillian Virginia Mountweazel" in Wikipedia, http://en.wikipedia.org/wiki/Lillian_Virginia_Mountweazel, as well as the link to the related entry, "Fictitious Entry," in Wikipedia, http://en.wikipedia.org/wiki/Nihilartikel.

9. As revealed below , I am purposely repeating the phrase "continued life" used by Walter Benjamin in his enigmatic, elegant, and much-quoted essay, "Task of the Translator," 71.

10. Besides the recognition his Sahitya Akademi award helped garner for Rajasthani as a distinct language, Lalas relied on the tales in Detha's multivolume *Baatan ri Phulwari* to compile entries for his Rajasthani dictionary.

11. Note, for example, the charges of Orientalism as the "fixing of . . . cultures" made in Niranjana, *Siting Translation*, 3, discussed further in Chapter 4.

12. See my translator's preface to Detha, *A Straw Epic*, for a more detailed account of this serendipitous circuit of the circulation from oral to written to oral (and—thanks in part to me—back to written).

13. Venuti makes a similar point about Amos Tutuola's *The Palm-Wine Drinkard:* "Tutuola's translating likewise prevents his narratives from being described as an expression of cultural authenticity. . . . For despite Tutuola's reliance on Yoruba folklore and literature, the calquing never rendered a specific Yoruba text; no purely indigenous original existed behind Tutuola's eccentric English"; Venuti, *Scandals of Translation*, 176.

14. Hobsbawm, "Introduction," 7.

15. Trumpener, *Bardic Nationalism*, 6 and 7.

16. Ibid., 33.

17. Sakai, *Translation and Subjectivity*, 15. See also the fortuitously named *Voices of the Past*, where he discusses language movements in nineteenth-century Japan and issues of framing.

18. Liu, "A Folksong Immortal"; Brennan, "National Longing for Form."

19. Trumpener, *Bardic Nationalism*, 7, 22, and 28.

20. Khanna, *Dark Continents*, 16.

21. Ibid., 16–7.

22. Ibid., 14–15.

23. Dipesh Chakrabarty argues that "the ideology of progress or 'development'" took hold from the nineteenth century and was the basis of narratives of social justice (including historicism) that "enabled European domination of the world" by making "modernity or capitalism look not simply global but rather as something that became global *over time*, by originating in one place (Europe) and then spreading outside of it"; Chakrabarty, *Provincializing Europe*, 7. As I discuss below, he proposes that we think around these center/periphery-as-original/derivative binaries underwriting what he labels "transition" narratives by looking to tropes of "translation." More salient to Khanna's point about haunted temporalities, he suggests that "It is only within some very particular traditions of thinking that we treat fundamental thinkers who are long dead not only as people belonging to their own times but also as though they were our own contemporaries"; ibid., 5.

24. Khanna, *Dark Continents*, 65.

25. I will use the term "writer" so as to avoid making a somewhat dubious distinction between author, translator, and folklorist.

26. Dundes, "Nationalistic Inferiority Complexes," 165.

27. Porter, "'Bring Me the Head of James Macpherson,'" 405.

28. Ibid., 396.

29. Ibid., 397.

30. Brennan, "National Longing for Form," 53.

31. Bassnett, *Comparative Literature*, 14 and 15. I wish to thank Jeffrey Grossman for pointing me to this reference.

32. Ibid., 18.

33. I understand the death drive in the Freudian sense of being ambivalently drawn toward death at the same time as life. For more on Melanie Klein's

application of this concept to acts of interpretation and its relevance as a heuristic strategy for understanding larger cultural movements, see Esther Sánchez-Pardo, *Cultures of the Death Drive.*

34. Chakrabarty's observation quoted in n. 23 above ("that we treat fundamental thinkers who are long dead not only as people belonging to their own times but also as though they were our own contemporaries") is part of his struggle to understand why, in his words, "Postcolonial scholarship is committed, almost by definition, to engaging with the universals . . . that were forged in eighteenth-century Europe and that underlie the human science"; Chakrabarty, *Provincializing Europe*, 5. Like Butler (especially in her 2000 essay, "Restaging the Universal"), Chakrabarty looks to the trope of translation to reclaim these intellectual traditions in a way that will keep them "alive" to issues of social justice in a more equitably universal sense.

35. Besides the 1985 and 1988 versions of "Can the Subaltern Speak?", in Spivak's self-consciously revised version in *Critique of Postcolonial Reason*, 269–308, she calls her "passionate lament" that "the subaltern cannot speak" an "inadvisable remark" (308).

36. Butler, "Values of Difficulty," 204.

37. Barthes, "Death of the Author," 49.

38. Here I am parodying Butler, *Gender Trouble*, 41.

39. Andrew Parker makes a similar argument, focusing, like Anderson in *The Spectre of Comparisons*, on Mario Vargas Llosa's novel (in English translation), *The Storyteller.*

40. Rita Copeland, *Rhetoric, Hermeneutics and Translation in the Middle Ages*, offers an engaging analysis of the European history of debates over "fidelity." Douglas Robinson, *Translator's Turn*, speaks to the ongoing legacy of such debates by offering an impassioned critique of the Christian mind-body dualisms haunting so many of our discussions of translation. Robinson's discussion in "The Ascetic Foundations of Western Translatology" shows even more specifically the ascetic overtones of the word-for-word versus sense-for-sense debates over translational fidelity.

41. Ernest Robert Curtius argues, "The word *transfertur* ('is transferred') gives rise to the concept of *translation* (transference) which is basic for medieval history. The renewal of the Empire by Charlemagne could be regarded as a transferal of the Roman *imperium* to another people. This is implied in the formula *translation imperii*, with which the *translation studii*." Curtius, *European Literature and the Middle Ages*, 29–29.

42. Ahmad, *In Theory*, 101–102. In response to Fredric Jameson's 1986 article, "Third World Literature in the Era of Multinational Capital," I cannot resist quoting Ahmad's later aside on translation: "Rare would be a major literary theorist in Europe or the United States who has ever bothered with an Asian or African language; and the enormous industry of translation which circulates texts among the advanced capitalist countries grinds erratically and slowly when it

comes to translation from Asian or African languages. The upshot is that major literary traditions—such as those of Bengali, Hindi, Tamil, Telugu and a half dozen others from India alone—remain, beyond a few texts here and there, virtually unknown to the American literary theorist"; Ahmad, *In Theory*, 97.

43. Chatterjee objects to the "sociological determinism" with which Anderson in *Imagined Communities* sees "in third-world nationalisms a profoundly 'modular' character . . . invariably shaped according to contours outlined by given historical models"; Chatterjee, *Nationalist Thought and the Colonial World*, 21. Years later, discussing the scene of "double vision" that Anderson describes in the opening to *Spectre of Comparisons*, Chatterjee writes that "the universalism that is available to Anderson to be refined and enriched through his anthropological practice could never have been available to Sukarno, [the object of that double vision,] regardless of the political power the latter may have wielded as a leader of a major postcolonial nation"; Chatterjee, "Anderson's Utopia," 168.

44. See James Holmes, "Images of Translation," for an engaging outline of these slavish tropes in Renaissance Europe.

45. I interrogate the politics of these metaphors of reproduction in global circulation in Merrill, "Seeds of Discontent."

46. See in particular Homi Bhabha, "How Newness Enters the World. Bhabha discusses Rushdie's novel, *The Satanic Verses*. In "Imaginary Homelands," published first in 1982, Rushdie calls himself and all who have been "borne across the world, . . . translated men." He adds, "It is normally supposed that something always gets lost in translation; I cling, obstinately, to the notion that something can also be gained." Rushdie, "Imaginary Homelands," 17.

47. Berman, *Experience of the Foreign*, 56, quoting Goethe, *Conversations with Eckermann*, 24 and 21.

48. Berman, *Experience of the Foreign*, 55.

49. Casanova, *World Republic of Letters*, 14, quoting Goethe, *Conversations*, 24. See also Nicholas Brown's interrogation of the terms of this "free exchange" in *Utopian Generations*, 5–6.

50. Damrosch, *What Is World Literature?* 4, quoting Karl Marx and Friedrich Engels, *Manifesto of the Communist Party*.

51. Damrosch, *What Is World Literature?* 5, quoting Janet Abu-Lughod, "Going beyond Global Babble," 131–37.

52. Bhabha, "How Newness Enters the World," 227.

53. Theorists are particularly interested in Walter Benjamin's notion of the "afterlife" of translation, which, he writes, signals "a transformation and a renewal of something living" by which "the original undergoes a change" (73). I will have a chance to refer to Paul de Man's famous performance of this translational *abîme* in Chapter 3.

54. In particular, Andrew Benjamin reads Walter Benjamin's "The Task of the Translator" in relation to his ideas in "The Storyteller" as a way of thinking through the relationship of "the temporality of the instant and the temporality

proper to after-life ([that is,] . . . primordial time)"; Andrew Benjamin, *Translation and the Nature of Philosophy*, 106.

55. Ibid., 98 and 100.

56. Ibid., 108.

57. Butler, *Gender Trouble*, xvii–xviii. For discussions of translation as an act of unequal exchange, see Talal Asad, "Concept of Cultural Translation"; Eric Cheyfitz, *Poetics of Imperialism*; Rita Kothari, *Translating India;* Lydia Liu, *Translingual Practice*, as well as the introduction to her edited volume, *Tokens of Exchange*, and the article "Legislating the Universal" in that same volume; Tejaswini Niranjana, *Siting Translation*; and Vicente Rafael, *Contracting Colonialism*. For utopic readings of the trope of translation, see Bhabha, "How Newness Enters the World"; Butler, "Restaging the Universal"; James Clifford, *Routes*; Robert J. C. Young's chapter "Translation" in *Postcolonialism: A Very Short Introduction*, 138–47.

58. Butler, "Values of Difficulty," 204–205.

59. While he does not attend specifically to the problematic of translation, Joseph Slaughter's careful and engaging study of the modern rhetoric of human rights in world literature is salient here. See Slaughter, *Human Rights, Inc.*

60. Spivak, "Can the Subaltern Speak?" 296.

61. Vicente Rafael, *Contracting Colonialism*, 21.

62. Liu writes that colonial historiography "refuses to assign meaning to events or confront contemporary face-to-face and day-to-day struggles outside the evolutionary conceptual models of tradition and modernity, backwardness and progress, particular and universal," while Marxist theory has "relied on a teleological view of history (the so-called transition from feudalism or the Asiatic mode of production to the capitalist mode of production) to characterize China's traumatic entrance into the modern international community"; Liu, "Legislating the Universal," 130.

63. Eagleton, *Walter Benjamin*, 171–72. He is quoting Walter Benjamin's "Theses on the Philosophy of History" (relying on a slightly amended translation) and Marx's *The Eighteenth Brumaire*.

64. Ibid., 149.

65. Ibid. Here he cites V. N. Volosinov, *Marxism and the Philosophy of Language*. To further the irony, there is, of course, debate over whether Bakhtin wrote under the fictitious name of Volosinov or whether this was an authentic author. See Morson and Emerson, *Mikhail Bakhtin*, 102–19.

66. Eagleton, *Walter Benjamin*.

67. Cheah, "Spectral Nationality," 226.

68. Apter, *Translation Zone*, 34.

69. By Detha's "minority" status, I refer to language and not necessarily ethnicity. See Chapter 3 for more on the link between minority and vernacular. I am particularly mindful of David Damrosch's critique of Deleuze and Guat-

tari's contention in their *Kafka: Toward a Minor Literature* that Kafka was a minority writer. Damrosch, *What Is World Literature*, 201–203.

70. Cheah, "Spectral Nationality," 227.

71. Chapman, trans., *Chapman's Homer*, 2:6.

72. Douglas Robinson, *Translation and Taboo*, 64–73, discusses "metempsychotic translation" with a different but related focus in terms of displacement of taboo subjects. For a more specific discussion of the limits of the ontological metaphors of translation as a question of reading a text as both singular and plural, see Merrill, "To Be or Not to Be a Gutter Flea."

73. It only enhances my argument to pursue the suggestion of Albert Lord in *The Singer of Tales* and Gregory Nagy in *Homeric Questions* that the name "Homer" refers to a plurality of oral composers.

74. Gayatri Spivak—a practicing translator herself—argues that the relationship between translator and text be thought of in complex, intimate terms, just as the bond between lovers; Spivak, "The Politics of Translation."

75. Detha, "A Dilemma," in *A Straw Epic and Other Stories*.

76. In another reverse circulation described in Chapter 2, I was introduced to Detha's work in Kabir's fine Hindi translations and began learning Rajasthani so that I might read more of his work.

77. In an even finer irony, the *India Abroad* Web site reports that the film did better in the box offices in the United States than in India; Rediff India Abroad, "Paheli is India's Oscar Nominee," September 26, 2005, http://www .rediff.com/movies/2005/sep/26paheli.htm.

78. For an incisive discussion on the imperial investments in translating property, see Cheyfitz, *Poetics of Imperialism*, 41–58.

79. I purposely avoid the more obvious rendering, "saying after," so as not to emphasize the implicit linear chronology such phrasing evokes.

2. A TELLING EXAMPLE

1. Cheah, *Spectral Nationality*; see especially "The Nation as a Community of Language and the Overcoming of Death," 121–25.

2. Lisa Mitchell, "Parallel Languages, Parallel Cultures," 446.

3. Brass, *Language, Religion and Politics in North India*.

4. "Independant [*sic*] Rajputstan," Web site of the Rajputana Liberation Front, http://rajputana.htmlplanet.com/rajput/indepraj.html.

5. Web site of the Rajputana Liberation Front. The listing of Dalits (formerly known as untouchables) and Mughals (one can assume this is a gloss for South Asian Muslims) as deserving of a separate nation is itself a deeply divisive maneuver.

6. Similar to this discussion of the question of Rajasthani nationalism in terms of tropes of silence, Ramaswamy relies on visual metaphors in her

discussion of Tamil nationalism; she opens her book by asking, "how one writes the history of something that is visible but not seen." Ramaswamy, *Passions of the Tongue*, 19.

7. Interestingly, A. K. Ramanujan includes a much shorter Tulu version of this tale in his collection; Ramanujan, ed., *Folktales of India*, 149–57. In their introduction to a 1996 collection of essays on riddling narratives, Galit Hasan-Rokem and David Shulman discuss this tale to comment on "the intricate relations between speech and silence" which "riddle-tales often map . . . in detail"; and while they admit that such a complex story "merits a full discussion beyond the limits of this introduction," they describe it succinctly as "a metanarrative on the riddle form"; Hasan-Rokem and Shulman, eds, *Untying the Knot*, 5–6. My hope is that this chapter will provide, in part, the fuller discussion they call for.

8. I discuss the *chougou* as an exercise in making sense of nonsense later in this chapter in comparison to an oral performance I attended. For now, it is enough to notice the formulaic cheerfulness of its meter and rhyme scheme:

bhale din padhara, pendai paki bor
ghar bhindak ghora jinera ladoo bhare chor
bat ri bat khurapat ri khurapata
khejari ro kantou sarhi solah hatha

9. My point is that we must be sure that our own tools of the trade do not unconsciously search out similarly elite cultural institutions and alienate precisely those people with whom we might also find common cause. Relevant here is Raymond Williams's critique of the elite and certainly lettered institutional formulations of the literary; Williams, *Marxism and Literature*, 46.

10. Such a perspective is influenced by the work of Jack Zipes, who places the Grimms in a similarly liminal category that is neither strictly that of "author" nor of "folklorist." Against charges of mindless nationalist pandering, Zipes writes that the Grimm Brothers collected the stories and then refined them in order "to *create* an ideal type for the *literary* fairy tale, one that sought to be as close to the oral tradition as possible, while incorporating stylistic, formal, and substantial thematic changes to appeal to a growing bourgeois audience." Zipes, *Brothers Grimm*, 12.

11. Andrew Benjamin, *Translation and the Nature of Philosophy*, 108.

12. Albert Lord makes a similar argument when discussing the bardic performers of Yugoslavia in *Singer of Tales* but argues instead that we should consider each performer an author:

It seems to me highly significant that the words "author" and "original" have either no meaning at all in oral tradition or a meaning quite different from the one usually assigned to them. The anonymity of folk epic is a fiction, because the singer has a name. We have created for ourselves in regard to both these terms problems that are not of any major importance. It should be clear from the foregoing that the author of an oral epic, that is, the text of a performance, is the performer, the singer before us. . . . A performance is unique; it is a creation, not a reproduction, and it can therefore have only one author. Albert Lord, *Singer of Tales*, 102.

13. Relevant here is Gayatri Spivak's discussion of the move of the Subaltern Studies collective (especially Ranajit Guha) to understand "the people or subaltern" within a master-slave dialectic that can define them categorically only in terms of "a difference from the elite." Spivak, *Critique of Postcolonial Reason*, 272.

14. See Komal Kothari, ed., *Premchand ke Patra*. Note too that we look more carefully at the contradictions in this agenda of Premchand's writing in particular in Chapter 5.

15. See the discussion of the Grimm brothers' creative writing process in Zipes, *Brothers Grimm*, as well as my article comparing Detha as author/folklorist to the Grimms; Merrill, "Are We the Folk in this Lok?"

16. Bora, *Contemporary Rajasthani Literature*, 1, 3, 4–5.

17. Ibid., 5.

18. In a September 2002 interview, he told me: "Volumes of *Phulwari* were sent out to the Pali schools and they were so popular [*prachalit*], one was saying I'll take this book and another was saying I'll take it, so there ended up being a fight among the students. Finally the teacher said that each class would get a copy. . . . And now in Rajasthan there is no teacher, no master, who has not read *Baatan ri Phulwari*."

19. Foucault, "What Is an Author?" 115, citing Samuel Beckett, *Texts for Nothing*, trans. Beckett (London: Calder & Boyars, 1974), 16. Given that Beckett is translating this riddling prose himself, its ironies double back endlessly.

20. Foucault, "What Is an Author?" 117.

21. Rao, "Texture and Authority," 204 and 205.

22. Ibid., 115 and 123.

23. Foucault, "What Is an Author?" 124.

24. Simon, *Gender in Translation*, 45.

25. Foucault writes:

It is well known that in a novel narrated in the first person, neither the first person pronoun, the present indicative tense, nor, for that matter, its signs of localization refer directly to the writer, either to the time when he wrote, or to the specific act of writing; rather, they stand for a "second self" whose similarity to the author is never fixed and undergoes considerable alteration within the course of a single book. It would be as false to seek the author in relation to the actual writer as to the fictional narrator; the "author-function" arises out of their scission—in the division and distance of the two.

Foucault, "What Is an Author?" At "second self" Foucault cites Booth, *Rhetoric of Fiction*, 67–77.

26. Ibid., 129.

27. Eagleton, *Walter Benjamin*, 149.

28. Chundavat, *"Ath Rani Chouboli ri baat."*

29. Joshi, *"Rani Chouboli ri vat."*

30. Prabhakar, *"Bat Raja Vikramaditya aur Chouboli ki,"* in Prabhakar, ed., *Rajasthani Baaten,* 5–15.

31. I would like to thank Richard Saran for alerting me to the existence of this unpublished manuscript and for spending many hours deciphering the difficult handwritten script and the equally unstandardized Rajasthani locutions.

32. Inden, *Imagining India,* 172 and 175. Inden quotes Tod: "We have nothing to apprehend from the Rajput States if raised to their ancient prosperity. The closest attention to their history proves beyond contradiction that they were never capable of uniting." From Tod, *Annals and Antiquities of Rajasthan,* 1:174.

33. Peabody, "Tod's Rajast'han and the Boundaries of Imperial Rule," 188.

34. Tod, *Annals and Antiquities of Rajasthan,* 1:xvi. That regional Rajasthan becomes synonymous with the broader category of India is a particularly colonial move, thus leading to the contradictory associations with nationalism still contentious today.

35. Ibid., 1:xv.

36. Ibid.

37. Dalmia, *Nationalization of Hindu Traditions,* 194.

38. Shukla, *Hindi Sahitya ke Itihas,* 27. See Wakankar, "Moment of Criticism in Indian Nationalist Thought," on Ramchandra Shukla for a detailed and thought-provoking reading of his efforts to promote a Brahminical version of Hindi nationalism at this crucial moment in history.

39. Motilal Menaria, *Rajasthani Bhasha aur Sahitya,* 63. Hiralal Maheshwari also lists *Prithiraja Rasau* as an example of Rajasthani poetry written in Pingal in Maheshwari, *History of Rajasthani Literature,* 7–8.

40. Dalmia, *Nationalization of Hindu Traditions,* 194 n. 70.

41. Ibid., 194.

42. I heard this story first in March 1989 from Vijay Dan Detha's younger cousin, Prakash Detha.

43. Tod., *Annals and Antiquities of Rajasthan,* 1:xvi.

44. Sakariya and Sakariya, *Rajasthani Hindi Shabd Kosh,* 1:460.

45. *Hunkara* will be discussed in more detail later in the chapter. They are the regular responses the listeners must give in order for the narrative to proceed in a storytelling session.

46. Recording of Abdul Rahman, February 20, 2003, Pipar City, Rajasthan. Compare with the published version of the chougou *"bhale din padhara"* that appears in Detha, *Baatan ri Phulwari,* 1:13–15.

47. An interesting comparison is the scene of Stephen Greenblatt in Tunisia hearing a version of *The Thousand and One Nights* recounted even though he

knew not a word of Arabic. See Greenblatt, *Marvellous Possessions*. This, perhaps, is another way of thinking of translation as performance.

48. Interviews on February 29, 2003, with Bhawani Bai and February 25, 2003, with Omprakash. Note that I am using their real names at their specific request.

49. The Rajasthani version of the chougou *"bhale din padhara"* written by Detha opens the first volume of Detha, *Baatan ri Phulwari*, and this version opens the English-language collection, Detha, *A Straw Epic*.

50. Stewart, *Nonsense*, 88.

51. Ibid., 4.

52. Ibid., 5.

53. Bateson, *Ecology of the Mind*, 71, cited in Stewart, *Nonsense*, 29.

54. Stewart, *Nonsense*, 29.

55. Ibid., 31.

56. Ibid. Likewise Bateson, *Ecology of the Mind*, 193, contends that without play "life would be an endless interchange of stylized messages, a game with rigid rules, unrelieved by change or humor."

57. Hutcheon, *Irony's Edge*, 37–56. Rather than arguing over the distinctions between humor and irony, as a critic such as C. D. Lang has, like Hutcheon I emphasize an understanding of irony that considers humor and playfulness as integral components.

58. Ibid., 30.

59. Ibid., 11–12 and 41–42.

60. Nancy, *Dis-Enclosure*, 127.

61. This notion relies on Jean-Luc Nancy's discussion in *Being Singular Plural* of the relationship between the individual and his community as one of being "singular plural," as well as M. M. Bakhtin's elaboration of the dialogic in *Dialogic Imagination* most particularly.

62. Note that the *Oxford English Dictionary* offers that the word "travesty" comes from Latin via the French, from a parodic translation of Virgil:

Originally a. F. *travesti*, fem. *travestie*, pa. pple. of (*se*) *travestir* (Montaigne *a*1592), "to disguise him, or take on another man's habit" (Cotgr.), ad. It. *travestire* to disguise (Florio), f. *tra-* = TRANS- + It., L. *vestīre* to clothe. The adoption from It. in 16th c. accounts for the retention of *s* in Fr., as opposed to *vêtir*, *revêtir*. Made known in England in the title of Scarron's *Le Virgile Travesty en vers burlesques* (= Vergil travestied in burlesque verses), 1648, whence occasionally in other connexions, and at length as a n., used first in Scarron's sense, and later in the etymological one.

63. Butler, *Gender Trouble*, 41.

64. While Tod popularized "Rajasthan" as an entity, most scholars agree that the term "Rajasthani" for the language was first coined in 1908 by the British linguist George Grierson as part of his vast, government-sponsored *Linguistic Survey of India*. However, Rama Sita Lalas, *Rajasthani Vyakaran*

[Rajasthani grammar] begins his history with the 1896 publication of Indian linguist Ramkaran Asopa's *Marwari Bhasha ra Vyakaran* [The grammar of the Marwari language], which he claims both Grierson and the equally foundational Italian linguist Tessitori based their research on. No doubt George Macalister's *Dictionary of the Dialects Spoken in the State of Jeypore* influenced Grierson to expand the definition of Rajasthani beyond Jodhpur, but Asopa's work is mentioned less often today in historical accounts of the language.

65. One can understand the point by looking through Lalas, *Rajasthani Vyakaran*, which uses Marwari and Rajasthani interchangeably.

66. Mitchell, "Parallel Languages, Parallel Cultures."

67. The main grammar book I relied on was a republication of Asopa, *Marwari Vyakaran*. I purchased it in the only shop in Jaipur that sold Rajasthani books.

68. See, e.g., Prabhakar, *Critical Study of Rajasthani Literature*; and Maheshwari, *History of Rajasthani Literature*; later I would see the same history repeated in Menaria, *Rajasthani Bhasha aur Sahitya*.

69. I follow Bahl, *Ādhunika Rājasthānī kā samracanātmaka vyākarana*, in calling Shekhavati and Marwari dialects of Rajasthani rather than of Hindi.

70. He wore the *pancharanga* turban popular among Rajputs. This reminds me of a version of that same saying: *har choubis kos pagari aur boli badalti hai* (every twenty-four miles the turban and the language change).

71. Usually working for a nongovernmental organization signifies working outside state control and therefore is usually more progressive. It certainly was in Dharmendar's case: at that point she was the press officer for the Rajasthan branch of the Indian National Trust for Artistic and Cultural Heritage (INTACH), which was working locally as a watchdog group to renovate architectural sites important to the community in a way that fostered artisanal skills and prevented environmental degradation.

72. Gayatri Spivak has published three different versions of the essay, "Can the Subaltern Speak? Speculations on Widow-Sacrifice," most recently in Spivak, *Critique of Postcolonial Reason*; also as a revised reprint in Nelson and Grossberg, eds., *Marxist Interpretations of Culture*, 271–313; it appeared originally in *Wedge* (Winter/Spring 1985):120–30. I am grateful to David Agruss for mentioning the work he and Indira Karemcheti are doing to compare the three versions.

73. Mani, "Contentious Traditions."

74. Rajan, *Real and Imagined Women*.

75. I first translated the story from a manuscript version Detha had photocopied for me. This Hindi version appeared in print years later in the March 1997 issue of *Kathadesh*.

76. For the full text in English, see my English version, Vijay Dan Detha, "A True Calling."

77. I explore the analogy between the sacrifice the *bhand* makes within the story and the sacrifice our institutions of authorship ask us to make as (multiple) writers of this story in Merrill, "Are We the Folk in this Lok?"

78. Purushottamlal Menaria. *Rājasthānnī bhāshā kī rūparekhā aura mānyatā kā prāsna*, 51. The words are for "here" and "there" in English, Hindi, Gujarati, and Rajasthani respectively. My thanks to Brajesh Samarth for discovering this couplet and sharing it with me.

79. An *anna* is a traditional form of measurement, especially when counting money: there are sixteen annas in a rupee, for example. This English translation is my own.

80. Devy, *In Another Tongue*, 135.

81. Booth, *Rhetoric of Irony*, 27–31. As I suggest above, Hutcheon considers such a reading of irony as focusing too much on the point of view of the ironist; see especially Hutcheon, *Irony's Edge*, 12. I argue that Booth's work figures an "implied author" in order to force us to account for the ways readers create such a figure in our own interpretations, to make the two positions quite complementary.

82. In English, Raymond Williams notes that literature refers not so much to the *making* of literature but to a level of social distinction based on literacy and education, given its etymological connection with the French word *litterature* from the Latin *littera*, letter (of the alphabet); literature is thus associated with "a condition of reading: of being able to read and of having read"; Williams, *Marxism and Literature*, 46. Pollock, "Cosmopolitan and Vernacular in History," 591–625, acknowledges that "the learned man in old India was . . . the *vāgmin*, the master of speech, and not, as in Europe, the *litteratus*, the lettered man," and yet cautions that "the contrast many draw between India and Europe on the place of writing in culture . . . should not be exaggerated" (83).

83. Monier-Williams, *Sanskrit-English Dictionary*, 1212. Note, e.g., the use of the word in India's premier institution, the Sahitya Academy.

84. Detha, "Chouboli," *Baatan ri Phulwari*, translated in Merrill as "Chouboli," *A Straw Epic and Other Stories*.

85. Ibid.

86. Ibid.

87. Ibid.

88. Mani, "Contentious Traditions," 88.

89. Detha, "Chouboli," *Baatan ri Phulwari*.

90. Another story written by Detha, "The Cannibal," is even more irreverent: the protagonist, an irascible temple priest, feels neglected by the goddess of the temple where he serves; she responds to him only when he threatens to smash her to pieces with a hammer. In that instance, the iconoclasm is nearly made literal.

91. Detha, "Chouboli," *Baatan ri Phulwari*.

92. Ibid.

93. Lutgendorf, *Life of a Text*, raises this question in his reading of the *Ram Charit Manas* and the triangle between Ram, Sita, and Lakshman, pointing to the danger implied in that relationship. He points out that in a traditionally exogamous culture, there is obviously a high premium on forcing the woman to conform to the demands of patriarchy and thus not disrupt the primary bonds holding the extended family together.

94. Detha, "Chouboli," *Baatan ri Phulwari*.

95. Butler, *Gender Trouble*, xvii–xviii.

3. FRAMED

1. Eagleton, *Walter Benjamin*, 150.

2. Eagleton writes: "on the one hand, prosaic contents seem cynically to hijack poetic forms; on the other hand, as the signifier transmits its energy to the signified, those forms cannot after all be quite as external to their contents as they seem to be"; ibid., 168.

3. Stallybrass and White, *Politics and Poetics of Transgression*, 13. They cite in particular Eagleton, *Walter Benjamin*, 148.

4. Stallybrass and White, *Politics and Poetics of Transgression*.

5. Bakhtin, *Rabelais and His World*, 11.

6. Ibid., 317.

7. Ibid., 167.

8. Eagleton, *Walter Benjamin*, 143, quoting Bertolt Brecht, *Flüchtlingsqespräche*.

9. Eagleton, *Walter Benjamin*, 154–55, quoting Benjamin, *One-Way Street*, 239.

10. Eagleton, *Walter Benjamin*, 154.

11. Ibid., 145.

12. Ibid., 155 n. 79, quoting Benjamin, *Briefe*, 1:132.

13. Eagleton, *Walter Benjamin*, 143.

14. Ibid., 168.

15. Marx and Engels, *Selected Works*, 100. Cited by Eagleton, *Walter Benjamin*, 168–69.

16. Eagleton, *Walter Benjamin*, 150–51.

17. Ibid., 151.

18. Bhabha, *The Location of Culture*, 227.

19. Eagleton, 150.

20. Florida, *Writing the Past*, 396–97.

21. Ibid., 396.

22. Bakhtin, *Speech Genres*, 7, cited in Morson and Emerson, 56.

23. Unlike Eagleton, Bakhtin warns us away from using a term like "dialectic" for such an interaction; for Bakhtin, the Hegelian-Marxist understanding

of dialectic and especially its culminating synthesis is limited and even reified because it "can be contained within a single consciousness and overcomes contradictions in a single, monologic view." Ibid.

24. Radhakrishnan, in *Theory in an Uneven World*, argues against the dangers of an extreme relativism and equally an extreme absolutism.

25. I use the word "intention" in reference to Bakhtin's writings, especially *Dialogic Imagination*. While concerns of space preclude me from engaging in a full discussion, I will say briefly that Bakhtin does not fall fully prey to the critiques of "the intentional fallacy" because of his emphasis on the many agents involved in the production of literary meaning. However, he does ascribe more agency to authorial genius than I do in my own work, and he seems oblivious to the inherent traps set by such institutions, as I discuss throughout this book, including in this chapter.

26. Unlike Naoki Sakai in his chapter on parodic literature in *Voices of the Past* (see esp. 178), I am expressly concerned with authorial intention in humorous texts.

27. Inden, "Introduction," in *Querying the Medieval*.

28. Mahadevan, "Switching Heads and Cultures," 25.

29. Here Mahadevan cites S. Schulz, "Hindu Mythology in Mann's Indian Legend." It would be interesting to map Charles Bernheimer's argument about disciplinary attitudes in the American academy toward non-Western literary sources in his 1995 report on the state of Comparative Literature by comparing Mahadevan's 2002 essay to Schulz's essay from three decades before.

30. Mahadevan, "Switching Heads and Cultures," 24–25.

31. See in particular ibid., 34 and 37.

32. See ibid., 37.

33. I refer to the work of Sheldon Pollock (particularly "Cosmopolitan and Vernacular in History"), which I discuss in the next section of this chapter. I should also note that Mahadevan makes explicit mention of "Nazi aggression in Europe" and Mann's use of this grotesque story to denounce German notions of Aryan supremacy; Mahadevan, "Switching Heads and Cultures," 34. On the history of Karnataka and Kannada, see Robert D. King, *Nehru and the Language Politics of India*, 71 and 98–110.

34. Karnad, "Theatre in India," 347.

35. Stallybrass and White use Rabelais an example of the ambivalence of our own literary institutions that encourage authors to disengage from the common people while still drawing on their vitality, to transcend their historical moment even while speaking from and for it; Stallybrass and White, *Politics and Poetics*, 123. Such a pressure becomes more understandable when you take into consideration their point that literary scholarship was most interested in following "ancient taxation categories" that "separated out a distinct élite set (the *classici*) from the commonality (the *proletarius*)"; ibid., 1.

36. Stallybrass and White tell us that "the classificatory body of a culture is always double, always structured in relation to its negation, its inverse"; ibid., 20.

37. Ibid., 26.

38. Karnad, "Theatre in India," 332.

39. Ibid., 339.

40. Ibid., 338.

41. Ibid., 339.

42. Ibid., 347.

43. Sudhanva Deshpande, "Text and Drama."

44. Mahadevan, "Switching Heads and Cultures," 37. See Karnad, "Theatre in India."

45. Somadeva, *Ocean of Story*, trans. Tawney, 1–2.

46. Ibid., 1.

47. Somadeva, *Tales from the Kathasaritsagara*, trans. Sattar, xviii–xix.

48. Florida, *Writing the Past*, 286. She notes that this inside-out move "invites the reader to re-read" the inside against the outside in such a way that serves "to inform (by fragmenting) her reading" dialectically and productively.

49. Somadeva, *Tales from the Kathasaritsagara*, 4, and *Ocean of Story*, 1:4.

50. Eagleton, 161.

51. Somadeva, *Tales from the Kathasaritsagara*, 5, and *Ocean of Story*, 1:6. In both versions, Kanabhuti is a *yaksha* who befriends a *raskhasa*, but Tawney goes so far as to have the god call the latter "that evil one."

52. Somadeva, *Tales from the Kathasaritsagara*, 29 and 31.

53. Ibid., 37–38.

54. Ibid., 47.

55. Ibid.

56. Pollock insists repeatedly that the introduction of writing technologies in South Asia just before the common era enable the literary (*kāvyā*) as a category to come into being, for writing "renders the discourse itself a subject for discourse for the first time, language itself an object of aestheticized awareness, the text itself an object to be decoded and a pretext for deciphering"; Pollock, *Language of the Gods*, 4. He dismisses the long Sanskrit tradition of venerating speech, including language philosopher Bhartrhari's contention that "Speech-informed awareness is the foundation of all knowledges, arts, and artisan practices," by calling orality in India "as much an ideology as a fact of practice, for the oral ideal persisted long after writing had become fundamental to the Sanskrit tradition itself"; ibid., 82–83.

57. Winternitz writes, "Unfortunately, this work has not come down to us in its original form, but it has been transmitted only in Sanskrit versions that are probably separated from the original by many centuries"; Winternitz, "Classical Sanskrit Literature," 347.

58. Ibid., 351.

59. Somadeva, *Tales from the Kathasaritsagara*, xxi. Dasgupta notes that the thirteenth-century Sanskrit literary critic Govardhana salutes Gunadhya alongside Valmiki and Vyasa (the gloriously reputed composers of the Ramayana and the Mahabharata) as the three great rivers of poetry. Dasgupta, *History of Sanskrit Literature*, 688, concurs with earlier scholars that there was a version of the *Brhatkatha* written by Gunadhya, but he is not convinced that the Kashmiri version that Somadeva and Ksemendra worked from was that one. Interestingly, for Dasgupta, one of the most convincing pieces of evidence is the *sloka* that M. S. Levi found in a ninth-century Cambodian inscription referring to Gunadhya's work in Prakrit.

60. Dasgupta, *History of Sanskrit Literature*, 690.

61. Ibid.

62. Somadeva, *Tales from the Kathasaritsagara*, xxi.

63. Ibid., xix.

64. Dasgupta, *History of Sanskrit Literature*, 690. This is the same line Tawney renders, "is precisely on the model of that from which it is taken . . . [without] even the slightest deviation."

65. Somadeva, *Ocean of Story*, 1:10–12; cited by Dasgupta, *History of Sanskrit Literature*, 690.

66. Pollock, *Language of the Gods*, 90 and 94.

67. Winternitz, "Classical Sanskrit Literature," 348, cites the sixth-century Sanskrit scholar Dandin calling it (in Winternitz's translator's English phrase) "the language of the goblins," and goes on to repeat turn-of-the-twentieth-century linguists such as George Grierson, *Indian Antiquary* 30 (1901): 556, and Pischel ("Grammatik de Prakrit-Sprachen") in conjecturing that it must have been a northwestern dialect or even a gypsy language.

68. Pollock, *Language of the Gods*, 92.

69. Ibid., 97.

70. Somadeva, *Tales from the Kathasaritsagara*, xix. Sattar cites J. A. B. van Buitenen, "Story Literatures."

71. Admittedly, Winternitz insists that "in the strict sense the word popular poetry can hardly designate the Brhatkatha" since "the work has never been a collection of popular tales (somewhat like the Brothers Grimm's Tales for children), but from its very beginning it had been an independent work of poetry in which stories after stories have gradually been added, many of which may have been in circulation among the people."; Winternitz, "Classical Sanskrit Literature," 354 n. 2.

72. Somadeva, *Tales from the Kathasaritsagara*, xx, citing Thapar, *History of India*, 121.

73. Pollock, "The Sanskrit Cosmopolis, 300–1300," 197; Pollock, "Cosmopolitan and Vernacular in History," 596 and 606.

74. Pollock, "Cosmopolitan and Vernacular in History," 614 and 599; Pollock, "The Cosmopolitan Vernacular," 13.

75. Pollock, "The Cosmopolitan Vernacular," 13.

76. Ibid., 13.

77. In the essay "Historical Change and the Theology of Eternal (Nitya) Sanskrit," Madhav Deshpande suggests that this is one of the central movements of Sanskrit: to claim an ongoing eternality in difference. That is, even when writers modulate for particular audiences that must necessarily shift over time and region, they still claim everything to be the same; any other claim diminishes one's authority. Significantly, he notes that "the lawmakers of ancient India said that such a statement must have existed in the 'original' Vedas, but that it was now lost. The existence of such a 'lost' Vedic statement was reasoned on the basis of the tradition (*smrti*) and from the practice and beliefs of the contemporary *sistas* 'social elites.'" Deshpande, *Sanskrit & Prakrit*, 53–82, 53.

78. Pollock, "Cosmopolitan and Vernacular in History," 596, 610, 611.

79. Pollock, *The Language of the Gods*, 6–7.

80. Pollock, "Cosmopolitan and Vernacular in History," 604; Pollock, "The Cosmopolitan Vernacular," 18.

81. Pollock, "The Cosmopolitan Vernacular," 16.

82. Pollock, "Cosmopolitan and Vernacular in History," 601.

83. Ibid., 625.

84. Stallybrass and White, *Politics and Poetics of Transgression*, 4–5. My thanks to Patsy Yaeger and Carol Bardenstein for referring me to this work.

85. Ibid., 27.

86. Ibid., 27–28.

87. Ibid., 28. This critique resonates with Partha Chatterjee's discussion in "Nationalist Resolution of the Women's Question" of the domestic space as traditional, feminine, "inside," and therefore protected from the influence of British imperialism and Western modernity. See also Chatterjee's discussion in *Nation and Its Fragments*, 119–121.

88. Pollock, "Cosmopolitan and Vernacular in History," 610. Pollock cites Gramsci, *Selections from Cultural Writings*, 188, 168; Bakhtin, *Rabelais and His World*, 465–74.

89. Pollock, "Cosmopolitan and Vernacular in History," 611.

90. Stallybrass and White, *Politics and Poetics of Transgression*, 30.

91. Ibid., 36.

92. Ibid., 38.

93. Ibid.

94. Ibid.

95. Ibid., 41.

96. Ibid., 41.

97. Ibid., 37.

98. Ibid., 30.

99. Ibid.

100. Ibid., 4–5.

101. Somadeva, *Tales from the Kathasaritsagara*, 190.

102. See Pollock, "The Cosmopolitan Vernacular," 14: "If the order of Sanskrit poetry was tied to the order of Sanskrit grammar, that order was itself a model or prototype of the moral, social and political order. A just king was one who himself used and promoted the use of correct language. . . . Sanskrit learning became a component of kingliness."

103. While Victor Turner, M. M. Bakhtin, and others have noted insightfully that the transgression of such fixed categories allows for a more intense, even if playful, reappraisal for the period of such a reversal, they are less interested in accounting for the actions of individual members of such groups except as an anonymous mass of people. See esp. the chapter "Betwixt and Between: Liminal Period" in Turner, *Forest of Symbols*, 93–111.

104. I suggest that such a distinction complicates the performative/constative distinction that has invited so much scholarly debate, following Austin's speech act theory. See also Parker and Sedgwick, eds., *Performativity and Performance*, 6.

105. Trikha, *Faiths and Beliefs in the Kathāsaritsāgara*, 179.

106. Kaviraj, "Two Histories of Literary Cultures in Bengal," 554.

107. Trikha, *Faiths and Beliefs in the Kathāsaritsāgara*, 178.

108. Ibid., 12.

109. Flood, *Tantric Body*, 14. He cites Abhinavagupta, *Tantrāloka*, 3:27, 10–13, 277–78.

110. Flood, *Tantric Body*, 41–42.

111. Somadeva, *Tales of Ancient India*, 12. Sattar translates the phrase "*mahāsattvo narpatih*" as "honourable king." In this case, we might also render the word "*mahāsattvo*" as "exceedingly genuine" or "of great truth."

112. Somadeva, *Tales of Ancient India*, 12.

113. Trikha, *Faiths and Beliefs in the Kathāsaritsāgara*, 180.

114. Flood, *Tantric Body*, 79.

115. Ibid., 80.

116. See as well the story of "The Delicate Feet," in Sattar's translation of the *vetala* storytelling cycle, where a king and his son wed a princess and her mother respectively. There, too, the question is one of relation: How are the children of these two unions related? Somadeva, *Tales from the Kathasaritsagara*, 228–32.

117. Somadeva, *Ocean of Story*, 2:234.

118. Somadeva, *Tales of Ancient India*, 12.

119. Somadeva, *Ocean of Story*, 2:234.

120. Somadeva, *Tales from the Kathasaritsagara*, 192.

121. Ibid., 192.

122. See my essay on multiple authorship and its connection to ideas of metempsychosis; Merrill, "To Be or Not to Be a Gutter Flea."

123. Flood, *Tantric Body*, 87–88. He cites the work of Freeman to suggest that possession is one of the central metaphors of a number of popular religions in South Asia, and acknowledges, too, the work of Frederick Smith.

124. Flood, *Tantric Body*, 18.

125. Silverstein and Urban, "Natural History of Discourse." In a separate essay in the same volume, Greg Urban compares original and copied discourse, and notes:

> entextualization is not synonymous with replication, since the former is primarily a matter of seeming. . . . The broader question of entextualization involves not only how or in what measure something is culture, in the sense of being shareable or transmittable, but also how it seems to be culture with or without evidence of actual sharing or transmission or even transduction.

Urban, "Entextualization, Replication, and Power," 21.

126. Silverstein and Urban, "Natural History of Discourse," 1.

127. Flood, *Tantric Body*, 23. He offers this discussion on the temporality of the body to counter Foucault's overemphasis on the body as a locus of contested power.

128. Ibid., 23.

129. Ibid., 88.

130. Ibid., 19.

131. See in particular the discussion of power: "power suffuses the concerns of the tantric traditions"; ibid., 9–10.

132. Ibid., 13.

133. Ibid., 18. See also on this page his references to Bakhtin's work and particularly the question of authorship.

134. Ibid., 12.

135. Ibid., 89.

136. Ibid., 13.

137. Urban, "The 'I' of Discourse," 41.

138. Ibid. I am interested in the connection between translation (as a carrying across) and anaphoric subjectivities: the Oxford English definition defines "anaphora" as "The repetition of the same word or phrase in several successive clauses," or "The use of a word which refers to, or is a substitute for, a preceding word or group of words," and gives its etymology as related to the Greek, αξαζοςα, for carrying back.

139. Somadeva, *Tales of Ancient India*, 13.

140. Somadeva, *Ocean of Story*, 2:234.

141. I refer here respectively to tales number six (261–64), ten (277–81), and two (242–45) in vol. 2 of Tawney's translation, Somadeva, *Ocean of Story*.

142. Somadeva, *Tales of Ancient India*, 15.

143. Somadeva, *Ocean of Story*, 2:241.

144. Ibid., 244.

145. Wayne Booth's work on irony and "pointed titling" is relevant here. See Booth, *Rhetoric of Irony*, 54.

146. Somadeva, *Ocean of Story*, 2:251.

147. Ibid.

148. Ibid., 2:257.

149. Ibid., 2:258.

150. I use the word "trickster" after reading about the scandalous and highly amusing antics of the trickster figure in the Winnebago tales documented and discussed in Radin, *Trickster*.

151. Somadeva, *Ocean of Story*, 2:232.

152. Ibid., 2:231.

153. Apter, *Translation Zone*, 90–91.

154. Barthes, *S/Z*, 90.

155. We should note the vast ambitions of such a project, as Barthes discusses it under the entry on "Antithesis I: The Supplement":

Far from differing merely by the presence of lack of a simple relationship . . . , the two terms of an antithesis are *marked:* their difference does not arise out of complementary, dialectical movement: the antithesis is the battle between two plenitudes set ritually face to face like two fully armed warriors. . . . Hidden in the *recess*, between outside and inside, installed at the interior limit of adversation, spanning the wall of the Antithesis, the narrator brings this figure into play: he induces or supports a transgression.

Ibid., 26–27.

156. Ibid., 41. The question is also repeated throughout Barthes, "Death of the Author," written contemporaneously.

157. Barthes, *S/Z*, 17. The protocol is laid out most clearly, however, in retrospect, in the essay "The Voice of Truth," in Barthes, *S/Z*, 209–10.

158. The elderly man who so intrigues the narrator and his date is introduced with the gossipy conjecture, "But it's now nearly six months since we've seen the Spirit. Do you think he's really alive?" Balzac, "Sarrasine," 227. And when he does appear, the young woman he brought as his date to the party clings to him and says, "He smells like a graveyard. . . . If I look at him again, I shall believe that death itself has come looking for me. Is he alive?" Ibid., 230–31. Soon she asks, "Why does Mme de Lanty allows ghosts to wander about in her house?" Ibid., 231.

159. Barthes, *S/Z*, 41.

160. See the French-to-English definition for *"abîme"* in *Harrap's French Dictionary*.

161. de Man, *Resistance to Theory*, 86.

162. Barthes, *S/Z*, 90. "Nested narratives" is another term for what I refer to as "embedded narratives."

163. Relevant here is the distinction R. Radhakrishnan makes: that we as scholars must learn to combine a focus on "the non-ideal . . . facticity of history"

(concerns he groups under the label "postcolonial") and "the utterly otherworldly and esoteric complexity of philosophy" (which he equates with [metropolitan] postmodern theory); Radhakrishnan, *Theory in an Uneven World*, viii.

164. Barthes, *S/Z*: 89.

165. Ibid.

166. Ibid., 3.

167. Barthes, "Death of the Author," 53. The first published version of "The Death of the Author" was in English translation, as one of several pamphlets in a multimedia cereal-box-like edition of the journal *aspen* no. 5–6 (1967). The first edition of *S/Z* appeared in French in 1970.

168. Ibid., 49, 52–53.

169. For a fuller discussion of the implications of copyright to translation in terms of this essay, see Merrill, "Death of the Authors a.k.a. Twilight of the Translators."

170. Barthes, *S/Z*, 4.

171. Ibid.

172. Ibid.

173. See, e.g., Peggy Kamuf's introductory notes to "Différance" in Derrida, *Derrida Reader*, 60.

174. William Jewett's note to de Man, *Resistance to Theory*, 73.

175. de Man, *Resistance to Theory*, 86. He adds: "The text is untranslatable: it was untranslatable for the commentators who talk about it, it is an example of what it states, it is a *mise en abyme* in the technical sense, a story within the story of what is its own statement." Not coincidentally, we find Barbara Johnson making a similar argument in her reading of Derrida reading Lacan reading Poe's story, "The Purloined Letter," in a chapter called "The Frame of Reference: Poe, Lacan, Derrida," in Johnson, *Critical Difference*, 110–46.

176. de Man, *Resistance to Theory*, 76.

177. Ibid., 84.

178. Ibid., 90–91. In discussing the broken vessel as "*tikkun*," de Man cites Jacobs, "Monstrosity of Language."

179. Holquist, "The Surd Heard," 138. I would like to thank Dominick LaCapra for suggesting the relevance of this riddle to my work.

180. Ibid.

181. Stewart, *Nonsense*, 42–43.

182. Ibid., 22.

183. See also his discussion of play and decentered knowledge; Radhakrishnan, *Theory in an Uneven World*, 13; and Niranjana's analysis of the de Man lecture, in particular where she is interested in asking: How might we redefine the trope of translation to eschew the Christian narrative of an eternal origin so that we may negotiate the demands of facticity and theory, the constative and the performative in a manner that acknowledges the asymmetry built into any such exchange? Niranjana, *Siting Translation*, 110–40.

184. Somadeva, *Ocean of Story*, 2:335.

185. Somadeva, *Tales of Ancient India*, 43, Somadeva, *Ocean of Story*.

186. Somadeva, *Tales of Ancient India*, 47–48. Strikingly, the demon adds, "He must be magnanimous of character and discriminating in judgment."

187. Ibid., 49.

188. Ibid.

189. Ibid., 50.

190. Ibid.

191. Ibid.

192. Ibid., 51.

193. Ibid.

194. Siegel, *Laughing Matters*, 292 and 148.

195. Ibid., 147.

196. Ibid.

197. Ibid., 148.

198. Khanna, *Dark Continents*, 30.

199. Ibid., 25.

200. "Demetaphorization" is a term used by Abraham and Torok, *Wolf Man's Magic Word*, to describe, in Khanna's words, "the material affect of loss as it manifests itself in language"; Khanna, *Dark Continents*, 24.

201. Freud, *Jokes and Their Relation to the Unconscious*, 121.

202. Flieger, "Purloined Punchline," 942.

203. Ibid., 945, citing Freud, *Standard Edition of the Complete Works*, 139.

204. Flieger, "Purloined Punchline," 945.

205. Ibid., 946.

206. Ibid., 947.

207. Ibid.

208. Ibid., 948.

209. Ibid.

210. Ibid., 958. While Flieger is most interested in the construction of gender in binaristic terms, I would suggest that tempering her insights with Butler's subsequent critique of Irigaray's "phallogocentric mode of signifying the female sex" (which Flieger cites approvingly) would make her insights into joking even more insightful and complex; Butler, *Gender Trouble*, 18.

211. Somadeva, *Ocean of Story*, 2:357.

212. Somadeva, *Tales of Ancient India*, 61–62.

213. Ibid., 62.

214. See the entry for *vidya-dhara* in Monier-Williams, *Sanskrit-English Dictionary*, 964.

215. Somadeva, *Tales of Ancient India*, 62.

216. Ibid., 62.

217. Ibid.

218. Ibid., 62–63.

219. Ibid., 63.
220. Ibid.

4. A DIVIDED SENSE

1. Pollock, "Cosmopolitan and Vernacular in History," 601.
2. See http://www.wordswithoutborders.org/article.php?lab=TrueCalling and http://www.commonwealthfoundation.com/culturediversity/writersprize/2007prize/Shortlist/index.cfm.
3. Damrosch, "World Literature in a Postcanonical, Hypercanonical Age," 48–49.
4. Ibid., 45.
5. Rushdie and West, *Vintage Book of Indian Writing 1947–1997*, ix–x.
6. Damrosch begins his article for the 2005 volume on the state of Comparative Literature by announcing that "World literature has exploded in scope during the past decade," but soon clarifies—quoting Rey Chow's article of a decade earlier—that "the concept of literature is strictly subordinated to a social Darwinian understanding of the nation" in which "'masterpieces' correspond to 'master' nations and 'master' cultures"; Damrosch then intones, "What Rey Chow warned about in the Bernheimer volume [of 1995] might have been averted at the level of the nation only to return at the level of the celebrity author." Damrosch, "World Literature in a Postcanonical, Hypercanonical Age," 43, 49–50, citing Chow, "In the Name of Comparative Literature," 109.
7. Rushdie and West, *Vintage Book of Indian Writing 1947–1997*, x.
8. The reference is to Rushdie's essay "Imaginary Homelands," in Rushdie, *Imaginary Homelands*, 9–21, 19.
9. Even the decision about what word to use for non-Indian languages has been controversial, especially since—as Sheldon Pollock, for one, points out—the English word "vernacular" derives from the Latin word for slave and so underscores the hierarchical master-slave dynamics implicit in the relationship between vernaculars and imperial or cosmopolitan languages in the West. We might note that the Bhasha Institute, Katha Press, and others mentioned in the opening chapter have made a self-conscious decision to use the Sanskrit term *"bhasha"* instead of "vernacular" to denote the indigenous languages of India.
10. The multilingual Tagore, like Ngũgĩ wa Thiong'o more recently, did most of his translation work himself. Mahasweta Sengupta's incisive 1990 essay, "Translation, Colonialism and Poetics: Rabindranath Tagore in Two Worlds," argues that Tagore had so little faith in the ability of his English-speaking audience to find common ground with him that his English version is an entirely different poem from the Bengali *Gitanjali*. See also Rita Kothari's discussion of Tagore's attempts to recreate himself afresh in the English version of the *Gitanjali* in Kothari, *Translating India*, 22–25; and the mention in

Merrill, "Translation from Indian/South Asian Languages (Modern)," of the significance of Tagore translating the *Gitanjali* while on a ship traveling to England, carrying across the text both literally and metaphorically at once.

11. Shankar, "Midnight's Orphans," 83.

12. Ibid., 71. He is responding to the essay "Of Mimicry and Man" in Bhabha, *Location of Culture*, 85–92.

13. Shankar, "Midnight's Orphans," 83–84, quoting Bhabha, "Editor's Introduction," 431-59.

14. Bhabha, "Editor's Introduction," 25, 26.

15. Mufti, "Aura of Authenticity," 100-101.

16. In much of his work, including the more recent *Enlightenment in the Colony*, Mufti does indeed discuss work in the vernacular—in Urdu, in his case—but does not attend to the movement between Urdu and English, except in the familiar melancholic mode that I discuss in the first chapter.

17. Bhabha, "Editor's Introduction," 440. MacIntyre discusses the concept of justice by comparing different English translations of Homer, observing, "Each translator cannot but, if he is to be intelligible to his intended audience, blend Homer's idiom with that of his own age, and the better the translator the more subtly it will be, transmuting Homer's quite alien preoccupations into more familiar ones." MacIntyre, *Whose Justice? Which Rationality?* 18.

18. Bhabha, "Editor's Introduction," 41.

19. Shankar, "Midnight's Orphans," 84.

20. Ibid., 88.

21. Ibid., 88.

22. Bhabha, "Editor's Introduction," 41.

23. Rushdie and West, eds. *The Vintage Book of Indian Writing 1947–1997*, x.

24. Ibid.

25. Ibid.

26. Mufti, *Enlightenment in the Colony*, 180.

27. Ibid., 2.

28. Kumar, *Limiting Secularism*, xvii (emphasis in original).

29. Ibid., 96. She writes, "I agree with Veena Das and Arthur Kleinman that a *double movement seems necessary* for remaking worlds shattered by violence." Ibid., 96, citing Das and Kleinman, et al., *Remaking a World*, 19. It is because of this emphasis and association that I use the phrase "shattered sense of provisional unity," but I realize that any term has unfortunate associations; in this context, "community" is often used to refer to a minority group, and "unity" invokes the jingoistic "unity in diversity" national slogan that Kumar herself suggests is self-serving and elitist. Kumar, *Limiting Secularism*, xiii. Both Kumar's tropes and her ethical concerns resonate with my discussion in the previous chapter of the utopic space of translation figured in terms of *tikkun* as a fragmented vessel.

30. Ibid., 96.

31. Bernard S. Cohn makes clear in his essay "The Command of Language and the Language of Command" that translation operating as division was a part of the English modus operandi in India not only in the era of Partition but as early as 1615, during the earliest days of the East India Company. Cohn, *Colonialism and Its Forms of Knowledge*, 16–56. Johannes Fabian makes a similar point with African examples in *Language and Colonial Power* (see, specifically, "A Question of Law and Rights: Language and the Colonial Charter," in Fabian, *Language and Colonial Power*, 44–49). In Chapter 5 I point to Dalmia, *Nationalization of Hindu Traditions*, and Pandey, "Hindi, Hindu, Hindustani," among other work, to discuss the historical link between "Hindu" as a legal category instituted by the British, based on notions of religious difference, and the Hinduized definition of the "Hindi" language.

32. In thinking about our own institutional hierarchies, we might note that Mufti and Kumar are literature scholars affiliated with English departments and not Asian Language and Literature departments, even if they read Manto in Urdu, for example.

33. Of a long list of relevant works on secularism, besides those already named, I recommend the special issue of *boundary 2* on "Critical Secularism," edited by Aamir Mufti, the collection *The Crisis of Secularism in India*, edited by Anuradha Dingwaney and Rajeshwari Sunder Rajan, as well as *Political Theologies: Public Religions in a Post-Secular World*, edited by Hent de Vries and Lawrence E. Sullivan. Besides Derrida's work generally and his essay "Theology of Translation," Naomi Seidman's *Faithful Renderings: Jewish-Christian Difference and the Politics of Translation* offers a useful historical perspective on the relationship between political theologies and translation in the European tradition.

34. Besides the work mentioned here, see Bhalla, ed., *Stories about the Partition*; and Ravikant and Saint, eds., *Translating Partition*.

35. Bose and Jalal, *Modern South Asia*, 198.

36. Pandey, *Remembering Partition*, 43.

37. Hasan, *India's Partition*.

38. Hasan, ed., *India Partitioned*, 8.

39. Ibid.

40. Spear, *India: A Modern History*, 422–23.

41. Chatterjee, *Nationalist Thought and the Colonial World*, 42.

42. Parker, however, argues that "Anderson has rejected in principle the ontologized distinction between origin and derivation on which Chatterjee's criticism depends: for Anderson there can be nothing authentic—East or West–with which to oppose the nation's constitutive secondariness." Parker, "Bogeyman: Benedict Anderson's 'Derivative' Discourse," 56.

43. Bose and Jalal, *Modern South Asia*, 198.

44. I reference obliquely Brown's intricate argument in her 1993 essay, "Wounded Attachments."

45. I reference in particular Culler and Cheah, *Grounds of Comparison*.
46. Chatterjee, "Anderson's Utopia," 161–70.
47. Ibid.
48. Culler and Cheah, *Grounds of Comparison*, 9.
49. Anderson, *Imagined Communities*, 24, thinks about the "simultaneity" of analogous nationalist enterprises in terms of "homogeneous, empty time," borrowing the term from Walter Benjamin, "Theses on the Philosophy of History" 265. Such perceived simultaneity thus gives rise to cross-border borrowings that Anderson calls "double visions" or "the spectre of comparisons"; Anderson, *Spectre of Comparisons*, 2. Parker and Chatterjee go on to argue whether such comparisons establish a perceived hierarchy between original and derivative, in their contributions to Culler and Cheah, *Grounds of Comparison*. I purposely play with these "specters" and "grounds" of comparison that are invoked in discussions of nationalism to think about the temporal and spatial bases of our own narratives of world literature in translation.
50. Sakai, *Translation and Subjectivity*, 15.
51. Ibid.
52. Pandey, *Remembering Partition*, 1.
53. Ibid., 4.
54. Pandey writes: "The discipline of history still proceeds on the assumption of a fixed subject—society, nation, state, community, locality, whatever it might be—and a largely pre-determined course of human development or transformation. However, the agent and locus of history is hardly pre-designated. Rather, accounts of history, of shared experiences in the past, serve to constitute these, their extent and their boundaries"; ibid., 4.
55. Ibid., 92.
56. Ibid., 5.
57. Cited in ibid., 97.
58. Cited in ibid., 105.
59. Ibid., 120.
60. Ibid.
61. Said, *Orientalism*, 7.

According to the traditional orientalists, an essence should exist—sometimes even clearly described in metaphysical terms—which constitutes the inalienable and common basis of all the being considered: this essence is both "historical," since it goes back to the dawn of history, and fundamentally a-historical, since it transfixed the being, "the object" of study, within its inalienable and non-evolutive specificity, instead of defining it as all other being, states, nations, peoples, and cultures—as a product, a resultant of the vection of the forces operating in the field of historical evolution.

62. Ibid., 98.
63. Niranjana, *Siting Translation*, 3.

64. Ibid.

65. By "transgressive," I refer obliquely to the controversies surrounding Manto and the accusations leveled against him that his work was pornographic, but more generally I mean to equate translational acts with transgressive acts, and open up the ways we think of such border crossings.

66. Aamir Mufti devotes an entire chapter to the question of what he calls "Manto's ironic relationship to the culture of Indian nationalism, particularly the bourgeois universalism of its 'moment of arrival'" and argues that Manto used the genre of the short story to question nationalism from within. Mufti, *Enlightenment in the Colony*, 178.

67. Derrida, "Des Tours de Babel," 171.

68. Ibid., 169.

69. Anderson, *Imagined Communities*, 6.

70. As mentioned in Chapter 2, Brass, *Language, Religion and Politics in North India*, discusses linguistic identity alongside religious identity as a cause for divisive violence in postcolonial India.

71. Macauley, "Indian Education," 722, cited in Niranjana, *Siting Translation*, 31.

72. Macauley, "Indian Education," 729, cited in Niranjana, *Siting Translation*, 30.

73. Ramaswamy, *Passions of the Tongue*, 1.

74. Ibid., 2.

75. Ibid., 3.

76. Ibid., 5–6. It is important to note that Ramaswamy investigates *Tamil-pparru* precisely to distinguish it from linguistic nationalism. She insists that "nationalism is not everywhere predicated on linguistic passions, nor does language loyalty necessarily or always induce a singular nation-state . . . passions of the tongue do not readily map onto the passions of the nation"; ibid., 4.

77. Ibid., 256.

78. Pollock, "Cosmopolitan and Vernacular in History," 612.

79. Ramaswamy, *Passions of the Tongue*, 63.

80. Lydia H. Liu and Naoki Sakai have each made a related argument in discussions of translating the notion of the self and of the subject, respectively. See Liu, *Translingual Practice*, 77–99; and Sakai, *Translation and Subjectivity*, 117–52.

81. Manto, "Toba Tek Singh," trans. Hasan, 11.

82. Manto, "Toba Tek Singh," trans. Naqvi, 281.

83. Booth, *Rhetoric of Irony*, 41.

84. See ibid., 30 n. 24, for example, where Booth likens an "ironic attack" to "flyting" (or "what some anthropologists have named 'joking relationships'").

85. In particular, Freud writes, "it is not the person who makes the joke who laughs at it and who therefore enjoys its pleasurable effect, but the inactive listener"; Freud, *Jokes and Their Relation to the Unconscious*, 118–19.

86. Booth, *Rhetoric of Irony*, 28.

87. Ibid., 34.

88. For a further elaboration of implied hierarchies in translations of irony, see Merrill, "Writing from Below," 32–54.

89. Manto, "Toba Tek Singh," trans. Asaduddin, 64.

90. Mufti, "Aura of Authenticity," 100-101.

91. Hutcheon, *Irony's Edge*, 66.

92. Ibid., 60.

93. Ibid.

94. Ibid., 89.

95. Ibid., 92.

96. Ibid., 89.

97. de Man, *Resistance to Theory*, 91.

98. White, "On the Virtues of Not Understanding," 333.

99. White, *Justice as Translation*, 252–53; cited in White, "On the Virtues of Not Understanding," 333.

100. White, "On the Virtues of Not Understanding," 335, in response to hooks, "'this is the oppressor's language,'" 295–301 in the same volume.

101. Manto, "Toba Tek Singh," trans. Haldane, 20.

102. Manto, "Toba Tek Singh," trans. Madan Gupta, 149.

103. Manto, "Toba Tek Singh," trans. Ratan, 23.

104. Stewart, *Nonsense*, 88.

105. Ibid.

106. As I discuss at some length in Chapter 5, Chakrabarty, *Provincializing Europe*, 17, distinguishes between "transition" narratives used in historiography and "translation."

107. Manto, "Toba Tek Singh," trans. Haldane, 20.

108. Manto, "Toba Tek Singh," trans. Trivedi, 215, 213.

109. Here I allude to the constant bilingual jokes one of the characters in *The Satanic Verses* makes on Saladin Chamcha's last name: "Spoono? You see her or you don't?" Rushdie, *Satanic Verses*, 7.

110. Chaussée performed his version at the Virginia Festival of the Book, March 2000. My thanks to him for so generously providing me with his notes.

111. Manto, "Toba Tek Singh," trans. Trivedi, 215–16.

112. Manto, "Toba Tek Singh," trans. Dougal.

113. A number of scholars have written moving, important accounts of the stories of women caught in these real-life riddles of belonging. See in particular Butalia, *Other Side of Silence*, as well as Menon and Bhasin, *Borders and Boundaries*. See also the chapter "Fictions of Violence" in Kumar, *Limiting Secularism*, 123–76.

114. Manto, "Toba Tek Singh," trans. Ratan, 25.

115. Manto, "Toba Tek Singh," trans. Gupta, 153.

116. Manto, "Toba Tek Singh," trans. Hasan, 16.
117. Manto, "Toba Tek Singh," trans. Dougal.
118. Manto, "Toba Tek Singh," trans. Pritchett.
119. Manto, "Toba Tek Singh," trans. Trivedi, 218.
120. Manto, "Toba Tek Singh," trans. Ratan, 26–27.
121. Manto, "Toba Tek Singh," trans. Naqvi, 287.
122. Manto, "Toba Tek Singh," trans. Hasan, 18.
123. Benjamin, *Illuminations*, 87.
124. Ibid., 84.
125. Ibid., 94.
126. Ahmad, *In Theory*, 102.
127. Nancy, *Dis-enclosure*, 121.
128. Ibid., 121–22.
129. Ibid., 126.
130. Ibid.
131. Ibid., 127.
132. Ibid., 124, 127.

5. PASSING ON

1. For a fun and far-ranging exploration of the topic, see Graeber, *Toward an Anthropological Theory of Value.*
2. Foster, "'Show Me the Zulu Tolstoy,'" provides a helpful overview of the controversy.
3. Said, *Culture and Imperialism*, 25. According to Foster, Martha Nussbaum, Charles Taylor, and Alfred Kazin each have different versions of the remark. Foster contends that it was Kazin's memoiristic essay about rightward-drifting Jewish intellectuals ("My heart sank when I heard that Bellow once said, 'Who is the Tolstoy of the Zulus? The Proust of the Papuans? I'd be glad to read him'") in the *New Yorker* that prompted Bellow to defend himself in the op-ed piece.
4. Bellow, "Papuans and Zulus."
5. Ibid.
6. Ibid.
7. Ahmad, *In Theory*, 101–102.
8. Amrit Rai, *Premchand*, 134–35.
9. Szanton, "Introduction."
10. Ibid.
11. Ibid.
12. Tansman, "Japanese Studies."
13. Ibid.
14. Ibid.
15. Damrosch, "World Literature in a Postcanonical, Hypercanonical Age," 45.

16. Bernheimer, "Bernheimer Report, 1993," 40.

17. Ibid., citing Levin, "Levin Report, 1965," 23.

18. Bernheimer, "Bernheimer Report, 1993," 40.

19. Greene, "Greene Report, 1975," 31–32.

20. Ibid., 30.

21. Bernheimer, "Bernheimer Report, 1993," 40, citing Greene, "Greene Report, 1975," 31.

22. Bernheimer, "Bernheimer Report, 1993," 44.

23. Ibid.

24. See in particular Edward Said's work on the legacies in the American academy of European exile—notably his introduction to the 2003 reprinting of Auerbach's *Mimesis* that Mufti reprinted in the edition of *boundary 2* on "Critical Secularism"; Said, "Erich Auerbach, Critic of the Earthly World." Moreover, Apter, "Global *Translatio*," argues that we should add Leo Spitzer to this list of founding scholars of Comparative Literature who are responding to their exilic condition.

25. Bernheimer, "Bernheimer Report, 1993," 44.

26. Ibid.

27. Spivak, *Death of a Discipline*, 19 and 9.

28. Ibid., 13.

29. Tolstoy, "Bhoot aur Roti." I purposely cite Premchand's title in Hindi rather than the original oral version in Russian, Tolstoy's written version, or the Maudes' English version, "The Crust and the Imp," to practice reading work without constant reference to a fixed original.

30. Tolstoy, "Bhoot aur Roti," 108.

31. Several of the contributions to Szanton, *Politics of Knowledge*, think through the complicated institutional histories of area studies in compelling detail. Of particular relevance here are the examples investigated in Dirks, "South Asian Studies"; and Bonnell and Breslauer, "Soviet and Post-Soviet Area Studies."

32. Lenin, "Articles on Tolstoy," 346.

33. One might consult, e.g., Bakhtin, *Dialogic Imagination;* Jameson, *Political Unconscious;* Lukács, *Theory of the Novel;* Moretti, *Atlas of the European Novel 1800–1900;* Watt, *Rise of the Novel.*

34. Mukherjee, *Realism and Reality*, 5.

35. Hutcheon, *Irony's Edge*, 41–42. The notion of authorial intention in Hutcheon's work is discussed in more detail in Chapter 2.

36. Mukherjee, *Realism and Reality*, 145.

37. Devi, *Premchand, ghar men*, 113; cited in Singh, "Premchand and Gandhism," 50.

38. Singh, "Premchand and Gandhism," 51.

39. Premchand, *Gift of a Cow*, 77; quoted in Singh, "Premchand and Gandhism," 49.

40. Singh, "Premchand and Gandhism," 52.

41. Ibid., 49.

42. Mukherjee, *Realism and Reality*, 145.

43. Ibid.

44. Ibid.

45. Ibid.

46. Premchand, "*Sahitya ka Uddeshya*," 17; translated and cited by Mukherjee, *Realism and Reality*, 145.

47. Mukherjee, *Realism and Reality*, 146.

48. Ibid.

49. "*Marna hi hai to jaldi mar kyon nahin jati!*"

50. "*Chamaron ka kunba aur sare ganv main badnam.*"

51. Anand, ed., *Touchable Tales*, 24.

52. Anand writes, "In the post-Ambedkar centenary period (1990–), political awareness of the specificity of dalit experiences came to be articulated across the country after the writings and speeches of Dr. Bhimrao Ramji Ambedkar were made available in various Indian languages." Ibid., 1.

53. Here I do not specify whether Dalit "identity" is ethnic or racial because the distinction has been the source of such controversy within the movement itself, as is evident in the bid to have caste-based discrimination included in the discussion at the U.N. World Conference Against Racism held in Durban, South Africa, August 2001. See the nuanced discussion of the institutional histories of this question in Visweswaran, "India in South Africa."

54. Anand, *Touchable Tales*, 24–25.

55. Sumanakshar, "*Rangbhoomi* ko 'Jangbhoomi' banane ke liye zimmedar kaun?"; trans. and cited in Brueck, "Dalit Chetna in Dalit Literary Criticism."

56. "*Vah baikunth main jayegi dada, baikunth ki rani banegi.*"

57. Spivak, "Can the Subaltern Speak?" (1988), 296. See discussion in Chapter 1.

58. The parallels with the ending of Detha's story "*Thakur rau Bhoot*," discussed in Chapter 6, are worth exploring.

59. Sara Rai, "Realism as a Creative Process," 40.

60. Ibid.

61. Premchand, *World of Premchand*, 191; quoted in Sara Rai, "Realism as a Creative Process."

62. Spivak, "Can the Subaltern Speak?" (1988), 292.

63. Chakrabarty, *Provincializing Europe*, 17.

64. Ibid.

65. Amrit Rai, *Premchand*, 113.

66. In his introduction, Gandhi writes, "The letter printed below is a translation of Tolstóy's letter written in Russian in reply to one from the Editor of *Free Hindustan*." Tolstoy, "Letter to a Hindu," 411. Martin Green identifies the original recipient of "Letter to a Hindu" as an Indian revolutionary and

exile named Taraknath Das who edited an insurrectionary magazine called *Free Hindustan*. Green writes that Das did not publish the letter at the time because he felt that "nonviolence was self-defeating and contradicted altruism as well as egotism"; Green, *Tolstoy and Gandhi*, 90–91.

67. Bilgrami, "Occidentalism, the Very Idea," argues that Gandhi's ideas on nonviolence were implicitly a critique of the violent histories of the West, or what today is thought of as (in Bilgrami's evocative phrasing) "the dehumanizing violence of the *jihadi* Occidentalist." Ibid., 395. See also Bilgrami, "Gandhi's Integrity," 49, on nonviolence as a critique of industrial civilization. Robert J. C. Young asserts that "the legacy of Gandhi's critiques of modernity, and his critique of an unquestioning, derivative use of western ideas, remains a powerful force in the thinking of certain contemporary thinkers" but notes the paradox that "Gandhi came to this position in large part through an eclectic synthesis of western counter-cultural thinkers." Young, *Postcolonialism: An Historical Introduction*, 320.

68. Majeed, "Gandhi, 'Truth' and Translatability," 303–32. Majeed also links this rhetorical positioning with Gandhi's humble autobiographical style.

69. See Gandhi's Introduction to Tolstoy, "A Letter to a Hindu," 414.

70. For a seminal history of the Négritude movement, see Kesteloot, *Les écrivains noirs de langue française*. See also Martin Puchner's discussion of Aimé Césaire's productive engagement with the "moving geography of surrealism" that inspired him to later coin the neologism *négritude*. Puchner, *Poetry of the Revolution*, 187–89. Puchner writes, "Césaire's particular fabrication, the neologism *négritude*, does not simply critique surrealist ethnography and primitivism but salvages from it the fact that geography is bound up with an imaginative enterprise, a locality that is never given, never natural, but always a product of movement, a project for the future." Ibid., 189.

71. The group that drafted the manifesto included an Urdu writer from Lahore named Sajjad Zaheer, who had studied at Oxford, a writer of Bengali and English named Jytormaya C. Ghosh, who had studied at the University of Edinburgh, and Mulk Raj Anand, a student from Peshawar who studied History of Art at the University of London and who would become president of the AIPWA. Mulk Raj Anand would later settle in Bombay and be the most celebrated among the Progressives; his first English-language novel *Untouchable*, was a moving account of the difficult life of a poor sweeper named Bhakha who hopes Western modernity will make substantive material changes in his life. Mulk Raj Anand has devoted his life as writer, editor, and activist to using literature to help ameliorate the suffering of India's downtrodden, including coediting an anthology of Dalit literature with Eleanor Zelliot that S. Anand in his introduction to *Touchable Tales* calls "the first of its kind." S. Anand, *Touchable Tales*, 1. Nevertheless, S. Anand himself uses Mulk Raj Anand as an example when critiquing the privileged upper-caste position from which non-Dalits often speak. For example, Sivakami's charge, quoted above, that "nondalit"

writers like Premchand use "dalits as toys to tickle a few strange nerves of their regular readers" and thus both behave like "self-styled autocrats passing adverse judgements on dalit life" is in response to S. Anand's question, "What has been your impressions of the literature produced by nondalits on dalits (from Mulk Raj Anand to Arundhati Roy)?" S. Anand, *Touchable Tales*, 24–25.

72. Many of the details of early AIPWA history and its analysis work are from Carlo Coppola's foundational 1974 article, "All-India Progressive Writers' Association," and the two-volume collection he edited, *Marxist Influences and South Asian Literature.*

73. Quoted in Coppola, "All-India Progressive Writers' Association," 4.

74. Cited in ibid., 9.

75. Coppola's work is unusual in the body of scholarship that analyzes translated work, since he sees the differences between original and translation as necessary interventions in what Premchand was fighting over, fighting for, and aspiring to honor in his practices of justice.

76. Wendy Brown's final chapter, "Specters and Angels," in Brown, *Politics Out of History*, focuses on the future-haunting ghosts of the past in Derrida, *Specters of Marx*, and the backward-looking, forward-blown angel of history in Walter Benjamin, "Theses on the Philosophy of History."

77. Brown, *Politics Out of History*, 155.

78. Ibid., 139.

79. The comparison is between the chapter, "Minority Histories, Subaltern Pasts," in Chakrabarty, *Provincializing Europe*, 97–113; and Brown, *Politics Out of History*, 155.

80. Andrew Benjamin, *Translation and the Nature of Philosophy*, 98 and 100.

81. Brown, *Politics Out of History*, 155.

82. Cheah, *Spectral Nationality*, 1.

83. Marx and Engels, *Communist Manifesto*, 20.

84. Damrosch, *What Is World Literature?* 284, comments wryly that world literature "doesn't lead to a transcendent universalism in which cultural difference is a mere heresy that should wither away as Marx and Engels expected the state to do." From this we might see that one of the contradictions of Marx and Engels's *Communist Manifesto* that so far has not been put to productive use is their vagueness on the issue of the national, linguistic identifications that must be transcended to achieve this idealized unity.

85. Coppola, "All-India Progressive Writers' Association," 9 and 11.

86. S. Anand, *Touchable Tales*, 24.

87. Robinson, *Who Translates?* 130, quoting Marx, *Portable Karl Marx*, 288.

88. Derrida, *Specters of Marx*, 109.

89. Robinson, *Who Translates?* 130.

90. Derrida, *Specters of Marx*, 110, Robinson, *Who Translates?* 131.

91. Coppola, "All-India Progressive Writers' Association," 5.

92. Ibid., 9.

93. Puchner, *Poetry of the Revolution*, 7.

94. Ibid., 12.

95. See Amrit Rai, *A House Divided*; and Christopher King, *One Language, Two Scripts*.

96. Besides those works already discussed in this chapter, I am referencing Dalmia, *Nationalization of Hindu Traditions*; Orsini, *Hindi Public Sphere 1920–1940*; Pandey, "Hindi, Hindu, Hindustani"; and Alok Rai, *Hindi Nationalism*.

97. Robert King, *Nehru and the Language Politics of India*, 28–29.

98. Ibid., 83.

99. We might rather call this exercise literary historiography, but in the case of Amrit Rai's work on Premchand, the historiography itself relies on literary technique, as Rai's son Alok Rai notes in the introduction to the English translation of the biography. Alok Rai, "Introduction," v.

100. Amrit Rai, *Premchand*, 385–88.

101. Ibid., 339–45. For a vivid account, see also the section "Inventing Hindustani: Gandhi and Premchand," in Trivedi, "Progress of Hindi, Part 2," 975–80.

102. Besides those titles already cited in this chapter, see Vijay Dan Detha's essay, *"Nām-samskār ke sarvashreshth purohit-premchand"* [The naming ritual of Priest-Premchand's favorite characters] in Kothari, *Premchand ke Pātra*; and Ram Vilas Sharma, *Premchand aur unka yug*.

103. This is perhaps not so very different from the notion of "effective history" that Niranjana proposes. But in this case I am more interested in a complex and critical literary reading of that story. See Niranjana, *Siting Translation*, 37; also cited in Liu, *Translingual Practice*, 22.

104. Foster, "Show Me the Zulu Tolstoy," 264.

105. Said, *Culture and Imperialism*, 25.

106. Ibid.

107. Ibid., 26.

108. Lukács, *Studies in European Realism*, 145.

109. Lukács, "Tolstoy and the Development of Realism," 291.

110. Ibid.

111. Ibid., 292.

112. *"Adharm ne ait prasann hokar bhoot ko pradhaan ki padvi de di"*; Tolstoy, "Bhoot aur Roti," 110.

113. Lukács, *Studies in European Realism*, 145, 146.

114. Lukács, "Tolstoy and the Development of Realism," 289.

115. Ibid., 290.

116. Ibid., 289.

6. NARRATION IN GHOST TIME

1. Chakrabarty, *Provincializing Europe*, 17.

2. Scholars today seem to share the same skepticism, whether we look to Stathis Gourgouris writing on modern Greece as a "dream nation" (Gourgouris, *Dream Nation*) or Susan Buck-Morss's reading of the fall of the Soviet "dreamworld" as "the passing of mass utopia" (Buck-Morss, *Dreamworld and Catastrophe*).

3. Walter Benjamin, *Arcades Project*, 267.

4. Eagleton, *Walter Benjamin*, 143, quoting Bertolt Brecht, *Flüchtlingsqespräche*; Marx, *Eighteenth Brumaire*, 15. Note that the publication details described in the notes (Marx, *Eighteenth Brumaire*, 141) outline a journey similar to that of Tolstoy, "Letter to a Hindu," outlined in the previous chapter: *The Eighteenth Brumaire* was published originally in the United States in English translation, and while the unnamed annotator considers it "one of the masterpieces of Marxism," the writer notes that at the time "only very few copies reached Europe."

5. Robinson, *Who Translates?* 131 (emphasis in original).

6. Ibid.

7. Ibid., 131, quoting Marx, *Der achtzehnte Brumaire des Louis Bonaparte*, 289. In German the phrase Robinsons works from is "nicht die alten zu parodieren."

8. Marx, *Portable Karl Marx*, 288; cited in Robinson, *Who Translates?* 130.

9. Marx, *Eighteenth Brumaire*, 8.

10. Ibid.

11. Rose, *Parody*, 8. She cites the work of Lelièvre. We might notice in the example Henry Louis Gates, Jr., offers in Gates, *Signifying Monkey*, of the parodic antics of the signifying monkey that such tales serve to undermine the entrenched authority with verbal performances that are funny (and therefore effective) only if the parody is both near to and yet different from the target of the humor.

12. Rose, *Parody*, 41.

13. Marx, *Eighteenth Brumaire*, 21.

14. Rose, *Parody*, 88.

15. Rose notes that parody is distinguished from satire in the way it uses the "preformed material of its 'target' as a constituent part of its own structure." Ibid., 81.

16. "U.S. Finishes 'A Strong Second' in Iraq War," *The Onion*; "Study: Iraqis May Experience Sadness When Friends, Relatives Die," *The Onion*.

17. "Loud and Clear," *Daily Show*.

18. Billionaires for Bush, "SMALL GOVERNMENT BIG WARS."

19. See DowEthics.com, "Dow Releases 'Acceptable Risk' at Banking Conference"; DowEthics.com, "Acceptable Risk"; and Yes Men, "Dow Discovers a Golden Skeleton!"

20. Stewart, *Nonsense*, 99, 90.

21. Richardson, "Language of Tactical Media."

22. Liu, "Legislating the Universal," 152, 148.

23. Walter Benjamin, *Arcades Project*, 267.

24. Yes Men, "Dow Discovers a Golden Skeleton!"

25. Richardson, "Language of Tactical Media."

26. Butler, *Gender Trouble*, 41.

27. Prakash, *Bonded Histories*, 203, 200. I would like to thank Jennifer Wenzel for pointing me to this reference.

28. Scott, *Weapons of the Weak*, 40–41.

29. Bakhtin, *Rabelais and His World*, 11–12.

30. Bhola Ram, interview January 17, 2003, at his home in Borunda, Rajasthan.

31. Detha, "*Thakur*'s Ghost."

32. Ranajit Guha, *Elementary Aspects of Peasant Insurgency in Colonial India*, 78.

33. Ibid.

34. Chakrabarty, *Provincializing Europe*, makes a more elaborate case for the ethical basis of such an approach. Here I focus instead on methods by which we might analyze the narrative structure of such relations.

35. The definition in the *Oxford English Dictionary Online* for "maund" is "A denomination of weight current in India and Western Asia, varying greatly in value according to locality. The standard maund of the Indian empire was = 100 lbs. troy, or 8227 lbs. avoirdupois." The entry in the dictionary thus poses another riddle of belonging: Is "maund" an English word, or Rajasthani? Is this translator repeating nonsense, or parodying tactfully?

36. British Broadcasting Corporation, "Fighting Poverty in India." The ironies of this were lovely: not just that I was hearing voices from Rajasthan—whole eloquent sentences decrying the corruption of the state and national government—while lying in bed in Michigan, but that I was hearing it via the radio service which itself started during the glory days of the British Empire to broadcast news between the colonies and the metropole.

37. It seems significant here that the word for this action in Hindi, *tulna*, the action of putting two objects in pans and scales to weigh them, is also the same verb used for acts of comparison. Comparative Literature is rendered in Hindi as *tulnaatmak saahityaa*.

38. For a fuller version of this story, see "Weigh Your Options" in Detha, *Straw Epic and Other Stories*, as well as a discussion of this incident in my introduction to that collection.

39. Dogra and Dogra, *Non-Party Political Process Profile of a People's Organization*, 4. The "difference" they refer to is this: they do not depend on outside funds and instead have devised a "replicable" system that relies on "the hidden potential of people themselves for initiating broad-based social change."

40. Ibid., 4.

41. Marx, *Eighteenth Brumaire*, 8.

42. Tactical, too, is my decision to repeat this technical vocabulary in Rajasthani in my translation to remind readers that they are reading a translation from a place with specific knowledge systems they likely have no direct access to. My thanks to Gill Kent for prompting me to consider this connection.

43. Relevant here is Derrida's work on the guest/host relationship in *Monolingualism of the Other*; in this instance it is important to note how topsy-turvy such an arrangement is when the host is a foreign national but is the one with the money to pay rent for a spacious flat to work in and fund the daily meals. A connection might be made between this essay and Derrida's thinking on *The Specter of Marx*, in particular the "furtive and untimely" comings and goings of specters, when we remember that the word in Sanskrit for guest is *atithi*, a joke on untimeliness because its etymology means "not according to a date." In the Sanskrit thinking, you never know when a guest will come or go and you have to be generous and hospitable regardless. The *atithi* is thought to be not just supernatural but godlike, divine.

44. Note here in particular Prasenjit Gupta's accusation that most translation teams involve a white translator and a native informant who usually receives little credit; Prasenjit Gupta, "Translator's Preface." In such an equation, only nationality, not class, gender, sexual orientation, or educational levels, is the operative distinction. See Chamberlain, "Gender and the Metaphorics of Translation"; and Simon, *Gender in Translation*.

45. Madhu Kishwar edited a collection of Ruth Vanita's translations; see Detha, *Dilemma and Other Stories*.

46. Throughout *Rhetoric, Hermeneutics and Translation in the Middle Ages*, Rita Copeland distinguishes between the two integral parts of the practice of translation: first the translator must interpret the text in an act she calls "hermeneutic" and then must express that interpretation in a performance she calls "rhetorical." While in most cases these two parts of the translation exercise take place in two different languages, having our respective areas of expertise so clearly in one language or the other made the double movement in our practice even more pronounced.

47. Detha, *"Thakur rau Bhoot,"* 214.

48. Detha, *"Thakur ka Bhoot."*

49. A metaphor, Stewart explains, is "a procedure for the interaction of two domains that ordinarily do not intersect. It is always involved in grouping, dismantling, and regrouping the semantic fields of social life"; Stewart, *Nonsense*, 34. According to Stewart, a dead metaphor is an especially edifying example to look at since it no longer offers a "fresh cut" across semantic domains but instead offers "short cuts" in social interaction that its users hardly think about. The way to "kill" a metaphor, Stewart suggests, "is to interpret it literally." Ibid., 36.

50. Lawrence Venuti's "foreignizing" method put forward in *The Translator's Invisibility* "seeks to restrain the ethnocentric violence of translation, . . . a cultural intervention in the current state of world affairs, pitched against the

hegemonic English-language nations and the unequal cultural exchanges in which they engage with their global others." Venuti, *Translator's Invisibility*, 20. Niranjana argues for a disruptive translation strategy that attempts to interrupt the "transparency" and "smoothness of a totalizing narrative," thereby marking the "displacement" inherent in language; Niranjana, *Siting Translation*, 185.

51. Shamma. "Exotic Dimension of Foreignizing Strategies."

52. See Rafael, *Contracting Colonialism*, 29.

53. Niranjana, *Siting Translation*, 3.

54. Karamcheti, "Aimé Césaire's Subjective Geographies," 184.

55. *Sud karno* is a farming technique that I translated in my first version as "to gather old grass as one ought." It's a kind of mulching technique, one that Bhola Ram would eventually refer to quite often in the version of the story he told in January 2003. The other two terms will be discussed shortly.

56. My note of November 18, 2003.

57. I should note that Vijay Dan Detha in particular finds copyright rules tiresome and overly imperialistic, but that all three of us—I think it could be safe to say—were not convinced that they worked to protect our creative interests, as has often been argued. For more on the history of copyright and translation, see Merrill, "Seeds of Discontent."

58. See, e.g., the entry for Lillian Virginia Mountweazel in the 1975 edition of the *New Columbia Encyclopedia*.

59. Bakhtin, *Rabelais and His World*, 3.

60. Interview with Shankar Singh, February 17, 2003, in Tilonia, Rajasthan.

61. Shiva, *Seeds of Suicide*, 113; Akhil Gupta, *Postcolonial Developments*, 310.

62. Buck-Morss, *Dreamworld and Catastrophe*, 68; quoting Walter Benjamin, *Das Passagen-Werk*, and Freud, *Interpretation of Dreams*, 84.

63. Bhola Ram, interview January 17, 2003, at his home in Borunda, Rajasthan.

A DOUBLE HEARING (TO CLOSE)

1. I use "translation" here specifically to resonate with Talal Asad's discussion of the term in 1995. He writes, "In ecclesiastical usage . . . the removal of a saint's remains, or his relics, from an original site to another is also known as translation," and points out that "what was transferred was note merely the relic but the power inherent in it." Asad, "A Comment on Translation, Critique, and Subversion," 325–26.

2. Arvind Rajagopal has a particularly incisive critique of Advani's *ratha yatra* as "spectacle" that drew in the upper-caste press. He observes, "Crowds were clearly drawn to the spectacle of a national leader speaking the language of religion, one that had not been seen in the northern region since Gandhi." Rajagopal, *Politics after Television*, 193.

3. For utopic readings of the trope of translation, see Bhabha, "How Newness Enters the World," 212–35; Butler, "Restaging the Universal"; Clifford, *Routes*; and "Translation" in Young, *Postcolonialism: A Very Short Introduction*, 138–47. For discussions of translation as an act of unequal exchange, see Asad, "Concept of Cultural Translation in British Social Anthropology"; Cheyfitz, *Poetics of Imperialism*; Kothari, *Translating India*; Liu, *Translingual Practice*; Liu, "Introduction"; Liu, "Legislating the Universal"; Niranjana, *Siting Translation*; and Rafael, *Contracting Colonialism*.

4. Detha, "*Dohari Zindagi*," 147.

Abdel-Malek, Anouar. "Orientalism in Crisis." *Diogenes* 44 (Winter 1963): 102–40.

Abhinavagupta. *Tantrāloka*. With *Viveka* by Jayaratha. 12 vols. Edited by M. S. Śāstrī (vol. 1) and M. S. Kaul (vols. 2–12). Srinagar, India: Kashmir Series of Texts and Studies, 1919–1938.

Abraham, Nicolas, and Maria Torok. *The Wolf Man's Magic Word: A Cryptonomy*. Translated by Nicholas Rand. Minneapolis: University of Minnesota Press, 1986.

Abu-Lughod, Janet. "Going beyond Global Babble." In *Culture, Globalization and the World-System: Contemporary Conditions for the Representation of Identity*, edited by Anthony King, 131–37. Minneapolis: University of Minnesota Press, 1997.

Ahmad, Aijaz. *In Theory: Classes, Nations, Literatures*. London and New York: Verso, 1992.

All-India Progressive Writers' Association. "All-India Progressive Writers' Association Manifesto." *Left Review*, February, 1935, 240.

Ambedkar, Bhimrao Ramji. "Gandhism: The Doom of the Untouchables." In *Essential Writings of B. R. Ambedkar*, edited by Valerian Rodrigues, 149–72. New Delhi: Oxford University Press, 2002.

———. *Mr. Gandhi and the Emancipation of the Untouchables*. Bombay: Thacker, 1943.

Anand, Mulk Raj. *Untouchable: A Novel*. Preface by E. M. Forster. London: Wishart, 1935.

Anand, Mulk Raj, and Eleanor Zelliot, eds. *An Anthology of Dalit Literature (Poems)*. New Delhi: Gyan, 1992.

Anand, S., ed. *Touchable Tales: Publishing and Reading Dalit Literature*. Pondicherry, India: Navayana, 2003.

Anderson, Benedict. *Imagined Communities: Reflections on the Origin and Spread of Nationalism*. London and New York: Verso, 1983.

———. *The Spectre of Comparisons: Nationalism, Southeast Asia and the World*. London and New York: Verso, 1998.

Apter, Emily. "Global *Translatio:* The 'Invention' of Comparative Literature, Istanbul, 1933." In *Debating World Literature*, edited by Christopher Prendergast, 76–109. London and New York: Verso, 2004.

———. *The Translation Zone: A New Comparative Literature*. Princeton, N.J.: Princeton University Press, 2006.

Asad, Talal. "A Comment on Translation, Critique, and Subversion." In *Between Languages and Cultures: Translation and Cross-Cultural Texts*, edited by Anuradha Dingwaney and Carol Maier, 325–32. Pittsburgh and London: University of Pittsburgh Press, 1995.

———. "The Concept of Cultural Translation in British Social Anthropology." In *Writing Culture: The Poetics and Politics of Ethnography*, edited by James Clifford and George E. Marcus, 141–64. Berkeley: University of California Press, 1986.

Asopa, Ramkaran. *Marwari Bhasha ra Vyakaran* [The grammar of the Marwari language]. Jaipur and Jodhpur: Vidya Shodh Samsthan, 1975 [1896].

Austin, J. L. *How to Do Things with Words*. Oxford: Clarendon Press, 1962.

Bahl, Kali Charan. *Ādhunika Rājasthānī kā samracanātmaka vyākarana* [Modern Rajasthani structural grammar]. Jodhpur, India: Rājasthānī Śodha Samsthāna, 1980.

Bakhtin, M. M. *Dialogic Imagination*. Translated by Caryl Emerson and Michael Holquist. Austin: University of Texas Press, 1981.

———. *Rabelais and His World*. Translated by Helene Iswolsky. Bloomington: Indiana University Press, 1984.

———. *Speech Genres and Other Late Essays*. Translated by Vern W. McGee, edited by Caryl Emerson and Michael Holquist. Austin: University of Texas Press, 1986.

Balzac, Honoré de. "Sarrasine." In *S/Z*, translated by Richard Howard, 221–54. New York: Hill and Wang, 1974.

Barthes, Roland. "The Death of the Author." In *The Rustle of Language*, translated by Richard Howard. Berkeley: University of California Press, 1986.

———. *S/Z*. Translated by Richard Howard. New York: Hill and Wang, 1974.

Bassnett, Susan. *Comparative Literature: A Critical Introduction*. Cambridge, Mass.: Blackwell, 1993.

Bateson, Gregory. *Ecology of the Mind*. New York: Ballantine, 1972.

Bellow, Saul. "Papuans and Zulus." *New York Times*, March 10, 1994, A25.

Benjamin, Andrew. *Translation and the Nature of Philosophy*. London and New York: Routledge, 1989.

Benjamin, Walter. *The Arcades Project*. Translated by Howard Eiland and Kevin McLaughlin. Cambridge, Mass.: Harvard University Press, 1999.

———. *Briefe*. 2 vols. Edited by Gershom Scholem and T. W. Adorno. Frankfurt am Main: Suhrkamp, 1966.

———. *One-Way Street and Other Writings*. Translated by Edmund Jephcott and Kingsley Shorter. London: NLB, 1979.

————. *Das Passagen-Werk.* Vol. 5 of *Gesammelte Schriften.* Edited by Rolf Tiedermann. Frankfurt: Suhrkamp Verlag, 1982.

————. "The Storyteller." In *Illuminations,* translated by Harry Zohn. New York: Schocken, 1968.

————. "The Task of the Translator." In *Illuminations,* translated by Harry Zohn. New York: Schocken, 1968.

————. "Theses on the Philosophy of History." In *Illuminations,* translated by Harry Zohn. New York: Schocken, 1968.

Bergson, Henri. "Laughter." Translator unnamed. In *Comedy,* edited by Wylie Sypher, 61–190. Baltimore, Md.: Johns Hopkins University Press, 1994 [1st English ed. 1956; French ed. 1884].

Berman, Antoine. *The Experience of the Foreign: Culture and Translation in Romantic Germany.* Translated by S. Heyvaert. Albany, N.Y.: SUNY Press, 1992.

Bernheimer, Charles. "Introduction: The Anxieties of Comparison." In *Comparative Literature in the Age of Multiculturalism,* edited by Charles Bernheimer, 1–17. Baltimore, Md.: Johns Hopkins University Press, 1995.

Bernheimer, Charles, chair, with Jonathan Arac, Marianne Hirsch, et al. "The Bernheimer Report, 1993: Comparative Literature at the Turn of the Century." In *Comparative Literature in the Age of Multiculturalism,* edited by Charles Bernheimer, 39–48. Baltimore, Md.: Johns Hopkins University Press, 1995.

Bhabha, Homi K. "Editor's Introduction: Minority Maneuvers and Unsettled Negotiations." *Critical Inquiry* 23, no. 3 (Spring 1997):431–59.

————. "How Newness Enters the World: Postmodern Space, Postcolonial Times and the Trials of Cultural Translation." In *The Location of Culture,* 212–35. New York: Routledge, 1994.

————. *The Location of Culture.* New York: Routledge, 1994.

Bhalla, Alok, ed., *Stories about the Partition.* New Delhi: HarperCollins, 1994.

Bharata Muni. *Nāṭyaśāstra: English Translation with Critical Notes.* Translated by Adya Rangacharya. Bangalore, India: IBH Prakashana, 1986.

Bilgrami, Akeel. "Gandhi's Integrity." *Raritan* 21, no. 2 (2001):48–67.

————. "Occidentalism, the Very Idea: An Essay on Enlightenment and Enchantment." *Critical Inquiry* 32, no. 3 (Spring 2006):381–411.

Bonnell, Victoria E., and George Breslauer. "Soviet and Post-Soviet Area Studies." In *The Politics of Knowledge: Area Studies and the Disciplines,* edited by David L. Szanton. University of California Press/University of California International and Area Studies Digital Collection, edited volume no. 3, 2003. http://repositories.cdlib.org/uciaspubs/editedvolumes/3/4.

Booth, Wayne C. *The Rhetoric of Fiction.* Chicago: University of Chicago Press, 1961.

————. *A Rhetoric of Irony.* Chicago: University of Chicago Press, 1974.

Bora, Ram Chandra. *Contemporary Rajasthani Literature.* Jodhpur, India: Books Treasure, 1995.

Borges, Jorge Luis. "Pierre Menard, Author of the *Quixote*." Translated by James E. Irby. In *Labyrinths: Selected Stories & Other Writings*, edited by Donald A. Yates and James E. Irby, 36–44. New York: New Directions, 1964.

Bose, Sugata, and Ayesha Jalal. *Modern South Asia: History, Culture, Political Economy*. London and New York: Routledge, 1998.

Brass, Paul. *Language, Religion and Politics in North India*. London: Cambridge University Press, 1974.

Brennan, Timothy. "The National Longing for Form." In *Nation and Narration*, edited by Homi K. Bhabha, 44–70. London and New York: Routledge, 1990.

Brown, Nicholas. *Utopian Generations: The Political Horizon of Twentieth-Century Literature*. Princeton, N.J.: Princeton University Press, 2005.

Brown, Wendy. *Politics Out of History*. Princeton, N.J.: Princeton University Press, 2001.

———. "Wounded Attachments." *Political Theory* 21, no. 3 (1993):390–410.

Brueck, Laura R. "Dalit Chetna in Dalit Literary Criticism." In "Dalit Perspectives: A Symposium on the Changing Contours of Dalit Politics." Special issue of *Seminar Magazine* (New Delhi) 558 (February 2006). http://www.india-seminar.com/2006/558/558%20laura%20r.%20obrueck.htm.

Buck-Morss, Susan. *Dreamworld and Catastrophe: The Passing of Mass Utopia in East and West*. Cambridge, Mass.: MIT Press, 2000.

Butalia, Urvashi. *The Other Side of Silence: Voices from the Partition of India*. Durham, N.C.: Duke University Press, 2000.

Butler, Judith. *Gender Trouble: Feminism and the Subversion of Identity*. New York and London: Routledge, 1999 [1990].

———. "Restaging the Universal: Hegemony and the Limits of Formalism." In Judith Butler with Ernesto Laclau and Slavoj Žižek, *Contingency, Hegemony, Universality: Contemporary Dialogues on the Left*. London and New York: Verso, 2000.

———. "Values of Difficulty." In *Just Being Difficult? Academic Writing in the Public Arena*, edited by Jonathan Culler and Kevin Lamb, 199–215. Stanford, Calif.: Stanford University Press, 2003.

Casanova, Pascale. *The World Republic of Letters*. Translated by M. B. DeBevoise. Cambridge, Mass.: Harvard University Press, 2004.

Chakrabarty, Dipesh. *Provincializing Europe: Postcolonial Thought and Historical Difference*. Princeton, N.J.: Princeton University Press, 2000.

Chamberlain, Lori. "Gender and the Metaphorics of Translation." In *Rethinking Translation: Discourse, Subjectivity, Ideology*, edited by Lawrence Venuti. London: Routledge, 1992.

Chapman, George. *The Poems of George Chapman*. Edited by Phyllis Bartlett. New York: Russell & Russell, 1962.

Chapman, George, trans. *Chapman's Homer: The Iliad, The Odyssey, and The Lesser Homerica*. Edited by Allardyce Nicoll. Princeton, N.J.: Princeton University Press, 1956.

Chatterjee, Partha. "Anderson's Utopia." In *Grounds of Comparison: Around the Work of Benedict Anderson*, edited by Jonathan Culler and Pheng Cheah, 161–70. New York and London: Routledge, 2003.

———. "The Nationalist Resolution of the Women's Question." In *Recasting Women: Essays in Indian Colonial History*, edited by Kumkum Sangari and Sudesh Vaid, 233–53. New Brunswick, N.J.: Rutgers University Press, 1999 [1989].

———. *Nationalist Thought and the Colonial World: A Derivative Discourse?* Minneapolis: University of Minnesota Press, 1998 [1986].

———. *The Nation and Its Fragments: Colonial and Postcolonial Histories*. Princeton, N.J.: Princeton University Press, 1993.

Cheah, Pheng. "Grounds of Comparison." In *Grounds of Comparison: Around the Work of Benedict Anderson*, edited by Jonathan Culler and Pheng Cheah, 1–20. New York and London: Routledge, 2003.

———. *Spectral Nationality: Passages of Freedom from Kant to Postcolonial Literatures of Liberation*. New York: Columbia University Press, 2003.

———. "Spectral Nationality: The Living On [sur-vie] of the Postcolonial Nation in Neocolonial Globalization." *Boundary 2* 26, no. 3 (1999):225–52.

Cheyfitz, Eric. *The Poetics of Imperialism: Translation and Colonization from* The Tempest *to* Tarzan. Philadelphia: University of Pennsylvania Press, 1997 [1991].

Chow, Rey. "In the Name of Comparative Literature." In *Comparative Literature in the Age of Multiculturalism*, edited by Charles Bernheimer, 107–16. Baltimore, Md.: Johns Hopkins University Press, 1995.

Chundavat, Lakshmi Kumari. "*Ath rani chouboli ri baat*" [Opening with the story of Rani Chouboli]. In *Chouboli*, edited by Kanhailal Sahal with Patramji Gaur, 11–25. Jaipur, India: Kitab Mahal, 1959.

Clifford, James. *Routes: Travel and Translation in the Late Twentieth Century*. Cambridge, Mass.: Harvard University Press, 1997.

Cohn, Bernard S. *Colonialism and Its Forms of Knowledge: The British in India*. New Delhi: Oxford University Press, 2002 [1996].

Copeland, Rita. *Rhetoric, Hermeneutics and Translation in the Middle Ages: Academic Traditions and Vernacular Texts*. Cambridge, U.K.: Cambridge University Press, 1995 [1991].

Coppola, Carlo. "The All-India Progressive Writers' Association: The European Phase." In *Marxist Influences and South Asian Literature*, edited by Carlo Coppola, vol. 1, 1–34. East Lansing: Asian Studies Center, Michigan State University, 1974.

Coppola, Carlo, ed. *Marxist Influences and South Asian Literature*. 2 vols. East Lansing: Asian Studies Center, Michigan State University, 1974.

Culler, Jonathan, and Pheng Cheah, eds. *Grounds of Comparison: Around the Work of Benedict Anderson*. New York and London: Routledge, 2003.

Curtius, Ernst Robert. *European Literature and the Middle Ages*. Translated by William R. Trask. New York and Evanston, Ill.: Harper and Row, 1963 [1953].

Dalmia, Vasudha. *The Nationalization of Hindu Traditions: Bharatendu Harischandra and Nineteenth-Century Banaras.* Delhi: Oxford University Press, 1999 [1997].

Damrosch, David. *What Is World Literature?* Translation/Transnation Series. Princeton, N.J.: Princeton University Press, 2003.

———. "World Literature in a Postcanonical, Hypercanonical Age." In *Comparative Literature in an Age of Globalization*, edited by Haun Saussy, 43–53. Baltimore, Md.: Johns Hopkins University Press, 2006.

Das, Veena, Arthur Kleinman, et al., eds. *Remaking a World: Violence, Social Suffering, and Recovery.* Berkeley, Calif.: University of California Press, 2001.

Dasgupta, S. N. *A History of Sanskrit Literature.* Calcutta: University of Calcutta Press, 1962.

Deleuze, Gilles, and Félix Guattari. *Kafka: Toward a Minor Literature.* Translated by Dana Polan. Minneapolis: University of Minnesota Press, 1986.

de Man, Paul. *Blindness and Insight.* Minneapolis: University of Minnesota Press, 1983.

———. *The Resistance to Theory.* Minneapolis: University of Minnesota Press, 1986.

Derrida, Jacques. *A Derrida Reader: Between the Blinds.* Edited by Peggy Kamuf. New York: Columbia University Press, 1991.

———. "Des Tours de Babel." Translated by Joseph F. Graham. In *Difference in Translation*, edited by Joseph F. Graham. Ithaca, N.Y.: Cornell University Press, 1985.

———. "Living On: Border Lines." In *Deconstruction and Criticism*, edited by Harold Bloom. New York: Continuum, 1979.

———. *Monolingualism of the Other; or, the Prosthesis of Origin.* Translated by Patrick Mensah. Stanford, Calif.: Stanford University Press, 1998 [1996].

———. *Specters of Marx: The State of the Debt, the Work of Mourning, and the New International.* Translated by Peggy Kamuf. New York: Routledge, 1994 [1993].

———. "Theology of Translation." Translated by Joseph Adamson. In *Eyes of the University: Right to Philosophy 2*, translated by Jan Plug et al., 64–80. Stanford, Calif.: Stanford University Press, 2004.

Deshpande, Madhav M. *Sanskrit & Prakrit: Sociolinguist Issues.* Delhi: Motilal Banarsidass, 1993.

Deshpande, Sudhanva. "Text and Drama." *Frontline* 23, no. 11 (June 3–6, 2006). http://www.flonnet.com/fl2311/stories/20060616000107100.htm.

Detha, Vijay Dan. *"Adamkhor"* [Cannibal]. In *Baataan ri Phulwari*, vol. 11, 25–29. Borunda, India: Rupayan Samsthan, 1985 [1976].

———. *"Adamkhor"* [Cannibal]. Translated by Kailash Kabir. In *Uljhan*, 61–64. New Delhi: Rajkamal Prakashan, 1982.

———. *Baataan ri Phulwari* [Garden of stories]. 14 vols. Borunda, India: Rupayan Samsthan, 1964–1985.

———. "Cannibal." Translated by Christi A. Merrill. *Oasis Quarterly*, Winter 1992, 14–23.

———. "Chouboli." In *Baataan ri Phulwari*, vol. 8, 177–225. Borunda, India: Rupayan Samsthan, 1987 [1966].

———. "Chouboli." Translated by Christi A Merrill with Kailash Kabir. In *A Straw Epic and Other Stories*. New Delhi: Katha Press; New York: Fordham University Press, 2008.

———. "A Dilemma." Translated by Christi Merrill. In *A Straw Epic and Other Stories*. New Delhi: Katha Press; New York: Fordham University Press, 2008.

———. "The Dilemma." In *The Dilemma and Other Stories*, translated by Ruth Vanita, edited by Madhu Kishwar, 145–169. New Delhi: Manushi Prakashan, 1997.

———. *The Dilemma and Other Stories*. Translated by Ruth Vanita, edited by Madhu Kishwar. New Delhi: Manushi Prakashan, 1997.

———. "*Dohari Zindagi*" [A double life]. Translated into Hindi by Kailash Kabir. In *Duvidha aur anya kahaniya*, 147–78. New Delhi: Rajkamal Prakashan, 1979.

———. "A Double Life." Translated by Christi Merrill. In *A Straw Epic and Other Stories*. New Delhi: Katha Press; New York: Fordham University Press, 2008.

———. "*Dovari Joon*" [A double life]. In *Lok Sanskriti* [Folk culture]. Borunda, India: Rupayan Samsthan, 1975.

———. "*Duvidhya*" [Dilemma]. In *Baataan ri Phulwari*, vol. 10, 172–210. Borunda, India: Rupayan Samsthan, 1987 [1972].

———. *Duvidha*. Dir. Mani Kaul. 1973.

———. "*Duvidha*" [Dilemma]. Translated by Kailash Kabir. In *Duvidha aur anya kahaniya*, 249–272. New Delhi: Rajkamal Prakashan, 1979.

———. "Off the Beaten Track." In *The Dilemma and Other Stories*, translated by Ruth Vanita, edited by Madhu Kishwar, 3–35. New Delhi: Manushi Prakashan, 1997.

———. *Paheli* [Riddle]. Dir. Amol Palekar. 2005.

———. "*Riayat*" [Freedom]. Translated into Hindi by Kailash Kabir. In *Duvidha aur anya kahaniya*, 175–78. New Delhi: Rajkamal Prakashan, 1979.

———. "*Rijak ka Maryada*" [A true calling]. *Kathadesh*, March 1997, 11–15.

———. *A Straw Epic and Other Stories*. Translated by Christi A Merrill with Kailash Kabir. New Delhi: Katha Press; New York: Fordham University Press, 2008.

———. "The *Thakur*'s Ghost." Translated by Christi A Merrill with Kailash Kabir. In *A Straw Epic and Other Stories*. New Delhi: Katha Press; New York: Fordham University Press, 2008.

———. "*Thakur ka Bhoot*" [The *thakur*'s ghost]. Translated by Kailash Kabir. In *Choudharain ki Chaturai* [The shrewdness of the farmer's wife], 98–107. Borunda, India: Sayar Prakashan, 1996.

————. *"Thakur rau Bhoot"* [The *thakur*'s ghost]. In *Baataan ri Phulwari*, vol. 9, 205–18. Borunda, India: Rupayan Samsthan, 1987 [1967].

————. "A True Calling." Translated by Christi A Merrill. *Words Without Borders: The Online Magazine for International Literature*. http://www.word-swithoutborders.org/article.php?lab=TrueCalling.

————. *"Uchal Panthi"* [Weigh your options]. In *Baataan ri Phulwari*, vol. 12, 99- . Borunda, India: Rupayan Samsthan, 1985 [1976].

————. "Weigh Your Options." Translated by Christi A Merrill with Kailash Kabir. *A Straw Epic and Other Stories*, translated by Christi A Merrill with Kailash Kabir. New Delhi: Katha Press; New York: Fordham University Press, 2008.

Devi, Shivrani. *Premchand, ghar men* [Premchand at home]. New Delhi: Anjuman Taraqi Urdu, 2007 [1956].

de Vries, Hent, and Lawrence E. Sullivan, eds. *The Crisis of Secularism in India and Political Theologies: Public Religions in a Post-Secular World*. New York: Fordham University Press, 2006.

Devy, G. N. *In Another Tongue: Essays on Indian English Literature*. Frankfurt am Main: Peter Lang, 1993.

Dingwaney, Anuradha, and Carol Maier, eds. *Between Languages and Cultures: Translation and Cross-Cultural Texts*. Pittsburgh and London: University of Pittsburgh Press, 1995.

Dingwaney Needham, Anuradha, and Rajeswari Sunder Rajan, eds. *The Crisis of Secularism in India*. Durham, N.C.: Duke University Press, 2007.

Dirks, Nicholas B. *Castes of Mind: Colonialism and the Making of Modern India*. Princeton, N.J.: Princeton University Press, 2001.

————. "South Asian Studies: Futures Past." In *The Politics of Knowledge: Area Studies and the Disciplines*, edited by David L. Szanton. University of California Press/University of California International and Area Studies Digital Collection, edited volume no. 3, 2003. http://repositories.cdlib.org/uciaspubs/editedvolumes/3/9.

Dogra, Madhu, and Bharat Dogra. *The Non-Party Political Process Profile of a People's Organization: MKSS: Mazdoor Kisan Shakti Sangathna (Rajasthan)*. New Delhi: Social Change Papers, n.d.

Dundes, Alan. "Nationalistic Inferiority Complexes and the Fabrication of Fakelore." Paper presented at the Eighth Congress of the International Society for Folk Narrative Research, Bergen, Norway, June 12–17, 1984.

Eagleton, Terry. *Walter Benjamin, or, Towards a Revolutionary Criticism*. London: Verso and NLB, 1981.

Fabian, Johannes. *Language and Colonial Power*. Berkeley: University of California Press, 1986.

Felman, Shoshana. *The Scandal of the Speaking Body: Don Juan with J. L. Austin, or Seduction in Two Languages*. Translated by Catherine Porter. Stanford, Calif.: Stanford University Press, 2002.

Flaubert, Gustave. *Bouvard et Pécuchet.* Translated by A. J. Krailsheimer. New York: Penguin Books, 1976.

Flieger, Jerry Aline. *The Purloined Punch Line: Freud's Comic Theory and the Postmodern Text.* Baltimore, Md.: Johns Hopkins University Press, 1991.

———. "The Purloined Punch Line: Joke as Textual Paradigm." *Modern Language Notes* 98, no. 5 (1983):941–67.

Flood, Gavin. *The Tantric Body: The Secret Tradition of Hindu Religion.* London and New York: I. B. Tauris, 2006.

Florida, Nancy K. *Writing the Past, Inscribing the Future: History as Prophecy in Colonial Java.* Durham, N.C.: Duke University Press, 1995.

Foster, John Burt, Jr. "'Show Me the Zulu Tolstoy': A Russian Classic between 'First' and 'Third' Worlds." *Slavic and East European Journal* 45, no. 2 (2001):260–74.

Foucault, Michel, "What Is an Author?" In *Language, Counter-Memory, Practice,* translated by D. Bouchard and Sherry Simon, 113–38. Ithaca, N.Y.: Cornell University Press, 1977.

Freeman, Rich. "The Teyyam Tradition of Kerala." In *The Blackwell Companion to Hinduism,* edited by Gavin Flood, 307–26. Oxford: Blackwell, 2003.

Freud, Sigmund. *The Interpretation of Dreams.* Translated by James Strachey. New York: Avon Books, 1965.

———. *Jokes and Their Relation to the Unconscious.* Translated by James Strachey. New York: W. W. Norton, 1960.

———. *Standard Edition of the Complete Works of Sigmund Freud.* Translated by James Strachey. London: Hogarth, 1955.

Gandhi, Leela. *Postcolonial Theory: A Critical Introduction.* New York: Columbia University Press, 1998.

Gandhi, M. K. *Evil Wrought by the English Medium.* Edited by R. K. Prabhy. Ahmedabad, India: Navajivan, 1958.

———. Introduction to "A Letter to a Hindu." In Leo Tolstoy, *Recollections & Essays,* translated by Aylmer Maude. London: Oxford University Press, 1937.

Gates, Henry Louis, Jr. *The Signifying Monkey: A Theory of Afro-American Literary Criticism.* New York: Oxford University Press, 1988.

Girard, René. *Violence and the Sacred.* Translated by Patrick Gregory. Baltimore, Md.: Johns Hopkins University Press, 1977 [1972].

Goethe, Johann Wolfgang von. *Conversations with Eckermann.* Translated by John Oxenford. San Francisco: North Point Press, 1984.

Gourgouris, Stathis. *Dream Nation: Enlightenment, Colonization and the Institution of Modern Greece.* Stanford, Calif.: Stanford University Press, 1996.

Graeber, David. *Toward an Anthropological Theory of Value: The False Coin of Our Own Dreams.* New York: Palgrave, 2001.

Gramsci, Antonio. *Selections from Cultural Writings.* Cambridge, Mass.: Harvard University Press, 1991.

Green, Martin. *Tolstoy and Gandhi: Men of Peace*. New York: Basic Books, 1983.

Greenblatt, Stephen. *Marvellous Possessions: The Wonder of the New World*. Chicago, Ill.: University of Chicago Press, 1991.

Greene, Thomas, chair, with Haskell Block, Nan Carpenter, Frederic Garber, et al. "The Greene Report, 1975: A Report on Standards." In *Comparative Literature in the Age of Multiculturalism*, edited by Charles Bernheimer, 28–38. Baltimore, Md.: Johns Hopkins University Press, 1995.

Grierson, George. "Specimens of the Rajasthani and Gujarati." Vol. 9, Part II, of *Linguistic Survey of India*. Calcutta, India: Office of the Superintendent of Government Printing, 1908.

Guha, Ramachandra. "Using and Abusing Gandhi." Bombay Sarvodaya Mandal/Gandhi Book Centre. http://www.mkgandhi.org/articles/abusing_gandhi.htm. Originally published in *Himal Magazine*, April 1996.

Guha, Ranajit. *Elementary Aspects of Peasant Insurgency in Colonial India*. Durham, N.C.: Duke University Press, 1999.

Gupta, Akhil. *Postcolonial Developments: Agriculture in the Making of Modern India*. Durham, N.C.: Duke University Press, 2000 [1998].

Gupta, Prasenjit. "Translator's Preface." In *Indian Errant: Selected Stories of Nirmal Verma*. New Delhi: Indialog, 2002.

Hasan, Mushirul. *India's Partition: Process, Strategy and Mobilization*. New Delhi: Oxford University Press, 1993.

Hasan, Mushirul, ed. *India Partitioned: The Other Face of Freedom*. New Delhi: Roli Books, 1995.

Hasan-Rokem, Galit, and David Shulman, eds. *Untying the Knot: On Riddles and Other Enigmatic Modes*. New York and Oxford: Oxford University Press, 1996.

Hobsbawm, Eric. "Introduction." In *The Invention of Tradition*, edited by Eric Hobsbawm and Terence Ranger. Cambridge and New York: Cambridge University Press, 1992.

Holmes, James. "Images of Translation: Metaphor and Imagery in the Renaissance Discourse on Translation." In *The Manipulation of Literature: Studies in Literary Translation*, edited by Theo Hermans, 103–35. Amsterdam: Croom Helm, 1985.

Holquist, Michael. "The Surd Heard." In *Literature and History: Theoretical Problems and Russian Case Studies*, edited by Gary Saul Morson. Stanford, Calif.: Stanford University Press, 1986.

hooks, bell. "'this is the oppressor's language / yet I need it to talk to you': Language, a Place of Struggle." In *Between Languages and Cultures: Translation and Cross-Cultural Texts*, edited by Anuradha Dingwaney and Carol Maier, 295–301. Pittsburgh: University of Pittsburgh Press, 1995.

Hutcheon, Linda. *Irony's Edge: The Theory and Politics of Irony*. London and New York: Routledge, 1995.

Inden, Ronald. *Imagining India*. Bloomington: Indiana University Press, 2000.

———. "Introduction: From Philological to Dialogical Texts." In *Querying the Medieval: Texts and the History of Practices in South Asia*, edited by Ronald Inden, Jonathan Walters, and Daud Ali, 3–28. Oxford and New York: Oxford University Press, 2000.

Irigaray, Luce. *This Sex Which Is Not One*. Translated by Catherine Porter with Carolyn Burke. Ithaca, N.Y.: Cornell University Press, 1985 [French ed. 1977].

Isaak, Jo Anna. *Feminism and Contemporary Art: The Revolutionary Power of Women's Laughter*. London and New York: Routledge, 1996.

Jacobs, Carol. "The Monstrosity of Language." In "Comparative Literature: Translation: Theory and Practice." Special issue of *Modern Language Notes* 90, no. 6 (1975):755–66.

Jameson, Fredric. *The Political Unconscious: Narrative as a Socially Symbolic Act*. Ithaca, N.Y.: Cornell University Press, 1981.

———. "Third World Literature in the Era of Multinational Capital." *Social Text* 15 (1986):65–88.

Johnson, Barbara. *The Critical Difference: Essays in the Contemporary Rhetoric of Reading*. Baltimore, Md., and London: Johns Hopkins University Press, 1980.

Joshi, Shrilal Nathamalji. "*Rani Chouboli ri Vat*" [The story of Rani Chouboli]. Edited by Manohar Sharma, 181–87. In *Rajasthani Vat Sangrah*. New Delhi: Sahitya Akademi, 2001 [1984].

Karamcheti, Indira. "Aimé Césaire's Subjective Geographies: Translating Place and the Difference It Makes." In *Between Languages and Cultures: Translation and Cross-Cultural Texts*, edited by Anuradha Dingwaney and Carol Maier, 181–98. Pittsburgh and London: University of Pittsburgh Press, 1995.

Karnad, Girish. *Hayavadana*. Translated by the author. In *Modern Indian Drama: An Anthology*, edited by G. P. Deshpande, 253–322. Delhi: Sahitya Akademi, 2000.

———. "Theatre in India." *Daedalus* 118, no. 4 (1989):330–52.

Kaviraj, Sudipta. "The Two Histories of Literary Cultures in Bengal." In *Literary Cultures in History: Reconstructions from South Asia*, edited by Sheldon Pollock, 503–66. New Delhi: Oxford University Press, 2003.

Kesteloot, Lilyan. *Les écrivains noirs de langue française: Naissance d'une littérature*. Brussels, Belgium: Université libre de Bruxelles, Institut de sociologie, 1965.

Khanna, Ranjana. *Dark Continents: Psychoanalysis and Colonialism*. Durham, N.C., and London: Duke University Press, 2003.

King, Christopher. *One Language, Two Scripts: The Hindi Movement in the Nineteenth Century North India*. Delhi: Oxford University Press, 1994.

King, Robert D. *Nehru and the Language Politics of India*. Delhi: Oxford University Press, 1998.

Kishwar, Madhu. "Gandhi on Women." *Race & Class* 28 (1986):43–61.

Kittler, Friedrich A. *Discourse Networks 1800/1900.* Translated by Michael Metteer with Chris Cullens. Stanford, Calif.: Stanford University Press, 1990.

Kothari, Komal, ed. *Premchand ke Pātra: Premchand ke Vashisht Katha-Patron ka Mahatwaparn Vishleshan* [Premchand's characters: A significant analysis of Premchand's special story characters]. Delhi: Akshar Prakashan, 1970.

Kothari, Rita. *Translating India: The Cultural Politics of English.* Manchester, U.K.: St. Jerome Publishing, 2003.

Kumar, Priya. *Limiting Secularism: The Ethics of Coexistence in Indian Literature and Film.* Minneapolis: University of Minnesota Press, 2008.

Lacôte, Félix. *Essai sur Guṇāḍhya et la Bṛhatkathā* [An Essay on Gunadhya and the Brhatkatha]. Paris: Ernest Leroux, 1908.

Lālas, Sītārām, ed. *Rajasthānī Sabad Kos* [Rajasthani dictionary]. Jodhpur, India: Chaupāsanī Śikśā Samiti, 1971.

———. *Rajasthani Vyakaran* [Rajasthani grammar]. Jodhpur, India: Rajasthani Shodh Samsthan, 1997.

Lang, Candace D. *Irony/Humor: Critical Paradigms.* Baltimore, Md.: Johns Hopkins University Press, 1988.

Légitime défense. Nendeln, Liechtenstein: Kraus Reprint, 1970 [1932].

Lelièvre, F. J. "The Basis of Ancient Parody." *Greece and Rome* ser. 2, no. 1/2 (June 1954):66–81.

Lenin, V. I. "Articles on Tolstoy." Translator not named. In *Marxists on Literature: An Anthology,* edited by David Craig. Middlesex, U.K.: Penguin, 1975.

Lessig, Lawrence. "CC in Review: Lawrence Lessig on Compatibility." Comment on Creative Commons Web site posted November 30, 2005. http://creativecommons.org/weblog/entry/5709.

———. *Code: And Other Laws of Cyberspace.* New York: Basic Books, 1999.

———. *Code: And Other Laws of Cyberspace, Version 2.0.* New York: Basic Books, 2006. Available in an editable wiki version as "Code v2." http://www.socialtext.net/codev2/index.cgi.

———. "Commons Misunderstandings: ASCAP on Creative Commons." Comment on Lessig Blog posted December 31, 2007. http://lessig.org/blog/2007/12/commons_misunderstandings_asca.html.

———. *The Future of Ideas: The Fate of the Commons in a Connected World.* New York: Vintage, 2002.

Levin, Harry, chair, with A. O. Aldridge, Chandler B. Beall, et al. "The Levin Report, 1965: Report on Professional Standards." In *Comparative Literature in the Age of Multiculturalism,* edited by Charles Bernheimer, 21–27. Baltimore, Md.: Johns Hopkins University Press, 1995.

"Lillian Virginia Mountweazel." *New Columbia Encyclopedia,* 1850. New York: Columbia University Press, 1975.

Liu, Lydia H. "A Folksong Immortal and Official Popular Culture in Twenti-eth-Century China." In *Writing and Materiality in China*, edited by Judith T. Zeitlin and Lydia H. Liu, 553–609. Cambridge, Mass.: Harvard University Press, 2003.

———. "Introduction." In *Tokens of Exchange: The Problem of Translation in Global Circulations*, edited by Lydia H. Liu, 1–12. Durham, N.C.: Duke University Press, 1999.

———. "Legislating the Universal: The Circulation of International Law in the Nineteenth Century." In *Tokens of Exchange: The Problem of Translation in Global Circulations*, edited by Lydia H. Liu, 127–64. Durham, N.C.: Duke University Press, 1999.

———. *Translingual Practice: Literature, National Culture, and Translated Modernity, China, 1900–1937*. Stanford, Calif.: Stanford University Press, 1995.

Lord, Albert. *The Singer of Tales*. Cambridge, Mass.: Harvard University Press, 1960.

Lukács, Georg. *Studies in European Realism: A Sociological Survey of the Writings of Balzac, Stendhal, Zola, Tolstoy, Gorki, and Others*. Translated by Edith Bone. London: Hillway, 1950.

———. *The Theory of the Novel: A Historico-Philosophical Essay on the Forms of Great Epic Literature*. Translated by Anna Bostock. Cambridge, Mass.: MIT Press, 1971 [1920].

———. "Tolstoy and the Development of Realism." In *Marxists on Literature: An Anthology*, edited by David Craig, 282–345. Harmondsworth, U.K.: Penguin Books, 1975.

Lutgendorf, Philip. *The Life of a Text: Performing the Ramcaritmanas of Tulsidas*. Berkeley: University of California Press, 1991.

Macalister, George. *A Dictionary of the Dialects Spoken in the State of Jeypore*. Allahabad, India: Allahabad Mission Press, 1898.

Macauley, Thomas Babington. "Indian Education (Minute of the 2nd of February, 1835)." In *Prose and Poetry*, edited by G. M. Young, 719–30. Cambridge, Mass.: Harvard University Press, 1967 [1952].

MacIntyre, Alasdair. *Whose Justice? Which Rationality?* London: Duckworth, 1988.

Mahadevan, Anand. "Switching Heads and Cultures: Transformation of an Indian Myth by Thomas Mann and Girish Karnad." *Comparative Literature* 54, no. 1 (2002):23–41.

Maheshwari, Hiralal. *History of Rajasthani Literature*. Delhi: Sahitya Akademi, 1980.

Majeed, Javed. "Gandhi, 'Truth' and Translatability." *Modern Asian Studies* 40, no. 2 (2006):303–32.

Mani, Lata. "Contentious Traditions: The Debate on *Sati* in Colonial India." In *Recasting Women: Essays in Colonial History*, edited by Kumkum Sangari and Sudesh Vaid, 88–126. New Brunswick, N.J.: Rutgers University Press, 1999 [1990].

Mann, Thomas. *Die vetauschten Köpfe: Eine indische Legende* (The transposed heads: An Indian legend). Stockholm: Bermann-Fischer Verlag, 1944.

Manto, Saadat Hasan. "Toba Tek Singh." Translated by Robert B. Haldane. *Journal of South Asian Literature* 6 (1970):20–23.

———. "Toba Tek Singh." In *Another Lonely Voice: The Life and Works of Saadat Hassan Manto*, introduction by Leslie A. Flemming, short stories translated by Tahira Naqvi, 281–288. Lahore, Pakistan: Vanguard, 1985.

———. "Toba Tek Singh." In Manto, *Kingdom's End and Other Stories*, translated by Khalid Hasan, 11–18. London and New York: Verso, 1987.

———. "Toba Tek Singh." In *Modern Urdu Short Stories*, selected and translated by Jai Ratan, 22–27. New Delhi: Allied, 1987.

———. "Toba Tek Singh." Translated by Harish Trivedi. In *Breakthrough: Modern Hindi and Urdu Short Stories*, edited by Sukrita Paul Kumar, 215–20. Shimla, India: Indian Institute of Advanced Studies, 1993.

———. "Toba Tek Singh." In *Selected Stories: Saadat Hasan Manto*, translated by Madan Gupta, 151–55. New Delhi, India: Cosmo, 1997.

———. "Toba Tek Singh." Translated by G. A. Chaussée. Read at the Virginia Festival of the Book, Charlottesville, Virginia, March 2000.

———. "Toba Tek Singh." Translated by M. Asaduddin. In *Translating Partition: Stories by Attia Hosain, et al.*, edited by Ravikant and Tarun K. Saint. New Delhi: Katha, 2001.

———. "Toba Tek Singh." Translated by Sundeep Dougal. *Outlook India*, August 16, 2001.

———. "Toba Tek Singh." Translated by Richard McGill Murphy. *Words without Borders: The Online Magazine for International Literature*. http://www.wordswithoutborders.org/article.php?lab=Toba.

———. "Toba Tek Singh." Translated by Frances W. Pritchett. Web site maintained by Frances Pritchett. http://www.columbia.edu/itc/mealac/pritchett/00urdu/tobateksingh/translation.html.

Marx, Karl. *Der achtzehnte Brumaire des Louis Bonaparte*. Vienna and Berlin: Verlag für Literatur und Politik, 1927.

———. *The Eighteenth Brumaire of Louis Bonaparte*. Translator not named. New York: International Publishers, 1998 [1963].

———. *The Portable Karl Marx*. Selected and translated by Eugene Kamenka. New York: Viking Press, 1983.

Marx, Karl, and Friedrich Engels, *Manifesto of the Communist Party*. Translator not named. New York: Pathfinder Press, 1987.

———. *Selected Works [of] Karl Marx and Frederick Engels in One Volume*. London: International Publishers, 1968.

Mayaram, Shail. *Against History, Against State: Counterperspectives from the Margins*. Delhi: Permanent Black, 2004 [2003].

McGregor, R. S., ed. *Oxford Hindi-English Dictionary*. Oxford: Oxford University Press, 1993.

Mehta, Uday Singh. *Liberalism and Empire: A Study in Nineteenth-Century British Liberal Thought*. Chicago: University of Chicago, 1999.

Melas, Natalie. *All the Difference in the World: Postcoloniality and the Ends of Comparison*. Stanford, Calif.: Stanford University Press, 2006.

Menaria, Motilal. *Rajasthani Bhasha aur Sahitya* [Rajasthani language and literature]. Jodhpur: Rajasthani Granthagar, 1999.

Menaria, Purushottamlal. *Rājasthānnī bhāshā kī rūparekhā aura mānyatā kā prāsna* [An outline of the Rajasthani language and an inquiry into acceptance]. Benares: Hindī Pracāraka Pustakālaya, 1953.

Menon, Ritu, and Kamala Bhasin. *Borders and Boundaries*. New Delhi: Kali for Women, 1998.

Merrill, Christi A. "Are We the Folk in This Lok?" In "Practice and Politics of Translation." Special issue of *Sagar* 8 (Spring 2002):105–19. Reprinted in *Translation: Poetics and Practice*, edited by Anisur Rahman, 67–79. New Delhi: Creative Books, 2002.

———. "The Death of the Authors a.k.a. Twilight of the Translators." In "Translation and Culture," edited by Katherine M. Faull. Special issue of *Bucknell Review* 47, no. 1 (2004):139–50.

———. "Seeds of Discontent: Re-Creation and the Bounds of Ownership." In *In Translation. Reflections, Refractions, Transformations*, edited by Prafulla Kar and Paul St. Pierre, 114–28. New Delhi: Pencraft International, 2004.

———. "To Be or Not to Be a Gutter Flea: Writing from beyond the Edge." In *Translating Others*, vol. 1, edited by Theo Hermans, 211–18. London: St. Jerome Press, 2006.

———. "Translation from Indian/South Asian Languages (Modern)." In *The Encyclopedia of Literary Translation into English*, edited by Olive Classe, 1:705–707. London: Fitzroy Dearborn.

———. "Writing from Below: Ironic Distance and the Location of Translation." In "Postcolonialism: The Dislocation of Culture." Special issue of *Genre* 22 (2001):32–54.

Mitchell, Lisa. "Parallel Languages, Parallel Cultures: Language as a New Foundation for the Reorganisation of Knowledge and Practice in Southern India." *Indian Economic and Social History Review* 42, no. 5 (2005):443–65.

Monier-Williams, Monier. *A Sanskrit-English Dictionary*. Delhi: Motilal Banarsidas, 1984 [1899].

Moretti, Franco. *Atlas of the European Novel 1800–1900*. London and New York: Verso, 1998.

Morson, Gary Saul, and Caryl Emerson. *Mikhail Bakhtin: Creation of a Prosaics*. Stanford, Calif.: Stanford University Press, 1990.

Mufti, Aamir. "The Aura of Authenticity." *Social Text* 18, no. 3 (2000):87–103.

————. *Enlightenment in the Colony: The Jewish Question and the Crisis of Postcolonial Culture.* Princeton, N.J.: Princeton University Press, 2007.

Mufti, Aamir, ed. "Critical Secularism." Special issue of *boundary 2: an international journal of literature and culture* 31, no. 2 (2004).

Mukherjee, Meenakshi. *Realism and Reality: The Novel and Society in India.* Delhi: Oxford University Press, 1985.

Nagy, Gregory. *Homeric Questions.* Austin: University of Texas Press, 1996.

Nancy, Jean-Luc. *Being Singular Plural.* Translated by Robert D. Richardson and Anne E. O'Byrne. Stanford, Calif.: Stanford University Press, 2000.

————. *Dis-enclosure: The Deconstruction of Christianity.* Translated by Bettina Bergo, Gabriel Malenfact, and Michael B. Smith. New York: Fordham University Press, 2007.

————. *The Inoperative Community.* Edited by Peter Connor, translated by Peter Connor, Lisa Garbus, Michael Holland, and Simona Sawhney. Minneapolis: University of Minnesota Press, 1991.

Ngũgĩ wa Thiong'o. *Decolonising the Mind: The Politics of Language in African Literature.* Portsmouth, U.K.: Heinemann, 1997.

Nimus, Anna. "Copyright, Copyleft and the Creative Anti-Commons." Article in the section on "Markets and Immaterial Labor" of the online journal *Subsol.* http://subsol.c3.hu/subsol_2/contributorso/nimustext.html.

Niranjana, Tejaswini. *Siting Translation: History, Post-Structuralism, and the Colonial Context.* Berkeley: University of California Press, 1992.

O'Gorman, Marcel. *E-Crit: Digital Media, Critical Theory, and the Humanities.* Toronto: University of Toronto Press, 2006.

Orsini, Francesca. *The Hindi Public Sphere 1920–1940: Language and Literature in the Age of Nationalism.* New Delhi: Oxford University Press, 2002.

Pandey, Gyanendra. "Hindi, Hindu, Hindustani." In *The Construction of Communalism in Colonial North India,* 201–32. New Delhi: Oxford University Press, 1990.

————. *Remembering Partition: Violence, Nationalism and History in India.* Cambridge, U.K.: Cambridge University Press, 2001.

Parker, Andrew. "Bogeyman: Benedict Anderson's 'Derivative' Discourse." In *Grounds of Comparison: Around the Work of Benedict Anderson,* edited by Jonathan Culler and Pheng Cheah, 53–73. New York and London: Routledge, 2003.

Parker, Andrew, and Eve Kosofsky Sedgwick, eds. *Performativity and Performance.* New York and London: Routledge, 1995.

Peabody, Norbert. "Tod's Rajast'han and the Boundaries of Imperial Rule in Nineteenth-Century India." *Modern Asian Studies* 30, no. 1 (1996):185–220.

Pollock, Sheldon. "Cosmopolitan and Vernacular in History." *Public Culture* 12, no. 3 (2000):591–625.

————. "The Cosmopolitan Vernacular." *Journal of Asian Studies* 57, no. 1 (1998):6–37.

————. *The Language of the Gods in the World of Men.* Delhi: Permanent Black, 2006.

————. "The Sanskrit Cosmopolis, 300–1300: Transculturation, Vernacularization, and the Question of Ideology." In *Ideology and Status of Sanskrit: Contributions to the History of the Sanskrit Language,* edited by Jan E. M. Houben, 197—247. Leiden, Netherlands: E. J. Brill, 1996.

Porter, James. "'Bring Me the Head of James Macpherson': The Execution of Ossian and the Wellspring of Folkloristic Discourse." *Journal of American Folklore* 114, no. 454 (2001):396–453.

Prabhakar, Manohar. *A Critical Study of Rajasthani Literature.* Jaipur, India: Panchsheel Prakashan, 1976.

Prabhakar, Manohar, ed. *Rajasthani Baaten* [Rajasthani stories]. Jaipur, India: Marughar Prakashan, 1975.

Prakash, Gyan. *Bonded Histories: Genealogies of Labor Servitude in Colonial India.* Cambridge, U.K.: Cambridge University Press, 1990.

Premchand. *The Gift of a Cow: A Translation of the Hindi Novel, Godaan, by Premchand.* Translated by Gordon C. Roadarmel. Bloomington: Indiana University Press, 1968.

————. *Sahitya ka Uddeshya* [The aim of literature]. Allahabad, India: Hans Prakashan, 1967.

————. *The World of Premchand.* Translated by David Rubin. Bloomington, Indiana University Press, 1969.

Premchand, trans. *"Landan mai Bharatiya Sahityakaron ki Ek Nayi Samstha"* [All-India Progressive Writers' Association manifesto]. *Hans,* October 1935. Reprinted in *Vividh Prasang,* edited by Amrit Rai. Allahabad, India: Hansa Prakashan, 1962.

Prins, Yopie. *Victorian Sappho.* Princeton, N.J.: Princeton University Press, 1999.

Puchner, Martin. *Poetry of the Revolution.* Princeton, N.J.: Princeton University Press, 2006.

Radhakrishnan, R. *Theory in an Uneven World.* Oxford: Blackwell, 2003.

Radin, Paul. *The Trickster: A Study in American Indian Mythology.* London: Routledge and Paul, 1955.

Rafael, Vicente. *Contracting Colonialism: Translation and Christian Conversion in Tagalog Society under Early Spanish Rule.* Durham, N.C., and London: Duke University Press, 1993.

Rai, Alok. *Hindi Nationalism.* Hyderabad, India: Orient Longman, 2001.

————. "Introduction." In Amrit Rai, *A House Divided: The Origin and Development of Hindi/Hindavi,* v–xxi. Delhi: Oxford University Press, 1984.

Rai, Amrit. *A House Divided: The Origin and Development of Hindi/Hindavi.* Delhi: Oxford University Press, 1984.

————. *Premacanda, kalama kā sipāhī* [Premchand, soldier of the pen]. Allahabad, India: Hamsa Prakāsana, 1981. Republished in English as *Premchand:*

His Life and Times, translated by Harish Trivedi. Delhi: Oxford University Press, 1990.

Rai, Sara. "Realism as a Creative Process: Features of Munshi Premchand's Ideology." *Social Scientist* 7, no. 84 (1979):32–42.

Rajagopal, Arvind. *Politics after Television: Hindu Nationalism and the Reshaping of the Public in India*. Cambridge, U.K.: Cambridge University Press, 2001.

Rajan, Rajeshwari Sunder. *Real and Imagined Women: Gender, Culture and Post-colonialism*. London and New York: Routledge, 1993.

Ramanujan, A. K., ed. *Folktales of India*. New York: Pantheon, 1991.

Ramaswamy, Sumathi. *Passions of the Tongue: Language Devotion in Tamil India, 1891–1970*. Berkeley: University of California Press, 1997.

Rao, Velcheru Narayana. "Texture and Authority: Telugu Riddles and Enigmas." In *Untying the Knot: On Riddles and Other Enigmatic Modes*, 191–207. Oxford and New York: Oxford University Press, 1996.

Ravikant and Tarun K. Saint, eds. *Translating Partition*. New Delhi: Katha, 2001.

Reichl, Susanne, and Mark Stein, eds. *Cheeky Fictions: Laughter and the Postcolonial*. Amsterdam and New York: Rodopi, 2005.

Richardson, Joanne. "The Language of Tactical Media." Article in the section on "Tactical Media" of the online journal *Subsol*. http://subsol.c3.hu/subsol_2/contributors2/richardsontext2.html.

Robinson, Douglas. "The Ascetic Foundations of Western Translatology: Jerome and Augustine." *Translation and Literature* 1 (1992):3–25.

———. *Translation and Taboo*. DeKalb: Northern Illinois University Press, 1996.

———. *The Translator's Turn*. Baltimore, Md.: Johns Hopkins University Press, 1991.

———. *Who Translates? Translator Subjectivities beyond Reason*. Albany, N.Y.: SUNY Press, 2001.

Rose, Margaret A. *Parody: Ancient, Modern, and Post-Modern*. Cambridge, U.K.: Cambridge University Press, 1993.

Rushdie, Salman. *Imaginary Homelands: Essays and Criticism 1981–1991*. New York: Granta Books with Viking Penguin, 1991.

———. *The Satanic Verses*. New York: Viking Penguin, 1989.

Rushdie, Salman, and Elizabeth West, eds. *The Vintage Book of Indian Writing 1947–1997*. New York: Vintage, 1997.

Said, Edward W. *Culture and Imperialism*. New York: Vintage, 1994.

———. "Erich Auerbach, Critic of the Earthly World." New introduction to Erich Auerbach, *Mimesis: The Representation of Reality in Western Literature*, translated by Willard R. Trask, ix–xxxii. Princeton, N.J.: Princeton University Press, 2003. Reprinted in "Critical Secularism." Special issue of *boundary 2: an international journal of literature and culture* 31, no. 2 (2004):11–34.

———. *Orientalism*. New York: Vintage, 1979.

Sakai, Naoki. *Translation and Subjectivity: On "Japan" and Cultural Nationalism.* Minneapolis: University of Minnesota Press, 1997.

———. *Voices of the Past: The Status of Language in Eighteenth-Century Japanese Discourse.* Ithaca, N.Y.: Cornell University Press, 1992.

Sakariya, Badri Prasad, and Bhupatiram Sakariya, eds. *Rajasthani Hindi Shabd Kosh* [Rajasthani-Hindi dictionary]. Jaipur, India: Panchsheel Prakashan, 1984.

Sánchez-Pardo, Esther. *Cultures of the Death Drive: Melanie Klein and Modernist Melancholia.* Durham, N.C., and London: Duke University Press, 2003.

Saussy, Haun. "Exquisite Cadavers: Stitched from Fresh Nightmares." In *Comparative Literature in an Age of Globalization*, edited by Haun Saussy, 3–42. Baltimore, Md.: Johns Hopkins University Press, 2006.

Schulz, S. "Hindu Mythology in Mann's Indian Legend." *Comparative Literature* 24, no. 2 (1962):129–42.

Scott, James C. *Weapons of the Weak: Everyday Forms of Peasant Resistance.* New Haven, Conn.: Yale University Press, 1985.

Sedgwick, Eve Kosofsky. *Between Men: English Literature and Male Homosocial Desire.* New York: Columbia University Press, 1985.

Seidman, Naomi. *Faithful Renderings: Jewish-Christian Difference and the Politics of Translation.* Chicago, Ill.: University of Chicago Press, 2006.

Sengupta, Mahasweta. "Translation, Colonialism and Poetics: Rabindranath Tagore in Two Worlds." In *Translation, History and Culture*, edited by Susan Bassnett and André Lefevere, 56–63. New York: Routledge, 1990.

Shamma, Tarek. "The Exotic Dimension of Foreignizing Strategies: Burton's Translation of the Arabian Nights." *The Translator* 11, no. 1 (2005):51–67.

Shankar, S. "Midnight's Orphans, or, a Postcolonialism Worth Its Name." *Cultural Critique* 56 (2003):64–95.

Sharma, Ram Vilas. *Premchand aur unka yug* [Premchand and his era]. New Delhi: Rajkamal Prakashan, 2002 [1993].

Shiva, Vandana. *Seeds of Suicide: The Ecological and Human Costs of Globalisation of Agriculture.* New Delhi: Research Foundation for Science, Technology, and Ecology, 2000.

Shukla, Ramchandra. *Hindi Sahitya ke Itihas* [The history of Hindi literature]. Varanasi, India: Nagaripracharini Sabha, 1988.

Siegel, Lee. *Laughing Matters: Comic Tradition in India.* Delhi: Motilal Banarsidass, 1987.

Silverstein, Michael, and Greg Urban. "The Natural History of Discourse." In *Natural Histories of Discourse*, edited by Michael Silverstein and Greg Urban, 1–17. Chicago and London: University of Chicago Press, 1996.

Simon, Sherry. *Gender in Translation: Cultural Identity and the Politics of Transmission.* London and New York: Routledge, 1996.

Singh, K. P. "Premchand and Gandhism." *Social Scientist* 9, no. 97 (1980):47–52.

Sinha, Mrinalini. *Specters of Mother India: The Global Restructuring of an Empire.* Durham, N.C.: Duke University Press, 2006.

Skaria, Ajay. *Hybrid Histories: Forests, Frontiers and Wildness in Western India.* New Delhi: Oxford University Press, 1999.

Slaughter, Joseph R. *Human Rights, Inc.: The World Novel, Narrative Form, and International Law.* New York: Fordham University Press, 2007.

Smith, Frederick M. *The Self Possessed: Deity and Spirit Possession in South Asian Literature and Civilization.* New York: Columbia University Press, 2006.

Somadeva Bhatt. *Die indische Weltmutter.* Translated by Heinrich Zimmer. Zürich: Eranos Jahrbuch, 1939 [1938].

———. *The Katha Sarit Sagara, or, Ocean of the Streams of Story.* Translated by C. H. Tawney, edited by N. M. Penzer. Delhi: Munshiram Manoharlal, 1992 [1880].

———. *The King and the Corpse.* Translated by Heinrich Zimmer, edited by Joseph Campbell. Princeton, N.J.: Princeton University Press, 1956 [1948].

———. *Tales of Ancient India.* Translated by J. A. B. van Buitenen. Chicago: University of Chicago Press, 1959.

———. *Tales from the Kathasaritsagara.* Translated by Arshia Sattar. Delhi: Penguin, 1994.

Sontag, Susan. "The World as India: Translation as a Passport within the Community of Literature." *Times Literary Supplement,* June 13, 2003, 13–5.

Spear, Percival. *India: A Modern History.* Ann Arbor: University of Michigan Press, 1961.

Spivak, Gayatri Chakravorty. "Can the Subaltern Speak? Speculations on Widow-Sacrifice." In *Marxist Interpretations of Culture,* edited by Cary Nelson and Lawrence Grossberg, 271–313. Basingstoke, U.K.: Macmillan Education, 1988. Previously published in *Wedge* (Winter/Spring 1985):120–30.

———. *A Critique of Postcolonial Reason: Towards a History of the Vanishing Present.* Cambridge, Mass.: Harvard University Press, 1999.

———. *Death of a Discipline.* New York: Columbia University Press, 2003.

———. "The Politics of Translation." In *Outside in the Teaching Machine,* 179–200. New York: Routledge, 1993.

Stallybrass, Peter, and Allon White. *The Politics and Poetics of Transgression.* Ithaca, N.Y.: Cornell University Press, 1986.

Stewart, Susan. *Nonsense: Aspects of Intertextuality in Folklore and Literature.* Baltimore, Md., and London: Johns Hopkins University Press, 1978.

Sumanakshar, S. "*Rangbhoomi* ko 'Jangbhoomi' banane ke liye zimmedar kaun?" [Who is responsible for turning *Rangbhoomi* (Premchand's novel, *The Land of Color*) into "Jangbhoomi" (The Land of War)?] *Apeksha* 10 (2005):16–18.

Szanton, David L. "The Origin, Nature, and Challenges of Area Studies in the United States." In *The Politics of Knowledge: Area Studies and the Disciplines,* edited by David L. Szanton. University of California Press/University of

California International and Area Studies Digital Collection, edited volume no. 3, 2003. http://repositories.cdlib.org/uciaspubs/editedvolumes/3/1.

Tagore, Rabindranath. *Gitanjali: Song Offerings.* Translated by the author. London: Macmillan, 1913.

Tansman, Alan. "Japanese Studies: The Intangible Act of Translation." In *The Politics of Knowledge: Area Studies and the Disciplines,* edited by David L. Szanton. University of California Press/University of California International and Area Studies Digital Collection, edited volume no. 3, 2003. http://repositories.cdlib.org/uciaspubs/editedvolumes/3/5.

Thapar, Romila. *A History of India.* Vol. 1. Harmondsworth, U.K.: Penguin Books, 1966.

Tod, James. *Annals and Antiquities of Rajasthan, or, the Central and Western Rajpoot States of India.* 2 vols. New Delhi: Munshiram Manoharlal, 2001.

Tolstoy, Leo. *"Bhoot aur Roti."* In *Talstay ki Kahaniyan,* translated by Premchand, 108–10. Allahabad and Delhi: Saraswati Press, 1986.

———. "The Imp and the Crust." In *Twenty-Three Tales,* translated by Louise Maude and Aylmer Maude, 202–206. London: Oxford University Press, 1928 [1886].

———. "A Letter to a Hindu." In *Recollections and Essays,* translated by Aylmer Maude with an Introduction by M. K. Gandhi, 413–39. London: Humphrey Milford, 1937.

Trikha, Nirmal. *Faiths and Beliefs in the Kathāsaritsāgara.* Delhi: Eastern Book Linkers, 1991.

Trivedi, Harish, and Susan Bassnett. "Introduction: Of Colonies, Cannibals and Vernaculars." In *Post-colonial Translation: Theory and Practice,* edited by Susan Bassnett and Harish Trivedi, 1–18. London and New York: Routledge, 1999.

———. "The Progress of Hindi, Part 2: Hindi and the Nation." In *Literary Cultures in History: Reconstructions from South Asia,* edited by Sheldon Pollock, 958–1022. New Delhi: Oxford University Press, 2003.

Trumpener, Katie. *Bardic Nationalism: The Romantic Novel and the British Empire.* Princeton, N.J.: Princeton University Press, 1997.

Tufte, Edward R. *Visual Explanations: Images and Quantities, Evidence and Narrative.* Cheshire, Conn.: Graphics Press, 1998.

Turner, Victor. *The Forest of Symbols: Aspects of Ndembu Ritual.* Ithaca, N.Y.: Cornell University Press, 1967.

Urban, Greg. "The 'I' of Discourse." In *Semiotics, Self, and Society,* edited by Benjamin Lee and Greg Urban, 27–51. Berlin and New York: Mouton de Gruyter, 1989.

van Buitenen, J. A. B. "Story Literatures." In *The Literatures of India,* edited by Edward Dimock, 198–211. Chicago: University of Chicago Press, 1974.

Vargas Llosa, Mario. *The Storyteller.* Translated by Helen Lane. New York: Penguin, 1990.

Venuti, Lawrence. *The Scandals of Translation: Towards an Ethics of Difference.* London and New York: Routledge, 1998.

———. *The Translator's Invisibility.* London and New York: Routledge, 1995.

Visweswaran, Kamala. "India in South Africa: Counter-Genealogies for a Subaltern Sociology?" in Murli Natarajan and Paul, eds. *Beyond Durban: Caste and Race Dialogues.* Delhi: Orient-Longman (forthcoming).

Volosinov, V. N. *Marxism and the Philosophy of Language.* Translated by Ladislav Matejka and I. R. Titunik. Cambridge, Mass.: Harvard University Press, 1986 [1973].

Wakankar, Milind. "The Moment of Criticism in Indian Nationalist Thought: Ramchandra Shukla and the Poetics of a Hindi Responsibility." *South Atlantic Quarterly* 101, no. 4 (2002):987–1014.

Watt, Ian. *The Rise of the Novel: Studies in Defoe, Richardson, and Fielding.* Berkeley: University of California Press, 1957.

White, James Boyd. *Justice as Translation: An Essay in Cultural and Legal Criticism.* Chicago: University of Chicago Press, 1990.

———. "On the Virtues of Not Understanding." In *Between Languages and Cultures: Translation and Cross-Cultural Texts*, edited by Anuradha Dingwaney and Carol Maier, 333–39. Pittsburgh: University of Pittsburgh Press, 1995.

Williams, Raymond. *Marxism and Literature.* Oxford and New York: Oxford University Press, 1977.

Winternitz, M. "Classical Sanskrit Literature." In *History of Indian Literature*, vol. 3, translated by Subhadra Jhā. Delhi: Motilal Banarsidas, 1963.

Young, Robert J. C. *Postcolonialism: An Historical Introduction.* Oxford: Blackwell, 2001.

———. *Postcolonialism: A Very Short Introduction.* Oxford, U.K.: Oxford University Press, 2003.

Zipes, Jack. *The Brothers Grimm: From Enchanted Forests to the Modern World.* New York and London: Routledge, 1988.

ONLINE SOURCES

Billionaires for Bush. http://billionairesforbush.com.

———. "SMALL GOVERNMENT BIG WARS." Bumper sticker. https://secure3 .ctsg.com/BforB/store/Product.asp?Product=175.

British Broadcasting Corporation. "Fighting Poverty in India." Report on Aruna Roy and the Association of Workers and Peasants. December 27, 2001. http://news.bbc.co.uk/1/hi/programmes/crossing_continents/1723539.stm.

DowEthics.com. "Acceptable Risk." http://www.dowethics.com/risk/.

———. "Dow Releases 'Acceptable Risk' at Banking Conference." Press release, May 3, 2005. http://dowethics.com/risk/pr.html.

Interview with Amartya Sen. Asia Source. New York: Asia Society. December 6, 2004. http://www.asiasource.org/news/special_reports/sen.cfm.

"Lillian Virginia Mountweazel." Wikipedia. http://en.wikipedia.org/wiki/
Lillian_Virginia_Mountweazel. See also http://en.wikipedia.org/wiki/
Nihilartikel.

"Loud and Clear." *The Daily Show*, October 9, 2007. http://www.thedailyshow
.com/video/index.jhtml?videoId=111129&title=loud-and-clear&byDate
=true.

"Maund." *Oxford English Dictionary Online*. 2nd ed. Oxford, U.K.: Oxford University Press, 1989. http://www.oed.com.

"Paheli Is India's Oscar Nominee." *India Abroad*, September 26, 2005. http://
www.rediff.com/movies/2005/sep/26paheli.htm.

Rajputana Liberation Front. "Independant [sic] Rajputstan." http://rajputana
.htmlplanet.com/rajput/indepraj.html.

"Study: Iraqis May Experience Sadness When Friends, Relatives Die." *The
Onion*, July 25, 2007, 43–30. http://www.theonion.com/content/news/study
_iraqis_may_experience.

"Travesty." *Oxford English Dictionary Online*. 2nd ed. Oxford, U.K.: Oxford
University Press, 1989. http://www.oed.com.

"U.S. Finishes 'A Strong Second' in Iraq War." *The Onion*, October 20, 2004,
40–42. http://www.theonion.com/content/node/30750.

Yes Men, The. http://www.theyesmen.org.

———. "Dow Discovers a Golden Skeleton!" http://www.theyesmen.org/en/
hijinks/acceptablerisk.